INTER-ASIAN LAW

What happens when Western law is no longer the default referent for legal modernity? This is a deceptively simple question, but its implications are significant for such fields as comparative law, international law, law and technology, and law and development. Whereas much of comparative law is predicated on the idea that modern law flows West to East and North to South, this volume proposes the paradigm of "Inter-Asian Law" (IAL), pointing to an emerging field of comparative law that explores the legal interactions between and among Asian jurisdictions. This volume is an experimental and preliminary effort to think through other beginnings and endings for law's movement from one jurisdiction to another, laying the grounds for new interactions between legal systems. In addition to providing an analytical framework to study IAL, the volume consists of fifteen chapters written by scholars from Asia and who study Asia that provide doctrinal and empirical accounts of IAL. This title is also available as Open Access on Cambridge Core.

Matthew S. Erie (JD, PhD) is an Associate Professor of Law at the American University Washington College of Law. A comparativist and anthropologist by training, he teaches international law, transnational business, comparative law, and law and development, and has taught law in the United States, United Kingdom, Singapore, Cambodia, Pakistan, and China.

Ching-Fu Lin is a Professor at the Institute of Law for Science and Technology, National Tsing Hua University, Taiwan. Trained as both a lawyer and an engineer, he teaches international law and global governance, law and technology, global health law, food law and policy, and artificial intelligence law and policy.

ASCL Studies in Comparative Law

ASCL Studies in Comparative Law publishes monographs and collections that broaden theoretical and practical knowledge of the world's many legal systems. Published under the direction of the American Society of Comparative Law, the *ASCL Studies* examine legal problems in a comparative light to advance legal science, develop technical insights, and promote greater cooperation across jurisdictional and cultural boundaries. This book series serves legal practitioners and those seeking to improve law and justice by publishing in-depth comparative studies of specific legal problems in every area of law.

The series has two general editors. David Gerber is Distinguished Professor of Law and Co-Director of the Program in International and Comparative Law at Chicago-Kent College of Law, Illinois Institute of Technology. He is past President of the American Society of Comparative Law. Mortimer Sellers is Regents Professor of the University System of Maryland and Director of the Baltimore Center for International and Comparative Law. He is past President of the Internationale Vereinigung für Rechts- und Sozialphilosophie.

Inter-Asian Law

Edited by

MATTHEW S. ERIE
American University

CHING-FU LIN
National Tsing Hua University, Taiwan

CAMBRIDGE
UNIVERSITY PRESS

CAMBRIDGE
UNIVERSITY PRESS

Shaftesbury Road, Cambridge CB2 8EA, United Kingdom

One Liberty Plaza, 20th Floor, New York, NY 10006, USA

477 Williamstown Road, Port Melbourne, VIC 3207, Australia

314–321, 3rd Floor, Plot 3, Splendor Forum, Jasola District Centre, New Delhi – 110025, India

103 Penang Road, #05–06/07, Visioncrest Commercial, Singapore 238467

Cambridge University Press is part of Cambridge University Press & Assessment, a department of the University of Cambridge.

We share the University's mission to contribute to society through the pursuit of education, learning and research at the highest international levels of excellence.

www.cambridge.org
Information on this title: www.cambridge.org/9781009580625

DOI: 10.1017/9781009580632

First published 2026

Cover image: © 2025 National Tsing Hua University. All rights reserved.

A catalogue record for this publication is available from the British Library

Library of Congress Cataloging-in-Publication Data
NAMES: Erie, Matthew S. editor http://id.loc.gov/rwo/agents/n2016003751 | Lin, Ching-Fu, 1982- editor http://id.loc.gov/rwo/agents/no2011072299
TITLE: Inter-Asian law / edited by Matthew S. Erie, University of Oxford; Ching-Fu Lin, National Tsing Hua University, Taiwan.
DESCRIPTION: Cambridge, United Kingdom ; New York, NY : Cambridge University Press, 2025. |
SERIES: ASCL studies in comparative law | Includes bibliographical references and index.
IDENTIFIERS: LCCN 2025018049 (print) | LCCN 2025018050 (ebook) | ISBN 9781009580625 hardback |
ISBN 9781009580601 paperback | ISBN 9781009580632 epub
SUBJECTS: LCSH: Comparative law–Asia | International and municipal law–Asia
CLASSIFICATION: LCC KM553.5 .I58 2025 (print) | LCC KM553.5 (ebook) | DDC 340/.2095–dc23/eng/20250421
LC record available at https://lccn.loc.gov/2025018049
LC ebook record available at https://lccn.loc.gov/2025018050

ISBN 978-1-009-58062-5 Hardback
ISBN 978-1-009-58060-1 Paperback

Contents

Acknowledgments

This volume was the result of collaboration by scholars, universities, and grant-making agencies from throughout the world, and the editors want to acknowledge that without their support, this book would not have been possible. *Inter-Asian Law* is the product of collective insights from scholars across a dozen jurisdictions who have explored, under a shared analytical framework, the origins, drivers, processes, mechanisms, and effects of Inter-Asian Law (IAL). Organized along four thematic dimensions – commercial law, constitutional law, law's movements, and emerging problems – this volume offers empirical, doctrinal, and theoretical contributions, and positions IAL as an emerging field and a new methodological approach within comparative and international law.

The broader institutional support for this book comes from the University of Oxford and National Tsing Hua University (NTHU). With funding from the National Science and Technology Council as well as the Ministry of Education of Taiwan, the Chiang Ching-kuo Foundation for International Scholarly Exchange, and the European Research Council (ERC, grant agreement No. 803763), both editors organized the Inter-Asian Law Workshop at NTHU in Hsinchu, Taiwan, in 2022, where most authors met in person and engaged in deep, reflective, and thought-provoking discussions. The editors and contributors are grateful to the chairs, discussants, and participants on various panels for their inputs, which fueled the momentum for our collective endeavor. In particular, we wish to thank Mindy Chen-Wishart and Teemu Ruskola for their keynote addresses, and Yu-Jie Chen and Joshua Karton for their insights as discussants. We would also like to acknowledge a number of promising graduate students at NTHU – I-Ching Chen, Hui-Hsuan Yang, Ting-Yu Huang, Yen-Yu Hung, Ta-Jung Chang, Shih-Hao Tsai, Kuan-Lin Ho, and Yun-Sheng Lin – for their assistance in organizing the workshop. The programmatic theme of the workshop animated our discussions and laid the groundwork for the framing of this volume. Our insights were further developed and refined through scholarly debates and discussions and are now the joint product of nineteen authors. The project was further refined through a presentation at the American Society of Comparative Law (ASCL) annual meeting in 2024, during which several contributors presented their chapters-in-progress, and we thank Margaret Woo for her moderation and comments.

We would like to express our gratitude to the anonymous reviewers of the book proposal for all their critical comments, and to Mortimer Sellers, General Editor, of the ASCL Studies in Comparative Law series, for his guidance. We thank Vicky Hayman for her careful editing of the final manuscript and two years of coordination efforts. Thanks also go to Michelle Ratton Sanchez Badin, Fabio Morosini, Olabisi Akinkugbe, Kevin Davis, and Mariana Pergendler for sharing their regional insights, and to the entire editorial team of ASCL Studies in Comparative Law at Cambridge University Press – Marianne Nield, Biju Singh, and Natasha Burton. Again, this collaborative project received generous financial and technical support, and we are particularly thankful to the ERC for enabling this volume to be made freely available online under a Creative Commons Open Access license.

The book was finalized while countries around the world are facing challenges of geopolitical tensions, trends of deglobalization and regionalization, and other lines of social, political, and economic realignment. While we noted in the conclusion that this volume is only a beginning, its focus on the contemporary landscape of IAL is already influencing domestic and transnational legal orders and will likely extend beyond the Asian region. It is our hope that this volume will stimulate future scholarly discourse on the relevance and implications of IAL as an emerging field and a new methodological approach, shedding light on other regional studies, as well as on comparative and international law.

Abbreviations

ABAC	APEC Business Advisory Council
ACCTS	Agreement on Climate Change, Trade and Sustainability
ACIA	ASEAN Comprehensive Investment Agreement
ADNDRC	Asian Domain Name Dispute Resolution Centre
ADR	alternative dispute resolution
AEC	ASEAN Economic Community
AFAS	ASEAN Framework Agreement on Services
AI	artificial intelligence
AIAC	Asian International Arbitration Centre
AILA	*Aliansi Cinta Keluarga* [Family Love Alliance] (Indonesia)
AMA	Arbitration–Mediation–Arbitration
APEC	Asia-Pacific Economic Cooperation
ASCL	American Society of Comparative Law
ASCN	ASEAN Smart Cities Network
ASEAN	Association of Southeast Asian Nations
ATISA	ASEAN Trade in Services Agreement
BICC	Bahrain International Commercial Court
BIT	bilateral investment agreement
BRI	Belt and Road Initiative
CAMP	Centre for Advanced Mediation Practice
CCIG	Geneva Chamber of Commerce and Industry
CCP	Chinese Communist Party
CDC Act	Communicable Disease Control Act
CECC	Central Epidemic Command Center
CFA	Court of Final Appeal
CIETAC	China International Economic and Trade Arbitration Commission
CPP	Cambodian People's Party

CPPCC	China's People's Political Consultative Conference
CPTPP	Comprehensive and Progressive Agreement for Trans-Pacific Partnership
CPV	Communist Party of Vietnam
CSO	civil society organization
CTMA	COVID-19 (Temporary Measures) Act
DB	dispute board
DEPA	Digital Economy Partnership Agreement
DIAC	Dubai International Arbitration Centre
DIFC	Dubai International Financial Centre
DNDR	Domain Name Dispute Resolution
DPR	*Dewan Perwakilan Rakyat* [Parliament] (Indonesia)
DRV	Democratic Republic of Vietnam
ERP	Essential Religious Practices
ESG	environmental, social, and governance
FCN	Friendship, Commerce and Navigation
FDI	foreign direct investment
FET	fair and equitable treatment
FPI	Forum Pembela Islam [Islamic Defenders Front] (Indonesia)
FTA	free trade agreement
GAR	Global Arbitration Review
GDP	gross domestic product
GPAI	Global Partnership on Artificial Intelligence
HKIAC	Hong Kong International Arbitration Centre
HKMC	Hong Kong Mediation Centre
HKNSL	Hong Kong National Security Law
HKSAR	Hong Kong Special Administrative Region
IAL	Inter-Asian Law
ICSID	International Centre for Settlement of Investment Disputes
ICT	information and communications technology
IDA	Infectious Diseases Act
IDCPA	Infectious Disease Control and Prevention Act
IEEE	Institute of Electrical and Electronics Engineers
IMDA	Infocomm Media Development Authority
IMF	International Monetary Fund
ISCPA	Infectious Disease Control and Prevention Act
ISDS	investor–state dispute settlement
ISO	International Organization for Standardization
JASCA	Japan Association for Smart Cities in ASEAN
JCAA	Japan Commercial Arbitration Association

JICA	Japan International Cooperation Agency
JIMC	Japan International Mediation Centre
KCAB	Korean Commercial Arbitration Board
KUHP	*Kitab Undang-Undang Hukum Pidana* (Indonesia)
LDII	Indonesian Islamic Propagation Institute
LGBT	Lesbian, Gay, Bisexual, or Transgender
LIPIA	Islamic and Arabic College of Indonesia
MERS	Middle East respiratory syndrome
METI	Ministry of Economy, Trade and Industry
MFA	Multi Fiber Agreement
MFN	most-favored nation
MIC	Ministry of Internal Affairs and Communications
MIFER	Ministry of Investment and Foreign Economic Relations
MLIT	Ministry of Land, Infrastructure, Transport, and Tourism (Japan)
MOLIT	Ministry of Land, Infrastructure and Transport (Japan)
MoU	memorandum of understanding
MR	menstrual regulation
MTI	Ministry of Trade and Industry
MUI	*Majelis Ulama Indonesia* [Indonesian Council of Ulema] (Indonesia)
NGO	non-governmental organization
NIEO	New International Economic Order
NPC	National People's Congress
NPC-SC	National People's Congress-Standing Committee
NTHU	National Tsing Hua University
NU	*Nahdlatul Ulama* (Indonesia)
ODA	official development assistance
ODR	online dispute resolution
OECD	Organisation for Economic Co-operation and Development
ORFS	Outcome Related Fee Structures for Arbitration
PAN	*Partai Amanat Nasional* [National Mandate Party] (Indonesia)
PDPC	Personal Data Protection Commission
PKB	*Partai Kebangkitan Bangsa* [National Awakening Party] (Indonesia)
PKS Party	*Partai Keadilan Sejahtera* [Prosperous Justice Party] (Indonesia)
POMH	public order, morality, and health
PPP	*Partai Persatuan Pembangunan* [United Development Party] (Indonesia)

PRC	People's Republic of China
RCEP	Regional Comprehensive Economic Partnership
RUU APP	*Rancangan Undang-Undang Anti Pornografi dan Pornoaksi* [Draft Law on Anti-pornography and Pornoaction] (Indonesia)
RUU PKS	*Rancangan Undang-Undang Penghapusan Kekerasan Seksual* [Draft Law of the Elimination of Sexual Violence] (Indonesia)
RUU TPKS	*Rancangan Undang-Undang Tindak Pidana Kekerasan Seksual* [Draft Law on Sexual Violence Crimes] (Indonesia)
SAR	Special Administrative Region
SARS	Severe Acute Respiratory Syndrome
SCCR	Supreme Council for Consultation and Recommendation
SCIA	Shenzhen Court of International Arbitration
SCO	Shanghai Cooperation Organization
SEZ	special economic zone
SIAC	Singapore International Arbitration Centre
SIArb	Singapore Institute of Arbitrators
SICC	Singapore International Commercial Court
SIMC	Singapore International Mediation Centre
Smart JAMP	Smart City Supported by Japan–ASEAN Mutual Partnership
SOE	state-owned enterprise
SRV	Socialist Republic of Vietnam
TPF	third-party funding
TPP	Trans-Pacific Partnership
TSMC	Taiwan Semiconductor Manufacturing Company
UDRP	Uniform Domain Name Dispute Resolution Policy
UNCITRAL	United Nations Commission on International Trade Law
UNCTAD	United Nations Conference on Trade and Development
UNESCAP	United Nations Economic and Social Commission for Asia and the Pacific
USSR	Union of Soviet Socialist Republics
UUTPKS	*Undang-Undang Tindak Pidana Kekerasan Seksual* [Law Number 12 of 2022 on Sexual Violence] (Indonesia)
VIAC	Vietnam International Arbitration Centre
VMC	Vietnam Mediation Centre
WTO	World Trade Organization

Introduction

The Emergence of Inter-Asian Law

Matthew S. Erie and Ching-Fu Lin

I THE QUESTION

What happens when Western law is no longer the default referent for legal modernity? This is a deceptively simple question, but its implications are significant for such fields as comparative law, international law, law and technology, and law and development. The question has moorings in legal history (the sources and models for legal development, colonialism, the predominance of certain "legal families," etc.) and, likewise, is twinned with the relationship between law and the economic relations between states (namely, trade and investment). It may further both reflect and influence geopolitics, the concentration of power and influence within certain states over others, and whether the world is organized under "unipolar" or "multi-polar" configurations.

Much of conventional comparative law and the sociology of law is predicated on the idea that modern law flows West to East and North to South.[1] Likewise, world systems theory, modernization theory, and new institutional economics all privilege Western institutions, norms, ideologies, and law as the center and non-Western systems as peripheral.[2] This same logic is sedimented into centuries of inter-state

[1] It is not hard to find traces of Western law and institutional bias in the thinking of the founders of such disciplines. See, e.g., Robert Launay, *Savages, Romans, and Despots: Thinking About Others from Montaigne to Herder* (Chicago University Press 2018) 127, 128–129 (noting that Montesquieu's portrayal of non-Western systems in *The Spirit of the Laws* is informed by his critique of monarchical absolutism); Max Weber, *On Law in Economy and Society*, trans. Edward Shils and Max Rheinsten (Clarion 1967 [1922]) 47 (implicitly using German law as comparative baseline); Karl Marx, "The Future Results of British Rule in India" in Robert C Tucker (ed), *The Marx-Engels Reader* (2nd edn, W. W. Norton 1978 [1853]) 659, 659 (observing that British rule was not only destructive but "regenerating" by "laying the material foundations of Western Society in Asia"). For more contemporary assessments, see, e.g., Mathias Siems, *Comparative Law* (2nd edn, CUP 2018) 43 ("The disregard of non-Western countries by traditional comparative law is . . . difficult to excuse.").

[2] Immanuel Wallerstein, The Rise and Future Demise of the World Capitalist System, in Immanuel Wallerstein (ed), *The Essential Wallerstein* (The New Press 2000 [1974]) 71, 76

behavior and foreign policy: first through the colonial projects and military expansionism of the nineteenth centuries, then the informal trade empires of the twentieth century, and in the twenty-first century, state projects centered on legal development assistance, "rule of law" programs, and, most recently, investor–state dispute settlement, digital development, and regulatory coherence.[3] States work alongside commercial lawyers, financial institutions, chambers of commerce, and civil society – not always in concert but in ways that dovetail – to ensure that legal ideas, choice of law in contracts, investment protection, international standards-setting, and bureaucracies become routinized.[4] The result – as exemplified in the "legal origins" approach to comparative law – is the continual minting of Western law as the blueprint for modernity.[5]

Consequently, Western law, namely, Anglo-American common law and European civil law, has spread the world over.[6] This diffusion was secured by the force of imperialism and associated forms of Enlightenment and industrialization, but also through the path dependence of everyday legal practice and the

(identifying the emergence of modern world-economy in sixteenth-century Europe); Robert A Packenham, *Liberal America and the Third World: Political Development Ideas in Foreign Aid and Social Science* (Princeton 1973) (arguing that modernization theory as applied to Latin American aid was infused with American-centric liberalism); Julio Faundez, "Douglass North's Theory of Institutions: Lessons for Law and Development" (2016) 8 HJRL 373, 387 ("North's focus on Western economies as the end model for all states led him to regard any institutional framework that do not meet the ideal standard as deviant cases and therefore not meriting close investigation.").

3 Teemu Ruskola, *Legal Orientalism: China, the United States, and Modern Law* (Harvard University Press 2013); Jedidiah J Kroncke, *The Futility of Law and Development: China and the Dangers of Exporting American Law* (OUP 2016); Yves Dezalay and Bryant Garth (eds), *Global Prescriptions: The Production, Exportation, and Importation of a New Legal Orthodoxy* (University of Michigan Press 2002); Nick Couldry and Ulises A Mejias, *The Costs of Connection: How Data Is Colonizing Human Life and Appropriating It for Capitalism* (Bloomsbury 2022); Gus Van Harten, *The Trouble with Foreign Investor Protection* (OUP 2020); Howard Mann, "International Investment Agreements: Building the New Colonialism?" (2003) 97 Proc ASIL Annual 247–250; Han-Wei Liu and Ching-Fu Lin, "The Emergence of Global Regulatory Coherence: A Thorny Embrace for China?" (2018) 40(1) U Pa J Int'l L 133–188. A note about Asian name order: we follow the normal practice pursuant to the language in which the author's work is published. Thus, we use Anglicized order (i.e., given name first, family name last) when the work is in English, but use the original Asian language order (i.e., family name first, given name last) when the work is published in the original Asian language.

4 Guy Fiti Sinclair, *To Reform the World: International Organizations and the Making of Modern States* (OUP 2017); William Easterly, *The White Man's Burden: Why the West's Efforts to Aid the Rest Have Done So Much Ill and So Little Good* (OUP 2006); Frank K Upham, *The Great Property Fallacy* (CUP 2018).

5 For a critique, see Mathias Siems, "Legal Origins" in Jan Smits, Jaakko Husa, Catherine Valcke and Madalena Narciso (eds), *Elgar Encyclopedia of Comparative Law* (Edward Elgar 2023) 478.

6 Antara Haldar, "Legal Emotions: Why Affect Matters for Law" in Sanjit Chakraborty (ed), *Human Minds and Culture* (Springer 2024) 123, 128.

institutionalization of power in international organizations and treaties. This power institutionalization and path dependence can be seen in the ways in which decolonial states draft their constitutions, international legal and financial organizations are created, and cross-border transactions are structured.[7]

The "what if" question posed by this volume is not to deny the relevance of Western law as the primary source for legal modernization, but to open up new and additional possibilities for alternative sources and methodologies. Hence, this volume is more a reformation than a refutation of orthodox thinking. It is an experimental and preliminary effort to think through other beginnings and endings for law's movement from one jurisdiction to another, laying the grounds for new interactions between legal systems.

Building on the paradigm of "Inter-Asia" which has gained ascendance in recent years across scholarly fields in the social sciences and humanities,[8] "Inter-Asian Law" (IAL) points to an emerging field of comparative and international law that explores the legal interactions – historical and contemporary – between and among Asian jurisdictions.[9] These interactions – through diverse actors, intermediaries, processes, and methods – may lead to a number of important formations including, legal transplantation, law and development, multilateralism and trade blocks, global value chains, transnational orders, judicial networks, legal educational exchange, and digital integration, to name a few.

IAL is particularly relevant in the post-pandemic period given shifting geopolitics, increased regionalization, and the importance of key Asian states including Japan, Singapore, South Korea, China, Taiwan, and India. These jurisdictions are both learning from each other through law and, in the process, reconfiguring the substance and procedure of a number of areas of law in the region, and posing ramifications that are felt well beyond Asia.[10] In parallel, a number of Asia-centric multilateral platforms, including the Association of Southeast Asian Nations (ASEAN) United Nations Convention on International Settlement Agreements Resulting from Mediation (the "Singapore Mediation Convention"), Regional Comprehensive Economic Partnership (RCEP), Asian Infrastructure Investment

7 Gordon Silverstein, *Law's Allure: How Law Shapes, Constrains, Saves, and Kills Politics* (CUP 2009); Jaakko Husa, "Developing Legal System, Legal Transplants, and Path Dependence: Reflections on the Rule of Law" (2018) 6 China J Comp L 129; John Bell, "Path Dependence and Legal Development" (2013) 87 Tulane L Rev 787; Bryant G Garth and Yves Dezalay, *Law as Reproduction and Revolution: An Interconnected History* (University of California Press 2021).

8 Engseng Ho, "Inter-Asian Concepts for Mobile Societies" (2017) 76 J Asian Studies 907–928; Prasenjit Duara, "Asia Redux: Conceptualizing a Region for Our Times" (2010) 69 J Asian Studies 963–983; Fahad Ahmad Bishara, *A Sea of Debt: Law and Economic Life in the Western Indian Ocean, 1780–1950* (CUP 2017).

9 See, e.g., Matthew S Erie, "The New Legal Hubs: The Emergent Landscape of International Commercial Dispute Resolution" (2020) 60(2) Va J Int'l 225–298.

10 Tom Ginsburg, "Eastphalia and Asian Regionalism" (2011) 44 UC Davis L Rev 859; Pasha L Hsieh, *New Asian Regionalism in International Economic Law* (CUP 2022); Guiguo Wang, *International Investment Law: A Chinese Perspective* (Routledge 2015).

Bank, Shanghai Cooperation Organization, Belt and Road Initiative, Digital Economy Partnership Agreement (DEPA), Global Development Initiative, and others, are further inflecting international law and the law of member states.[11] The salience of these countries, their multilateral organizations, the dynamic flows of law, capital, and legal professionals, and the region as a whole generate legal creativity that warrants interdisciplinary research through doctrinal analyses, case studies, empirical approaches, historical assessments, and other methods of comparative and international law.

IAL is of increasing importance given the ongoing tension between the US and China and the resulting regionalization of trade and investment. IAL is not divorced from Western legal systems but demonstrates a complex set of relationships with Western law, such as post-colonialism, "late-comer advantages," path dependency, and divergence. While there is inheritance, there is also modification and innovation. To be clear, IAL may not only have Asian origins; it may borrow from non-Asian law but also extensively reform said law such that it finds new applications; it may even loop back to and co-evolve with said law through global norm diffusion and interaction.

The 2008 Global Financial Crisis and the COVID-19 pandemic cast doubt on Western liberal forms of law and governance, and calls for decolonizing comparative law have become more urgent.[12] It is no longer the case that legal change derives exclusively from Anglo-American common law or European civil law; rather, IAL shows how the Asian region is a dynamic field of legal modernization and experiment, an observation particularly germane during the COVID-19 pandemic and the emergence of data-driven economies and artificial intelligence (AI).[13]

IAL spotlights not only comparative law, but also international law, law and history, and law and society. More specifically, IAL touches on such fields as inter alia constitutional law, labor, property, contract, trade and investment, dispute

[11] Wang Guiguo [王贵国], Li Wulin [李鋈麟] and Liang Meifen [梁美芬], *Yidaiyilu zhengduan jiejue jizhi* [A Belt and Road Initiative Dispute Resolution Mechanism] (Zhejiang University 2017); Guiguo Wang and Rajesh Sharma, "The International Commercial Dispute Prevention and Settlement Organization: A Global Laboratory of Dispute Resolution with an Asian Flavor" (2021) 115 AJIL Unbound 22–27; Tom Ginsburg, "Authoritarian International Law" (2020) 114 AJIL 221–260; David Suter, *The Shanghai Cooperation Organisation: A Chinese Practice of International Law* (Schulthess 2015); Pasha L Hsieh, "Against Populist Isolationism: New Asian Regionalism and Global South Powers in International Economic Law" (2018) 51 Cornell Int'l L J 683–729.

[12] Lena Salaymeh and Ralf Michaels, "Decolonial Comparative Law: A Conceptual Beginning" (2022) 86 Rabel J Comp & Int'l Private L 166–188.

[13] Henry S Gao, "Data Regulation with Chinese Characteristics" in Mira Burri (ed), *Big Data and Global Trade Law* (CUP 2021); Jeanne Huang, "Applicable Law to Transnational Personal Data: Trends and Dynamics" (2020) 21(6) German Law J 1283–1308; Matthew S Erie and Thomas Streinz, "The Beijing Effect: China's 'Digital Silk Road' as Transnational Data Governance" (2021) 54 NYU JILP 1–92; Anu Bradford, *Digital Empires: The Global Battle to Regulate Technology* (OUP 2023).

resolution, data governance, law and technology, civil and criminal procedure, human rights, gender, and law and religion. Most fundamentally, at the epistemological level, IAL asks what it means if Asia – and not the West – is the referent for Asia's own legal modernity.

This volume, the first of its kind, is premised on a collective and experimental effort to provide an analytical framework to understand IAL and think through its possibilities and limits. It charts out the main origins, drivers, trajectories, and mechanisms of IAL, their effects at the national, regional, and transnational levels, and broader consequences for the political economy of the Asian region and beyond. It refers to IAL as both an empirical mapping and assessment as well as a new methodology of comparative and international legal studies. It seeks to unpack IAL as a phenomenon, to assess whether it is unique, and the extent to which the interactions traced demonstrate discernible patterns of influence. It presents empirical, doctrinal, and theoretical contributions thematically organized into commercial law, constitutional law, law's movements, and emerging problems. Specifically, the contributions examine both state-led initiatives at legal harmonization, commercial causes for convergence, many of which are driven by lawyers and their corporate clients, judges' citations to and networks with neighboring courts, and the role of other non-state actors. Hence, the volume's individual contributions assess different units and layers of analysis, among them, states, transnational networks, and company towns that effect legal and regulatory change across multiple jurisdictions.

The volume explicitly endeavors a form of deep interdisciplinarism to understand the nature and operation of IAL; it tracks between secular and religious law, private and public law, and national and international law. The operating assumption is that hyper-specialization in legal analysis has created siloed thinking which sacrifices historical and cultural perspectives and macroregional breadth for doctrinal minutiae. It hence eschews the safety of blinkered thinking and boldly recenters causation. As such, the volume takes a diachronic view of IAL, ranging from historical approaches that lay a groundwork for understanding the origins and trajectories of legal modernization in the region to contemporary doctrinal and policy analyses that assess how national legal systems have responded to current crises, whether in the forms of pandemics or wars. This emphasis on robust comparison facilitates thinking across disciplinary and national distinctions to show the evidence of and possibilities for legal pasts, presents, and futures that may benefit from Western precedents but also create new bases for solving regional and global dilemmas. While we argue that IAL elucidates broader rules rather than the "law of the horse,"[14] we are also conscious of the problem of overclaiming and recognize that IAL remains nascent whereas there is significant path dependency in choice of law throughout world legal systems which, in many aspects, still favor Anglo-American and Western European laws.

[14] See the final chapter of this volume, "A Beginning."

II BACKGROUND AND CORE CONCEPTS

The legacy of empires, formal and informal, has assured that the West, namely, the United Kingdom (UK), Europe, and the United States (US), has defined legal modernity throughout the world.[15] Empires functioned to export, transplant, and reproduce variants of common law and continental civil law throughout Latin America, Africa, and Asia. Pursuant to the relationship between power and modern knowledge, the disciplines of international law and comparative law have further concretized such binaries as the Global North produces "legal subjects" whereas the Global South features "legal barbarians."[16]

However, decolonization, globalization, and the economic ascendance of former (semi-)colonized territories, including Hong Kong, Taiwan, Singapore, Japan, China, and India, have challenged long-standing orthodoxies about the nature and directionality of legal modernity. Scholars have developed critiques of existing knowledge about law and modernization, through, for example, the Third World Approaches to International Law,[17] Critical Race Theory,[18] subaltern studies,[19] the study of international law as empire,[20] and the so-called

[15] Maïa Pal, *Jurisdictional Accumulation: An Early Modern History of Law, Empires, and Capital* (CUP 2020); Lauren Benton and Richard J Ross, "Empires and Legal Pluralism: Jurisdiction, Sovereignty, and Political Imagination in the Early Modern World" in Lauren Benton and Richard J Ross (eds), *Legal Pluralism and Empires, 1500–1850* (New York University Press 2013).

[16] Daniel Bonilla Maldonado, *Legal Barbarians: Identity, Modern Comparative Law and the Global South* (CUP 2021). See also David W Kennedy, "New Approaches to Comparative Law: Comparativism and International Governance" (1997) *Utah L Rev* No. 2, 545; Günter Frankenberg, "Critical Comparisons: Re-Thinking Comparative Law" (1985) 26 HILJ 411.

[17] Antony Anghie, *Imperialism, Sovereignty, and the Making of International Law* (CUP 2004); Olabisi D Akinkugbe, "Africanization and the Reform of International Investment Law" (2021) 53 Case W Res J Int'l L 7; B S Chimni, "The World of TWAIL: Introduction to the Special Issue" (2011) 3 TL&D 1.

[18] Ruth Gordon, "Critical Race Theory and International Law: Convergence and Divergence" (2000) 45(5) Villanova L Rev 827; Makau Mutua, "Critical Race Theory and International Law: The View of an Insider-Outsider" (2000) 45 Villanova L Rev 841; Vijah Prashad, *Darker Nations: A People's History of the Third World* (The New Press 2008); Barbara Young Welke, *Law and the Borders of Belonging in the Long Nineteenth Century United States* (CUP 2010).

[19] Dianne Otto, "Subalternity and International Law: The Problems of Global Community and the Incommensurability of Difference" in Eve Darian-Smith and Peter Fitzpatrick (eds), *Laws of the Postcolonial* (University of Michigan Press 1999).

[20] Karen J Alter, "From Colonial to Multilateral International Law: A Global Capitalism and Law Investigation" (2021) *iCON* 1–67; Lauren Benton and Lisa Ford, *Rage for Order: The British Empire and the Origins of International Law, 1800–1850* (Harvard University Press 2016); Kate Miles, *The Origins of International Investment Law: Empire, Environment and the Safeguarding of Capital* (CUP 2013); Karen Alter, "The Empire of International Law?" (2019) 113 AJIL 183–199; Luis Eslava, "The Moving Location of Empire: Indirect Rule, International Law, and the Bantu Educational Kinema Experiment" (2018) 31 Leiden JIL 539–567; Martti Koskenniemi, Walter Rech and Manuel Jimenez Fonseca, *International Law and Empire: Historical Explorations* (OUP 2017).

BRICS.[21] In recent years, the spread of nationalism, protectionism, xenophobia, and dedemocratization have greatly weakened the global footprint of the erstwhile epicenter of legal modernity, most visibly, the US, but also, to various degrees, the UK, France, and Germany.[22] All of these trends have opened up more spaces for both Asian economic powers, not only China, but also India, Singapore, and Japan, to expand their regional and global influence.

The foregoing lays the backdrop for the study of IAL. As a definition of "Inter-Asian law," we propose the following: *a conceptual framework for comparative and international law that underscores the interactions between Asian jurisdictions at bilateral, regional, or transnational levels which introduce legal, regulatory, or normative change*. Under this definition, several concepts require unpacking, including "Asia," "Inter-Asia," and, more centrally, "Inter-Asian law."

A. "*Asia*"

First, "Asia " can be understood as a geographical megaregion, a juxtaposition of legal systems, or a discursive conceit. These interpretations are not necessarily mutually exclusive. Geographical understandings of Asia include East Asia, South Asia, Central Asia, Southeast Asia, and Western Asia.[23] In the geographic sense, Asia is a place in the world defined by physical boundaries, culture, and populations. A legal systems approach recognizes that Asia is a mixture of diverse legal systems including common law, civil law, and hybrid legal systems, including Islamic law.[24] These systems are a result of historical processes, including imperialism and decolonization. The discursive understanding takes these historical and contemporary relationships further to underscore the historical construction of "Asia" as that which is "not Europe."[25] In this understanding, Asia is both a product of Western knowledge production (diplomatic, academic, etc.) and one that has also sought

[21] William W Burke-White, "Power Shifts in International Law: Structural Realignment and Substantive Pluralism" (2015) 56 HILJ 1–79; David Wilkins and Mihaela Papa, "The Rise of the Corporate Legal Elite in the BRICS: Implications for Global Governance" (2013) 54 B C L Rev 1149–1184; David B Wilkins, Virkramaditya S Khanna and David M Trubek, *The Indian Legal Profession in the Age of Globalization: The Rise of the Corporate Legal Sector and Its Impact on Lawyers and Society* (CUP 2017); Gregory Shaffer, *Emerging Powers and the World Trading System: The Past and Future of International Economic Law* (CUP 2021).

[22] Tom Ginsburg and Aziz Huq, *How to Save a Constitutional Democracy* (University of Chicago Press 2019); Steven Levitsky and Daniel Ziblatt, *How Democracies Die: What History Reveals About our Future* (Penguin 2018); Cass R Sunstein, *Can It Happen Here? Authoritarianism in America* (Day Street Books 2018).

[23] World Atlas, "Asia", www.worldatlas.com/webimage/countrys/as.htm, accessed March 5, 2024.

[24] Christoph Antons, "What Is 'Asian Law'? Asia in Law, the Humanities and Social Sciences" in Christoph Antons (ed), *Routledge Handbook of Asian Law* (Routledge 2017) 3–27.

[25] Edward W Said, *Orientalism* (Vintage 1978); Amitav Archarya, "Asia Is Not One" (2010) 69(4) J Asian Studies 1001; Teemu Ruskola, "Where Is Asia? When Is Asia? Theorizing Comparative Law and International Law" (2011) 44 UC Davis L Rev 879.

redefinition and agency.[26] These different understandings build on each other and provide different lenses through which to study Asia as place, system(s), and image. While Asia attains some coherence when contrasted against the West, Asia itself is highly heterogeneous, both in terms of law and politics, and thus diversity, including diverse interests, must be central to any analysis of Asia.

B. *"Inter-Asia"*

Second, and in part pursuant to this observation of heterogeneity, the idea of "Inter-Asia" grows out of a number of efforts across the humanities and social sciences to rethink area studies. Area studies as a field underwent attack in the 1980s as a vestige of colonial thinking, that is, the idea of bounded culture-units that are "other" than the West. Contrary to this idea, scholars such as Prasenjit Duara and Engseng Ho have explained the idea of Inter-Asia as one of circulation of migrants, ideas, and capital between and among Asian jurisdictions.[27] In his formulation, Ho identifies Inter-Asia as "an old world crisscrossed by interactions between parts that have known and recognized one another for centuries . . . ."[28] Hence, Inter-Asia is not just an effect of modernity; rather, it has deep historic roots, roots that work both down and outward, connecting origins, nationalisms, and modernizations, across the region.[29] Further, Inter-Asia builds on but is conceptually different from "pan-Asianism" and "Asian regionalism," concepts that have gained traction in Asian political thought and academic study, respectively.[30]

While the defining movements of Asian nationalism and anti-colonialism were both reactions against Western imperialism and selective appropriations of Western political forms (e.g., Mahatma Gandhi's *satyagraha* ("holding to truth"), Liang Qichao's *ziqiang yundong* ("self-strengthening"), and Sun Yat-sen's *minzu* ("nationality")), there were also extensive borrowings between and among Asian polities. For instance, many of the efforts to reform the Qing Empire were borrowed from the Meiji restoration and even Mustafa Kemal took Japan as a model for reform.[31] Manchukuo, Japan's puppet state in northeast China from 1932 to 1945, cross-fertilized ideas of governance between Europe, Japan, and China.[32] Through the

[26] Gayatri Chakravorty Spivak, "Subaltern Studies: Deconstructing Historiography" in Ranajit Guha and Gayatri Chakravorty Spivak (eds), *Selected Subaltern Studies* (OUP 1988) 3–24.

[27] Duara (n 8); Ho (n 8).

[28] Ho (n 8) 907.

[29] Christine R Yano, "Global Asias: Improvisations on a Theme" (2021) 80 J Asian Studies 845–864.

[30] See, e.g., Kakuzō Okakura, *The Awakening of Japan* (Adamant Media Corp 2001 [1904]); Mark Beeson and Richard Stubbs, *Routledge Handbook of Asian Regionalism* (Routledge 2021).

[31] Pankaj Mishra, *From the Ruins of Empire: The Revolt against the West and the Remaking of Asia* (Penguin 2012) 1.

[32] Prasenjit Duara, *Sovereignty and Authenticity: Manchukuo and the East Asian Modern* (Rowen & Littlefield 2004).

push and pull of exile and diaspora, Chinese traders, merchants, and businesspeople created interlinked ecosystems of commerce, religion, and politics throughout the South Pacific from Southeast China to Taiwan, the Philippines, Vietnam, Malaysia, Sumatra, Cambodia, Thailand, and overland into Myanmar.[33] Likewise, decolonization and political movements fomented a diaspora throughout South Asia.[34] There were further overlapping commercial and religious links between the present-day Gulf States and South Asia;[35] China, Taiwan, and the Middle East;[36] the Middle East and Southeast Asia;[37] and Turkey and Central Asia.[38] In many cases, and chiefly, China and India, diasporas served to channel foreign direct investment into nascent nation-states allowing them to become the economic behemoths they are today.[39]

Inter-Asia as a concept has a rich intellectual history. One starting point is the work of Yoshimi Takeuchi, a major intellectual in post-war Japan, who proposed as early as 1960, "Asia as Method," by which he sought to trace the Chinese and Japanese approaches to modernization.[40] Takeuchi's method, then, is both comparative and reflexive; he shifts the analysis away from Euro-American models to juxtapose Chinese and Japanese ones, assessing their mutual inheritance and differences. Takeuchi's approach has been influential in Asian studies and has been taken up by several key intellectuals, including the Taiwanese scholar Kuan-Hsing Chen. Chen is a leading figure in the "Inter-Asian Cultural Studies project," which founded the academic journal *Inter-Asian Cultural Studies* in the late 1990s and a number of conferences that have "worked toward the imagination and possibilities

33 Gungwu Wang, *China and the Chinese Overseas* (Times Academic Press 1992); Laurence J C Ma and Carolyn L Cartier, *The Chinese Diaspora: Space, Place, Mobility, and Identity* (Rowan & Littlefield 2003); Melissa Macauley, *Distant Shores: Colonial Encounters on China's Maritime Frontier* (Princeton University Press 2021); Santasombat Yos, *Chinese Capitalism in Southeast Asia: Cultures and Practices* (Palgrave Macmillan 2017); Aihwa Ong, *Flexible Citizenship: The Cultural Logics of Transnationality* (Duke University Press 1999).

34 Papiya Ghosh, *Partition and the South Asian Diaspora: Extending the Subcontinent* (Routledge 2007).

35 Engseng Ho, *The Graves of Tarim: Genealogy and Mobility across the Indian Ocean* (University of California Press 2006).

36 Hyeju Jeong, "A Song of the Red Sea: Communities and Networks of Chinese Muslims in the Hijaz" (2016) 12 Dirasat 1–29; Zvi Ben-Dor Benite, "*Nine Years in Egypt*": *Al-Azhar University and the Arabization of Chinese Islam*. HAGAR: Studies in Culture, Polity & Identities (Ben Gurion University 2008).

37 Michael Gilsenan, "Topics and Queries for a History of Arab Families and Inheritance in Southeast Asia: Some Preliminary Thoughts" in Eric Tagliacozzo (ed), *Southeast Asia and the Middle East: Islam, Movement, and the Longue Durée* (National University of Singapore Press 2009).

38 Magnus Marsden, *Trading Worlds: Afghan Merchants across Modern Frontiers* (Hurst 2015).

39 Min Ye, *Diasporas and Foreign Direct Investment in China and India* (CUP 2014).

40 Yoshimi Takeuchi, "Asia as Method" in Richard F Calichman (ed), *What Is Modernity? Writings of Takeuchi Yoshimi* (Columbia University Press 2005) 149–166.

of diverse forms of intellectual integration in Asia."[41] Building on Takeuchi, Chen argues for "Asia as method" by which he means that by "using the idea of Asia as an imaginary anchoring point, societies in Asia can become each other's points of reference, so that the understanding of the self may be transformed, and subjectivity rebuilt."[42] With such genealogies in mind, it is clear that "Inter-Asia" speaks not of "one Asia" but, rather, many.[43]

C. *"Inter-Asian Law"*

Third, IAL builds on the foregoing concepts to highlight law as a mobile normative resource between and among Asian jurisdictions. Crucially, the prefix *inter*-points to the relationship between and among Asian jurisdictions rather than taking them as independent case studies.[44] There is, of course, a premodern history to such exchanges, for example, in the legal borrowing of Qing China and Joseon Korea from Meiji Japan.[45] Contemporary assemblages may build on these historical precedents but may likewise operate across new configurations.

There is a growing literature that examines such legal comparisons, some of which may challenge conventional comparative law theory[46] and demonstrate degrees of harmonization of modern commercial law in different Asian jurisdictions.[47] As a theoretical or practical matter, private law may demonstrate greater convergence given that the interests of stakeholders may be aligned to optimize their respective rules.[48] Yet even in public law, there is a growing literature on such

[41] Inter-Asian Cultural Studies, "About Us", https://culturalstudies.asia/about-us/, accessed March 5, 2024.

[42] Kuan-Hsing Chen, *Asia as Method: Toward Deimperialization* (Duke University Press 2010) 212.

[43] Sanjay Subrahmanyam, "One Asia, or Many? Reflections from Connected History" (2016) 50 Modern Asian Studies 5–43.

[44] This phenomenon may not be unique to Asia; for example, Latin American states have experienced their own degree of intra-regional law. See, e.g., Maximo Langer, "Revolution in Latin American Criminal Procedure: Diffusion of Legal Ideas from the Periphery" (2007) 55 AJCL 617.

[45] See, e.g., Tay-sheng Wang, *Legal Reform in Taiwan under Japanese Colonial Rule, 1895–1956* (University of Washington Press 2000); Marie Seong-Hak Kim, *Law and Custom in Korea: Comparative Legal History* (CUP 2012).

[46] Dan W Puchniak, Harald Baum and Michael Ewing-Chow (eds), *The Derivative Action in Asia: A Comparative and Functional Approach* (CUP 2021); Dan W Puchniak, Harald Baum and Michael Ewing-Chow (eds), *Independent Directors in Asia: A Historical, Contextual and Comparative Approach* (CUP 2017).

[47] Anselmo Reyes and Weixia Gu (eds), *The Developing World of Arbitration: A Comparative Study of Arbitration Reform in the Asia Pacific* (Hart 2018).

[48] Gary F Bell, "Harmonisation of Contract Law in Asia – Harmonising Regionally or Adopting Global Harmonisation – The Example of the CISG" (2005) *Singapore J Legal Studies* 362; Gary F Bell, *The UNCITRAL Model Law and Asian Arbitration Laws: Implementation and Comparisons* (CUP 2018); Oliver Gaillard and Krista Nadakavukaren Schefer, *Private International Law in East Asia: From Imitation to Innovation and Exportation* (Hart

comparisons. Several collections of comparative Asian constitutional law have been published in recent years demonstrating this trend.[49] These volumes evince the increasing relevance of comparative Asian law to "mainstream" legal scholarship. This volume builds on these studies but provides a substantial innovation by creating a conceptual foundation for the study of IAL as a field of widespread interest.

The recentering of law in Asian studies and Asian law within legal studies must overcome histories of marginalization. Historically, the disciplines that study law have denigrated the place of law in Asian societies giving rise to what Teemu Ruskola has called "legal orientalism."[50] There is, in fact, a long history of negating Asian law, dating back at least to Max Weber's sociology of law, and his treatment of law in India, China, and Muslim societies.[51] That it was mainly European, British, and, later, American officials, diplomats, traders, and scholars who denied Asia law, and who epistemologically foreclosed the possibility of law in Asian communities has not gone unchallenged.[52]

In their place, legal scholars who work on Asian law, some from the region and others based in Western academies, have put forth their own perspectives – theoretical, doctrinal, ethnographic, and comparative – on Asian law. In an early example of Inter-Asian legal scholarship, the Japanese legal sociologist and anthropologist Masaji Chiba made canonical contributions to the study of what he alternately called "customary law," "living law," and "unofficial law" of Japan, eventually building out conceptual frames taken up by scholars from not just Japan but also Egypt, Iran, Sri Lanka, India, and Thailand.[53] One of his collaborators, Upendra Baxi developed his own sociology of Indian law.[54] The "raw material" of Asian law(s) included ethics, religious law, social norms, market principles, social networks, and other functional equivalents of "law." Expanding the parameters of legal analysis coupled with ongoing deimperializing projects called for new epistemological approaches. Exemplifying the idea that both the substance and study of Asian law demand a new set of analytical tools, Chinese legal scholar Suli Zhu has called attention to China's "native resources" (*bentu ziyuan*) as foundational to its legal

Publishing 2024). On the potential for developing states to develop "heterodox" approaches to private law that diverge from Global North prescriptions, see Kevin E Davis and Mariana Pargendler, *Legal Heterodoxy in the Global South: Adapting Private Law to Local Contexts* (CUP 2025).

49 Wen-Chen Chang et al (eds), *Constitutionalism in Asia: Cases and Materials* (Bloomsbury 2014); Rosalind Dixon and Tom Ginsburg (eds), *Comparative Constitutional Law in Asia* (Edward Elgar 2014); Ngoc Son Bui and Mara Malagodi (eds), *Asian Comparative Constitutional Law, Volume 1: Constitution-Making* (Bloomsbury 2023).

50 Ruskola (n 3).

51 Max Weber, *Economy and Society* (University of California Press 1978 [1922]).

52 Li Chen, *Chinese Law in Imperial Eyes: Sovereignty, Justice, and Transcultural Politics* (Columbia University Press 2016); Kroncke (n 3); Douglas Clark, *Gunboat Justice: Volume 2* (Earnshaw 2015).

53 Masaji Chiba (ed), *Asian Indigenous Law: In Interaction with Received Law* (Routledge 1986).

54 Upendra Baxi, *Toward a Sociology of Indian Law* (Satvahan Publications 1986).

culture and path for development,[55] and has inveighed polemically against what he deems the Western monopoly on knowledge production about Asian law, and Chinese law in particular, calling for the birth of Asian law and social sciences.[56] Contributions by Asian scholars occurred in conjunction with those Western scholars who were trained in Asian law and studied, in particular, the relationships between Asian legal systems, including state, religious, and customary ones.[57]

Ideas of Asian law, of course, have not evolved in an apolitical space. One historical data point is the 1955 Asian Lawyers' Conference in Calcutta. While overshadowed in the academic literature by the Bandung Conference, of the same year, the Calcutta Conference shared many of the key themes as Bandung but focused particularly on their legal aspects. Thus, the lawyers discussed sovereignty, mutual respect, and non-interference, among other topics, within the frame of international law.[58] The Calcutta conference was thus one meeting ground for lawyers to share ideas in the context of anti-colonial struggles.

There would be other moments where Asian leaders would attempt to differentiate themselves from the West. For example, first the Singaporean and Malaysian governments and then the Chinese one espoused discourses on "Asian values." Drawing opportunistically from (Neo-)Confucian communitarianism, Chinese Marxism, and cultural relativism, "Asian values" were also seen as unique to Asia and born of the ether of Asian culture.[59] While the content of Asian values varied according to the regime in question, they often stood for several claims including that rights are culturally determined, the community should be prioritized over the individual, social and economic rights are more important than civil and political ones, and rights are ultimately a matter of national sovereignty.[60] Proponents of Asian values hold that the relationship between rights, governance, and capitalism is fundamentally different in Asian countries given their unique histories and philosophies.[61] Critics, however, hold that Asian values demonstrate states self-orientalizing themselves to legitimate authoritarian rule[62] or other political agendas. Some of the

55 Zhu Suli [朱苏力], *Fazhi jiqi bentu ziyuan (Rule of Law and Native Resources)* (China University of Political Science and Law 2004 [1996]).

56 Zhu Suli [朱苏力], *Songfa xiaxiang: Zhongguo jiceng sifa zhidu yanjiu (Sending the Law down to the Countryside: Research on China's Grassroots Judicial System)* (Peking University 2011).

57 See, e.g., M B Hooker, "The Relationship between Chinese Law and Common Law in Malaysia, Singapore, and Hong Kong" (1969) 28 J Asian Studies 723–742.

58 Amrit S Pradhan, Vice-President, All-India Association of Democratic Lawyers and President of Bombay Branch, Asian Lawyers' Conference: To the Editor, *Times of India* (March 5, 1955) 6.

59 Wm. Theodore De Bary, *Asian Values and Human Rights* (Harvard University Press 1998).

60 Xiaorong Li, "'Asian Values' and the Universality of Human Rights" in Patrick Hayden (ed), *The Philosophy of Human Rights* (Paragon 2001 [1996]) 399–400.

61 See, e.g., Morishima Michio, "Confucianism as a Basis for Capitalism" in Daniel I Okimoto and Thomas P Rohlen (eds), *Inside the Japanese System: Readings on Contemporary Society and Political Economy* (Stanford University Press 1988) 36–38.

62 Jack Donnelly, "Human Rights and Asian Values: A Defense of "Western" Universalism" in Joanne R Bauer and Daniel A Bell (eds), *The East Asian Challenge for Human Rights* (CUP

logic of Asian values can be seen in other politicized discourses, such as the promotion of a "China model"[63] and various strains of Hindu nationalism.[64] Whereas Asian values as a legitimating discourse have largely peaked, these other ideologies continue to have traction in their respective corners.

Law has become a privileged domain for modernization projects in Asia. Whereas the gravitational center of international and comparative law has long been held to be Europe, across a number of contemporary fields of law, including constitutional law, international economic law, data law/cyber law, dispute resolution, and religious law, among others, Asia has become a new fulcrum for legal dynamism and co-evolution. Innovation takes several forms.

First, linking the political discourses on sovereignty and decolonization with the remarkable economic performances of many Asian economies in the latter half of the twentieth century (i.e., Japan's post-WWII economic recovery, the "Asian tigers," China's economic ascendance, and India's rise), scholars have noted that many Asian jurisdictions have developed their own approaches to international law, and international economic law, in particular.[65] It is in the field of commercial law where harmonization across Asian jurisdictions is most apparent. Asian jurisdictions have strong incentives to reduce cross-border transaction costs and facilitate inter-regional trade and investment.

Second, Asian jurists and lawyers have led IAL harmonization projects, such as the Principles of Asian Contract Law[66] led by scholars at Keio University in Japan and Tsinghua University in China, the Asian Principles of Private International Law, based out of Ritsumeikan University in Japan,[67] and the work of the Asia Business Law Institute in Singapore.[68] While not all of these have led to legal or policy innovation, they demonstrate intellectual projects of and for Asian law, in particular its co-evolution across Asian jurisdictions. Third, and related, Asian

1999); Inoue Tatsuo, "Liberal Democracy and Asian Orientalism" in Joanne R Bauer and Daniel A Bell (eds), *The East Asian Challenge for Human Rights* (CUP 1999) 27–59.

63 Francis Fukuyama and Weiwei Zhang, "The China Model: A Dialogue between Frances Fukuyama and Zhang Weiwei" (2011) 4 NPQ 41.

64 Balraj Madhok, *Indianization? What, Why and How* (S Chand 1970).

65 Muthucumaraswamy Sornarajah and Jiangyu Wang, *China, India and the International Economic Order* (CUP 2010); Muthucumaraswamy Sornarajah, "Review of Asian Views on Foreign Investment Law" in Vivienne Bath and Luke Nottage (eds), *Foreign Investment and Dispute Resolution and Practice in Asia* (Routledge 2011).

66 Shinyuan Han, "Principles of Asian Contract Law: An Endeavor of Regional Harmonization of Contract Law in East Asia" (2013) 28 Villanova L Rev 589; Naoki Kanayama, "Principles of Asian Contract Law" (2010) 1406 Jurist 102.

67 Uematsu Mao, "APPIL (Asian Principles of Private International Law) and Its Perspective Regarding International Jurisdiction" (2019) 37 Ritsumeikan L Rev 35.

68 Asia Business Law Institute, "Convergence of Laws and Frameworks for Cross-Border Personal Data transfers in Asia", https://abli.asia/abli-projects/convergence-of-data-privacy-laws-and-frameworks-for-cross-border-transfers-of-personal-data-in-asia/, accessed March 5, 2024.

jurisdictions including, chiefly, Singapore and Hong Kong have led the global race for institutional optimality among dispute resolution venues.[69]

Fourth, middle- and high-income Asian states (e.g., China, Singapore, and Japan) may serve as "intermediaries" for lower-income Asian jurisdictions during legal transplantation. The former may have adapted transplants from the West, and these countries are now transplanting their ideas, through further adaptation and interpretation, to recipient states elsewhere in Asia and Africa. A new generation of Asian legal exporters has subsequently emerged, including India, Singapore, and Vietnam. Hence, law and development requires attention to these "second-order transplants."[70] Tying these strands together, recent multilateral agreements have shifted the world's focus to Asia as a center for advancements in trade law and conflict resolution, as in the example of the RCEP and the Singapore Mediation Convention. The Chinese-led Belt and Road Initiative has also been widely viewed as a novel form of megaregional ordering, connected through bilateral investment treaties, free trade agreements, and soft law.[71] Hence, Asian states may contribute to their own bodies of regional law and transnational law.[72]

Yet another dynamic area for Asian legal revival is the question of religious law. Buddhism, Confucianism, Daoism, Islam, and Christianity all have their own normative sources, including ethical and legal orders.[73] Migrants, missionaries, proselytizers, and refugees have promoted these orders, sometimes not wholly disconnected from secular law and its institutions.[74] Lastly, it bears mentioning that Asian scholarly organizations have served to foment not just academic but also policy change in these areas of law, including the Asian Society of International Law, Asian Academy of International Law, and the Asian Law and Society Association, to name a few. In summary, Asian jurisdictions are emerging as catalysts for academic study (knowledge) and legal practice (power) through both competition and collaboration, and, collectively, they are changing the nature of law in the region and beyond.

69 Reyes and Gu (n 47).

70 Matthew S Erie and Do Hai Ha, "Law and Development Minus Legal Transplants: The Example of China in Vietnam" (2021) 8 Asian J L & Soc 372–401.

71 Gregory Shaffer and Henry Gao, "A New Chinese Economic Order?" (2020) 23 J Int'l Econ L 607–635; Jiangyu Wang, "China's Governance Approach to the Belt and Road Initiative (BRI): Partnerships, Relations, and Law" (2019) 14(4) Glob Trade Cust J 222; Matthew S Erie, "Chinese Law and Development" (2021) 62 HILJ 51.

72 Ngoc Son Bui, "Vertical Law and Development" (2021) 54 Cornell Int'l L J 1; Hsieh (n 11, 2018); Benedict Kingsbury et al (eds), *Megaregulation Contested: Global Economic Ordering after TPP* (OUP 2019).

73 Peter van der Veer, *The Modern Spirit of Asia: The Spiritual and the Secular in China and India* (Princeton University Press 2014).

74 Matthew S Erie, "Shari'a as Taboo of Modern Law: Halal Food, Islamophobia, and China" (2019) 33(3) J L & Rel 390; Fernanda Pirie, *The Rule of Laws: A 4,000-Year Quest to Order the World* (Profile Books 2021); Tom Ginsburg and Benjamin Schonthal (eds), *Buddhism and Comparative Constitutional Law* (CUP 2022).

By way of summary, there are thus three caveats to IAL and its study. First, and echoing insights from the study of Inter-Asia, IAL does not assume that Asia is a homogenous jurisprudential space. Rather, IAL is premised upon the understanding that Asia (and Asian law) is highly heterogenous and dynamic, sometimes contested. As Evan Feigenbaum and Robert Manning have argued, there are (at least) "two Asias": The first is one of economic integration, and the second is characterized by security dilemmas.[75] As to the latter, to take China as an example, the country is nearly surrounded by non-allies; Japan, South Korea, Taiwan, and India all have antagonistic relationships with China, and other countries like Vietnam have historically complicated relationships with China. Hence, any degree of IAL between China and these neighbors is precarious, although there are examples to the contrary.

The second caveat, also drawing on the above, is that IAL does not assume Asia is hermetically sealed. There are ongoing relationships with Western jurisdictions defined by learning, exporting, transplantation, co-evolution, and transnational harmonization. Yet, as mentioned, the East–West relationship is complicated in several ways. The role of "intermediary" states means that legal borrowings, transplantations, or translations may be sequential. Likewise, vertical transplants vis-à-vis regional, megaregional, or transnational law further show Asian jurisdictions informing law beyond the state, and vice versa, those sources of law may shape domestic or "municipal" law in Asia. These interactive relationships – horizontal and vertical – require mapping and analysis.

The third caveat is that IAL is only just emerging; hence, this volume is an early attempt to make sense of embryonic trends that may deepen, evolve, or diverge in the future. Pushback against globalization and enhanced regionalization, including Asian regionalism, may promote more IAL. Without flattening the Asian region, it is likely that increased intra-regional dependence with its economic incentives (e.g., reducing transaction costs and minimizing conflicts between legal systems) may further stimulate the conditions for IAL. Commercial law is one area that already suggests such increased activity.[76] Increased interactions may lead to more legal convergence, sometimes divergence, or innovation. In order to understand these emerging dynamics, the next section provides an analytical framework for the study of IAL.

[75] Evan A Feigenbaum and Robert A Manning, "A Tale of Two Asias" (2012) Foreign Policy. https://foreignpolicy.com/2012/10/31/a-tale-of-two-asias/, accessed March 5, 2024.

[76] Dan W Puchniak, "The False Hope of Stewardship in the Context of Controlling Shareholders: Making Sense Out of the Global Transplant as a Legal Misfit" (2024) 72 AJCL 109–169, 159 ("In Asia, some jurisdictions may even decide to follow the Singapore Family Code model and claim that they are tailoring their approach to a new form of Asian corporate governance – with family owners as the natural stewards of a significant portion of listed companies.").

III THE ANALYTICAL FRAMEWORK

Comparative law scholar Ralf Michaels concludes his study of Asian law with the assertion that what he calls "intra-Asian comparison" holds perhaps the most promise to create a pathway that steers the study of Asian law away from its own essentialization, providing a durable basis for future study.[77] This IAL volume starts where Michaels leaves off, asking: Why study IAL? What insights does it provide? How does one engage in its study?

As part of the process of building a conceptual framework for the study of IAL, on December 16–17, 2022, a group of scholars convened the Inter-Asian Law workshop in Hsinchu, Taiwan, at the National Tsing Hua University. Participants included scholars who focus on several fields including corporate law, international economic law, dispute resolution, constitutional law, comparative law, and interdisciplinary approaches. The participants were united in their study of Asian law; most are from the region and teach in law schools in Asian countries, and a minority are from the US, UK, and Australia and likewise teach Asian law in law schools in their universities. The participants were tasked with addressing one or more of the following questions, which cohere the volume:

1. How and why have specific Asian jurisdictions borrowed or adapted legal innovations, procedures, institutional designs, and techniques from neighbors?
2. What have been the main mechanisms for the flow of ideas about legal change between Asian jurisdictions and who/what have been the agents for that change?
3. How has legal change responded to crisis and transformation (epidemiological, environmental, socioeconomic, political, technological, etc.) in the Asian region?
4. What are the trajectories and dimensions of IAL relationships in various fields? How may IAL relationships necessitate new methods and theories of comparative law?
5. In examining the relationship between law and economic growth as well as technological advances, how has development in specific Asian jurisdictions or the region at large spurred particular types of legal modernization and innovation? Why and how have such types of legal modernization and innovation spilled over to other Asian jurisdictions?
6. Is the Asian region growing indigenous models of law that diverge from Western law? If so, how? In this vein, are there new forms and channels of legal interactions emerging between Asia and the rest of the world?

[77] Ralf Michaels, "How Asian Should Asian Law Be?" in Gary Low (ed), *Convergence and Divergence of Private Law in Asia* (CUP 2022) 227–251.

Over the course of the two-day workshop, participants stimulated synergies between their papers through discussion and elaboration. Comparative cases, literatures, and theoretical frames were identified and used as touchstones to unite the pieces. Discussion between panel members was facilitated by additional commentators who the organizers invited to help round out knowledge on specific areas of Asian law, with a focus on the mechanisms of legal integration, their effects at different levels of analysis, and broader consequences for the political economy of the region. At the end of the workshop, the organizers assessed its findings and contributions but also the gaps. Subsequently, the organizers contacted a small number of additional scholars to fill those gaps.

Over the course of both the Hsinchu workshop and resulting conversations, it became clear that IAL is a broad field, with different types of discernible patterns among specific configurations of jurisdictions, and that, also, the field itself has its own set of limitations. The conversations coalesced around a set of themes that structure this volume.

Types and methods of interactions: These include cooperation, competition, mimicry, diffusion, norm innovation, and export. They are not mutually exclusive types or methods. They also may not be limited to Asia but show inheritance and borrowing from or co-evolution with Western jurisdictions even if the crucible of the interaction resides in Asia. History of inter-state relations, types of legal systems (e.g., common law, civil law, Islamic law, hybrid, etc.), geopolitical and economic contexts, and types of political regimes are important variables explaining which type of interaction prevails and its relative success.

Actors and intermediaries: The role of the experts, platforms, or institutions that facilitate the movement (and translation) of law is pivotal. Specific intermediaries include judiciaries, administrative officials, lawyers, regulators, and scholars. Institutional actors include trade agreements, international and regional organizations, and bilateral platforms. Such actors and intermediaries have different catalytic functions and processes at various levels. These different individual and institutional intermediaries may have different capacities, interests, influences, constraints, and agendas, which may, in turn, structure IAL.

Effects, consequences, and conflicts: IAL may result in harmonization and convergence, which can catalyze economic, judicial, or political relations. IAL may just as probably lead to inter-jurisdictional borrowing that does not result in harmonization given that the effects of localization may trump convergence. The ultimate effect may be that legal exchange effectively promotes reinforcement or retrenchment of local identity, politics, or institutional design. IAL may even lead to conflicts that can generate friction between and among jurisdictions. Effects may be more or less pronounced in substantive or procedural areas of law, domestic or transnational levels. Just as equally, would-be norm exporters may encounter obstacles to such normative work. Differences in political systems, cultures, languages, legal orders, and long-standing sensitivities and even hostilities can greatly complicate outcomes.

These themes, which, broadly speaking, provide a conceptual scaffolding for the volume, are taken up by the individual contributions. By using these themes as touchstones for their individual contribution, the writers explicitly and implicitly generate conversations across their respective studies. In short, through this analytical framework, the writers assess the merits and potential, as well as limitations and even shortcomings, of IAL as a mode of conducting comparative (and international) legal analysis.

IV ORGANIZATION OF THE VOLUME

The volume is structured to reflect the results of this work. It includes, in addition to this Introduction, which provides the background to and analytical framework for IAL, four sections: *Commercial Law: From Firms to International Economic Law* (hereinafter "Commercial Law"); *Constitutional Law: Judicial Practices, Inter-Court Dialogue, and Democratic Resilience* (hereinafter "Constitutional Law"); *Law's Movements: Transnational Networks, Religious Donors, and Institutional Co-Learners* (hereinafter "Law's Movements"); and *Emerging Problems: Between Technology and Authoritarianism* (hereinafter "Emerging Problems"). These sections capture the main legal domains of interaction.

Part I, *Commercial Law*, features contributions that analyze innovations in private or business law in Inter-Asia, a hallmark of this new field of inquiry. For example, Gen Goto and Dan W. Puchniak examine the corporate law frameworks for Asian jurisdictions with a focus on independent directors, derivative actions, and stewardship codes. They argue that alleged convergence with Anglo-American law is superficial; rather, they point to local factors as shaping corporate governance reform in Asian jurisdictions. In their analysis, IAL becomes a lens through which to explore this adaptive diversity.

In a similar vein, Trang (Mae) Nguyen explores the role of "company towns" in Inter-Asian global supply chains and their role as legal entrepôts as they are both formed by and formative of various sources of law, including sub-national, national, and transnational. She finds that such company towns mark divergence from earlier American versions that were vertically integrated; rather, inter-Asian ones demonstrate horizontal (and indeed regional) integration.

Tran Hoang Tu Linh analyzes what happens when things go wrong and disputes arise between corporate and other parties. In particular, she assesses Inter-Asian hubs for alternative dispute resolution, including arbitration, and their modeling for second-tier (smaller market) Asian states in the region. In the same spirit as the other contributions, she concludes that while Asian hubs may not displace the dominant centers of international commercial dispute resolution (e.g., London and Paris), they demonstrate more frequent and tighter interaction, showing causal connections in design and implementation as in the example of Singapore's influence in Vietnamese arbitration.

Lastly, Pasha Hsieh provides an assessment above the firm or national level to show how ASEAN members are building international economic law. They do so in a way that is distinct in procedural rather than substantive terms; they create multilayered investment agreements for the region. For Hsieh, the uniqueness of IAL at the international level is its procedural aspects, consensus-building and interest-alignment. Such a perspective casts light on how Asian regionalism may foment IAL. The section thus shows across a number of units (sub-national, national, and supranational) how IAL operates to support cross-border business.

Part II, *Constitutional Law*, shifts the focus from private law matters to public ones and the central role of courts in establishing legal norms for their respective jurisdictions. Yvonne Tew, Deepa Das Acevedo, and Gauri Pillai each provide different accounts of national courts' cross-citations on specific questions of law, including judicial review, essential religious practices, and reproductive rights, respectively. Each focuses on the importance of India (and, for Pillai, Nepal) as an epicenter of case law that has gained traction outside of the home state, in neighboring common law South Asian and Southeast Asia countries. Whereas Tew and Das Acevedo provide empirical accounts of cross-citation and doctrinal migration arguing for deep localization driven by IAL rather than homogenization, Pillai takes a hypothetical approach to show how IAL can be a wellspring of legal imagination. The authors draw different conclusions about how borrowing jurisdictions may deploy case citations to Indian (or Nepali) decisions and what such practices mean for judicial empowerment, regionalism, and women's rights, broadly construed.

Wen-Chen Chang and Yi-Li Lee take a different tack in their contribution. Contrary to the notion that Asian states are dedemocratizing, the co-authors suggest that several states, South Korea, Taiwan, and Singapore among them, feature courts that resist authoritarian or illiberal trends. As such, the co-authors examine the constitutional foundations, jurisprudential developments, and democratic processes that allowed such jurisdictions to do so despite trends in other states – including Western ones – to exercise various emergency measures during the COVID-19 pandemic that may have laid the groundwork for states of exception. In particular, building on the shared constitutional norms underlying their pandemic responses, the authors point to the learning among the three jurisdictions in pandemic legal framework, multi-level governance between central and local governments, and the involvement of non-governmental organizations (NGOs). In summary, the section demonstrates various forms of interaction – explicit or implicit – between Asian jurisdictions and among their courts in particular which suggest diffusion of constitutional norms and principles.

Part III, *Law's Movements*, provides inter-disciplinary studies of how law "moves" throughout Inter-Asia. Contributions spotlight several such ways, including through transnational IAL networks, religious donations, and institutional co-learning. These insights, in turn, help reflect on conventions in comparative law more generally, for example, the focus on "legal transplants." For instance, Matthew S. Erie shows how China has emerged as a would-be norm exporter to developing countries in Asia. It does so through creating transnational networks, although this is hardly a facile process. China has taken the lead in several areas including cyber law and data regulation but also in terms of how political authorities use law – all of which may be attractive (to varying degrees) to other states in Asia or Africa.

Examining a different set of relationships, Theodora Yuni Shah Putri and Veronica L. Taylor focus on inter-regional legal influence between Middle Eastern and Southeast Asian communities. Specifically, they examine the case of Saudi influence on criminal law reform in Indonesia. Putri and Taylor are thus also interested in transnational networks and ones that, in their understanding of IAL, transgress the sacred–secular divide of law. Lastly, Valerie Hans focuses on the diffusion of models of lay participation in trial systems across Asia. She observes that some of these represent "legal translations," a concept that she prefers over transplants. Legal translation, for Hans, is a mode of institutional co-learning as states studied each other's advancements in lay participation. For example, Japan studied systems throughout the world and other East Asian states like Korea and Taiwan studied Japan's modifications, among those of other states. Repeating earlier historical patterns, established during the Meiji Period, Japan has been a first mover in adapting Western law into local law, which was, in turn, adapted by other Asian states. In summary, the section demonstrates different modalities for the diffusion of IAL and diverse normative effects.

Part IV, *Emerging Problems*, begins where the previous section left off, by taking stock of some of the key issues facing the region, including emerging technologies and creeping authoritarianism, issues that are all endogenous to the Asian region and global in scope. First, many Asian states, such as China, Japan, Korea, Taiwan, and Singapore, have led the global race in integrating AI and other "smart" technologies like smart cities into their commercial and legal systems, which have caused their own challenges (e.g., privacy protection). Two contributions in this section place these innovations in context, national, transnational, and comparative. Ching-Fu Lin explores how East Asian countries have been shaping law and policy initiatives in response to the complex and multifaceted challenges posed by AI and how such jurisdictions interact through regulatory cross-referencing, learning, and competition. Lin further points out new regional forums such as DEPA as potential venues for IAL policy dialogue, best practices exchanges, and the co-development of AI governance. In parallel, Yoshiko Naiki examines the role of Japan, in competition with Singapore, and China, and the forms and substance of their policies in shaping smart cities in ASEAN states. These smart cities are built through hard and soft infrastructure, and also legal infrastructures in the sense of IAL. Naiki shows how Japanese proponents of the technology engage with questions of law in their construction of smart cities outside of Japan.

Jacques deLisle draws attention to an extreme case of the impact of one Asian jurisdiction on another: the increasing footprint of Chinese governance in Hong Kong. DeLisle diagnoses the different types of this influence as a "field guide" to IAL, including the informal methods that are adopted by Hong Kong in the shadow of China's influence. While the administrative relationship between China and Hong Kong is distinct, DeLisle's contribution offers insights for IAL, suggesting that the social, political, and economic weight of one jurisdiction may lead to legal and judicial change in another. Through its studies on emerging challenges such as advanced technology and authoritarianism, this section highlights that IAL is not a seamless or given process, but rather, encounters tension between cross-border work and domestic priorities, including protectionism and sovereignty.

In lieu of a conclusion, "A Beginning" summarizes and synthesizes these findings. It notes the potential for IAL as a comparative lens but also recognizes its limitations. It further suggests that the thematic domains of law covered in the four sections are not exclusive. There are more than likely additional domains and questions to which the IAL analytical framework can be applied. It further suggests that intra-regional comparison may not be unique to Asia, and that IAL may provide a template for considering Inter-Latinx law, Inter-African law, and Inter-European law. In summary, IAL and its derivates may suggest pathways to rethink comparative and international law from the vantage of the former peripheries that have, in a period of geo-economic flux and ideological doubt, to varying degrees, become center.

PART I

Commercial Law

From Firms to International Economic Law

1

Faux Convergence in Asian Corporate Governance

Unmasking the Illusion of Anglo-American Transplants

Gen Goto and Dan W. Puchniak

I INTRODUCTION

Over the past few decades, corporate governance in Asia has undergone dramatic changes. On the surface, many Asian jurisdictions appear to have converged toward Anglo-American corporate governance laws and practices. Independent directors, a corporate governance mechanism invented in the United States (US) in the 1970s, are now ubiquitous in boardrooms across the region.[1] Stewardship codes, a United Kingdom (UK) corporate governance solution to the 2008 Global Financial Crisis, exhort institutional investors to be active owners in most of Asia's important economies.[2] Derivative actions, a historical hallmark of US and UK company law, are now enshrined in company laws across Asia – ironically being more consequential in Japan than almost anywhere else in the world, despite Japan's civil law roots and ostensible culture of non-litigiousness.[3] To a casual observer, it may seem that corporate law and governance in Asia has converged on the Anglo-American-cum-global corporate law

[1] Dan W Puchniak and Kon Sik Kim, "Varieties of Independent Directors in Asia: A Taxonomy" in Dan W Puchniak, Harald Baum and Luke Nottage (eds), *Independent Directors in Asia: A Historical, Contextual and Comparative Approach* (CUP 2017) 89, 89–93.

[2] Gen Goto, Alan K Koh and Dan W Puchniak, "Diversity of Shareholder Stewardship in Asia: Faux Convergence" (2020) 53 Vand J Transnat'l L 829, 832–833; Alan K Koh, Dan W Puchniak and Gen Goto, "Shareholder Stewardship in Asia: Functional Diversity Within Superficial Formal Convergence" in Dionysia Katelouzou and Dan W Puchniak (eds), *Global Shareholder Stewardship* (CUP 2022) 613, 614; Dan W Puchniak, "The False Hope of Stewardship in the Context of Controlling Shareholders: Making Sense Out of the Global Transplant of a Legal Misfit" (2024) 72 AJCL 109, 127–132.

[3] Harald Baum and Dan W Puchniak, "The Derivative Action: An Economic, Historical and Practice Oriented Approach" in Dan W Puchniak, Harald Baum and Michael Ewing-Chow (eds), *The Derivative Action in Asia: A Comparative and Functional Approach* (CUP 2012) 1–89; Dan W Puchniak, "The Derivative Action in Asia: A Complex Reality" (2012) 9 Berkeley Bus L J 1, 2–5; Dan W Puchniak and Masafumi Nakahigashi, "Japan's Love for Derivative Actions: Irrational Behavior and Non-Economic Motives as Rational Explanations for Shareholder Litigation" (2012) 45 Vand J Transnat'l L 1, 4–8.

and governance model. From this perspective, as predicted by two of the most prominent corporate law scholars in the US, maybe we have reached, or at least are very close to, "The End of History for Corporate Law."[4]

However, this superficial convergence masks a far more complex reality. As this chapter will demonstrate, the adoption of Anglo-American corporate governance laws and mechanisms in Asia often amounts to "faux convergence" – a phenomenon where jurisdictions implement foreign laws and corporate law and governance mechanisms in name and form, but not in substance or function.[5] By closely examining three key areas – independent directors, derivative actions, and stewardship – we can see how Asian jurisdictions have selectively borrowed and adapted Anglo-American corporate law and governance concepts to fit their own unique jurisdiction-specific contexts, producing outcomes that often diverge significantly from Anglo-American corporate governance practices.

Crucially, this chapter goes beyond merely highlighting the divergence between Asian and Anglo-American practices. It emphasizes the rich diversity within Asia itself, advocating for the power of inter-Asian comparisons in advancing our understanding of comparative corporate law.[6] By examining how different Asian jurisdictions have adapted and implemented similar governance mechanisms, we can uncover nuanced insights into the dynamics of formal legal transplants and functional jurisdiction-specific practices in comparative corporate law and governance that are often overlooked in broader East–West comparisons. Using Erie and Lin's taxonomy of analytical frameworks for Inter-Asian Law (IAL) the theory of faux convergence could be seen as an attempt to carve out an overlooked form of "types and methods of interactions" among Asian jurisdictions and between them and Western jurisdictions by analyzing the superficial nature of convergence achieved as "effects, consequences, and conflicts" caused by such interactions.[7]

The theory of faux convergence, coupled with a focus on inter-Asian comparisons, provides a powerful lens for understanding the true nature of corporate governance reforms and practices in Asia. It reveals how policymakers and companies in the region have responded to global pressures for governance reform while maintaining systems that reflect deep-seated local norms, power structures, and institutional logics. Faux convergence allows Asian jurisdictions to signal compliance with international standards while preserving space for locally appropriate governance models. Meanwhile, inter-Asian comparisons illuminate the diverse strategies employed by different jurisdictions in this process of adaptation and localization.

4 Henry Hansmann and Reinier Kraakman, "The End of History for Corporate Law" (2001) 89 Geo L J 439.

5 Goto, Koh and Puchniak (n 2) 876.

6 See generally Matthew S Erie and Ching-Fu Lin, "Introduction: The Emergence of Inter-Asian Law", this volume.

7 See Ibid 17.

This chapter develops the theory of faux convergence and demonstrates its explanatory power through an in-depth examination of independent directors, derivative actions, and stewardship codes across major Asian jurisdictions.[8] It builds on our previous work analyzing the complex reality of these mechanisms in Asia,[9] which challenged oversimplified notions of legal transplants and convergence. By synthesizing insights across these areas and emphasizing inter-Asian variations, we can construct a more nuanced understanding of how corporate governance actually functions in Asian contexts.

The faux convergence framework, combined with inter-Asian comparative analysis, makes several important contributions. First, it provides a more accurate picture of the state of corporate law and governance in Asia, moving beyond surface-level observations to uncover the underlying dynamics and diversity within the region. Second, it offers a new theoretical perspective that transcends the traditional convergence–divergence debate in comparative corporate law and governance. Third, it yields practical insights for policymakers, investors, and companies seeking to navigate Asia's complex and varied corporate law and governance landscape.

Ultimately, embracing the reality of faux convergence and the value of inter-Asian comparisons pushes us to rethink fundamental assumptions about the evolution of corporate law and governance around the world. It highlights the persistent diversity and path-dependence of national systems, even as globalization drives superficial harmonization. And it underscores the need for nuanced, contextual analysis rather than universalist theories in the field of comparative corporate law and governance.

The rest of this chapter proceeds as follows. Section II elaborates on the theory of faux convergence, explaining its core elements and how it differs from existing frameworks. Section III examines independent directors, derivative actions, and stewardship codes in Asia through the lens of faux convergence, with a particular emphasis on inter-Asian variations. Section IV concludes by synthesizing key insights from these case studies, highlighting the power of inter-Asian comparisons, and discussing broader implications for comparative corporate law and governance scholarship.

8 The authors first coined the term "faux convergence" in their articles with Alan K Koh (see Goto, Koh and Puchniak (n 2) and Koh, Puchniak and Goto (n 2). This chapter significantly develops the theory of "faux convergence" by providing a more detailed explanation of the concept and applying it to multiple areas of corporate law in Asia.

9 See generally, Puchniak (n 3); Puchniak and Nakahigashi (n 3); Dan W Puchniak, "Multiple Faces of Shareholder Power in Asia: Complexity Revealed" in Randall Thomas and Jennifer Hill (eds), *The Research Handbook on Shareholder Power* (Edward Elgar 2015) 511; Puchniak and Kim (n 1); Gen Goto, "The Logic and Limits of Stewardship Codes: The Case of Japan" (2019) 15 Berkeley Bus L J 365; Dan W Puchniak and Umakanth Varottil, "Related Party Transactions in Commonwealth Asia: Complicating the Comparative Paradigm" (2020) 17 Berkeley Bus L J 1; Goto, Koh and Puchniak (n 2); Koh, Puchniak and Goto (n 2); Puchniak (n 2).

II THE THEORY OF FAUX CONVERGENCE

Faux convergence refers to the phenomenon where jurisdictions adopt the outward form of foreign corporate governance practices, without implementing their substance or intended function.[10] It involves the selective borrowing and adaptation of governance mechanisms to fit local jurisdiction-specific contexts, often producing outcomes that diverge significantly from the source model.[11] Faux convergence allows jurisdictions to signal compliance with global norms while maintaining governance systems that reflect deep-seated local power structures, norms, and institutional logics.[12]

Several key elements characterize faux convergence. To begin, there is superficial adoption, where jurisdictions implement the basic form or structure of a foreign governance mechanism, but not its underlying substance. For instance, independent directors may be mandated, but lack true independence.[13] This is often accompanied by functional divergence, where the adopted mechanism serves different purposes or functions than in its jurisdiction of origin. For example, stewardship codes may aim to entrench rather than challenge corporate insiders.[14]

Contextual adaptation is another hallmark of faux convergence.[15] Foreign practices are modified to fit local jurisdiction-specific contexts, power structures, and cultural norms. This reshaping fundamentally alters how the mechanism operates in practice. A key driver of adoption is often the motivation to signal adherence to global governance standards, rather than a genuine desire for reform. This signaling function allows jurisdictions to gain legitimacy in international markets.[16]

Importantly, faux convergence involves the preservation of local practices. Core features of the local governance system are often maintained beneath a veneer of foreign practices. This allows jurisdictions to balance external pressures for reform with internal resistance to fundamental change.[17]

10 Goto, Koh and Puchniak (n 2) 876.

11 This can be seen in Asian jurisdictions selectively adopting prominent Anglo-American-cum-global corporate governance mechanisms – such as independent directors and stewardship codes – and then using them for their own purposes. See, Goto, Koh and Puchniak (n 2) 877; Puchniak and Kim (n 1) 90–93.

12 Goto, Koh and Puchniak (n 2) 877.

13 For example, in Indonesia, see Royhan Akbar, Nathaniel Mangunsong and Dan W Puchniak, "The Abolition of Independent Directors in Indonesia: Rationally Autochthonous or Foolishly Idiosyncratic?" (forthcoming) AJCL. https://ssrn.com/abstract=4941189.

14 Dan W Puchniak and Samantha S Tang, "Singapore's Embrace of Shareholder Stewardship: A Puzzling Success" in Dionysia Katelouzou and Dan W Puchniak (eds), *Global Shareholder Stewardship* (CUP 2022) 297, 298–300.

15 Goto, Koh and Puchniak (n 2) 880.

16 Puchniak (n 2) 143–147.

17 See Katharina Pistor, "The Standardization of Law and Its Effect on Developing Economies" (2002) 50 AJCL 97, 98–99 (noting the tendency of domestic players to resist imposed rules from outside).

Faux convergence differs from several existing theoretical perspectives on comparative corporate governance. Unlike traditional convergence theory, which posits movement toward a single optimal model (usually Anglo-American shareholder primacy),[18] faux convergence recognizes persistent functional diversity in governance outcomes. It goes beyond the notion of "divergence within convergence"[19] by highlighting how adopted practices may serve entirely different functions than in their source jurisdictions.[20]

The concept of faux convergence also moves past simplistic cultural or legal origins explanations for governance differences. Instead, it emphasizes how local actors strategically adapt foreign practices to serve their interests within jurisdiction-specific contexts.[21] This produces complex hybrid models rather than wholesale transplantation or rejection of foreign approaches. The faux convergence framework builds on institutional approaches to comparative corporate law and governance, which emphasize how governance practices are shaped by their broader institutional environment.[22] However, it particularly highlights the agency and strategic behavior of local actors in selectively implementing and reshaping governance mechanisms to work within their local jurisdiction-specific contexts.

Crucially, the theory of faux convergence builds upon, but importantly differs from, Ronald Gilson's influential distinction between formal and functional convergence in corporate law and governance.[23] Gilson posited that while formal convergence of corporate law rules might be impeded by path dependence, jurisdictions could achieve functional convergence by developing substitutes that fulfill similar economic functions.[24] However, the concept of faux convergence turns Gilson's theory on its head in several crucial ways.

First, faux convergence suggests that even when there is apparent formal convergence in corporate governance laws or mechanisms, this may mask significant functional divergence. Unlike in Gilson's framework, where functional convergence could occur without formal similarity,[25] faux convergence highlights cases where there is surface-level formal adoption without true functional alignment.[26]

18 Hansmann and Kraakman (n 4).

19 Jeffrey N Gordon, "Convergence and Persistence in Corporate Law and Governance" in Jeffrey N Gordon and Wolf-Georg Ringe (eds), *The Oxford Handbook of Corporate Law and Governance, Oxford Handbooks* (OUP 2018) 28, 41–44.

20 Goto, Koh and Puchniak (n 2) 876.

21 Ibid 877–878.

22 See, for example, Masahiko Aoki, *Information, Incentives, and Bargaining in the Japanese Economy* (CUP 1988); Curtis J Milhaupt and Katharina Pistor, *Law and Capitalism: What Corporate Crises Reveal about Legal Systems and Economic Development Around the World* (University of Chicago Press 2008).

23 Ronald J Gilson, "Globalizing Corporate Governance: Convergence of Form or Function" (2001) 49 AJCL 329.

24 Gilson (n 23) 334–340.

25 Ibid 336–337, 337–340.

26 See Goto, Koh and Puchniak (n 2) 879–880 (see figure 1 describing differences of formal, functional, and faux convergences).

Second, while Gilson's theory assumes that functional convergence is driven by efficiency imperatives and will ultimately lead jurisdictions to similar economic outcomes,[27] faux convergence recognizes that adopted mechanisms may be repurposed to serve entirely different economic or political functions than in their jurisdictions of origin. The motivations behind faux convergence often have more to do with signaling conformity to the global norm than with achieving functionally similar governance outcomes.[28]

Third, faux convergence goes beyond Gilson's binary of formal versus functional convergence, coined in the subtitle of his seminal article,[29] by illuminating the complex ways in which governance mechanisms are strategically adapted and reconfigured as they move across borders. It emphasizes how local actors may deliberately subvert the intended functions of adopted practices to serve their own interests, rather than simply finding alternate means to achieve similar functional ends.[30]

Finally, whereas Gilson's theory suggests that functional convergence might be a pathway toward more fundamental formal convergence over time,[31] the concept of faux convergence highlights how superficial formal adoption may actually serve to prevent deeper functional changes.[32] By creating the illusion of convergence, faux convergence can relieve pressure for more substantive reforms while allowing core features of local governance systems to persist.[33]

Ultimately, faux convergence provides a more nuanced and realistic account of how corporate law and governance evolves in the face of global and local pressures. It moves beyond simplistic narratives of convergence or resistance to foreign models. Instead, it illuminates the complex processes through which governance practices are negotiated, contested, and reconfigured as they move across borders.

The concept of faux convergence is particularly valuable for understanding corporate law and governance developments in Asia. As we will see in Section III, the adoption of independent directors, derivative actions, and stewardship codes across Asian jurisdictions exemplifies the dynamics of faux convergence. While these mechanisms may superficially resemble their Anglo-American counterparts, their actual implementation and impact often diverge dramatically from Anglo-American models. The faux convergence lens reveals how Asian jurisdictions have strategically responded to global governance pressures while maintaining systems that reflect local jurisdiction-specific realities. Moreover, the faux convergence

27 Gilson (n 23) 338.

28 Puchniak (n 2) 140–141, 143–147.

29 Gilson (n 23).

30 Puchniak (n 2) 149.

31 Gilson (n 23) 338 ("Functional convergence is likely the first response to competitive pressure because changing the form of existing institutions is costly.").

32 Puchniak (n 2) 149, 158–159.

33 Dan W Puchniak and Luh Luh Lan, "Independent Directors in Singapore: Puzzling Compliance Requiring Explanation" (2017) 65 AJCL 265, 274. See also Puchniak (n 2) 156–157.

framework helps explain why decades of governance reforms modeled on Anglo-American practices have often failed to fundamentally reshape corporate behavior in many Asian markets.[34] By recognizing how adopted mechanisms are reconfigured to serve local purposes, we can better anticipate their actual impact and limitations.

In the next section, we will examine how faux convergence dynamics have played out in the implementation of independent directors, derivative actions, and stewardship codes across major Asian jurisdictions. This analysis will demonstrate the explanatory power of the faux convergence concept and yield insights into the true nature of corporate governance in Asia.

III THE COMPLEX REALITY OF CORPORATE GOVERNANCE IN ASIA: INDEPENDENT DIRECTORS, DERIVATIVE ACTIONS, AND STEWARDSHIP CODES

As briefly highlighted in Section I, corporate law and governance mechanisms that originated in Anglo-America have been widely adopted across Asia, often with the encouragement of international organizations and experts advocating for "global best practices."[35] At first glance, this trend appears to provide evidence of formal convergence in corporate law and governance. However, a closer examination reveals a much more complex reality.

This section will explore three key corporate governance mechanisms that have been widely adopted across Asia – independent directors, derivative actions, and stewardship codes – to demonstrate how their implementation and function often diverge significantly from their Anglo-American origins. This analysis reveals that while there may be superficial convergence in the formal adoption of these mechanisms, there is substantial divergence in how they actually operate within Asia's unique jurisdiction-specific contexts. Understanding this "faux convergence" is critical for developing a more nuanced view of comparative corporate law and governance.

A. *Independent Directors*

The independent director, a corporate governance mechanism with roots in the US,[36] has become ubiquitous across Asia's leading economies over the past few

34 Puchniak (n 9) 512–515.

35 For the increasing influence of international organizations in the global corporate governance discussion, see Mariana Pargendler, "The Rise of International Corporate Law" (2021) 98 Wash U L Rev 1765.

36 For the development of independent directors in the US, see Jeffrey N Gordon, "The Rise of Independent Directors in the United States, 1950–2005: Of Shareholder Value and Stock Market Prices" (2007) 59 Stan L Rev 1465.

decades.[37] On the surface, this appears to be a clear example of corporate law and governance convergence, with Asian jurisdictions adopting a key feature of the Anglo-American model. Indeed, most Asian jurisdictions now mandate that public companies have a certain number or percentage of independent directors on their boards.[38] However, a closer examination reveals that the form and function of independent directors in Asia often diverge significantly from the US model.

While the original US concept of the independent director focuses primarily on independence from management, most Asian jurisdictions have adopted definitions that require independence from both management and significant shareholders.[39] This reflects the prevalence of concentrated ownership structures in Asia, where controlling shareholders rather than management often dominate corporate governance.[40] The position of independent directors within corporate law and governance structures also varies widely. While some jurisdictions like Hong Kong and Singapore have adopted one-tier board structures similar to the US, others like Japan and China have unique board structures that create different roles for independent directors.[41]

In many Asian jurisdictions, controlling shareholders retain significant influence over the selection and removal of ostensibly "independent" directors, potentially compromising their true independence in their intended role as monitors of controlling shareholders on behalf of minority shareholders.[42] In addition to the powerful role played by controlling shareholders in most of Asia's leading economies, independent directors in Asia are driven by unique local factors, which often have resulted in them serving significantly different purposes than their US counterparts. For example, in China, many independent directors are academics who may lack business expertise to be effective independent directors, but provide legitimacy and government connections.[43] In Singapore's family-controlled firms, independent directors often act as mediators in family disputes rather than as monitors of management.[44] In Japan, which is one of the latest among Asian jurisdictions to promote or require independent directors, independent directors are now expected to champion investors' interests in the boardroom, which has been traditionally dominated by managerial directors.[45] This might sound similar to the role of

37 Puchniak and Kim (n 1) 89.

38 Ibid 90–93.

39 Ibid 97–99, 102–104.

40 Puchniak (n 2) 132–134.

41 Puchniak and Kim (n 1) 104–107.

42 For an Indonesian example, see Akbar, Mangunsong and Puchniak (n 13). See also Lucian A Bebchuk and Assaf Hamdani, "Independent Directors and Controlling Shareholders" (2017) 165 U Pa L Rev 1271.

43 Puchniak and Kim (n 1) 107–108.

44 Ibid 117.

45 Gen Goto, "Recent Boardroom Reforms in Japan and the Roles of Outside/Independent Directors" in Hiroshi Oda (ed), *Comparative Corporate Governance: The Case of Japan, Journal of Japanese Law Special Issue No.12* (Carl Heymanns/Wolters Kluwer 2018) 33, 45–53.

independent directors in the US, but the difference is that independent directors are promoted by the Japanese government as a part of its policy to overcome Japan's long-time economic malaise.[46]

Equally important as illuminating the distinction between independent directors in Asia from the original US concept of the independent director, is the insight that the "faux convergence" lens provides into the functional diversity of independent directors *within* Asia. As one of us observes in a summary chapter in a book on independent directors in Asia:

> Although there are important similarities in the form and function of "independent directors" within Asia, there are also significant intra-Asia jurisdictional differences. While intra-Asia comparisons of 'independent directors' may have more utility than Asia–US comparisons, jurisdictional differences in the form and function of "independent directors" within Asia must also be recognised and accounted for in comparative analyses.[47]

This diversity in the actual implementation and function of independent directors across Asia demonstrates how a corporate law and governance mechanism can be formally adopted while being adapted to serve very different purposes across jurisdictions and cautions against assuming that the mere presence of independent directors indicates convergence toward an Anglo-American model of corporate law and governance.[48]

B. *Derivative Actions*

The derivative action, which allows shareholders to pursue a lawsuit for and on behalf of the company, is another corporate law and governance mechanism that has been widely adopted across Asia. Again, this appears on the surface to demonstrate convergence toward Anglo-American corporate governance norms. However, a closer examination reveals significant divergences in both the legal frameworks and practical utilization of derivative actions across Asian jurisdictions.

While common law jurisdictions in Asia inherited the restrictive English rule in *Foss v. Harbottle*, many have since adopted statutory derivative actions to facilitate minority shareholders' utilization of the derivative action.[49] Meanwhile, civil law jurisdictions have often created derivative action mechanisms without this historical baggage. Jurisdictions vary widely in who can bring derivative actions.[50] Some

[46] Hideaki Miyajima and Takuji Saito, "Corporate Governance Reforms under Abenomics: The Economic Consequences of Two Codes" in Takeo Hoshi and Phillip Y Lipscy (eds), *The Political Economy of the Abe Government and Abenomics Reforms* (CUP 2021) 357, 363–366.

[47] Puchniak and Kim (n 1) 96–97.

[48] Ibid 131.

[49] Puchniak (n 3) 14–15.

[50] Ibid 14.

impose minimum shareholding requirements, while others allow any shareholder to sue.[51] This significantly impacts the practical availability of the mechanism. The specific procedures for initiating and maintaining derivative actions differ substantially across jurisdictions, affecting their accessibility and effectiveness.[52]

The allocation of legal costs and the availability of contingency fees greatly influence the economic incentives for shareholders to pursue derivative litigation. These factors vary significantly across Asia.[53] The types of corporate wrongdoing that can be addressed through derivative actions and the available remedies differ across jurisdictions.[54]

Despite similar formal rules in some cases, the actual use of derivative actions varies dramatically. Japan and Korea saw a significant spike in derivative actions after they lay moribund for decades,[55] while the derivative action has remained rare in listed companies in many other Asian jurisdictions throughout its history.[56] As one of us notes in an article on the derivative action in Asia:

> The point is simple. There are a myriad of complex factors which result in varying levels of derivative litigation in Asia's leading economies. Ironically, the one factor that is conspicuously absent as a defining force of derivative litigation in all of Asia's leading economies is Asia's ostensibly non-litigious culture.[57]

This diversity in the implementation and use of derivative actions across Asia demonstrates how transplanted legal mechanisms can evolve in unexpected ways when introduced into different jurisdiction-specific contexts.[58] It also highlights the danger of making broad generalizations about "Asian" approaches to corporate law and governance or litigation.

[51] Ibid 18.

[52] See, for example, Meng Seng Wee and Dan W Puchniak, "Derivative Actions in Singapore: Mundanely Non-Asian, Intriguingly Non-American and at the Forefront of the Commonwealth" in Dan W Puchniak, Harald Baum and Michael Ewing-Chow (eds), *The Derivative Action in Asia: A Comparative and Functional Approach* (CUP 2012) 323, 341–346 and Gen Goto, "Legally 'Strong' Shareholders of Japan" (2014) 3 MJPVL 125, 138–139.

[53] Puchniak (n 3) 17–18.

[54] For example, the liability of controlling shareholders cannot be exercised by shareholders' derivative suits in Japan. See Goto (n 52) 138.

[55] Japan is also known for having court decisions imposing a substantial monetary liability on defendant directors from time to time. For a recent case where former directors of Tokyo Electric Power Company were held liable for more than 13 trillion Japanese Yen, see Gen Goto, "ESG, Externalities, and the Limits of the Business Judgment Rule: TEPCO Derivative Suit on Fukushima Nuclear Accident and the Expansion of Caremark" (2024) 12 Chinese J Comp L 1.

[56] Puchniak (n 3) 4–5, 18–19.

[57] Ibid 5.

[58] Ibid 24–28.

C. *Stewardship Codes*

The rapid adoption of stewardship codes across Asia since 2014 appears, at first glance, to be a clear example of corporate law and governance convergence. These codes, inspired by the UK Stewardship Code of 2010, ostensibly aim to promote active ownership by institutional investors.[59] Their widespread adoption has been hailed by some as evidence that Asian jurisdictions are embracing a more shareholder-centric model of corporate law and governance with a focus on less managerial risk-taking and maximizing long-term shareholder value.[60] However, a closer examination reveals that the adoption of UK-style stewardship codes in Asia often represents a form of "faux convergence." While the codes may be similar in form,[61] their intended and actual functions often diverge significantly from the UK model, the purpose of which is to motivate institutional investors to monitor corporate management to prevent them from engaging in the type of excessive risk-taking and short-termism that led to the Global Financial Crisis and, more recently, to promote an environmental, social, and governance (ESG) agenda.[62]

Unlike the UK, most Asian jurisdictions do not have dispersed ownership structures dominated by institutional investors. Many listed companies have controlling shareholders, fundamentally altering the context in which stewardship operates.[63] The types of investors targeted by stewardship codes also vary among Asian jurisdictions. While most focus narrowly on traditional institutional investors, Singapore stands out for its code that focuses on controlling families – a unique attempt to make the UK's idea of stewardship "fit" Singapore's (and most of Asia's) local context.[64]

The goals driving the adoption of stewardship codes differ widely across Asian jurisdictions. In Japan, the stewardship code was part of a broader economic growth strategy aimed at making companies take *more* risk to use capital more efficiently.[65] In Korea, the code was seen as a tool to address governance issues in family-controlled conglomerates (*chaebols*).[66] In Singapore and Hong Kong, the adoption

59 Goto, Koh and Puchniak (n 2) 842.

60 See Goto, Koh and Puchniak (n 2) 844–846 (citing perceptions of OECD, Ernst & Young, and Institutional Shareholder Services).

61 Dionysia Katelouzou and Mathias Siems, "The Global Diffusion of Stewardship Codes" in Dionysia Katelouzou and Dan W Puchniak (eds), *Global Shareholder Stewardship* (CUP 2022) 631.

62 Goto, Koh and Puchniak (n 2) 833–836, 840–841.

63 Puchniak (n 2) 111–112.

64 Puchniak and Tang (n 14) 310–314.

65 Goto (n 9) 396–397.

66 Sang Yop Kang and Kyung-Hoon Chun, "Korea's Stewardship Code and the Rise of Shareholder Activism: Agency Problems and Government Stewardship Revealed" in Dionysia Katelouzou and Dan W Puchniak (eds), *Global Shareholder Stewardship* (CUP 2022) 239, 241–244. From an IAL perspective, it is also noteworthy that Korea did not just copy

of stewardship codes appears driven more by a desire to signal compliance with global governance norms – a form of "halo signaling" than to address specific domestic issues.[67]

The concept of "halo signaling" as a driver for adopting stewardship codes has now received empirical support. Nguyen and Wang find evidence consistent with stewardship codes acting as a "halo" signal that attracts broader equity ownership by US institutional investors in adopting countries, particularly in firms that previously had less US investor presence.[68]

While all Asian stewardship codes are technically voluntary, the level of regulatory pressure for adoption varies. Some jurisdictions have used soft governmental pressure to encourage compliance,[69] while others have left it entirely to market forces.[70] The actual impact of stewardship codes on investor behavior and corporate governance practices varies widely across jurisdictions, often differing significantly from their stated ambitions.[71] As we observe elsewhere:

> It appears that a variety of jurisdiction-specific factors – including market signalling, politics, and ESG considerations – drove governments in Asia to adopt UK-style stewardship codes. As a result, the intended and actual functions of UK-style stewardship codes in Asia have significantly departed from – and in some cases run counter to – the intended and actual functions of the UK Code.[72]

This divergence in the function of stewardship codes across Asia, despite their similar form, highlights the importance of understanding the specific jurisdiction-specific contexts in which corporate law and governance mechanisms operate. It also demonstrates how jurisdictions can use the adoption of "global standards" strategically to serve local purposes, a phenomenon that extends beyond stewardship codes to other areas of corporate law and governance.

The above examination of independent directors, derivative actions, and stewardship codes in Asia reveals a common pattern: formal adoption of corporate law and governance mechanisms originating in Anglo-America, followed by significant divergence in their implementation and function. This pattern of "faux convergence" – superficial similarity in form masking significant diversity in function – creates

the UK Stewardship Code, but deliberately took in some aspects of the Japanese Stewardship Code upon drafting its code. Ibid 243 and 247.

67 Puchniak (n 2) 143–146.

68 Trang T Nguyen and Charles C Y Wang, *Stewardship Codes and Shareholder Voting on Contested Ballot Measures*, Harvard Business School Working Paper (October 2024), https://papers.ssrn.com/sol3/papers.cfm?abstract_id=4986759, accessed 20 May 2025.

69 Gen Goto, "The Japanese Stewardship Code: Its Resemblance and Non-Resemblance to the UK Code" in Dionysia Katelouzou and Dan W Puchniak (eds), *Global Shareholder Stewardship* (CUP 2022), 222, 232, 234.

70 Puchniak and Tang (n 14) 306–309.

71 See generally, Goto, Koh and Puchniak (n 2); Koh, Puchniak and Goto (n 2); Puchniak (n 2).

72 Koh, Puchniak and Goto (n 2) 623.

challenges for both academics and policymakers in accurately assessing corporate law and governance practices globally. As we argue elsewhere:

> Faux convergence turns this assumption on its head. As the Asian jurisdiction case studies canvassed in this chapter have demonstrated, mechanisms originally intended as tools of "good" corporate governance can be subverted by elites for their own ends. A superficially adopted corporate governance tool can be simultaneously wielded to maintain or reinforce a jurisdiction's existing corporate governance system, to further the jurisdictional elites' own agendas and to signal to the world – notwithstanding little to no commitment to real change – that the jurisdiction's elites have adopted "good corporate governance".[73]

For scholars of comparative corporate law and governance, these findings emphasize the need for nuanced, context-specific analysis that goes beyond surface-level comparisons. As Asian jurisdictions often adapt and repurpose corporate law and governance mechanisms to serve local needs and goals, including "halo signaling," rather than simply emulating Anglo-American models, significant diversity in corporate law and governance practices persists both between Asia and Anglo-America, and within Asia itself. Local contexts, including ownership structures, legal systems, and domestic and international political economies, significantly shape how these mechanisms operate in practice. Surface-level comparisons based solely on the presence or absence of certain mechanisms without knowledge of such local jurisdiction-specific contexts can be misleading. For policymakers and international organizations promoting corporate law and governance reform, they highlight the limitations of one-size-fits-all approaches and the importance of understanding local dynamics.

Ultimately, the experience of corporate law and governance reform in Asia suggests that while globalization has led to some convergence in form, the substance of corporate law and governance remains deeply embedded in local contexts. Understanding this complex reality is crucial for developing more effective approaches to corporate law and governance both within Asia and globally.[74] This is especially the case as globalization appears to be moving toward a more regional approach to corporate law and governance around the world.[75]

[73] Ibid 629–630.

[74] See also Puchniak and Kim (n 1) 131–132.

[75] See Roza Nurgozhayeva and Dan W Puchniak, "Corporate Purpose beyond Borders: A Key to Saving Our Planet or Colonialism Repackaged?" (2024) 57 Vanderbilt J Trans Law 1339 ("Amid clearly global institutional efforts to tackle sustainability concerns, there has been a rise in the power and ambition of regional organizations to create models of corporate governance that are bespoke for a region – particularly in Asia."). See also Curtis J Milhaupt, "Corporate Governance in an Era of Geoeconomics" (2024) European Corporate Governance Institute – Law Working Paper No. 790/2024, https://ssrn.com/abstract=4888623, accessed 20 May 2025. See also Puchniak (n 2) 159.

IV THE POWER OF INTER-ASIAN COMPARISONS AND FAUX CONVERGENCE IN RESHAPING COMPARATIVE CORPORATE LAW

Our examination of independent directors, derivative actions, and stewardship codes across Asia demonstrates the explanatory power of the faux convergence framework and the untapped potential of inter-Asian comparisons for enriching comparative corporate law scholarship more broadly.

The concept of faux convergence, as introduced earlier, provides a powerful lens through which to understand the complex reality of corporate law and governance in Asia. It explains how Asian jurisdictions have adopted the outward form of Anglo-American corporate law and governance mechanisms while strategically adapting their substance and function in various ways to serve local purposes. Notably, the adoption of globally recognized corporate law and governance mechanisms can serve important signaling functions, allowing jurisdictions to demonstrate compliance with international norms, which may sometimes be more important than the actual function of the mechanism. This phenomenon results in superficial similarity masking significant functional diversity, challenging simplistic narratives of global convergence.

The diverse implementation and functions of these corporate law and governance mechanisms within Asia provide a unique laboratory for understanding how similar legal transplants evolve in different yet related contexts, exemplifying faux convergence in action. For instance, while both Japan and Korea had derivative actions that lay dormant for decades and then suddenly saw a spike in activity, the driving forces behind this trend differed significantly,[76] illustrating how seemingly similar legal mechanisms can serve distinct purposes in different local contexts.

Inter-Asian comparisons also reveal the diverse strategies jurisdictions employ when adapting foreign corporate law and governance concepts, further highlighting the dynamics of faux convergence. The case of independent directors is particularly illustrative.[77] While most Asian jurisdictions have formally adopted independent director requirements, their roles vary significantly across the region. In Japan, independent directors are expected to champion investors' interests in the boardroom as a part of the government's policy to overcome the long-time economic malaise, while in Singapore's family-controlled firms, they frequently act as mediators in family disputes. These functional variations within Asia demonstrate the creative ways in which jurisdictions can repurpose corporate law and governance mechanisms to serve local needs, often diverging significantly from their original intended functions.

Furthermore, the adoption of stewardship codes across Asia showcases how seemingly similar reforms can serve vastly different purposes in different

[76] See *supra* Section III, B.
[77] See *supra* Section III, A.

jurisdictions, epitomizing faux convergence.[78] While Japan's stewardship code aims to promote shareholder-centric governance to promote more risk-taking as part of a broader economic strategy, Korea's code was seen as a tool to address governance issues in family-controlled conglomerates (*chaebols*). These inter-Asian differences provide rich insights into how global corporate law and governance norms are negotiated and reconfigured within diverse jurisdiction-specific contexts.

By focusing on these inter-Asian variations through the lens of faux convergence, scholars can move beyond simplistic East–West comparisons and develop a more sophisticated taxonomy of convergence for understanding legal transplants and governance evolution.[79] This approach, which aligns with broader trends in comparative law toward more contextual, pluralistic frameworks,[80] allows us to identify local factors that shape corporate law and governance outcomes, which might be overlooked in broader global comparisons.

Moreover, inter-Asian comparisons offer valuable lessons for other regions grappling with similar challenges. As many Asian jurisdictions navigate the tension between global pressures and local institutional logic, their experiences with faux convergence provide a roadmap for other emerging economies seeking to reform their corporate law and governance systems while maintaining local relevance. This may be especially relevant as globalization appears to be moving toward a more regional approach to corporate law and governance around the world – a trend that may accelerate with the election of Donald Trump in the US.

V CONCLUSION

Ultimately, embracing the complexity revealed through inter-Asian comparisons and the faux convergence framework can significantly advance the field of comparative corporate law and governance. It pushes us to develop more robust and nuanced taxonomies that capture the true state of convergence and diversity of global corporate law and governance practices. The time has come to recognize the reality of "faux convergence" as an important lens for understanding corporate law and governance within Asia and beyond.

[78] See *supra* Section III, C.

[79] See also Erie and Lin (n 6).

[80] Ralf Michaels, "The Functional Method of Comparative Law" in Mathias Reimann and Reinhard Zimmermann (eds), *The Oxford Handbook of Comparative Law* (OUP 2006) 339. [This source is relevant because it critiques the traditional functional method in comparative law and argues for a more nuanced approach that uses functionalist comparisons as "critical tools" to challenge assumptions and reveal alternatives, aligning with the chapter's advocacy for more contextual, pluralistic frameworks in comparative corporate governance.]

2

Inter-Asia's Company Towns

Trang (Mae) Nguyen

I INTRODUCTION

The employer provided everything – wages, housing, post office, parks, canteens. Such a model of the "company town," where a single corporation dominates in multiple capacities as employer, landlord, service provider, and quasi-regulator over a dwelling area, has endured across borders and time. The term can portray textile mills in eighteenth-century England or coal and steel towns in early twentieth-century America just as fittingly as it does today's network of "supply chain cities" that span East and Southeast Asia and beyond. Unlike the old towns of the industrializing West, which largely served a single, vertically integrated conglomerate, today's factory towns are transboundary, interconnected, and designed to take advantage of various legal regimes, most notably trade, tariff, investment, and labor laws. Built to settle workers around job sites such as mills, mines, or factories, these manufacturing industrial parks manifest an evolving, expansive exercise of corporate power – once confined to national boundaries, now at once local and transnational thanks to the demands of global supply chains.

This chapter conceptualizes Inter-Asia's supply chain cities as modern company towns. In particular, it studies manufacturing sites in East and Southeast Asia and their business and legal links. More than just towering physical spaces, these sites represent a form of legal entrepôt – created by law and capable of shaping laws and norms through diverse pathways, including regulatory fragmentation and coordinated advocacy. In comparison with another gilded-age moment of industrial development – early twentieth-century United States (US) – these modern company towns exemplify the uniqueness of Inter-Asia's corporate forms, exercise of power, and regional integration.

II A BRIEF HISTORY: FROM CLASSIC COMPANY TOWNS TO SUPPLY CHAIN CITIES

A. *The Classic Company Towns*

If "seeing like a state" was about the statecraft of rendering societies' complexity into "legible" patterns in the name of bureaucratic administration,[1] company towns are, arguably, the craft for seeing and planning like an industrialist. Two key features set them apart from other towns and enterprises. First and foremost, the raison d'être of company towns was, and is, economic activities – as one scholar puts it, they are "physical expressions of economic enterprise."[2] Second, company towns facilitated an expansive corporate control order that spread through and blurred the lines between work and personal space, enabled by the corporation's multifaceted role – most visibly as employers, but also as landlords, property owners, and quasi-regulators of the town's life. Functionally, as explored elsewhere, this corporate control order manifested through at least three mechanisms: the physical link between workplace and housing; the financial link between workers' wages and rent; and heavy monitoring of private activities. Each represents, in turn, physical control, resource constraint, and social and moral control.[3] As we shall see, these key features have translated well into the business model of modern factory towns, despite very different settings.

Classic company towns, such as those that emerged during the Industrial Revolutions in the West, are broadly defined as "communities dominated by a single company, typically focused on one industry."[4] This domination started in the towns' very names, often eponymous to the particular companies or entrepreneurs (most often men) that founded them.[5] Beyond a general definition, however, company towns were as diverse as their industries, designs, locations, and their founders' ethos. Resource-extraction towns supporting coal mining and metal ores often sprang up from scratch in remote areas, necessitated by the need to stay close to natural resources.[6] Towns in lighter manufacturing industries such as textiles might have begun as small settlements that then expanded alongside a growing

1 James C Scott, *Seeing Like a State: How Certain Schemes to Improve the Human Condition Have Failed* (Yale University Press 2020) 11–15.

2 J D Porteous, "The Nature of the Company Town" (1970) 51 Transactions of the Institute of British Geographers 127.

3 See Trang (Mae) Nguyen, "Global Company Towns" (2025) 96 U Colorado L Rev 75.

4 H Green, *The Company Town: The Industrial Edens and Satanic Mills That Shaped the American Economy* (Basic Books 2010) 1. Notably, this definition is broader than those that require corporate property ownership. Margaret Crawford, *Building the Workingman's Paradise: The Design of American Company Towns* (Verso 1996) 1.

5 Famous examples include Pullman, Ill.; Lowell, Mass.; and Hershey, Pa.

6 Linda Carlson, *Company Towns of the Pacific Northwest* (University of Washington Press 2003) 194–195.

corporation that served as each town's primary employer.[7] Either way, it was critical for housing to locate near the worksite, especially in remote locations, to attract and retain labor, reduce turnover, and maximize efficiency.[8]

It was this peculiar arrangement – where work lives and private lives were deliberately, physically entwined – that defined the towns. Companies would build not only housing but also stores, parks, roads, churches, and medical clinics. Many strived to cultivate the image of "a working family's paradise," complete with public amenities and social programs.[9] Benevolent motives aside, business owners certainly had ample incentives to keep workers content.[10] Towns with on-site amenities and a sense of community created through social groups and religious services were better able to attract and retain workers to an otherwise unattractive hard-labor life.[11] Providing robust activities and entertainment to keep workers on-site also lowered the risk of off-site temptations, consistent with the paternalistic attitude that companies held over their workforce.[12] More broadly, social control was part of industrial capitalism's ideals of the virtuous worker: "Early to bed, early to rise, makes a man healthy, wealthy, and wise."[13] In this vision of corporate paternalism, running a business came with moral and economic responsibilities. By advocating for "industrious virtues" such as thrift, diligence, and obedience, corporate owners argued that the enterprises were safekeepers of not only industrialist productivity but also the larger social project of eradicating vice.[14] Corporate regulations, enforced through the physical insulation and architecture of company towns, were deemed critical to improve workers' welfare, both for their own and for societal goods.[15]

In their heydays, company towns' physical architecture, so comprehensive in its fusion of capitalist efficiency with labor management, thus exemplified legal scholars' conception of "infrastructure as regulation" – that is, spatial constructions that shaped behaviors and created social ordering.[16] As we will see below, this

7 Ibid.

8 Margaret Mulrooney, *Legacy of Coal: The Coal Company Towns of Southwestern Pennsylvania* (US National Park Service 1989) 9–10; J Allen, *The Company Town in the American West* (University of Oklahoma Press 1966) 7.

9 John S Garner (ed), "Introduction" in *The Company Town: Architecture and Society in the Early Industrial Age* (OUP 1992) 4.

10 M Todd Henderson, "The Nanny Corporation" (2013) 76 U Chicago L Rev 1517, 1536.

11 See Allen (n 8) 6–7.

12 See Carlson (n 6) 10.

13 David Blanke, "Thrift and Thriving in America: Capitalism and Moral Order from the Puritans to the Present" (2012) 99 J Am Hist 561–563 (quoting Benjamin Franklin, *Poor Richard's Almanack* (1733)).

14 See Mulrooney (n 8) 10–11.

15 Ibid.

16 See Benedict Kingsbury, "Infrastructure and InfraReg: On Rousing the International Law 'Wizards of Is'" (2019) 8 Cambridge Intl LJ 171, 177–184; Benedict Kingsbury, "Introduction to the Symposium on Infrastructuring International Law" (2023) 117 AJIL Unbound 1, 2. For some salient examples in the context of infrastructure and racial discrimination in US laws, see Sarah Schindler, "Architectural Exclusion: Discrimination and Segregation through Physical

feature has remained constant even as the business model of company towns globalized and adapted.

B. *Company Towns Go Global*

By the 1950s, traditional industrial towns had slowly receded in the US due to a confluence of colliding forces.[17] The development of cars and railroads, changes in technology, and new, robust state and federal regulations in response to the Great Depression all contributed to what became known as the beginning of America's great deindustrialization.[18] But as company towns started to phase out in the West, globalization enabled their reincarnation abroad as manufacturing outposts, first mainly catering to Western economies. An early example – and a spectacular failure – was Ford Motor Co.'s establishment of the Fordlandia rubber plantation in 1920s' Brasilia.[19] Modeled after Ford's flagship plant in Dearborn, Michigan, Fordlandia featured an extensive compound built amidst isolated nature and a similar system of control over local workers, including whistles, time-punch clocks, and routine investigations.[20] Fordlandia's eventual abandonment stood in history as an expensive lesson on multiple fronts: a failed attempt to export Ford's famed assembly line to a jungle ecology, the complexity of going multinational, and the politics of bringing "white man's magic" to other parts of the world.[21] Relevant to this chapter, it also epitomizes the challenges of attempting to exercise corporate control over an increasingly intricate global production process. As detailed in the next section, critical for modern company towns in Inter-Asia, that task was soon outsourced to a new crop of companies, who took over not only the human

Design of the Built Environment" (2015) 124 Yale LJ 1934; Deborah Archer, "'White Men's Roads through Black Men's Homes': Advancing Racial Equity through Highway Reconstruction" (2020) 73 Vand L Rev 1259.

17 Some have argued that employer-owned planned communities (such as the Walt Disney Company's Celebration in Florida) and Big Tech's campuses (such as those owned by Google and Facebook) function similarly to company towns. The wealthy nature of these towns, however, sets them apart from the industrial settlements at the heart of this chapter, characterized by stark power imbalance between workers and enterprises. As such, this chapter focuses on *industrial towns*, where economic activities center on large-scale manufacturing and the management of blue-collar workers, whether during the Industrial Revolutions or in supply chain contexts.

18 Deindustrialization in the US is the subject of a large interdisciplinary literature. One example compares two former steel towns in the US and Canada in the aftermath of globalization: Tracy Neumann, *Remaking the Rust Belt: The Postindustrial Transformation of North America* (University of Pennsylvania Press 2016); another presents case studies on how various cities coped with job loss and factory closedown: James Connolly (ed), *After the Factory: Reinventing America's Industrial Small Cities* (Lexington Books 2010).

19 For a captivating portrait of Henry Ford's saga in the Amazon, see Greg Grandin, *Fordlandia: The Rise and Fall of Henry Ford's Forgotten Jungle City* (Picador Books 2009) 5–25.

20 Ibid.

21 Heather Barrow, "The Reach of an Automotive Giant: Urban Implications of an Industrial Policy" (2011) 37 J Urban History 207–301.

management of supply chains, but also the legal and economic arbitrage of structuring global production itself.

III INTER-ASIA'S COMPANY TOWNS

This part conceptualizes today's "supply chain cities," prolifically built in Asia, but also popular elsewhere, as modern reincarnation of the old company town model. At first blush, this may seem an unintuitive comparison. The fundamental qualities – the time and space, the companies, the states, the products, and the production process – have all changed. Yet, from Pullman, Illinois, to Foxconn's "iphone city" in Shenzhen, China, the "keywords" remain starkly similar: economic productivity, labor–capital tension, corporate control. Such similarity, as I have argued elsewhere, is not a coincidence but the result of a global economic integration process that prioritizes efficiency and large-scale productivity.[22] Put differently, the company town business model, then and now, facilitates a mode of capital accumulation and labor management that caters to industrial development.

To be sure, factory towns of the present operate in a very different world from the past. Instead of textile mills and coal mines, modern industrial towns, especially in Asia, specialize in distinct functions of their industries, ranging from labor-intensive tasks such as part assembly and packaging to high-value technology-related manufacturing. Unlike the old industrial towns of the West, which largely served single, vertically integrated corporations, modern factory towns, as demanded by global supply chains, are transboundary, interconnected, and designed to take advantage of various legal regimes, most notably trade, tariff, investment, and labor laws. This part explores some of the critical features that pave the way for Inter-Asia's company towns: the rise to prominence of transnational suppliers, the proliferation of special zones, the creation of modern industrial towns, and the horizontal networks across Inter-Asia's supply base.

A. *Rise of Transnational Suppliers*

The gravitation toward a "made in the world" manufacturing model[23] paved the way to the rise of a largely hidden new crop of multinational enterprises – which I call "Big Suppliers."[24] By Big Suppliers, I refer to large-contract manufacturing corporations, public and private, with presence in multiple jurisdictions, whether through

[22] Nguyen (n 3).

[23] See Pol Antràs, *Global Production: Firms, Contracts, and Trade Structure* (Princeton University Press 2015) 4–5.

[24] Trang (Mae) Nguyen, "Hidden Power in Global Supply Chains" (2023) 64 Harv Int' L J, 45–60.

subsidiaries or contracting networks.[25] Though not always, they tend to be headquartered outside of Global North economies, most dominantly in Asia, as a product of outsourcing trends, trade regulations, and individual nations' industrial policies.[26] As brands and retailers in the US, Europe, and elsewhere divested, their foreign-based contracting partners increasingly scaled up and consolidated to meet the complex demands of global production.[27] When each part of a product might come from different countries and even different continents, control, coordination, task management, and compliance were critical to ensure a smoothly run supply chain.[28] This, in turn, spurred demands for a professional logistics industry capable of the herculean tasks of optimizing complex cross-border processes.

Transnational suppliers thus emerged as a new, quiet crop of corporate powers, whose presence transformed the economic and legal organization of global trade.[29] By virtues of size and scale, they sit atop a robust global supply base spanning Asia, Latin America, and beyond.[30] As laid bare by the COVID-19 pandemic, this global supply base, while transboundary and expansive, is also concentrated, both geographically to a small number of key countries and economically to a small group of key firms.[31] Well-known examples include Foxconn, the world's largest electronics contract manufacturer; the Taiwan Semiconductor Manufacturing Company (TSMC), the world's biggest semiconductor manufacturing foundry, known for its ability to make the most advanced nanochip; TAL Apparel, which produces one out of every eight dress shirts bought worldwide; Luen Thai, a textile conglomerate; Yue Yuen, the world's largest manufacturer of athletic shoes; and Li & Fung, the world's biggest apparel trading house, once called "the most important company that most American shoppers never heard of."[32]

Transnational suppliers' quiet rise to prominence in a highly interdependent system has resulted in a relative shift in the locus of power in global supply chains, long assumed to be dominated by Western brands.[33] Relevant to this chapter, they are also the employers of modern company towns, having taken over the tasks of manufacturing and labor management. Like the corporate giants of the past, they act at once as employers, landlords, and quasi-regulators to manage the employment,

[25] Ibid. In this chapter, the terms *Big Suppliers*, *first-tier suppliers*, *top-tier suppliers*, and *lead suppliers* are used interchangeably to refer to these large companies.

[26] Ibid.

[27] Ibid.

[28] See Michael P Vandenbergh, "The New Wal-Mart Effect: The Role of Private Contracting in Global Governance" (2007) 52 UCLA L Rev 913, 925–929.

[29] See Nguyen (n 24) 68–80.

[30] See Timothy Sturgeon, John Humphrey and Gary Gereffi, "Making the Global Supply Base" in Gary Hamilton and others (eds), *The Market Makers: How Retailers Are Reshaping the Global Economy* (OUP 2011).

[31] See Nguyen (n 24) 56–58.

[32] Ibid.

[33] Ibid 60–68.

housing, mobility, and social lives of millions of workers whose labor sustains global consumption. As argued elsewhere, the emergence of these companies has implications for a suite of public and private law issues, including cross-border contracts, corporate social responsibility designs, trade regulations, private regulatory functions, and more.[34] Before turning to transnational suppliers' management of modern industrial towns, it is first helpful to understand the type of law-made soil on which these towns stand – the special economic zones (SEZs).

B. *SEZs*

Special economic zones, at a fundamental level, are a form of regulatory laboratories – aptly defined as "demarcated geographic areas contained within a country's national boundaries where the rules of business are different from those that prevail in the national territory."[35] Their history dates back to the Roman Empire, whose authorities bestowed free trade–like conditions on ports and islands to encourage trade.[36] Early SEZs included European colonial outposts such as Macau and Hong Kong, as well as China's numerous "treaty ports," through which it ceded territories and granted broad concessions to Western powers in the aftermath of the Opium Wars.[37] In the 1970s and 1980s, SEZs were catapulted to holy grail status thanks to several highly successful utilizations, first by the "Asian Tigers" economies, then by the People's Republic of China as part of Deng Xiaoping's "Open Door" policy.[38] Urged on by a coalition of national governments, private sectors, and international organizations hoping to replicate such successes, other developing countries quickly seized on the model, resulting in a rapid spread of SEZs around the globe.[39] Though widespread, zone distributions are highly concentrated, both in geography and in economic activities. Nearly 90 percent of the world's SEZs are located in developing nations, with China hosting nearly half and a substantial number spreading across East and Southeast Asia.[40]

[34] Ibid 69–81.

[35] See Thomas Farole and Gohkan Akinci (eds), "Introduction" in *Special Economic Zones: Progress, Emerging Challenges, and Future Directions* (World Bank 2011) 3.

[36] See Clause Baissac, "Brief History of SEZs and Overview of Policy Debates" in Thomas Farole (ed), *Special Economic Zones in Africa: Comparing Performance and Learning from Global Experience* (World Bank 2011) 31–35.

[37] Dong Wang, *China's Unequal Treaties: Narrating National History* (Lexington Books 2005). For a legal perspective on the oppressive terms of these treaties, see Cornelius Murphy, "Economic Duress and Unequal Treaties" (1970) 11 Va J Int'l L 51–54.

[38] See, e.g., Douglas Zhihua Zeng, "How Do Special Economic Zones and Industrial Clusters Drive China's Rapid Development?" in *Building Engines for Growth and Competitiveness in China* (World Bank 2010) 9. https://documents1.worldbank.org/curated/en/310891468018256346/pdf/WPS5583.pdf.

[39] From just under 200 zones in the 1980s, today there are over 7,000 SEZs in 145 countries, employing an estimated workforce of 100 million. Farole and Akinci (n 35) 5.

[40] Farole and Akinci (n 35) 5.

Functionally, SEZs allow states to move beyond the old economic wisdom of national competitive advantage to create modern one-stop-shop "location-specific advantages."[41] The goal, as made clear by policymakers, is to create more liberal, effective business environments, insulated from the larger national context, in order to attract foreign investments and boost economic development.[42] Common regulatory incentives include preferential customs duties and taxes; streamlined administrative procedures; and one-stop integrated offices to ease compliance.[43] Benefiting from SEZs' well-defined spatial boundaries, states may also test controversial policies such as land auctions, wholly foreign-owned companies, or labor market liberalization, without having to commit to large-scale changes.[44] Legal and regulatory learning was well documented among states, for example, Vietnam and Ethiopia in emulating mainland Chinese and Taiwanese experience.[45]

C. *Special Towns*

Modern company towns retain key vestiges of the old model – large-scale economic activities, comprehensive infrastructure planning, and tight control over workers' lives – but operate in a vastly different context. Thanks in part to transnational suppliers' rapid expansion, modern factory towns no longer resemble the old model's discrete islands of economic activities. Instead, they belong to transnational networks operating at different nodes of global production, strategically located to take advantage of trade, tariff, and other favorable laws. Much has been written about the meticulous infrastructure planning, extensive control, and labor plights in modern factory cities, most infamously Foxconn's "forbidden iPhone city" in Longhua.[46] This part focuses instead on a different facet, that is, the roles of supply chain cities as innovation hubs in advancing both business norms and certain quasi-public functions.

On advancing innovative business norms, consider, for example, the Luen Thai Liz Claiborne facility in Dongguan, China. Luen Thai, a Hong Kong–based apparel manufacturer, first experimented with supply chain cities in 2007, on the heels of the expiration of the Multi Fiber Agreement (MFA) – a multilateral regime

[41] Rajneesh Narula and James X Zhan, "Using Special Economic Zones to Facilitate Development: Policy Implications" (2019) 26 Transnational Corp J 1, 2.

[42] Ibid.

[43] Ibid.

[44] Sebastian Heilmann, "Policy Experimentation in China's Economic Rise" (2008) 43 Stud Comp Int'l Dev 1–26.

[45] See, e.g., Keyi Tang, "The Political Economy of Special Economic Zones: The Cases of Ethiopia and Vietnam" (2023) 30 Rev Intl Poli Econ 1957, 1968–1973 (detailing the learning experience of SEZ "rising stars" such as Ethiopia and Vietnam).

[46] See Pun Ngai and Jenny Chan, "Global Capital, the State, and Chinese Workers: The Foxconn Experience" (2012) 38 Modern China 383–410; Jason Dean, "The Forbidden City of Terry Gou" (August 11, 2007) *Wall Street Journal*, www.wsj.com/articles/SB118677584137994489 [https://perma.cc/K3BX-D4W7], accessed October 1, 2024.

that carved out special quotas for trade in textiles from 1973 to 2005.[47] By imposing country-specific quotas on textile exports by developing countries, the MFA contributed to a proliferation of supply bases around the world, and its end brought about a consolidation of the apparel supply chains.[48] With Liz Claiborne's backing, Luen Thai relocated the raw material suppliers and product manufacturers into one mega-factory located in Dongguan, in the province of Guangdong – known for its convenient transportation access.[49] From there the company built a campus comprised of product development centers, factories totaling 2 million square feet, a 4,000-person dormitory, a movie theater, gyms, hotels, and showrooms for visiting clients.[50] All parties follow a highly standardized scan-and-track inventory system to allow goods to move seamlessly across production stages and from the factory floors into Liz Claiborne stores in the US and elsewhere.[51] "A buyer, a marketer, a brander from the [United States] can go to Supply Chain City and never have to leave the complex," explains Luen Thai's US president. "They can make their samples, they can buy their fabrics, they can do everything they want under one roof."[52] Luen Thai's restructuring resulted in a corresponding change at Liz Claiborne, which at the time sourced from over 250 suppliers in thirty-five countries.[53] The retailer started to consolidate its supplier base and relocate its designers from Hong Kong, New York City, and elsewhere to the Dongguan complex so that they could closely collaborate with Luen Thai's technicians from the factory and fabric mills.[54] The one-stop-shop, comprehensive nature of Luen Thai's industrial site thus fosters collaboration, information sharing, and innovation – an arrangement that mirrors the "technology cluster" concept of high-tech locales like Silicon Valley.[55]

Equally significant, corporate functions in modern factory towns can extend well beyond commercial activities – a phenomenon amplified by the COVID-19

47 The MFA created a special quota regime as an exception to the trade framework set up by the General Agreement on Tariffs and Trade (GATT), the precursor to the World Trade Organization (WTO). See WTO, *Textiles: Back in the Mainstream*, www.wto.org/english/thewto_e/whatis_e/tif_e/agrm5_e.htm [https://perma.cc/UZ28-R38R], accessed October 1, 2024.

48 See Nguyen (n 24) pt I.B (describing the impact of the MFA).

49 See Staci Kusterbeck, "China Appeals to U.S. Buyers with 'Supply Chain Cities'" (*Retail Info Systems*, August 1, 2005), https://perma.cc/6BMF-4WLN, accessed October 1, 2024.

50 "From Fashion to Fish: How Hong Kong's Luen Thai Holdings Learned to Shift with the Wind" (*Knowledge@Wharton*, March 31, 2010), https://knowledge.wharton.upenn.edu/article/from-fashion-to-fish-how-hong-kongs-luen-thai-holdings-learned-to-shift-with-the-wind [https://perma.cc/GYE5-4FF3], accessed October 1, 2024.

51 Ibid.

52 Ibid.

53 See Richard P Appelbaum, "Transnational Contractors in East Asia" in Gary Hamilton, Benjamin Senauer and Misha Petrovic (eds), *The Market Makers: How Retailers Are Reshaping the Global Economy* (Oxford Academic 2011) 255, 258.

54 Ibid.

55 See William R Kerr and Frederic Robert-Nicoud, "Tech Clusters" (2020) Working paper 20-063 Harvard Business School 3.

pandemic. In the 2019–2021 period, as the pandemic traveled around the globe, transnational suppliers, as operators of supply chain cities, took on surprising and dramatic roles as providers of public health and pandemic response, even as diplomats to secure scarce vaccines. In Vietnam, for example, after waves of COVID-19 outbreaks, electronic factories turned to a model of "sleepover manufacturing" to insulate workers from infections, greenlit by a national leadership anxious to keep the country's reputation as a supply chain rising star.[56] Pou Chen – Yue Yuen's Vietnamese subsidiary – advanced its own contact tracing, testing, and medical reporting system,[57] while Samsung Vietnam provided free dormitories and food to encourage workers to stay within its industrial park.[58] When COVID-19 inevitably reached the factory floors, these suppliers, sanctioned by regulators, turned their plants into quarantine space, where thousands of workers spent time away from their families isolating in clusters.[59] This was an exception to Vietnam's highly rigid regulation that COVID exposures were subject to mandatory quarantine in military-operated camps.[60] Suppliers also mounted fierce lobbying efforts to prioritize factory workers for vaccine eligibility.[61] In Taiwan, in an extraordinary development, Foxconn and TSMC took on diplomatic and political roles as they represented the Taiwanese government in its negotiation to purchase COVID vaccines directly from BioNTech.[62] By outsourcing the negotiation to its two most powerful companies, Taiwan was able to sideline a conflict with the People's

[56] See Chia Woon Eunice Chua and Nguyen Dieu Tu Uyen, "Factory Sleepovers Help Guard Vietnam's Workers from Virus Outbreaks" (Bloomberg, July 6, 2021), www.bloomberg.com/news/newsletters/2021-07-06/supply-china-latest-vietnamese-workers-avoid-virus-by-sleeping-at-work [https://perma.cc/NB73-4Z5V], accessed October 1, 2024.

[57] See "Pou Chen Group's Efforts in Response to COVID-19 Pandemic" (*Pouchen ESG News*, May 31, 2021), www.pouchen.com/index.php/en/csr/esg-news/56-csr_2020/803-pcc-csr-news-200531-en [https://perma.cc/734Q-EGPM], accessed October 1, 2024.

[58] See "Samsung Viet Nam Day Manh Cac Bien Phap Phong Dich COVID-19 [Samsung Vietnam Increases Measures to Prevent Covid-19]" (*Samsung Newsroom*, May 14, 2021), https://news.samsung.com/vn/samsung-viet-nam-day-manh-cac-bien-phap-phong-dich-covid-19 [https://perma.cc/KQ5R-7VV5], accessed October 1, 2024.

[59] See Lien Hoang, "Samsung Suspends Vietnam Factories Hit by COVID: Health Ministry" (*Nikkei Asia*, July 14, 2021), https://asia.nikkei.com/Spotlight/Coronavirus/Samsung-suspends-Vietnam-factories-hit-by-COVID-health-ministry [https://perma.cc/6ANJ-QFA6], accessed October 1, 2024; Phuong Nguyen and James Pearson, "Vietnam Coronavirus Outbreak Threatens to Disrupt Tech Supply Chains" (*Reuters*, May 28, 2021), www.reuters.com/technology/vietnam-coronavirus-outbreak-threatens-disrupt-tech-supply-chain-2021-05-28 [https://perma.cc/8KLB-FP2R], accessed October 1, 2024.

[60] See Trang (Mae) Nguyen and Edmund Malesky, "Reopening Vietnam: How the Country's Improving Governance Helped It Weather the COVID-19 Pandemic" (*Brookings Institute*, May 20, 2020), www.brookings.edu/blog/order-from-chaos/2020/05/20/reopening-vietnam-how-the-countrys-improving-governance-helped-it-weather-the-covid-19-pandemic [https://perma.cc/M7NR-U328], accessed October 1, 2024.

[61] See Hoang (n 59); Nguyen and Pearson (n 59).

[62] See "Taiwan Tech Giants Foxconn and TSMC to Buy 10m COVID Jabs" (*BBC*, July 12, 2021), www.bbc.com/news/business-57801031 [https://perma.cc/M58P-RPT9], accessed October 1, 2024.

Republic of China, which insisted that Taiwan needed to wait for vaccine distribution from the central government, just like other Chinese provinces.[63] In Vietnam, suppliers also played critical roles in securing vaccine supplies for their workforce early in the pandemic, spurring a heated public debate on vaccine equity.[64] In their defense, these enterprises argued that the infrastructure of their industrial sites acted as built-in regulation for vaccine compliance and should be prioritized both for public health and economic reasons.[65] To be sure, the desire to maintain production, at a time when global supply chains became heavily scrutinized, factored into these governments' delegation of critical foreign policy and public health functions to transnational suppliers.[66]

D. *Horizontal Networks*

Distinct from past company towns, a key feature of today's manufacturing sites in East and Southeast Asia is their deep links as part of a global supply base. This phenomenon arose well before the COVID-19 pandemic and subsequent geopolitical changes, thanks in part to transnational suppliers' history of expansion. In labor-intensive textile and footwear industries, for example, as the cost of living rose in China, major suppliers such as TAL Apparel and Yue Yuen sought out manufacturing bases in labor-rich Southeast Asia and South Asia, with a high concentration in Vietnam, Indonesia, and Cambodia.[67]

Changing geopolitics and post-pandemic reordering have accelerated at least two trends: efforts to reindustrialize Global North economies and pressure to divert manufacturing out of China into other manufacturing bases. The latter has spurred a new wave of factories and industrial clusters in Southeast Asia and South Asia as suppliers attempted to hedge unstable geopolitics and legal uncertainties. Apple, for example, has announced plans to move some of its core production operations to

63 See Joyu Wang and Chao Deng, "Tech Firms to Buy Covid-19 Vaccines on Behalf of Taiwan's Government" *Wall Street Journal* (July 12, 2021), www.wsj.com/articles/tech-firms-to-buy-covid-19-vaccines-on-behalf-of-taiwans-government-11626020496 [https://perma.cc/J9VA-UWNC], accessed October 1, 2024.

64 See, e.g., Lien Hoang, "Intel Staff Vaccinated as Vietnam Prioritizes Tech Exports" (*Nikkei Asia*, July 13, 2021), https://asia.nikkei.com/Business/Companies/Intel-staff-vaccinated-as-Vietnam-priori tizes-tech-exports [https://perma.cc/TT6N-BKB6], accessed October 1, 2024.

65 Ibid.

66 See Huong Le Thu, "Delta Variant Outbreak Challenges Vietnam's COVID-19 Response Strategy" (*Brookings Institute*, August 11, 2021), www.brookings.edu/blog/order-from-chaos/2021/08/11/delta-variant-outbreak-challenges-vietnams-covid-19-response-strategy [https://perma.cc/76X9-889W], accessed October 1, 2024.

67 See "Corporate Information" (Yue Yuen Industrial (Holdings) Ltd.), www.yueyuen.com/en/corporate_information.html [https://perma.cc/R88U-XG8B], accessed October 1, 2024; "Manufacturing Business" (Yue Yuen Industrial (Holdings) Ltd.), www.yueyuen.com/en/iframe-manufacturing-business.html [https://perma.cc/6WYN-NFRX], accessed October 1, 2024.

India and Vietnam, triggering its "Big Three" suppliers – Foxconn, Luxshare, and Goertek – to set up subsidiaries, secure land leases, and announce construction plans in these destinations.[68] In the textile and apparel industries, the passage of the Uyghur Forced Labor Prevention Act and other sanctions has driven brands to seek out alternative cotton resources, effectively creating new demand for labor and cotton plants in Pakistan, Bangladesh, and India.[69]

Inter-Asia's supply base is not catering to Western brands alone. Homegrown brands from China and Southeast Asia are increasingly a driver of the region's growth and economic integration. Chinese EV manufacturer BYD, for example, recently announced a $1.3 billion investment in new manufacturing facilities in Thailand and Indonesia, to be completed by 2026.[70] Vietnam's EV brand VinFast has announced a $1.2 billion investment in Indonesia for an assembly plant, further underlining the attractiveness of Indonesia as a manufacturing base for the EV industry.[71]

As a result, new factories and industrial clusters are being created across Inter-Asia. Efforts to divest from China have, in essence, strengthened the region's interdependence as Chinese suppliers seek nearby offshore locations to restructure their own supply chains. This flexibility in supply chain architecture underscores the key difference between today's global supply base and past company towns. Instead of the old model's discrete islands of economic activities, today's factory towns are part of a transnational, cross-boundary network that can coordinate, share legal and business practices, and learn from one another in the face of uncertainties. The next part explains some of these dynamics by turning to the concept of infrastructure sites as "legal entrepôts."

68 Iris Deng, "Apple's Supply Chain in China Evolves as Foxconn Hires, Compal Invests in Vietnam and MacBook Production Relocates to Thailand" *South China Morning Post* (June 12, 2023), www.scmp.com/tech/tech-trends/article/3223802/apples-supply-chain-china-evolves-foxconn-hires-compal-invests-vietnam-and-macbook-production, accessed October 1, 2024; Chi Trung, "Apple's Deepening Roots and Flourishing Partnerships" (*Vietnam Investment Review*, May 9, 2024), https://vir.com.vn/apples-deepening-roots-and-flourishing-partnerships-110987.html, accessed October 1, 2024; "Supply Chain Exodus from China to India, Vietnam Far Faster Than Anticipated" (*Telecom*, March 8, 2023), https://telecom.economictimes.indiatimes.com/news/supply-chain-exodus-from-china-to-india-vietnam-far-faster-than-anticipated/98496252, accessed October 1, 2024.

69 "Beyond China: US' Xinjiang Cotton Ban Has Far-Reaching Implications, Even for Asian Alternatives" *South China Morning Post* (July 27, 2022), www.scmp.com/economy/china-economy/article/3186664/beyond-china-us-xinjiang-cotton-ban-has-far-reaching [https://perma.cc/UFK5-HWJ7], accessed October 1, 2024.

70 "BYD Launches in Indonesia with New Cars and a Promised $1.3 Billion Factory as It Continues Its March to Global EV Dominance" (*Fortune*, January 19, 2024), https://fortune.com/asia/2024/01/19/byd-launches-indonesia-new-cars-factory-ev-global-expansion/, accessed October 1, 2024.

71 "Vietnam's VinFast to Establish EV Assembly Plant in Indonesia This Year" (*Jakarta Globe*, February 19, 2024), https://jakartaglobe.id/business/vietnams-vinfast-to-establish-ev-assembly-plant-in-indonesia-this-year, accessed October 1, 2024.

IV INTER-ASIA'S COMPANY TOWNS AS LEGAL ENTREPÔTS

Entrepôt is derived from the French words *entre* (among, between) and *poser* (to place).[72] Historically, the term referred to warehouses and shipment centers, where goods were deposited as part of trade flows.[73] More broadly, like a gateway or a port, an entrepôt is a physical place in-between, connecting local commerce with the wider world, providing a space for processing, documenting, and organizing the migration of goods and people.[74] Borrowing from this concept, a legal entrepôt is legal in two ways. First, its nature is legal in that it is law-made, designated as a cross-border entrance by the relevant authorities from which it derives legitimacy. In this sense, any official port, SEZ, or factory town is necessarily a law-made space, sanctioned by law and created with specific policy goals, often to encourage regulatory and economic experiments without having to commit to large-scale change.[75] Indeed, scholars have argued that these specially designated spaces represent a regime of capitalist "micro-ordering" – that is, "political arrangements at a small scale," separate from the structure of the nation-states.[76]

Second, equally noteworthy, the concept of a legal entrepôt underscores how laws and norms, like other commodities, flow through and are shaped within the physical space. When transnational suppliers operate supply chain cities that resemble past company towns, how they organize their buildings, factory floors, and work shifts becomes the de facto regulation of significant aspects of individual lives. As transnational suppliers often operate in "regulatory laboratory" spaces such as SEZs with more leeway given to local authorities and private actors, their roles in private governance are especially pronounced. The first example below, on regulatory fragmentation through production lines, illustrates the power of suppliers in taming regulations by "splitting" production lines. Yet, the transboundary, porous nature of global supply chains, while facilitating the extraterritorial reach of corporate private governance, can also present new opportunities for transnational solidarity among workers across disparate supply bases. The second example, on efforts to coordinate labor actions, exemplifies transnational advocacy that leverages the very nature of business-friendly global supply chains (admittedly in a limited way) for labor causes.

A. *Regulatory Fragmentation*

Regulatory fragmentation refers to a phenomenon in which a transnational supplier, by virtue of its control over dispersed industrial sites, can choose to

72 See "entrepôt," Oxford-Hachette French Dictionary (1994).

73 See "entrepôt," Merriam-Webster Dictionary, www.merriam-webster.com, accessed October 1, 2024.

74 See J Russell Smith, "The World Entrepôt" (1910) 18 J of Pol Econ 697.

75 Ibid.

76 See Quinn Slobodian, *Crack-Up Capitalism: Market Radicals and the Dream of a World Without Democracy* (Metropolitan Books 2023) 4.

"fracture" its production lines to comply with stringent standards only where required. Take, for example, Yue Yuen's operation model of customer-specific production lines. A major athletic footwear manufacturer, Yue Yuen is the main supplier for Nike, Adidas, Reebok, and other brands.[77] As one of Nike's major suppliers, Yue Yuen became embroiled in the anti-sweatshop campaign against Nike during the late 1990s, including major exposés on its factories in Vietnam.[78] In the aftermath, Nike became an early adopter of corporate social responsibility, with some of the most stringent standards on workers' rights in the industry.[79] As a supplier to multiple brands, Yue Yuen increasingly needs to comply with not only varying manufacturing specifications but also a variety of codes of conduct and labor and safety standards. Yue Yuen organizes its production lines according to specific merchandisers, producing specific items in batches.[80] As a result, Nike's more stringent labor standards are effectively "quarantined" within its own production line. Meeting the more stringent requirements for a customer like Nike does not necessarily result in positive spillover effects on Yue Yuen's other processes.[81]

Solar suppliers utilize the same tactic when faced with US import sanctions regarding polysilicon – a critical component for photovoltaic cells that make up solar panels. The Xinjiang Autonomous Region in Northwestern China is home to four of the five largest polysilicon factories in the world.[82] In 2021, President Biden signed into law the Uyghur Forced Labor Prevention Act, which creates a rebuttable presumption that imports from Xinjiang – polysilicon included – are made with forced labor unless importers can produce "clear and convincing" evidence demonstrating otherwise.[83] In a concerted move, US Customs and Border Protection, which, in addition to immigration, is also in charge of the admission of goods into the US, issued a series of "withhold release orders" to detain solar components suspected of being "tainted"

[77] See n 67 (Yue Yuen's corporate materials).

[78] See, e.g., Steven Greenhouse, "Nike Shoe Plant in Vietnam Is Called Unsafe for Workers" *New York Times* (November 8, 1997), www.nytimes.com/1997/11/08/business/nike-shoe-plant-in-vietnam-is-called-unsafe-for-workers.html [https://perma.cc/D6F9-KYRZ], accessed October 1, 2024; Burhan Wazir, "Nike Accused of Tolerating Sweatshops" *Guardian* (May 19, 2001), www.theguardian.com/world/2001/may/20/burhanwazir.theobserver [https://perma.cc/HHV2-SQVF], accessed October 1, 2024.

[79] See Lynn S Paine, "Sustainability in the Boardroom: Lessons from Nike's Playbook" (July–August 2014) Harvard Business Review 87, 90 (crediting Nike's creation of a board-level corporate responsibility committee for its success in turning around Nike's image).

[80] See Jeroen Merk, "Restructuring and Conflict in the Global Athletic Footwear Industry: Nike, Yue Yuen and Labour Codes of Conduct" in Marcus Taylor (ed), *Global Economy Contested: Power and Conflict Across the International Division of Labour* (Routledge 2008) 79, 90.

[81] Ibid.

[82] See Aitor Hernandez-Morales and others, "Fears over China's Muslim Forced Labor Loom over EU Solar Power" (*Politico*, February 10, 2021), www.politico.eu/article/xinjiang-china-polysilicon-solar-energy-europe/ [https://perma.cc/HY3P-UCD5], accessed October 1, 2024.

[83] See HR 1155, 117th Congress (2021).

with Xinjiang labor.[84] In response, solar component manufacturers have started "splitting" their production lines, with dedicated "clean" lines – that is, clearly free of Xinjiang inputs – slated for export to the US.[85] By an example, Jinko Solar, a solar module manufacturer headquartered in Shanghai, is reportedly ramping up its Xinjiang-free production in Vietnam to serve the US market, noting that it is only using German and US polysilicon for these production lines.[86]

B. *Supply Chain Solidarity*

The transboundary, porous nature of global supply chains, while facilitating the extraterritorial reach of corporate private governance, also presents new opportunities for transnational solidarity. As the examples below demonstrate, thanks to the interconnectedness of global production, strategic coordination is possible among workers who might be in different countries or industries but are linked through the global supply base.

The prime example so far has been in Europe rather than Asia: the coordinated strike against Tesla by Scandinavian workers, first started in October 2023 by four Swedish technicians.[87] Since then, thousands of workers across countries and industries have joined in, including Norwegian and Finnish port workers, Danish truck drivers, as well as Swedish postal workers, cleaners, and garbage collectors who declined to service Tesla offices.[88] While Northern Europe is a relatively small market, these labor actions have garnered attention across the globe as a renewed form of transnational solidarity that capitalizes on the very business-friendly nature of global production and strikes at key nodes of supply chains.[89]

[84] US Customs and Border Protection, "CBP Issues Region-Wide Withhold Release Order on Products Made by Slave Labor in Xinjiang" (press release, January 13, 2021), www.cbp.gov/newsroom/national-media-release/cbp-issues-region-wide-withhold-release-order-products-made-slave [https://perma.cc/T3SL-J5M7], accessed October 1, 2024 (citing section 307 of the Tariff Act of 1930, which prohibits the import of any product that was mined, produced, or manufactured wholly or in part by forced labor, including forced or indentured child labor and which delegates enforcement authority to US Customs and Border Protection).

[85] See Alan Crawford and others, *Over-Exposed, Uyghur Region Exposure Assessment for Solar Industry Sourcing* (Sheffield Hallam University, November 2023) 1–5, www.shu.ac.uk/helena-kennedy-centre-international-justice/research-and-projects/all-projects/over-exposed [https://perma.cc/38NL-YQYX], accessed October 1, 2024.

[86] Ibid 17–19. In response to US import sanctions, Jinko already sold off its ingot (crystalline silicon) manufacturing factory in Xinjiang and reported that it only used ingot produced elsewhere for its solar wafers.

[87] See Gerrit De Vynck, "Tesla Strike in Sweden Is Biggest Test Yet of Elon Musk's Anti-Union Stance" *Washington Post* (December 29, 2023), www.washingtonpost.com/world/2023/12/29/tesla-strike-sweden-elon-musk/ [https://perma.cc/7DH9-ARN6], accessed October 1, 2024.

[88] Ibid.

[89] See Melissa Eddy, "Tesla Strike Is a Culture Clash: Swedish Labor vs. American Management" *New York Times* (December 28, 2023), www.nytimes.com/2023/12/27/business/tesla-sweden-strike-labor.html [https://perma.cc/7DH9-BCN6], accessed October 1, 2024.

The coordinated strikes against Tesla are reminiscent of earlier efforts by Asian supply chain workers in China and Vietnam against shoe giant Yue Yuen. In 2014, in what turned out to be one of the largest industrial strikes in Chinese history, 40,000 workers from multiple Yue Yuen factories in Dongguan, China, took to the street to protest the company's failure to pay worker benefits.[90] It started with a single worker at a Yue Yuen factory in Dongguan, who, in seeking compensation for a workplace injury, learned that the shoe giant had failed to contribute to workers' social insurance funds.[91] Within a week, the strike had spread to 1,000 workers; within two weeks, an estimated 40,000 workers from all seven of Yue Yuen factories in the region had joined in – marking a rare regional effort.[92] The unusual size, length, and reach of the unrest triggered a violent response from local authority.[93] By the end of the month, most workers accepted a settlement and returned to work.[94] Without the counterweight of an independent union, the massive strike, like a wave, surged but then dissipated without long-lasting gains for Chinese workers.[95] Even then, the legacy of the Yue Yuen strikes prompted the central government to announce an investigation into Yue Yuen's books and records, eventually resulting in a $90 million settlement to replenish its social insurance and workers' housing funds.[96]

In Vietnam, strike coordination can happen not through workers but, perhaps somewhat ironically, through business and political networks. To avoid competition, employers in the same industrial clusters – especially East Asian companies from Taiwan, Japan, and Korea – often coordinate on wage rates and workers' benefits.[97] A successful strike that raised wage rates would thus impact the equilibrium of the entire industrial zone and even region. To maintain stability and discourage further strikes, provincial union officials often inform their counterparts in neighboring zones and provinces about the successful strike and the resulting new wage rates.[98] They may even advise employers to engage in preemptive negotiations, rather than waiting for workers' reactions, which may halt production and cause

90 See Cynthia Estlund, *A New Deal for China's Workers?* (Harvard University Press 2017) 10–15 (recounting the origin and legacy of the Yue Yuen strikes).

91 Ibid. The social insurance fund is a legally mandated fund set aside to pay for workers' health care premiums, work-related injuries, unemployment, and housing needs.

92 For a firsthand account by a Yue Yuen worker, see "Defeat Will Only Make Us Stronger: Workers Look Back at the Yue Yuen Shoe Factory Strike" *China Labour Bulletin* (May 22, 2014), https://clb.org.hk/en/content/defeat-will-only-make-us-stronger-workers-look-back-yue-yuen-shoe-factory-strike [https://perma.cc/QA6B-ARN6], accessed October 1, 2024 (translating from an interview transcript published in a Chinese blog, *Worker View Point* (工评社)).

93 Ibid.

94 See Estlund (n 90) 10–15.

95 Ibid.

96 Ibid.

97 See Do Quynh Chi, "The Regional Coordination of Strikes and the Challenge for Union Reform in Vietnam" (2017) 48 Development and Change 1063–1064.

98 Ibid.

missed deadlines.[99] In effect, through business and political networks, local officials in Vietnam have informational advantages regarding strike activities, allowing them to act as a kind of broker to set the bargaining terms and preempt potential conflicts. This practice is certainly not labor-led negotiation. But it still represents a way in which the interconnected nature of industrial zones and supply chains can be leveraged for higher wages, albeit tamed through political and business interests.

V CONCLUSION

Inter-Asia's company towns are both starkly similar and different to the old model. Now and then, these manufacturing clusters are the physical manifestation of the capital accumulation and labor management that cater to and facilitate industrial development. Then and now, they reflect the expansiveness of private governance. But unlike past models, today's modern factory towns are transboundary and interconnected as demanded by global supply chains, as part of their designs to capitalize on legal and economic advantages across borders. The horizontal links among Inter-Asia's industrial clusters facilitate their roles as legal entrepôts – made by law and capable of shaping laws. While suppliers' locational advantages enable regulatory fragmentation through practices such as supply chain splitting, modern factory towns' interconnectedness can also open up opportunities for learning and coordination among workers who are linked through regional supply chains. As changing geopolitics create new, rapid demands for industrial sites in Asia and beyond, this volume chapter thus offers a timely, if limited, study on the pathologies of and perhaps even hopes for Inter-Asia's modern company towns.

99 Ibid.

3

International Commercial Alternative Dispute Resolution in Asia

Charting the New Inter-Asian Dynamics

Tran Hoang Tu Linh

I INTRODUCTION

Alternative dispute resolution (ADR), which is a process of offering alternatives to traditional court litigation in which an impartial third party, such as an arbitrator and mediator, helps disputing parties reach a settlement, is not a new phenomenon. However, the development of modern-day ADR only dates back to the twentieth century in Western countries,[1] with London and Paris traditionally being the most active players, followed by Geneva, New York, and Stockholm.[2] The adaptation of international commercial ADR in Asia was even more recent, a trend that has its beginnings in colonial ties.[3] Despite the late start, Asia has witnessed explosive growth in the ADR field, leveling the international playing field. For example, in terms of international commercial arbitration institutions, the Singapore International Arbitration Centre (SIAC) and the Hong Kong International Arbitration Centre (HKIAC) are consistently ranked among the leading institutions in the world.[4] With Singapore and Hong Kong as the current leaders, several other centers in Asia (Seoul, Tokyo, Kuala Lumpur, Abu Dhabi, Dubai, Beijing, and Shanghai, among others) are actively trying to draw more attention from contracting parties.[5] The success of the first-tier Asian cities (e.g., Singapore and Hong Kong)

[1] Katie Shonk, "What Is Alternative Dispute Resolution?" (Program on Negotiation at Harvard Law School, April 4, 2024), www.pon.harvard.edu/daily/dispute-resolution/what-is-alternative-dispute-resolution/, accessed May 15, 2024; Ronán Feehily, *International Commercial Mediation: Law and Regulation in Comparative Context* (Cambridge University Press 2022) 6.

[2] Piyush Prasad, "Arbitration in Singapore and Hong Kong" (2017) 83 International Immersion Program Papers 1, 4.

[3] Gary B Born, *International Commercial Arbitration* (2nd edn, Kluwer Law International 2014) 58.

[4] Queen Mary University of London Survey, "2021 International Arbitration Survey: Adapting Arbitration to a Changing World" (2021) 10.

[5] Gary L Benton, "The Whispered Conversation: Hong Kong v. Singapore" (*Kluwer Arbitration Blog*, January 2, 2009), https://arbitrationblog.kluwerarbitration.com/2019/01/02/whispered-conversation-hong-kong-v-singapore/, accessed May 15, 2024.

and the growth of the second-tier cities (e.g., Seoul, Tokyo, etc.) and the relationship between and among them suggest a new era of Inter-Asian ADR.

This chapter approaches Inter-Asian ADR from two categories: arbitration and mediation. Arbitration is currently Asia's most popular type of ADR and therefore deserves a thorough exploration. Mediation, however, is noteworthy given the strong cultural aspects of the practice, particularly as such aspects are most pronounced in Asia. These cultural practices include a greater emphasis on consensus than in Western countries, as evidenced by, for instance, the preference for mediation and conciliation or the incorporation of amicability into arbitration procedures.[6] Although mediation has yet to receive as much activity as arbitration, its presence has undoubtedly caused significant reforms across Asia. Other types of ADR include adjudication, dispute review boards, and domain name dispute resolution (DNDR). While Asian jurisdictions have also grown these ADR fields, there has, to date, been less written about them. Nonetheless, the prevalence of these other types of ADR gives further credence to the idea of Inter-Asian ADR. Starting from the first two dragons Singapore and Hong Kong, the fever for ADR now spreads wide and deep in Asia. Today, Asia is causing the center of the world's ADR market to shift eastward, and, despite some challenges on the horizon, this trend will only likely continue.

II THE RACE BETWEEN SINGAPORE AND HONG KONG

A. *Singapore's Status*

Background

Singapore's history as a hub for international commerce is closely linked to its colonial past. When British governor Stamford Raffles secured the port that would become modern-day Singapore in 1810 and later established it as a colony in 1824, he laid the foundations for a thriving trading post.[7] Unlike Hong Kong, which serves as a gateway to China, Singapore's strategic position as a crossroads of busy sea lanes has uniquely positioned it to become a premier arbitration hub in Asia.[8] Despite its small area, less than a third of the size of Hong Kong, Singapore boasts three-quarters of Hong Kong's population, resulting in a higher population density.[9]

Building on its colonial roots, Singapore's evolution into a major trading hub has continually fueled the demand for ADR. The flow of trade through Singapore,

6 Born (n 3) 59.

7 Matthew S Erie, "The New Legal Hubs: The Emergent Landscape of International Commercial Dispute Resolution" (2020) 60 Va J Int'l L 225, 262.

8 Prasad (n 2) 4.

9 "Country comparison: Hong Kong vs Singapore" (World Data, 2023), www.worlddata.info/country-comparison.php?country1 = HKG&country2 = SGP, accessed May 15, 2024.

initiated during its colonial era, has only intensified over the years. This historical trend set the stage for the development of sophisticated ADR mechanisms to address the commercial disputes arising from the bustling trade activity. The culmination of this growth was marked by Singapore's independence in 1965, which further solidified its status as a leading center for international commercial arbitration in the region.

Singapore's attempt to promote ADR started in the 1980s when it began internationalizing its commercial dispute resolution system.[10] Singapore acceded to the United Nations Convention on the Recognition and Enforcement of Foreign Arbitral Awards (New York Convention) in 1986, set up SIAC in 1991 and the Singapore Mediation Centre in 1997, and consolidated the United Nations Commission on International Trade Law (UNCITRAL) Model Law on International Commercial Arbitration in its International Arbitration Act in 2002. Many policy reforms have been implemented over the years, such as the 2004 amendment of the Legal Profession Act to allow anyone to represent a party in an arbitration seated in Singapore and perform work that was previously reserved for advocates and solicitors.[11] Singapore aimed to be the number one forum for international commercial arbitration in Asia and, achieving that, has subsequently sought to be a leading center in the world.[12] Pursuant to the Queen Mary Survey on international commercial arbitration in 2021, Singapore has now proven successful in making it to the top.[13]

Singapore's Establishment

ADR Promotion Strategy – Specializing and Networking: Instead of promoting all models of international commercial ADR, Singapore tends to focus on two models: arbitration and mediation. Singapore is known for its wide variety of service offerings within those models. With the availability of the trio of SIAC (est. 1991), Singapore International Mediation Centre (SIMC, est. 2014), and Singapore International Commercial Court (SICC, est. 2015), Singapore has proven it has the institutional capacity to meet international parties' dispute resolution needs. Firstly, in collaboration with SIMC, SIAC offers an Arbitration–Mediation–Arbitration (AMA) procedure, which allows parties to utilize the strengths of each method. The parties can attempt mediation after initiating arbitration proceedings and return to arbitration if the mediation does not result in a settlement. In other cases, a mediated settlement agreement can be turned into an award through arbitration. The mediated settlement is then referred to the arbitrator for approval, and the arbitrator then assesses the consent terms and makes an award, thereby converting the mediated agreement

10 Erie (n 7).
11 Prasad (n 2) 10.
12 Erie (n 7).
13 Queen Mary Survey 2021 (n 4) 6.

into an arbitration award. The arbitration award is, therefore, enforceable under the New York Convention to enhance its recognition and enforcement in member jurisdictions.

Another collaborative service is the SICC–SIMC Litigation–Mediation–Litigation, whereby parties can refer to SIMC for mediation after the disputes commence SICC. In recent years, the commercial attitude toward mediation has been getting more positive; for example, the inclusion of SIMC into SICC has earned positive feedback from the business community. Secondly, SIAC collaborated with SICC to publish a model clause, allowing parties to select the SICC as the supervisory court rather than the default General Division of the Singapore High Court.[14] With this model, parties can make a more compelling decision by benefiting from SIAC's renowned arbitration mechanism[15] and SICC's extensive expertise.[16] Thirdly, Singapore also connects ADR services providers, professional standards bodies, and research institutions to exchange information and offer well-rounded regulations, as evidenced by the different rules for different entities participating in third-party funding (TPF).[17] The multiple connections among institutions in Singapore can further reinforce the impression of an ecosystem made from dispute resolution networks rather than individual institutions. These linkages make it possible for one to combine many of the ADR services that may be available in order to improve the capability of dispute resolution. They can also contribute to creating trust and credibility among international actors in the event such an ecosystem is provided, which demonstrates that all actors are committed to high standards and best practices. Moreover, the consolidation of sources within this network may encourage practices for resource sharing and collaboration, which might enhance the methods used and boost dependability and forecasting. This interconnectedness could promote Singapore as taking a more expansive role in the international dispute resolution system.

State-of-the-art Institutions and Infrastructure: The *SMU SIDRA Report 2022* pointed out six major factors influencing the choice of venue: efficiency, administrative support, in-person hearing facilities, virtual hearing facilities,

[14] "Singapore International Commercial Court Launches Initiative to Hear Arbitration Matters with Support from Singapore International Arbitration Centre" (SG Courts, January 12, 2023), www.judiciary.gov.sg/news-and-resources/news/news-details/joint-media-release-singapore-international-commercial-court-launches-initiative-to-hear-arbitration-matters-with-support-from-singapore-international-arbitration-centre, accessed May 15, 2023.

[15] Pamela K Bookman and Matthew S Erie, "Experimenting with International Commercial Dispute Resolution" (2021) 115 AJIL Unbound 5.

[16] Prasad (n 2) 12.

[17] For example, Singapore established SIAC and SIMC as service providers, SIArb and the Singapore International Mediation Institute as the professional bodies, and SIDRA as the research institution. See Eunice Chua, "The Singapore Convention on Mediation – A Brighter Future for Asian Dispute Resolution" (2019) 9 AsianJIL 195, 204.

additional facilities, and convenience of location.[18] Singapore knew this early on[19] and has worked to not only meet but also excel in each criterion through the development of the Maxwell Chambers arbitration complex since 2010.[20] The Maxwell Chambers hosts most major Singapore institutions and several international ones while featuring a corresponding number of rooms of various sizes, allowing both on-site conferences and virtual hearings. Thus, despite Singapore's small area, it manages to "enable a certain degree of cross-institutional coordination."[21] Furthermore, as the leader in international commercial ADR infrastructure, Singapore continuously renovates the Maxwell Chambers in terms of advanced technology and infrastructure, as shown by the 2018 "SMART Maxwell" program. This program established an app that allows parties to do a variety of functions, from gaining access to hearing rooms to tracking expenditures for a more efficient finance and administrative process.[22] The program's effectiveness can be evidenced by the sharp increase in the caseload of SIAC in 2020,[23] as well as the preference of parties to resolve disputes at Maxwell Chambers.[24]

Recent Development – TPF: Singapore has taken one step after another to liberalize the legal industry and promote the city as a preferred arbitration venue. A recent example is passing new legislation such as the Civil Law (Third-Party Funding) Regulations 2017, to allow parties to seek TPF.[25] This legislation also marked Singapore's abandonment of the common law doctrines of maintenance and champerty. These doctrines are legal rules of decision originating from English common law, which has forbidden third parties from funding legal actions. Maintenance is concerned with preventing a third party from assisting in a litigation case in which they have no professional or personal interest, while champerty is supporting a case for a share of the litigants' gains.

18 Singapore International Dispute Resolution Academy, "SIDRA International Dispute Resolution Survey: 2022 Final Report" (SMU SIDRA Report 2022) 19.

19 In 2015, the Legal Services Working Group of the Economic Review Committee put emphasis on "good infrastructure and facilities" in making Singapore an ADR spotlight in Asia. See Legal Business, "Singapore v Hong Kong: The Arbitration Battle Intensifies" *Thomson Reuters* (November 30, 2011), www.legalbusinessonline.com/features/singapore-v-hong-kongthe-arbitration-battle-intensifies/57638, accessed May 15, 2023.

20 Prasad (n 2) 5.

21 Erie (n 7) 265.

22 Ilyda Chua, "Maxwell Chambers to be world's first smart hearing facility" *The Strait Times* (April 4, 2018), www.straitstimes.com/singapore/courts-crime/maxwell-chambers-to-be-worlds-first-smart-hearing-facility, accessed June 15, 2024.

23 "2021 Singapore International Arbitration Centre Statistics Return to Pre-Pandemic Trends" (*Conventus Law*, July 7, 2022), https://conventuslaw.com/report/2021-singapore-international-arbitration-centre-statistics-return-to-pre-pandemic-trends/, accessed June 15, 2024.

24 "SMU SIDRA Report 2022" (n 18) 20.

25 "Third-Party Funding to Be Permitted for More Categories of Legal Proceedings in Singapore", www.mlaw.gov.sg/news/press-releases/2021-06-21-third-party-funding-framework-permitted-for-more-categories-of-legal-preceedings-in-singapore/, accessed June 15, 2024.

These doctrines sought to reduce the chances of filing baseless cases and manipulation of the court process. At first, Singapore initially applied TPF only to international arbitration and related court procedures, but TPF has been subsequently officially embraced for domestic arbitration and other procedures. Notably, Singapore also gives parties freedom by not limiting the amount funded and paid. Non-binding regulations on TPF are present as well, specifically (i) SIAC Practice Note 31/3/2017; (ii) The Law Society of Singapore Guidance Note 10.1.1 on Third-party Funding; and (iii) the Singapore Institute of Arbitrators (SIArb) Guidelines for Third Party Funders. These regulations act as guidelines for the best practices of lawyers and funders, respectively. In short, what has distinguished Singapore's TPF regulations from other competitors are: (i) the underlying supportive and detailed legislation, (ii) the funded parties' protection from malpractice, using guidelines regulating lawyers and funders, and (iii) the absence of limitations on the amount funded and paid, which has greatly increased the use of TPF.[26]

National Endeavor – Neutral, Incorruptible, and Binding System: Singapore is often considered a neutral arbitration seat. But what makes a seat "neutral" and why is Singapore considered one? A forum is considered neutral when none of the parties is at an actual or perceived disadvantageous jurisdiction.[27] Singapore satisfied this requirement when it established a reputation for having accessible and impartial justice.[28] Singapore is also known for its fight against corruption, which is supported by the country's consistently high ranking in anti-corruption indices.[29] Recently, pursuant to its anti-corruption efforts, Singapore ranked fifth globally and first among Asian countries in the Corruption Perceptions Index 2022.[30]

Furthermore, the enforceability of foreign and domestic awards in Singapore is almost guaranteed. Since Singapore is a party to both the New York Convention and the United Nations Convention on International Settlement Agreements resulting from Mediation (Singapore Convention),[31] its arbitration awards and mediation agreements are widely enforceable in other member states. Likewise, the national

[26] Lianjun Li and others, "Implementation of ORFS in Hong Kong: A Comparative Look at Mainland China and Singapore" (*Reed Smith*, January 5, 2023), www.reedsmith.com/en/perspectives/2023/01/implementation-of-orfs-in-hong-kong, accessed March 15, 2024.

[27] Andrea K Bjorklund, "Chapter 7: Enforcement" in Thomas Schultz and Federico Ortino (eds), *The Oxford Handbook of International Arbitration* (OUP 2020) 190.

[28] Sreenivasan Narayanan, Raja Bose and Henry Kim, "International Arbitration and the Singapore International Arbitration Centre" (*Lexology*, June 7, 2022), www.lexology.com/library/detail.aspx?g = c6c23bc6-1369-47aa-8bc8-fe95b596bc7c, accessed March 15, 2023.

[29] Prasad (n 2) 5.

[30] "Corruption Perceptions Index: Singapore" (*Transparency International*, 2023), www.transparency.org/en/cpi/2022/index/sgp, accessed July 15, 2024.

[31] The Singapore Convention on Mediation is named so to commemorate the fact that it was adopted and opened for signing in Singapore in August 2019 as part of showcasing Singapore's commitment to international ADR. This naming brings to focus the role of Singapore as an initiator in present-era facilitation techniques and consolidates its position as a significant contributor and mediator in the sunrise field of international commercial mediation.

courts of Singapore have shown their support for the arbitration procedure, stating that their function is to support the procedure, not to replace it.[32]

Thus, Singapore's strength comes primarily from its achievements – both the government's success in establishing Singapore's status as a neutral seat and the private sector's achievements in creating new facilities and services.

B. *Hong Kong's Status*

Background

Hong Kong's story started in 1842 when Britain established it as a colony.[33] Because of its connection to two jurisdictions China and Britain, Hong Kong is often regarded as an important "gateway" to mainland China.[34] As a gateway, Hong Kong's strength lies in having access to an enormous market – China.[35] Moreover, Hong Kong has both a common law legal system and friendliness toward the English language, which attracts an enormous source of investors including from the United States (US) and United Kingdom (UK).[36] Hong Kong's status as a colony terminated in 1997, when it was handed over to the People's Republic of China (PRC) and established its status as a "special administrative region" (SAR). This did not remove Hong Kong's status as the gateway connecting China and the rest of the world since the common law legal system of Hong Kong would be expected to last at least fifty years after the handover.[37] Furthermore, the handover allowed trade to flow both ways, as Hong Kong now also serves Chinese outbound investment, including that related to the recent Belt and Road Initiative (BRI), providing international banking and financial services.[38]

As a legal hub, Hong Kong is considered "organic" thanks to existing trade activities, rather than needing to build its hub reputation from the ground up – or "artificial" like Shanghai or Dubai.[39] In terms of regulations, Hong Kong offers its own signature common law, which has the advantage of being the "middleman" since it has both Chinese and Western influence.[40] Hong Kong is also unique for being the only venue outside China that allows parties to seek interim measures

[32] Prasad (n 2) 5.
[33] Erie (n 7) 253.
[34] Ibid.
[35] Benton (n 5).
[36] Erie (n 7) 254. Hong Kong has the "Basic Law," which is their mini-constitution, and while the judicial system operates in a common law manner, Hong Kong is only a special administrative region (SAR) and the PRC legal system (a civil law system) has various points of oversight over Hong Kong SAR – the "one country two systems" approach.
[37] Jan K Schaefer, "Leaving the Colonial Arbitration Laws Behind: Southeast Asia's Move Into the International Arbitration Arena" (2000) 16 Arb. Int'l 297, 300–301.
[38] Erie (n 7) 255.
[39] Ibid 261.
[40] Ibid 256.

from mainland courts and is thus more favorable than other jurisdictions when seeking mainland enforcement.[41] Thanks to its strong background, talented legal community, and modern arbitration institutions, Hong Kong is a solid contestant for Asia Pacific-based international arbitration.[42]

Hong Kong's Establishments

ADR Promotion Strategy – Centralizing, Diversifying, and Pioneering: Unlike Singapore, Hong Kong incorporates different types of international commercial ADR into one institution – HKIAC, which was established in 1985.[43] The Hong Kong International Arbitration Centre offers several ADRs, including arbitration, mediation, DNDR, and adjudication.[44] Mediation at HKIAC is administered by the Hong Kong Mediation Centre (HKMC) division, which was set up in 1999.[45] Domain name dispute resolution is administered by the Asian Domain Name Dispute Resolution Centre (ADNDRC), which HKIAC jointly established with the China International Economic and Trade Arbitration Commission (CIETAC) in 2002. This remained the only institution in Asia to resolve disputes under the Uniform Domain Name Dispute Resolution Policy (UDRP) until 2013.[46]

While adopting a centralist approach, Hong Kong has sought inspiration from other jurisdictions in terms of innovating its ADR offerings. These adaptations are emblematic of Hong Kong's role as a centripetal force for borrowing ADR innovations from other systems. For example, the expedited procedure was first the product of the Geneva Chamber of Commerce and Industry (CCIG) in 1992[47] before being adopted by HKIAC in 2008. Other leading Asian institutions, such as SIAC or the Asian International Arbitration Centre (AIAC), have only adopted the expedited procedure since 2010. Similarly, consolidation of arbitration upon the party's request, introduced by the International Criminal Court (ICC) in 2012, has been adopted by HKIAC and AIAC since 2013, and SIAC since 2016. Thus, Hong Kong can be seen as not only a geographical gateway to China but also a gateway for ADR services and regulations – connecting Asia with Western countries.

Transparency and Technological Innovation: As a gateway, Hong Kong consistently introduces new innovations to Asia. Most recently, in 2021, HKIAC introduced

[41] Arrangement Concerning Mutual Enforcement of Arbitral Awards.

[42] Benton (n 5).

[43] Herbert Smith Freehills, "ADR in Asia Pacific: Spotlight on Mediation in Hong Kong" (Issue 1, Herbert Smith Freehills 2015) 2–4.

[44] See HKIAC Arbitration Rules 2018, HKIAC Mediation Rules, HKIAC Adjudication Rules, and The Guide to HKIAC Domain Name Dispute Resolution 2022.

[45] HKIAC "HKIAC Mediation Rules", www.hkiac.org/mediation/rules/hkiac-mediation-rules, accessed May 15, 2023.

[46] In 2013, the Arab Center for Dispute Resolution became the second institution in Asia to resolve disputes under the UDRP.

[47] Joséphine Hage Chahine, "Fast Track Arbitration: A Time-Efficient Procedure That Could Hinder the Award?" (*Jus Mundi*, May 29, 2020), https://blog.jusmundi.com/fast-track-arbitration-a-time-efficient-procedure-that-could-hinder-the-award/, accessed May 16, 2023.

two new services: HKIAC Case Digest and HKIAC Case Connect. The first service, HKIAC Case Digest, is a database for redacted and summarized past arbitration awards, which only subscribers can access. This follows the movement of arbitration centers around the world to improve the consistency and predictability of the arbitral process by using precedents.[48] However, compared to other institutions' corresponding services, the awards published by HKIAC Case Digest are more limited, shown only partially and to subscribers only. Nonetheless, HKIAC earned the Best Innovation award at the 12th annual Global Arbitration Review (GAR) Awards ceremony in 2022 for this service, thus, proving its effectiveness.[49]

The second innovation – HKIAC Case Connect – is a secure and convenient platform allowing parties to manage all their documents and communicate more efficiently.[50] This is another huge success for HKIAC since it inspired not only Asian but also international institutions (i.e., ICC, with 2022 ICC Case Connect) to build an online case management platform).[51] With these innovations, Hong Kong proved itself to be an innovator in the field of international commercial ADR.

Recent Development – TPF: Similar to Singapore, TPF was traditionally prohibited in Hong Kong due to the common law doctrine of maintenance and champerty. However, in 2017, Hong Kong legalized TPF in international arbitration, making Hong Kong a TPF-friendly jurisdiction.[52] In 2021, the Hong Kong Law Reform Commission published a report on Outcome Related Fee Structures for Arbitration (ORFS) recommending further legalizing lawyer fee structures. In December 2022, the regime became effective, allowing lawyers to arrange conditional fee agreements, damages-based agreements, and hybrid damages-based agreements.[53] Therefore, Hong Kong's legal framework on TPF

48 Noah Rubins, Ezequiel Vetulli, and Rohit Bhat , "Drive Towards Greater Transparency" (Freshfields 2023), www.freshfields.com/en-gb/our-thinking/campaigns/international-arbitration-in-2023/drive-towards-greater-transparency/, accessed May 10, 2024.

49 "HKIAC Case Digest Wins GAR Award for Best Innovation" (*HKIAC*, April 6, 2022), www.hkiac.org/news/hkiac-case-digest-wins-gar-award-best-innovation, accessed May 10, 2023. HKIAC also previously won 2015 GAR Awards for inclusion of a choice of law provision in its model clauses and the introduction of a tribunal secretary service. See "And the GAR Innovation Award goes to . . . HKIAC" (*HKIAC*, February 27, 2015), www.hkiac.org/news/and-gar-innovation-award-goes-%E2%80%A6-hkiac, accessed May 10, 2023.

50 "HKIAC Launches HKIAC Case Connect" (*HKIAC*, November 1, 2021), www.hkiac.org/news/hkiac-launches-hkiac-case-connect, accessed May 10, 2022.

51 Marc Labgold and Megan Labgold, "Arbitration Tech Toolbox: ICC Case Connect – A User Perspective" (*Kluwer Arbitration Blog*, February 21, 2023), https://arbitrationblog.kluwerarbitration.com/2023/02/21/arbitration-tech-toolbox-icc-case-connect-a-user-perspective/, accessed April 15, 2024.

52 See Arbitration and Mediation Legislation (Third Party Funding) (Amendment) Ordinance 2017 of Hong Kong.

53 Hiroko Yamamoto and others, "2022 Year in Review: Key Developments in East and Central Asia" (*Kluwer Arbitration Blog*, January 4, 2023), https://arbitrationblog.kluwerarbitration.com/2023/01/04/2022-year-in-review-key-developments-in-east-and-central-asia/, accessed May 10, 2024.

provides a broader variety of services than Singapore's despite being more limited in terms of the amount funded.[54]

National Endeavor – Perseverance through Crisis: Despite all the above, Hong Kong is not without problems. Hong Kong's proximity to China has been both a blessing and a curse since Western-based parties can be nervous about getting too close to China.[55] In 2020, this fear turned into a crisis when China enacted the new National Security Law[56] to safeguard China's security and protect the "one party, two systems" policy of Hong Kong by enforcing sanctions on offenders.[57] Reacting to this situation, the US announced that it would terminate Hong Kong's special trading status, effectively treating Hong Kong similarly to mainland China.[58] These events have caused international companies to avoid choosing Hong Kong as the seat of arbitration and resort to rival hubs like Singapore, fearing China's increasing influence in Hong Kong would erode trust in its legal system.[59] Amidst the chaos, Hong Kong authorities have sought to offer assurances that these developments have had only minor effects on trade and ADR.[60] The main argument is that the Chief Executive's ability to select judges in litigation does not affect arbitration or other ADR systems since parties or the institution makes appointments or nominations.[61] While Hong Kong has held onto its status as a dominant seat of arbitration[62], its position remains less certain than earlier.

To summarize, Hong Kong's strength originates mainly from its status as a geographical and jurisdictional gateway to mainland China and as a gateway for international commercial ADR services in Asia. Hong Kong's strong, established legal culture also continues to attract ADR activities. Despite facing a crisis in terms

[54] Li (n 26).

[55] Legal Business (n 19).

[56] In full, the Law of the People's Republic of China on Safeguarding National Security in the Hong Kong Special Administrative Region (National Security Law). See Adrian Wong and Kelvin Poon, "Are Arbitrations Shifting Away from Hong Kong and Towards Singapore? Impact of the Hong Kong National Security Law" (*Lexology*, October 29, 2020), www.lexology.com/library/detail.aspx?g=3cfc2411-fd99-4d64-93ce-a8976c764b3b, accessed May 10, 2023.

[57] Ibid.

[58] Denise Tsang, "United States Ending Hong Kong's Special Trading Status Will Hurt US Firms, City's American Chamber of Commerce Says" *South China Morning Post* (July 17, 2020), www.scmp.com/news/hong-kong/hong-kong-economy/article/3093573/united-states-ending-hong-kongs-special-trading, accessed May 15, 2023.

[59] Erie (n 7).

[60] Elizabeth Law, "Chinese President Xi Signs Hong Kong National Security Law Into Effect" *The Strait Times* (June 30, 2020), www.straitstimes.com/asia/east-asia/beijing-passes-hong-kong-national-security-law-government-adviser, accessed May 12, 2023.

[61] Wong and Poon (n 56).

[62] In 2022, 344 arbitration cases were submitted to HKIAC, a 24.2 percent increase from 2021. This number is even higher than it was before the National Security Law (i.e., 2019, 2020). See "2022 Statistics" (HKIAC, 2023), www.hkiac.org/about-us/statistics, accessed May 10, 2024.

of its reputation in the business community for impartial dispute resolution services, Hong Kong will likely continue to contribute to the ADR ecosystem of Asia.

C. *Inter-Asian Comparisons*

Starting Point Revisited

In comparing Singapore and Hong Kong, while, broadly, the two city-states have similarities, Hong Kong historically came out on top due to its market access to China. In terms of their core similarities, both are former British colonies and with legal systems based on English common law.[63] There was a separate legal regime for international and national arbitration under both systems, which is paradoxical considering English law does not make such a distinction.[64] Since both are city economies with limited internal markets and with finance as the main sector,[65] they also share the tendency to formulate international centers rather than national ones.[66] Despite being Asian institutions, SIAC and HKIAC pay great attention to the Western principle of party autonomy,[67] where parties can agree on the appointment of arbitrators and how the proceedings are carried out (i.e., using rules from other institutions) if so requested by the parties. However, because mainland China's court provided Hong Kong with a better chance of award recognition and enforcement for matters related to China, it was Hong Kong where parties who do business in China chose to arbitrate in the beginning.[68] In what follows, I trace the inter-Asian rivalry between Hong Kong and Singapore.

The Road Traveled

Beginning in the early 2000s, while Hong Kong was the first Asian jurisdiction to obtain international renown as a center for international commercial ADR, Singapore has been catching up. By 2000, Singapore had already established all the necessary requirements for an attractive seat of arbitration, including signing the New York Convention (1986), consolidating the Model Law (2002), setting up institutions, increasing the court's familiarity with the arbitration procedure, holding arbitration events, and publishing modern legislations on arbitration.[69] Singapore also drew its strength externally, thanks to the rise of up-and-coming economies like India and other Southeast Asian neighbors. Meanwhile, Hong Kong has obtained

63 Schaefer (n 37) 300.
64 Ibid 306.
65 Erie (n 7) 255.
66 Schaefer (n 37) 319–320.
67 Kun Fan, "International Dispute Resolution Trends in Asia" (2013) 10 Transnat'l Dispute Manag 8.
68 Legal Business (n 19).
69 Singapore Ministry of Law, "Background Brief on International Arbitration in Singapore", www.mlaw.gov.sg/files/news/press-releases/2009/07/linkclickf8e7.pdf, accessed May 16, 2023.

an advantage in terms of other types of international commercial ADRs (even if under a centralized model). With HKMC and ADNDRC, Hong Kong made ADR in Asia much livelier. Nonetheless, by 2010, Singapore had become a formidable challenger to Hong Kong for the crown, as shown by the Queen Mary International Arbitration Survey.[70]

It appears that Singapore's efforts have given Hong Kong an incentive to hold onto the crown. Since 2008, Hong Kong redoubled its efforts, starting with adopting new arbitration rules on expedited procedures or consolidation of arbitration. Hong Kong also unified legal regimes for domestic and international arbitration with the Arbitration Ordinance 2011.[71] In 2014, Hong Kong introduced the Advisory Committee on the Promotion of Arbitration to advise the Department of Justice in promoting arbitration. For its part, Singapore has improved its institutions apace. The institution of the Maxwell Chambers in 2010 quickly boosted Singapore's reputation not only as a reliable seat but also as a modern venue of arbitration. Mediation in Singapore also received more attention with the establishment of SIMC in 2014. The result of the rivalry between the two jurisdictions during this time favored Hong Kong, as evidenced by another Queen Mary International Arbitration Survey: HKIAC took the lead as the third-best institution worldwide and the most improved seat, while SIAC followed as the fourth-best institution and second-most improved.[72]

Since 2015, the battle has intensified as each jurisdiction has put maximum effort into improving its respective international commercial ADR. Notably, both Singapore and Hong Kong adopted monumental regulations on TPF at approximately the same time to attract more activities in ADR. On Singapore's part, collaborative hybrid procedures and other networks have been created during this period. Online dispute resolution infrastructure was also developed by Maxwell Chambers, resulting in SIAC's symbolic achievement of the 1,000-cases milestone in 2020. In Hong Kong, the 2020 National Security Law had serious implications for the city-state's reputation and allowed Singapore to leap ahead. Hong Kong authorities have downplayed investor concerns, and Hong Kong's institutions have continued to innovate, including the HKIAC Case Digest and HKIAC Case Connect. Still, these efforts may not be enough to counter the widespread perception that Hong Kong's judicial integrity has been compromised by Chinese national security. Meanwhile, Singapore continues to create new paradigms for international

70 Queen Mary University of London Survey, "2010 International Arbitration Survey: Choices in International Arbitration" (2010) 19, 23.

71 David Holloway and others, "Strengthening Hong Kong's Position as an Arbitration Hub in the Belt and Road Initiative" (2018) Research Centre for Sustainable Hong Kong Policy Paper 8, 2, www.cityu.edu.hk/cshk/files/PolicyPapers/CSHK%20Policy%20Paper%208.pdf, accessed May 10, 2023.

72 Queen Mary University of London Survey, "2015 International Arbitration Survey: Improvements and Innovations in International Arbitration" (2015) 12, 17.

commercial ADR, including, for example, the 2018 Singapore Convention. Singapore, as one of the first parties to this Convention, is taking the lead with SIMC and does so through the networks that it has established across the world.[73] A surging Singapore's status is reflected in the Queen Mary International Arbitration Survey 2018 and 2022, wherein Singapore unsurprisingly holds the crown.

After reviewing the race between Singapore and Hong Kong, one may ask what exactly "the crown" is. In terms of which jurisdiction is the preferred seat of arbitration or has more attractive institutions, "Singapore" may be the immediate answer. However, there is more to the role of a state and its institutions than just satisfying customers. From the perspective of practitioners and academics, Hong Kong comes out on top as it plays a vital role in implementing innovations, which lay the ground for the rest of Asia to follow, including Singapore. For example, in 2009, Singapore followed Hong Kong's example in adopting Option 1 of the 2006 UNCITRAL Model Law.[74] Singapore and Hong Kong should be viewed as complementary[75] because they offer different alternatives to suit parties' needs. The constant competitiveness between Hong Kong and Singapore thus only results in a net positive for Asia,[76] making a more exciting battle of ADR Asia versus the rest of the world.[77]

III THE IMPLICATIONS OF SINGAPORE'S AND HONG KONG'S MOVEMENTS FOR ASIA

A. *Across Asia*

In theory, to enhance international commercial ADR attractiveness, six aspects should be covered: (i) accession to the international treaties (i.e., the New York Convention, Singapore Convention); (ii) adoption of UNCITRAL Model Law (on Arbitration or Mediation); (iii) establishment of institutions with up-to-date practices; (iv) courts' support of arbitration and familiarity with recognition and enforcement process; (v) activities (e.g., training and seminars); and (vi) competent and attractive legislation.[78] In practice, I find that the presence of leading international

73 SIMC is preferred by 61 percent of respondents, while HKIMC and HKIAC received 11 percent and 6 percent, respectively. See (n 18) 33.

74 Darius Chan, "Singapore's International Arbitration Act 2012 vs Hong Kong's Arbitration Ordinance 2011" (*Kluwer Arbitration Blog*, April 5, 2012), https://arbitrationblog.kluwerarbitration.com/2012/04/05/singapores-international-arbitration-act-2012-vs-hong-kongs-arbitration-ordinance-2011/, accessed May 15, 2023.

75 Legal Business (n 19).

76 Erie (n 7) 245.

77 Legal Business (n 19).

78 Anselmo Reyes and Weixia Gu, "Introduction: Towards a Model of Arbitration Reform in the Asia Pacific" in Anselmo Reyes and Weixia Gu (eds), *The Developing World of Arbitration: A Comparative Study of Arbitration Reform in the Asia Pacific* (Hart Publishing 2018) 3.

commercial ADR hubs in Singapore and Hong Kong has inspired changes in Asia mostly on the third, fifth, and sixth counts. In particular, in this section, I first examine general patterns of convergence across Asia in regard to international commercial ADR and the Singapore–Hong Kong competition in particular, then examine Singapore's influence in Vietnam, and lastly, conjecture some possible future outcomes of the mixture of competition and convergence in inter-Asian international commercial ADR.

Rules

In the past few decades, changes have been made to international commercial ADR across Asia in terms of rules. The UAE, or more specifically, Dubai, is the most potent example. In 2021, Dubai abolished the Dubai International Financial Centre (DIFC)–London Court of International Arbitration Centre and breathed new life into the Dubai International Arbitration Centre (DIAC). Following the event, DIAC also established the new Arbitration Rules of 2022, allowing procedures to be done electronically and adopting provisions on joinder and consolidation, emergency arbitration, expedited procedure, and TPF.[79] DIAC's supervisory court is the DIFC Courts, which operate independently from its domestic judiciary system.[80] This is similar to the SIAC–SICC relationship since DIFC is also an international commercial court with arbitration expertise; however, the difference is that the DIAC–DIFC Courts relationship does not require parties' agreement. This movement has shown Dubai's determination to become the leading legal hub in the Middle East.

In addition to development in Dubai, several new ADR institutions have been set up across Asia to follow the rise of SIAC and HKIAC. India recently established the International Arbitration and Mediation Centre in 2021. It includes Med-Arb, emergency arbitration, and online dispute resolution among its services to compete with leading institutions. Some other institutions chose to update existing rules, drawing inspiration from HKIAC and SIAC. The Korean Commercial Arbitration Board (KCAB) has been influenced by SIAC and HKIAC in developing the 2016 International Arbitration Rules. Aside from the popular provisions, KCAB now also allows the nomination of arbitrators (as opposed to appointment), which is a method used by SIAC,[81] and mandates arbitrators who accept an

[79] Soraya Corm-Bakhos, "DIAC 2022 Rules of Arbitration: A Modernised Set of Rules for a New Era" (*Kluwer Arbitration Blog*, March 21, 2022), https://arbitrationblog.kluwerarbitration.com/2022/03/21/diac-2022-rules-of-arbitration-a-modernised-set-of-rules-for-a-new-era/, accessed May 10, 2024.

[80] Silvana Cinari, "The Emergence of International Commercial Courts: The Rationale and Key Features" (2022) 9 S Eur LJ 82, 93.

[81] Jae-Hyun Kim and Bryan E. Hopkins, "Recent Changes to the Korean Arbitration Act and Its Comparison with Singapore: Korea's Potential to Become an Arbitration Hub" (2016) 26 J Arb Stud 27, 36.

appointment or nomination to sign and submit a Statement of Acceptance and a Statement of Impartiality and Independence, which is a requirement provided by HKIAC.[82]

Notably, Singapore's institutions also make an impact by offering collaborative services with foreign institutions. For example, in 2021, SIMC collaborated with India's Centre for Advanced Mediation Practice (CAMP) and the Japan International Mediation Centre (JIMC)[83] to offer more economical, efficient, and effective mediation during COVID-19. The JIMC–SIMC Joint COVID-19 Protocol also allows each institution to appoint a co-mediator, which is well-received by both customers and mediators.[84] Furthermore, in 2022, SIMC and the Shenzhen Court of International Arbitration (SCIA) established the Mediation–Arbitration Protocol, which allows parties to utilize SIMC mediation while increasing the enforceability of SIMC mediation outcomes in China.[85] Last but not least, in 2024, Singapore and Bahrain signed a bilateral treaty to establish the Bahrain International Commercial Court (BICC) and allow appeals from this new institution to be heard by SICC. This collaboration builds on the previous Memorandum of Understanding on Cooperation and Memorandum of Guidance as to the Enforcement of Money Judgments by the Singapore and Bahrain judiciaries in May 2023. The BICC aims to leverage Bahrain's regional growth, while the SICC's involvement offers a transnational dispute resolution mechanism.[86] Not only do these protocols offer better quality services to customers, but they also bring Asian institutions closer together and share any expertise along the way.

The eastward shift of international commercial ADR also prompts Asian institutions to take bold steps in an attempt to break through in a field historically dominated by European centers. For example, the Japan Commercial Arbitration Association (JCAA) established the new Interactive Arbitration Rules 2019, where the tribunal and parties took a more active role in swiftly resolving disputes.[87] This new procedure is based on dialogues among all participants rather than traditional one-way communication. Parties share their views on each of the matters and comment on each other's views, while arbitrators can elaborate their own opinions.[88] Due to

82 Ibid.
83 See SIMC–CAMP Joint Covid-19 Protocol and JIMC–SIMC Joint Covid-19 Protocol.
84 Yoshihiro Takatori, "Online Practice and Activation of ADR – Further Progress of Arb. Med. Arb." (2022) 3 Japan Comm Arb 64, 66.
85 "Med-Arb" (SIMC 2022), https://simc.com.sg/dispute-resolution/med-arb/, accessed May 10, 2024.
86 "Singapore and Bahrain Sign Bilateral Treaty on Appeals from the Bahrain International Commercial Court", www.mlaw.gov.sg/news/press-releases/singapore-bahrain-sign-treaty-on-appeals-from-bicc/, accessed May 10, 2024.
87 Douglas K Freeman, "The New JCAA Arbitration Rules – Japan's Attempt in Innovative Dispute Resolution" (2020) 1 Japan Comm Arb J 4, 7.
88 Masato Dogauchi, Shinji Ogawa and Jieying Peng, "New Style of Arbitration – The First Case under JCAA Interactive Arbitration Rules" (2022) 3 Japan Comm Arb 7, 8.

how parties communicate, they are more likely to gain mutual information, resulting in a higher chance of negotiation, saving time and costs, and, most importantly, fulfilling certain Japanese disputants' expectations of amicability. While this idea is unique to Japan, it shows that the playground for new ideas is no longer exclusive to Singapore and Hong Kong. With the rise of mediation after the Singapore Convention, consensual procedures like interactive arbitration can inspire other countries to adopt the same approach.

Supplementary Activities

Since 2016, SIAC has been actively signing memoranda of understanding (MoUs) with institutions around the world to collaborate on organizing conferences, seminars, and workshops; providing marketing support for each other's international arbitration events; and granting complimentary admission to each other's paid or members-only events, training courses, and workshops.[89] Currently, there are at least twenty-seven MoUs between SIAC and Asian institutions from ten jurisdictions, including Cambodia, China, India, Japan, Korea, Malaysia, Russia, Thailand, Timor-Leste, and the UAE. For comparison, HKIAC has only signed a handful of cooperation agreements with Asian centers. The overwhelming number of SIAC's MoUs secure its place as the leading hub in Asia.

Outside SIAC's influence, Asian institutions have been more active than ever in conferences, workshops, and seminars, especially during the COVID-19 pandemic. Furthermore, Asian institutions are now publishing their own journals. A few years back, SIAC's *Asian International Arbitration Journal* (est. 2005) and HKIAC's *Asian Dispute Review* (est. 1999) were the two journals in Asia that major arbitration institutions published. However, the picture has evolved recently, with the introduction of KCAB's *Korean Arbitration Review* in 2010, JCAA's *Japan Commercial Arbitration Journal* in 2020, and AIAC's *Alternative Dispute Resolution Journal* in 2022. The new journals bring more extensive research to both ADR in individual countries and the view on Asian ADR practice from different perspectives. This undeniably enriches the conversations on arbitration, makes knowledge more accessible, and encourages Asian institutions to collaborate and innovate further.

National Legislations

To ensure a vibrant ecosystem for international commercial ADR, countries must have a solid legal framework. In recent years, Asia has witnessed constantly changing laws on ADR in an attempt to keep regulations up to date. India stands out as an example of amending laws, as India has passed three Amendments to the Arbitration

89 Alvin Yeo, Chou Sean Yu and Lim Wei Lee, "Singapore: Latest Arbitration Developments" in David Samuels (ed), *The Asia-Pacific Arbitration Review 2023* (Global Arbitration Review 2022) 279–280.

and Conciliation Act in 2015, 2019, and 2021.[90] By tackling the lengthy procedures and fixing several issues, such as time extensions and substitution of arbitrators, India has shown its endeavor to establish an arbitration hub.[91] However, the 2021 amendment is unlikely to be the last,[92] as academics are anticipating further revision because some issues have yet to be resolved.[93]

Aside from "typical" ADR regulations (Arbitration Act, Mediation Act, etc.), Japan and Korea also have unconventional legislation promoting ADR. Specifically, Japan passed the Act on Promotion of the Use of Alternative Dispute Resolution, which came into effect in 2007, while Korea enacted the new Arbitration Industry Promotion Act in 2017.[94] Japan's Act focuses on establishing general provisions applicable to all ADRs, such as requirements for ADR services or obligations of ADR institutions. This is comparable to Hong Kong's approach to ADR since Hong Kong also tries to incorporate all forms of ADR. On the contrary, the Korea Arbitration Industry Promotion Act took a more Singaporean approach, focusing on only one form of ADR – arbitration. Furthermore, the Arbitration Industry Promotion Act established how Korea deals with matters contributing to the growth of arbitration, such as funding for the arbitration industry and training arbitrators.

Regarding substantive law, one of Singapore and Hong Kong's most significant impacts on Asian regulations is TPF. This trend has sparked a lot of conversation among academics. However, depending on each country's legal system (or rather, the presence of the common law doctrine of maintenance and champerty), the impact of TPF can be different. For common law and mixed legal system countries like India and Malaysia, respectively, they first have had to draw a line between illegal acts of champerty and legal TPF, similar to how Singapore and Hong Kong dealt with the problem. For civil law countries like Korea and Japan, the legislators instead only have to consider clarifying the status of TPF, whether such conducts are legal or prohibited. Japan, for example, also

[90] Ashish Dholakia, Ketan Gaur and Kaustub Narendran, "India's Arbitration and Conciliation (Amendment) Act, 2021: A Wolf in Sheep's Clothing?" (*Kluwer Arbitration Blog*, May 23, 2021), https://arbitrationblog.kluwerarbitration.com/2021/05/23/indias-arbitration-and-conciliation-amendment-act-2021-a-wolf-in-sheeps-clothing/, accessed May 10, 2023.

[91] Satyendra Wankhade, "India Closer Than Ever to Becoming an International Arbitration Hub: Former UK Attorney General Lord Peter Goldsmith" (*Bar and Bench*, February 17, 2023), www-barandbench-com.cdn.ampproject.org/c/s/www.barandbench.com/amp/story/news/india-closer-than-ever-to-becoming-an-international-arbitration-hub-lord-peter-goldsmith, accessed May 15, 2024.

[92] Dholakia, Gaur and Narendran (n 90).

[93] Akash Gupta and Tarazi Mohammed Sheikh, "Legal Challenges of ADR in India and Bangladesh: A Comparison" *The Daily Star* (February 19, 2023), www.thedailystar.net/law-our-rights/news/legal-challenges-adr-india-and-bangladesh-comparison-3249936, accessed June 10, 2024.

[94] Takatori (n 84).

intends to clarify the status of TPF, following the trend set by Singapore and Hong Kong.[95]

B. *Case Study: Vietnam*

Background

Vietnam presents one case study of how a second-tier Asian jurisdiction's international commercial ADR has been influenced by a first-tier jurisdiction, in this instance, that of Singapore. Vietnam's modern arbitration history began in 1994, with the Government's release of Decree No. 116-CP on the organization and activities of economic arbitration. This laid the ground for Vietnam's accession to the New York Convention in 1995. In 2003, Vietnam established the Ordinance on Commercial Arbitration to fulfill Vietnam's obligations as a member state – marking the first time Vietnam regulated commercial arbitration by law. This was soon replaced by the Law on Commercial Arbitration of 2010, which has not been amended since. Despite certain compatibility with the Model Law, Vietnam is not considered a Model Law jurisdiction.[96]

Vietnam's Development

Among jurisdictions, Vietnam most turns to trends in, firstly, Singapore and, secondarily, Hong Kong, in terms of studying the cutting edge of international commercial ADR. This applies to several aspects, such as (i) whether or not Vietnam should base its legislation on the UNCITRAL Arbitration Model Law,[97] (ii) recognizing emergency arbitration in Vietnam,[98] or (iii) whether Vietnam should focus on arbitration and mediation instead of ADR all-around. On these points, Vietnam frequently looks to Singapore. For example, on the issue of the scope of international commercial ADR, Vietnam has followed Singapore in focusing on arbitration and mediation. Dispute boards (DBs) and DNDRs are mostly not used in Vietnam. In fact, it was not until 2017 that the first legislation on commercial ADR besides arbitration was established, Decree No.22/2017/ND-CP on Commercial Mediation ("Decree 22"), which is based mainly on the UNCITRAL

[95] Theresa Tseung and Hiroko Yamamoto, "2021 Year in Review: Key Developments in East and Central Asia" (*Kluwer Arbitration Blog*, January 20, 2022), https://arbitrationblog.kluwerarbitration.com/2022/01/20/2021-year-in-review-key-developments-in-east-and-central-asia/, accessed May 10, 2023.

[96] Van Dai Do, "Amending the Law on Commercial Arbitration So That Vietnam Become a Country Under the Model Law" (2021) 140 Vietnamese J. Legal Sci 26.

[97] Ibid.

[98] Huynh Quang Thuan and Tran Hoang Tu Linh, "The Possibility of Recognizing Emergency Arbitration in National Laws of Countries with Developing Commercial Arbitration: Experience from Vietnam" (2021) 14 Contemp Asia Arb J 185.

Model Law on Mediation.[99] Although Vietnam has had a history of importing regulations from China,[100] this is not the case here since the PRC has yet to enact any legislation on commercial mediation.[101]

From the institutional point of view, the traces from Singapore are visible. First, the Vietnam International Arbitration Centre (VIAC) Rules tend to internalize the norms set by SIAC to make arbitration at VIAC more attractive. Most recently, the 2017 version of the VIAC Rules made the following changes: (i) allowing parties to bring claims relating to more than one contract in a single request; (ii) allowing the consolidation of arbitrations; (iii) enabling the new expedited procedure.[102] Correspondingly, these are also the significant changes the SIAC made in 2016 to Rules 6, 8, and 5 of its Arbitration Rules, respectively.[103] However, these transplantations are partial since the VIAC only sets out general rules, contrasting with the comprehensive SIAC rules. Despite that, the VIAC still managed to administer cases according to these new rules (e.g., in 2018, the VIAC administered twenty-three multiple contract cases).[104] This transplant method can benefit the VIAC since the Vietnamese courts are more likely to interfere with the recognition and enforcement procedure.[105] By regulating lightly, the VIAC keeps its procedural rules simple and can better maintain the enforceability of its award, avoiding any denial based on due process.

Secondly, the VIAC offers hybrid dispute resolutions in a manner similar to SIAC. Following the publication of Decree 22 in 2018, the Vietnam Mediation Centre (VMC) was established. In 2020, the VIAC and VMC collaborated and introduced the first hybrid procedures in Vietnam, Med-Arb/Arb-Med and the Arb-Med-Arb Protocol. These procedures mirror Singapore's establishment of SIMC in 2014 and the introduction of collaborative SIAC-SIMC Arb-Med-Arb the following year. The difference between Vietnam and Singapore lies in the independence of SIMC from the SIAC since VMC remains a division of the VIAC. Thus, institutions

99 Nguyen Manh Dzung and Dang Vu Minh Ha, "Enforcement of Mediated Settlement Agreements in Vietnam: A Step Forward the International Trend?" (*Vietnam Mediation Centre*, January 3, 2020), www.vmc.org.vn/en/mediation/enforcement-of-mediated-settlement-agreements-in-vietnam-a-step-forward-the-international-trend-a118.html, accessed May 10, 2022.

100 Matthew S Erie and Do Hai Ha, "Law and Development Minus Legal Transplants: The Example of China in Vietnam" (2021) 8 AsianJLS 372, 383.

101 Guodong Du, "A Decade of Rise: How Commercial Mediation in China Evolved in the 2010s" (*China Justice Observer*, February 19, 2023), www.chinajusticeobserver.com/a/a-decade-of-rise-how-commercial-mediation-in-china-evolved-in-the-2010s, accessed May 10, 2024.

102 See Article 6, 15 and 37 of VIAC Rule 2017, respectively.

103 Alastair Henderson, Daniel Waldek and Emmanuel Chua, "Singapore International Arbitration Centre Arbitration Rules 2016: Key Changes and Potential Impact" (Herbert Smith Freehills, July 13, 2016), https://hsfnotes.com/arbitration/2016/07/13/singapore-international-arbitration-centre-arbitration-rules-2016-key-changes-and-potential-impact/, accessed June 16, 2024.

104 Vietnam International Arbitration Centre, "Annual Report 2018" (2019) 5.

105 Erie and Hai Ha (n 100).

in Vietnam have been learning from Singapore's experience to enhance the efficiency of dispute resolution and attract more parties.

Concerning the structure of institutions, Vietnam shows some degree of similarity with the Hong Kong-style approach. Similar to how HKIAC established several divisions to deal with specific matters (HKMC for mediation, ADNDRC for domain name disputes), the VIAC also established VMC for mediation and the Vietnam Institute for Arbitration Research and Training for researching and training in ADR fields.

These observations raise the question as to why Singapore has mostly been the jurisdiction of choice for Vietnam to study in the field of international commercial ADR. In other areas of law, China is generally the best fit due to being adjacent to Vietnam, sharing similar cultural values, and having a frequent trade relationship.[106] To answer that question, it should be noted that transplantation from a jurisdiction can take two (or more) forms: direct exportation from one institution or (city-)state to another or socialization of practices among the users (in this case, of international commercial ADR centers).[107] Both of these conditions are present to a higher degree in the Singapore–Vietnam ADR relationship. Singapore has been known as one of the leaders in arbitration and, recently, mediation, and thus, the implications could, as noted above, go beyond its borders, affecting Asian countries and even beyond.

However, what truly creates the trend of studying Singapore in Vietnam is the reciprocal socialization of users of international commercial ADR into both systems. Singapore ranked second among foreign users at VIAC in 2020 and 2021,[108] while Vietnam ranked 6th and 8th among SIAC foreign users in 2021 and 2022, respectively.[109] In contrast, Vietnam is not among the top ten users of ICC, HKIAC, or CIETAC.[110] Singapore attracts Vietnamese parties more than Hong Kong, likely due to Singapore being a fellow Association of Southeast Asian Nations state and a more neutral seat.

C. *The Future of ADR Centers*

The Emerging Asian Landscape: Over-Concentration or Decentralization?

As Singapore and Hong Kong charge forward, it begs the question: Will other Asian jurisdictions have any chance of making their name? Currently, other than

[106] Ibid.

[107] Kun Fan, "Glocalization of Arbitration: Transnational Standards Struggling with Local Norms through the Lens of Arbitration Transplantation in China" (2013) 18 Harv Negot L Rev 175, 218.

[108] Vietnam International Arbitration Centre, "Annual Report 2021" (2022) 11.

[109] Singapore International Arbitration Centre, "Annual Report 2022" (2023) 25.

[110] China International Economic and Trade Arbitration Commission, "Annual Report on International Commercial Arbitration in China (2020~2021)" (Wolters Kluwer China (tr), 2021) 16–17.

Singapore and Hong Kong, the attention paid to other Asian seats of arbitration is relatively insignificant.[111] Over-concentration of capacity and cases in one or two centers may become a serious issue if the gap between the first-tier cities of Singapore and Hong Kong and the rest of Asia continues to grow. Asia is known for its cultural diversity. The region of Southeast Asia alone contributed significantly to this diversity due to the vast differences in religions, languages, and histories. Thus, if over-concentration happens, ADR in Asia may become a one-size-fits-all model, which can damage both the businesses in the region and Asia's competitive edge.

So, is over-concentration real in this case? The good news is that it is unlikely to come to pass. In the recent Queen Mary Survey, several interviewees suggested they might be willing to use the new or emerging lesser-known institutions instead of the well-established ones, SIAC and HKIAC.[112] Interestingly, the reasoning behind such a choice is that they acknowledged the risk of over-concentration. They are willing to discount the established names of the leading institutions and seek underlying quality to help institutions receive the reputation they deserve.[113] The numbers also partially support this idea, as the *Singapore International Dispute Resolution Academy International Dispute Resolution Survey: 2022 Final Report (SMU SIDRA Report 2022)* introduced several new competitors to the favored arbitration institutions, including the Philippines Dispute Resolution Centre, JCAA, SCIA, Beijing Arbitration Commission, and VIAC.[114] This signals a slight decentralization in the ADR market, which, from a normative view, is desirable. Furthermore, as the history of Singapore and Hong Kong has proven, the crown is not permanent. Therefore, although there remains a gap between Singapore and Hong Kong, on the one hand, and the rest of Asia, on the other, it is too soon to predict which will bear the crown ten years from now.

Singapore and Hong Kong: What Can Be Expected?

Since Singapore and Hong Kong are currently the two leaders in international commercial ADR in Asia, the question is, what should we expect from them? First, since they attract ADR activities at the international level, the initial answer would be that they should maintain their flexible procedure so that both Asian and Western parties can find common ground.[115] Furthermore, it has long been predicted that Singapore and Hong Kong would soon witness new challengers coming onto the

[111] See Queen Mary Survey 2021 (n 4) 6; "SMU SIDRA Report 2022" (n 18) 34. The only other seats are Beijing, Shanghai, and Dubai, but the former two are related to China and thus, related to Hong Kong.

[112] "Queen Mary Survey 2021" (n 4) 11–12.

[113] Ibid.

[114] "SMU SIDRA Report 2022" (n 18) 18. See also Singapore Management University, Singapore International Dispute Resolution Academy International Dispute Resolution Survey: 2022 Final Report (SMU SIDRA Report 2020), 39.

[115] Benton (n 5).

stage (e.g., Korea, Japan, Malaysia, and mainland China). Now that these second-tier jurisdictions are waiting for their chance to break through, Singapore and Hong Kong must establish their competitive advantage – consolidating their ability to bridge East–West divides, markets, and politics.

Secondly, on Hong Kong's part, the short-term answer would be dealing with the crisis caused by the National Security Law and, more broadly, the increasing presence of mainland PRC governance in Hong Kong. To date, there is no concrete evidence that parties are opting out of Hong Kong and using Singapore because of the former's political situation, even if there are general concerns about such a shift happening. With the BRI, HKIAC can still grow in terms of its number of cases, even if there may be cases of a certain threshold amount. Hong Kong will, in the foreseeable future, remain more attractive to China-related disputes than mainland PRC.[116] In the long run, on the other hand, Hong Kong should establish modern dedicated hearing venues as, according to the SMU SIDRA 2022 report, the quality of hearing facilities is one of the top factors affecting the choice of venue of arbitration to satisfy the needs of businesses. Currently, the HKIAC office doubles as the hearing venue for arbitration, but that leaves plenty of room for improvement.[117] Other ADR systems in the region, like Singapore, Korea, Japan, or Dubai, have specialized state-of-the-art hearing centers. By establishing a dedicated, high-quality arbitration venue, Hong Kong can also increase its appeal as a seat of arbitration.

Thirdly, for Singapore, the problem lies in the very crown it is holding. Now that Singapore is widely known as a reliable seat of arbitration, it has to live up to its name. Singapore cannot stop innovating or risk being overthrown by emerging competitors. The answer for Singapore in this situation would be to continue growing its network with other providers in Asia. Only by continuing to grow a larger and deeper network can SIAC maintain its relevance and irreplaceability.[118] Even when other competitors rise to the challenge, Singapore still has an advantage in knowledge and experience.

IV CONCLUSION

If the significance of international commercial ADR is measured as the outcome of a race between Asian jurisdictions, the lead is currently in favor of Singapore. Thanks to its constant development in infrastructure, services, and regulations, Singapore has secured its place as the most preferred seat of arbitration not only in Asia but also in the world. If, however, one measures a jurisdiction's significance by its contribution to Asian ADR culture, both Singapore and Hong Kong can be

[116] Benton (n 5).
[117] "SMU SIDRA Report 2022" does not show HKIAC among the most favored hearing facilities.
[118] Benton (n 5).

considered to be influential. While Singapore functions as a blueprint for the future development of other countries, exemplified by Vietnam adopting Singaporean ADR practices, Hong Kong functions like a test drive to see if a service is compatible with the Asian culture. Singapore and Hong Kong's success with international commercial ADR has encouraged new contestants such as Korea, Japan, Malaysia, UAE, and Vietnam to break through. By diversifying ADR providers, businesses will benefit more from the competition, getting to choose whichever suits them most. Furthermore, with the rise of mediation, parties worldwide will turn to Asia – where consensual culture resonates. Thus, Asia would likely continue to develop a healthy ecosystem of international commercial ADR.

4

Transforming the ASEAN Way in Inter-Asian Law

The RCEP and Beyond

*Pasha L. Hsieh**

I INTRODUCTION

Global crises are rapidly transforming the international regime. The neoliberal international order that underpins the normative foundation of postwar economic institutions is facing unprecedented threats. The collapse of the World Trade Organization (WTO) appeals mechanism, the COVID-19 pandemic, intensifying United States (US)–China conflicts, and Ukraine and Taiwan Strait confrontations have aggravated diverse forms of trade protectionism.[1] New trade and investment roadmaps prompted the Indo-Pacific strategies of the US, the European Union (EU), the Association of Southeast Asian Nations (ASEAN), as well as China's Belt and Road Initiative.[2] Regional and global supply chains for commodities ranging from raw materials to semiconductor chips are imperative to these stakeholders.

Amid geopolitical challenges, international law has evolved to reflect the reality of the multipolar world. A new dynamic is evolving: Inter-Asian Law (IAL), which

* I thank Matthew Erie, Ching-Fu Lin, and the participants of the IAL Workshop at National Tsing Hua University for their insights and comments. I also acknowledge the research assistance of Han Xin Yi and Bill Puah, as well as the research support provided by the Lee Kong Chian Fellowship and the Taiwan Studies Project grant.

1 As the US blocked the appointments and reappointments of Appellate Body Members, the appeals mechanism ceased to function in December 2019. See generally, Jean Galbraith, "United States Continues to Block New Appellate Body Members for the World Trade Organization, Risking the Collapse of the Appellate Process" (2019) 113(4) AJIL 822, 822–823. In August 2022, Beijing conducted large-scale military exercises around Taiwan in response to former US House Speaker Nancy Pelosi's visit to Taipei. Jude Blanchette and others, "Speaker Pelosi's Taiwan Visit: Implications for the Indo-Pacific" (*Center for Strategic & International Studies*, August 15, 2022), www.csis.org/analysis/speaker-pelosis-taiwan-visit-implications-indo-pacific, accessed May 1, 2025.

2 Key policy statements on Indo-Pacific strategies include Indo-Pacific Strategy of the United States (2022), Joint Communication to the European Parliament and the Council: The EU Strategy for Cooperation in the Indo-Pacific (2021), and ASEAN Outlook on the Indo-Pacific (2021).

reinforces the cross-fertilization of legal developments between different regional agreements in Asia and between these agreements and domestic legal reforms. Pursuant to the conceptual framework of the volume this chapter explores how IAL has developed procedurally through multilayered investment agreements. It argues that the legalization of the so-called ASEAN way has propelled the normative evolution of IAL, which departs from the Western approach premised on the Washington Consensus.[3] In other words, the ASEAN way has served as a formula, resulting in IAL as the product.

The chapter sheds light on core questions under the book's analytical framework. It illustrates the types and methods of interactions among Asian jurisdictions and beyond, as well as actors and intermediaries that enable Asian governments to align interests via non-Western-dominated plurilateral platforms. This development demonstrates Asian countries' pursuit of their own legal models, which will decrease their past dependency on transplanting EU and US rules and fortify Asia's collective power in shaping international law. Markedly, the Asian model for constructing IAL in the context of investment law has been more prominent in the unique procedure of making multilateral law rather than in creating new substantive legal requirements.

The rise of Asia provides the contextual background for IAL. Undoubtedly, Asian economies have become the locomotives of global trade. Asia will contribute to over half of global gross domestic product (GDP) by 2050, restoring the region to the dominant economic status that it once possessed before the Industrial Revolution.[4] Moreover, in the next decade, China will overtake the US to be the world's largest economy.[5] As a ten-country bloc, ASEAN will ascend to the equivalent of the fourth largest economy and is expected to admit Timor-Leste as the eleventh member.[6] Complementary to the ASEAN Economic Community (AEC), the six "ASEAN Plus One" free trade agreements (FTAs) have built the legal architecture of new Asian regionalism.[7]

The ASEAN-centered framework culminated in the fifteen-party Regional Comprehensive Economic Partnership (RCEP), which entered into force in

3 See, generally, John Williamson, "A Short History of the Washington Consensus" in Narcís Serra and Joseph E. Stiglitz (eds), *The Washington Consensus Reconsidered: Towards a New Global Governance* (OUP 2008) 14, 15–17.

4 Asian Development Bank, "Asia 2050: Realizing the Asian Century: Executive Summary" (2011) 3–5.

5 Centre for Economics and Business Research, "World Economic League Table 2021" (2020) 70–71.

6 ASEAN "agreed: In-principle to admit Timor-Leste to be the 11th member of ASEAN" at the 40th and 41st ASEAN Summits and Related Summits in November 2022. See ASEAN, "ASEAN Leaders' Statement on the Application of Timor-Leste for ASEAN Membership" (*ASEAN*, November 11, 2022), https://asean.org/asean-leaders-statement-on-the-application-of-timor-leste-for-asean-membership/, accessed May 1, 2025.

7 From 2002 to 2017, the ASEAN signed six FTAs sequentially with seven economies, including China, Japan, India, Korea, Australia, New Zealand, and Hong Kong.

January 2022 and became the world's largest FTA by economic scale.[8] This mega-FTA constitutes 30 percent of global GDP and 26.2 percent of foreign direct investment (FDI) inflows.[9] In contrast to Brussels' focus on bilateral pacts with Asian countries and Washington's Indo-Pacific Economic Framework for Prosperity without market access, ASEAN and the RCEP manifest Asian approaches to global governance.

Investment law provides a unique case study for IAL. The absence of consensus among WTO members removed investment from the WTO Doha agenda. The ambit of present WTO negotiations on "investment facilitation for development" is limited and excludes investment liberalization and protection.[10] A core issue concerning investment is investor–state dispute settlement (ISDS) that has encountered massive backlash from the Global South. The United Nations Commission on International Trade Law (UNCITRAL) entrusted Working Group III to discuss procedural reforms for ISDS under investment treaties.[11] Asian governments seem to lack common positions on these reforms at the multilateral level.[12] Hence, it is vital to examine their agendas on investment law at the regional and national levels to comprehend the evolution of IAL. These experiences exhibit ASEAN's and the RCEP's legal approach of pragmatic incrementalism and provide valuable lessons for developing countries to consider alternatives to the Washington Consensus.

After this introduction, Section II unveils the development of investment issues during three waves of global regionalism. It also explores salient features of investment rules in modern FTAs, bilateral investment agreements (BITs), key domestic laws, and ISDS cases. Section III explores the evolution of ASEAN law with a focus on the AEC's new investment rules and services commitments on foreign equity restrictions, as well as the ISDS mechanism. Section IV examines the RCEP's investment and services rules and its omission of ISDS that reflect the new consensus forged under the ASEAN Plus One structure. Section V concludes by highlighting the legal and political implications of investment reforms on IAL.

8 ASEAN, "RCEP Agreement Enters into Force" (*ASEAN*, January 1, 2022), https://asean.org/rcep-agreement-enters-into-force/, accessed May 1, 2025.

9 ASEAN, "Joint Leaders' Statement on the Regional Comprehensive Economic Partnership (RCEP)" (*ASEAN*, November 15, 2020), https://asean.org/joint-leaders-statement-on-the-regional-comprehensive-economic-partnership-rcep-2/, accessed May 1, 2025; United Nations Conference on Trade and Development (UNCTAD), "World Investment Report 2021: Investing in Sustainable Recovery" (*UNCTAD*, April 1, 2021) 6.

10 WTO, "Annual Report 2021" (*WTO*, 2021) 58.

11 Malcolm Langford and others, "Special Issue: UNCITRAL and Investment Arbitration Reform: Matching Concerns and Solutions: An Introduction" (2020) 21 J World Invest Trade 167, 172–177.

12 See submissions from Asian governments, UNCITRAL, "Working Group III: Investor-State Dispute Settlement Reform", https://uncitral.un.org/en/working_groups/3/investor-state, accessed May 1, 2025.

II INTER-ASIAN LAW IN GLOBAL REGIONALISM

After World War II, three waves of global regionalism shaped international law and trade. IAL is paramount in the latest wave of regionalism, which I called the "Third Regionalism," that has yielded a significant impact on investment rules.[13] During the previous periods, Asian countries predominantly followed the normative requirements that the US created. The Bretton Woods system and the Washington Consensus underscored the neoliberal international order that enabled Asian countries to recover from the devastating war.

Asian nations had neither the intention nor the power to challenge the rules to sustain "embedded liberalism."[14] However, the Asian financial crisis and the overriding disappointment with West-dominated monetary institutions invigorated paradigm shifts. The subsequent formation of "ASEAN Plus Three" and "ASEAN Plus Six" frameworks and rising populist protectionism in the US prompted Asia to embark on a divergent path, expediting the growth of IAL. To verify this analysis, I explain below the investment law developments in the three waves of global regionalism.

In particular, the evolution to the Third Regionalism demonstrates the emphasis on legal cooperation and harmonization, which feature the major type and method of interaction among Asian states. The ASEAN-centered architecture, including ASEAN agreements and the RCEP, has become institutional, plurilateral platforms for Asian governments to develop IAL. Divergent from the first two waves of regionalism, these platforms reflect the Asian or ASEAN way, at least procedurally, in shaping the regional order. The notable procedural dimension is pragmatic incrementalism, distinct from the legalization concept commonly understood in the West.

Coined by Jagdish Bhagwati, the term "First Regionalism," refers to trade pacts in the 1950s and 1960s.[15] Although Washington was preoccupied with multilateralism in the Kennedy Round, it supported the European Economic Community for countering Soviet influences.[16] ASEAN's founding signified the inception of Asian regionalism, but the bloc was built predominantly for security purposes of resisting

[13] Pasha L Hsieh, *New Asian Regionalism in International Economic Law* (CUP 2021) 5–12.

[14] John Gerard Ruggie, "International Regimes, Transactions, and Change: Embedded Liberalism in the Postwar Economic Order" (1982) 36(2) Intl Organ 379, 392–398.

[15] Jagdish Bhagwati, *Termites in the Trading System: How Preferential Agreements Undermine Free Trade* (OUP 2008) 29–32.

[16] WTO, "World Trade Report 2011" (WTO, 2011) 52l; Sungjoon Cho, "Breaking the Barrier between Regionalism and Multilateralism: A New Perspective on Trade Regionalism" (2001) 42(2) Harvard ILJ 419, 427; Fredrik Söderbaum and Luk van Langenhove, "Introduction: The EU as a Global Actor and the Role of Interregionalism" (2005) 27(3) J Eur Int 249, 255.

Communist expansions rather than for economic integration.[17] As Bhagwati noted, most trade initiatives merely achieved a marginal trade-creation effect owing to political interventions.[18] ASEAN was not an exception.

In this era, investment pacts began to surface. Asian countries often succumbed to the normative demands of the Global North.[19] To illustrate, US Friendship, Commerce and Navigation (FCN) Treaties incorporated investment issues.[20] A key objective of FCN Treaties was to ensure the protection and security of foreign investment and to guarantee prompt, adequate, and effective compensation in the case of expropriation. Compared with modern investment treaties, a major enforcement weakness of FCN Treaties is the absence of detailed procedural rules for dispute settlement.

The 1965 Convention on the Settlement of Investment Disputes between States and Nationals of Other States (ICSID Convention) was a breakthrough in international law, as the ISDS mechanism became available at the multilateral level. While the first BIT was concluded between West Germany and Pakistan in 1959, the 1968 Netherlands–Indonesia BIT marked the first investment pact with ISDS provisions, allowing an investor to bring claims against the host state to the Center created under the ICSID Convention.[21] Many Asian countries joined the Group of 77 in passing UN resolutions to establish "a New International Economic Order (NIEO)" in the 1970s.[22] Premised on absolute sovereignty over natural resources, NIEO principles departed from the West-preferred compensation standards and mandated that local courts rather than international tribunals settle investment disputes.[23] Nevertheless, the NIEO movement quickly failed due to objections from the powerful trans-Atlantic alliance. The Bretton Woods institutions and modern, neoliberal BITs reinforced the Washington Consensus.

During the Uruguay Round, the "Second Regionalism" occurred in the 1980s and 1990s. The EU and the North American Free Trade Agreement (NAFTA)

[17] Amita Acharya, "Foundations of Collective Action in Asia: Theory and Practice of Regional Cooperation" (2012) ADBI Working Paper Series, No. 344, 5–10; Rodolfo C Severino, *Southeast Asia in Search of an ASEAN Community: Insights from the Former ASEAN Secretary-General* (Inst Southeast Asian Stud 2006) 1–11.

[18] Bhagwati (n 15) 29.

[19] UNCTAD, "UNCTAD's Reform Package from The International Investment Regime" (2018) 14.

[20] Joshua P Meltzer, "Investment" in Simon Lester and others (eds), *Bilateral and Regional Trade Agreements: Commentary and Analysis* (2nd edn, CUP 2015) 245, 246.

[21] Julien Chaisse and others, "The Changing Patterns of Investment Rule-Making Issues and Actors" in Julien Chaisse and others (eds), *Asia's Changing International Investment Regime: Sustainability, Regionalization, and Arbitration* (Springer 2017) 13, 14; UNCTAD (n 19) 14.

[22] Resolution adopted by the General Assembly: 3201 (S-VI): Declaration on the Establishment of a New International Economic Order, A/RES/S-6/3201 (1974); Resolution adopted by the General Assembly: 3202 (S-VI): Programme of Action on the Establishment of a New International Economic Order, A/RES/S-6/3202 (1974).

[23] United Nations General Assembly Resolution 3281 (XXIX): Charter of Economic Rights and Duties of States (1975), art 2(c); Meltzer (n 20) 246–248.

PART II

Constitutional Law

Judicial Practices, Inter-Court Dialogue, and Democratic Resilience

In 2010, the Chaudhry court considered a challenge to the Eighteenth Amendment introducing a judicial appointments process requiring nominations to be put forward by a Judicial Commission and vetted by a Parliamentary Committee, which was not required to provide reasons for rejecting the Commission's nominees.[15] The Court issued an interim order recommending that Parliament make specific changes to the appointments process, including increasing the number of judges on the Judicial Commission and empowering the Commission to overrule the decision of the Parliamentary Committee.[16]

The following year, Parliament incorporated most of the judiciary's proposed changes by passing the Nineteenth Amendment, which increased judicial representation on the Commission and required the Parliamentary Committee to provide reasons for rejecting judicial nominees put forward by the Judicial Commission.[17] In 2011,[18] the Court upheld the Nineteenth Amendment in form, but not in substance, by ruling that the Parliament Committee's reasons for refusing a nomination put forward by the Judicial Commission were reviewable.[19]

Then came the Pakistan Supreme Court's landmark decision in the 2015 case of *District Bar Association v Federation of Pakistan* (*Rawalpindi*).[20] The case involved a challenge to the Eighteenth Amendment on the judicial appointments process as well as to the Twenty First Amendment, which authorized terrorist suspects to be tried by military court martials.

In this decision, a majority of the Supreme Court of Pakistan expressly recognized substantive limits on Parliament's amending power.[21] Thirteen out of seventeen justices agreed that the judiciary could review the substance of constitutional amendments to protect the Constitution's core, endorsing the court's power to strike down constitutional amendments passed by Parliament. According to the plurality opinion joined by eight justices, Pakistan's Constitution contains "salient features," including democracy, a parliamentary form of government, and the independence of the judiciary, and it was for the Court to review constitutional amendments "to determine whether any of the Salient Features of the Constitution has been repealed, abrogated, or substantively altered."[22] Five other justices also held that

15 *Nadeem Ahmed v Fed'n of Pakistan*, (2010) PLD (SC) 1165 (Pakistan).

16 Ibid [10], [13], [14], [17]. See Sadaf Aziz, *The Constitution of Pakistan: A Contextual Analysis* (1st edn, Bloomsbury Publishing 2017) 148 (noting that "while the committee structure still stands, the balance has tipped toward the judicial branch in terms of effective power").

17 See Constitution (Nineteenth Amendment) Act, 2010 §4 (Pakistan).

18 *Munir Hussain Bhatti v Fed'n of Pakistan*, (2011) PLD (SC) 407, [22], [24]–[26], [32], [59].

19 See Po Jen Yap and Rehan Abeyratne, 'Judicial Self-Dealing and Unconstitutional Constitutional Amendments in South Asia' (2021) 19(1) Int J Const Law 127.

20 *District Bar Association v Fed'n of Pakistan*, (2015) PLD (SC) 401 (hereinafter *Rawalpindi*).

21 See Ibid (Saeed J, joined by Jamali, Muslim, Bandial, Osmany, Ahmed, Alam, Baqar JJ); see also *Rawalpindi* (n 20) (Khawaja, joined by Isa, Ejaz Afzal Khan, Chaudhry, and Dost Muhammad Khan).

22 Ibid [180(d)] (Saeed J, joined by Jamali, Muslim, Bandial, Osmany, Ahmed, Alam, Baqar JJ).

the Court had the power to determine the legality of constitutional amendments, although they located the basis for judicially enforceable limits on Parliament's power in the Constitution and its preamble.[23] Thus, a clear majority on the Supreme Court explicitly held that the judiciary could strike down procedurally valid constitutional amendments passed by Parliament.

Still, despite laying out a broad power to declare unconstitutional constitutional amendments, the Supreme Court refrained from directly exercising that power. Indeed, it did not seek to invalidate either of the two challenged constitutional amendments.[24] The amendment providing for military court trials was upheld as a proportionate response to terrorist threats.[25] The Supreme Court also left intact the Eighteenth Amendment on the judicial appointments process in its current form – that is, as amended by the Nineteenth Amendment in line with the Court's interpretation in previous precedent – where "the power to initiate and the primacy of decisiveness with regard to the final outcome of the process must vest in the Chief Justices and the Members of the Judiciary."[26]

Even so, the *Rawalpindi* plurality opinion sounded a warning note for the government. If the provision "was to be amended or reinterpreted, compromising either of the two limbs of the test mentioned above," it warned, "it may not be possible to hold that the provisions so amended or interpreted are not in conflict with the Independence of the Judiciary, which is a Salient Feature of the Constitution."[27]

The Supreme Court of Pakistan's decision laid the framework for establishing an expansive judicial power to review constitutional amendments as unconstitutional. At the same time, the narrow ruling in *Rawalpindi* left the constitutional amendments intact, avoiding immediate political or public backlash.

B. *Malaysia*

We see another illustration of judicial statecraft at play in the Malaysian Federal Court. For six decades of the country's history, Malaysia, like the neighboring state of Singapore, operated as a dominant-party political system. Since Malaysia's independence in 1957, the country had been governed by a single ruling coalition, until it lost to the opposition coalition in an unprecedented election outcome in 2018. After the new government alliance was dismantled in a political kerfuffle in 2020, Malaysia's political landscape has remained volatile. Once an

[23] See Ibid [40]–[41], [51]–[55] (Khawaja J). The other four justices were Justices Isa, Ejaz Afzal Khan, Chaudhry, and Dost Muhammad Khan.

[24] Ibid.

[25] Ibid [178] (Saeed J).

[26] Ibid [104]. See *Munir Hussain Bhatti* (n 18).

[27] Ibid [104].

exemplar of a dominant-party system, Malaysia is now better characterized as a fragile democracy.[28]

For many decades, the Malaysian judiciary employed a highly passive, rigidly formalistic approach marked by extensive deference to the consolidated political branches.[29] Courts in "Asian nonliberal democracies," like Malaysia, Singaporean scholar Thio Li-ann has observed, play "a relatively marginal role in constitutional politics" and "do not play a primary role in shaping constitutional understandings."[30]

The Malaysia Federal Court's approach shifted, however, in a number of assertive judicial decisions delivered in 2017 and 2018.[31] In a sequence of landmark cases, the Malaysian apex court carved out a power for courts to nullify constitutional amendments that would undermine the constitution's foundational structure. Through this carefully staged process, the Malaysian Federal Court sought to establish the power to review unconstitutional constitutional amendments in a fraught political context.

The 2017 decision in *Semenyih Jaya* appeared to be a seemingly prosaic case over land acquisition compensation.[32] The dispute, on its face, involved a provision in the Land Acquisition Act that enabled lay assessors, sitting with a High Court judge, to determine the amount of compensation for land acquisition. Dissatisfied landowners challenged the statute's provision allowing lay assessors to make a conclusive determination on land compensation, arguing that this infringed the constitutional judicial power vested in the courts under Article 121(1). The challenge thus brought into play the clause in Article 121(1) of Malaysia's Federal Constitution regarding the judicial power – long the site of tension between the judiciary and the government.

Some history is in order: In 1988, the Malaysian Parliament, under the administration of then Prime Minister Mahathir Mohamad, had amended Article 121(1) to remove the provision that "the judicial power . . . shall be vested" in the courts. The clause was amended to state that the courts "shall have such jurisdiction and powers as may be conferred by or under federal law." The year 1988 also saw the highly controversial removal of the head of the judiciary and five other Supreme Court justices by the Mahathir administration, widely viewed as a moment of judicial crisis in Malaysia.

[28] See Yvonne Tew, 'Malaysia' in David Law, Alex Schwartz and Holning Lau (eds), *The Oxford Handbook of Constitutional Law* (OUP 2023) https://doi.org/10.1093/oxfordhb/9780198825463.013.9.

[29] See Yvonne Tew, 'On the Uneven Journey to Constitutional Redemption: The Malaysian Judiciary and Constitutional Politics' (2016) 25 Wash Int'l L J 674, 681–91.

[30] See, e.g., Li-Ann Thio, 'Soft Constitutional Law in Nonliberal Asian Constitutional Democracies' (2010) 8 Int'l J Const L 766, 767; see alsoPo Jen Yap, *Courts and Democracies in Asia* (1st edn, Cambridge University Press 2017) 2 (observing that in jurisdictions such as Malaysia, 'where a dominant political party has remained in power since independence,' courts are 'at a fringes of the entity's political life').

[31] For an in-depth discussion of these cases, see Yvonne Tew, *Constitutional Statecraft in Asian Courts* (OUP 2020).

[32] *Semenyih Jaya v Pentadbir Tanah Daerah Hulu Langat* [2017] 3 MLJ 561.

For decades after the legislature's aggressive move to cull judicial power by amending the Constitution's judicial power provision, Malaysian courts took on a subservient position toward the political branches. In the 2007 case of *Kok Wah Kuan*, for example, the Federal Court affirmed that the scope of judicial power "depends on what federal law provides," ruling that the amended Article 121(1) meant that the courts' powers and jurisdictions were indeed subject to federal law.[33]

The Malaysian Federal Court's *Semenyih Jaya* decision was a remarkable about-turn, marking a robust assertion of judicial power. In a unanimous decision, the Federal Court struck down a land acquisition statutory provision as unconstitutional – the first time in twenty years it had struck down a federal statute – for infringing the judicial power and separation of powers. The Federal Court renounced the 1988 constitutional amendment in uncategorical terms, declaring that "the judicial power of the court resides in the Judiciary and no other as is explicit in [Article] 121(1) of the Constitution."[34] Malaysia's apex court embraced the notion of the basic structure doctrine as inherent to the Malaysian Constitution, explicitly stating that "Parliament does not have power to amend the Federal Constitution to the effect of undermining the features" of the doctrine of separation of powers and the independence of the judiciary.[35]

Still, it is worth noting that the Malaysian Federal Court did not expressly invalidate the 1988 constitutional amendment; instead, it interpretively nullified the amendment so that the amended provision had no effect on the judicial power of the courts. In short, as a matter of constitutional interpretation, the Federal Court effectively returned Article 121(1) to the position it had before 1988.

Another curious feature of the *Semenyih Jaya* decision lies in its remedy: The Malaysian Federal Court provided a detailed set of procedural guidelines to replace the statutory provision that it invalidated, but stated that its decision would only have prospective effect.[36] Thus, even as it issued a maxi-minimalist ruling that mitigated the immediate impact of its decision and helped insulate the court from any immediate political ramifications, the Malaysian apex court embedded the seeds for a broad doctrine of judicial authority over fundamental constitutional features.

The following year, in 2018, the Malaysian Federal Court built on the foundations it had laid earlier to further entrench the doctrine of protecting the constitution's basic structure. Unlike *Semenyih Jaya*, *Indira Gandhi* was a blockbuster case. This time, the judiciary asserted itself in one of the most highly charged area of Malaysian law and politics: the authority of civil courts vis-à-vis religious courts.

The challenge in the case was brought by Indira Gandhi, a mother of three children; unknown to her, her ex-husband had converted to Islam and then

33 *Kok Wah Kuan v Public Prosecutor* [2008] 5 MLJ [11].
34 Ibid [86].
35 Ibid [76].
36 Ibid [126].

officially converted all their children to Islam and obtained custody orders from the Sharia courts. At stake was another constitutional provision that had been inserted along with the 1988 amendments to the Article 121(1) judicial power provision. Article 121(1A) provides that the civil courts "shall have no jurisdiction in respect of any matter within the jurisdiction of the Sharia courts." For many years, the civil courts had relied on Article 121(1A) to justify their extensive deference of jurisdiction to the Sharia courts, even in cases with religious freedom implications, vastly expanding the reach of the religious courts.[37]

The Malaysian Federal Court in *Indira Gandhi* – in another unanimous decision written by Justice Zainun Ali, the author of the *Semenyih* judgment – relied on the basic structure doctrine it had articulated in its earlier decision to nullify the Article 121(1A) constitutional amendment on the basis that the amendment undermined the civil courts' power of judicial review.[38] The Court quashed the children's conversion certificates, ruling that the Malaysian Constitution's equal protection guarantee requires that both parents consent to changing their children's religion.

More broadly, and significantly for the judiciary's own institutional position, the Federal Court held that the civil courts have jurisdiction over constitutional matters even when questions of Islamic law are involved.[39] Affirming the basic structure doctrine, the Federal Court declared that powers of judicial review and constitutional interpretation are "part of the basic structure of the constitution," which "cannot be abrogated from the civil courts or conferred upon the Syariah Courts, whether by constitutional amendment, Act of Parliament or state legislation."[40]

On display here is the Malaysian Court's careful endeavor building on the foundations it had laid earlier in *Semenyih Jaya* in order to assert its judicial power in *Indira Gandhi*, this time with a highly charged issue at stake. The Federal Court laid the foundation for the basic structure doctrine in its 2017 *Semenyih Jaya* judgment, which the Court would then cite as precedent in its decision nullifying the constitutional amendment a year later in *Indira Gandhi*. In a multistage sequence of a *maxi*-minimalist decision followed by a *mini*-maximalist one, the once-passive Malaysian court established and expanded a basic structure doctrine empowering the judiciary to protect the Constitution's core from legislative intrusion.

IV JUDICIAL RHETORIC AND THE USE OF CONSTITUTIONAL COMPARATIVISM AMONG ASIAN COURTS

Courts in Pakistan and Malaysia have long operated in challenging political systems with dominant regimes under which the judiciary has been thought of

37 See Yvonne Tew, 'Stealth Theocracy' (2018) 58 Va J Int'l L 31, 50–58.

38 *Indira Gandhi v Pengarah Jabatan Agama Islam Perak* [2018] 1 MLJ 545 (FC) (hereinafter *Indira Gandhi* (FC)).

39 Ibid [104].

40 Ibid [48].

as a passive institution. Yet these two apex courts rendered decisions that displayed statecraft in strengthening judicial power.[41] What kinds of mechanisms have these Asian courts employed in rendering these decisions that helped expand their institutional power?[42] What features do these judgments share and in what aspects are they distinct?

I want to focus here on a particular mechanism that judges tend to employ in issuing self-empowering decisions: judicial rhetoric in crafting opinions that have popular salience – in particular, judicial engagement with constitutional comparativism in these Asian courts. Have these judiciaries sought to engage with the jurisprudence generated by other courts in Asia? How have these Asian courts used citations of foreign case law, especially when seeking to assert high-stakes judgments?

We begin with the Indian Supreme Court's decision in *Kesavananda Bharati*, the epicenter of jurisprudence in Asia on the doctrine of a constitutional basic structure.[43] Both the apex courts of Pakistan and Malaysia referred to *Kesavananda* in their judgments establishing judicial review of unconstitutional constitutional amendments. What is striking is the distinct manner in which the Pakistan Supreme Court and the Malaysian Federal Court treated the Indian Supreme Court's jurisprudence on unconstitutional constitutional amendments.

Consider the Malaysian Federal Court's 2017 and 2018 decisions in *Semenyih Jaya* and *Indira Gandhi*. In both cases, the Federal Court referred to the Indian Supreme Court's jurisprudence on the basic structure doctrine to endorse the basic structure doctrine for the Malaysian context. In *Semenyih Jaya*, the Malaysian Federal Court declared that: "The principles laid down in *Kesavananda Bharati v State of Kerala* were reviewed and affirmed by the Supreme Court in *Indira Nehru Gandhi v Shri Raj Narain*. The Supreme Court emphasized the sanctity of the doctrine of separation of powers and the exclusivity of judicial power."[44] It then cited the

[41] Scholars have also explored strategic maneuvers by other Asian courts. In East Asia, Wen-Chen Chang has shown how the constitutional courts of Korea and Taiwan have strategically responded to highly politically charged cases by creating "win–win" situations for all parties, using the literal interpretive techniques, adopting self-empowering legal doctrines, and delivering single-voice decisions. See Wen-Chen Chang, 'Strategic Judicial Responses in Politically Charged Cases: East Asian Experiences' (2010) 8 Int J Const Law 885.

[42] It is significant to note, though, that while many of these judicial maneuvers focus on the court acting as an institution, particular individual judges may have an impact on a judiciary's broader agenda. For work on judges that have had a unique impact on the constitutional trajectory of their jurisdiction, see generally Rehan Abeyratne and Iddo Porat (eds), *Towering Judges: A Comparative Study of Constitutional Judges* (1st edn, Cambridge University Press 2021). Whether a court's long-term strategy of self-empowerment survives after such towering judicial personalities step down may depend on the nature of the institution, particularly the degree to which the bench is cohesive or fragmented, as well as the external political climate. See also Kureshi (n 11) 153–219 (discussing the Pakistani Supreme Court's confrontational relationship with the military in seeking to play a more expansive political role).

[43] *See* Part I above.

[44] *Semenyih Jaya* (n 32) [87].

Kesavananda majority's opinion (with emphasis added, for good measure) that "*it is not permissible for the legislature to encroach upon the judicial sphere.*"[45] The Malaysian court concluded with a forceful proclamation of judicial power: "The Judiciary is thus entrusted with keeping every organ and institution of the state within its legal boundary. Concomitantly the concept of the independence of the Judiciary is the foundation of the principles of the separation of powers. This is essentially the basis upon which rests the edifice of judicial power."[46]

A year later, in its 2018 judgment in *Indira Gandhi*, the Malaysian Federal Court in its unanimous opinion cited its own decision in *Semenyih Jaya* as precedent, as well as comparative case law from numerous jurisdictions.[47] The judgment written by Justice Zainun Ali also cited *Kesavananda* as precedent for it being "well settled that features of the basic structure cannot be abrogated or removed by a constitutional amendment."[48] According to the Court, the judiciary is the "ultimate arbiter of the lawfulness of state action" and the power of the civil courts is a "natural and necessary corollary" of the rule of law and constitutional supremacy.[49] In addition to the Indian case law, Justice Zainun Ali drew on cases from other common law jurisdictions, including Canada,[50] Singapore,[51] the United Kingdom,[52] and New Zealand,[53] as well as the Judicial Committee of the Privy Council in relation to Ceylon,[54] to support the conclusion: "That judicial power is vested exclusively in the Judiciary is implicit in the very structure of a Westminster model constitution itself . . ."[55] The Court's judgment then relies on "the landmark case of *Kesavananda Bharati* [in which] the Supreme Court of Indian found the power of judicial review to be indispensable in a Constitution that is federal in character" to declare that "the power of judicial review is essential to the constitutional role of the courts, and inherent in the basic structure of the Constitution."[56] Thus, "the power of judicial review is essential to the constitutional role of courts and cannot be abrogated or altered by Parliament by way of a constitutional amendment."[57]

It is especially noteworthy that the Malaysian Federal Court in *Indira Gandhi* cites to foreign cases in seeking to establish the basic structure doctrine as part of Malaysian constitutional jurisprudence given that the Malaysian courts have

45 Ibid (emphasis in original).
46 Ibid [88]–[89].
47 Ibid [42], [48]–[49].
48 *Indira Gandhi* (FC) (n 38) [39].
49 Ibid [33].
50 Ibid [29]–[31], [34], [38].
51 Ibid [32], [37], [39]–[41].
52 Ibid [35]–[36], [50].
53 Ibid [41].
54 Ibid [44].
55 Ibid [44].
56 Ibid [48]. See also [39].
57 Ibid [48].

traditionally been far less receptive – even hostile – to constitutional comparisons outside of the "four walls" of the Malaysian Constitution.[58] Indeed, the Malaysian Court of Appeal's majority opinion in *Indira Gandhi*, delivered in 2015, had forcefully rebuked the lower High Court for considering Malaysia's commitments under international law. According to the Court of Appeal's decision, which was overturned by the Federal Court's decision three years later, the court was not free "to stretch or pervert the language of the Constitution in the interest of any legal of constitutional theory," nor to decide whether a legislative act is "in contravention of generally acknowledged principles of international law."[59] The Federal Court's judgment is striking for its explicit and extensive discussion of foreign and comparative sources.

Compare, on the other hand, the Pakistan Supreme Court's *Rawalpindi* decision. Here, the Pakistani judiciary rejected the idea that its power to review unconstitutional constitutional amendments owed anything to the Indian Supreme Court's basic structure doctrine jurisprudence. Justice Sheikh Azmat Saeed, in the plurality opinion joined by eight justices, warned that:

> Though wisdom may not recognize any national borders, yet it may not be safe to rely too much on the Constitutional Jurisprudence of other Countries, especially as Countries practicing in generic terms, the same Legal System and having a written Constitutions, when confronted with the question of implied restrictions on power to amend the Constitution have come to diametrically opposite conclusions.[60]

Noting that "India, Belize and Bangladesh have accepted and enforced the doctrine, while Sri Lanka, Malaysia and Singapore have rejected the same," Justice Saeed stated that "we must primarily draw from our own Constitutional history and Jurisprudence to answer the questions that we are currently confronted with."[61] The plurality opinion concluded therefore that the Pakistan Supreme Court's power to review unconstitutional constitutional amendments was drawn from the Pakistan Constitution's own "salient features."[62]

Justice Jawad Khawaja's separate opinion was forceful in its dismissal of the Indian "basic structure doctrine," calling it a project that "took root in an alien soil under a distinctly different constitution."[63] Observing that "the Indian preamble does not

58 *Government of the State of Kelantan v Government of the Federation of Malaya* [1963] 29 MLJ 355 (noting that '[t]he Constitution is primarily to be interpreted within its own four walls and not in the light of analogies drawn from other countries such as Great Britain, the United States of America or Australia'). On the 'four walls' approach in Malaysian constitutional adjudication, see generally Tew (n 31) 46–49.

59 *Pathmanathan a/l Krishnan v Indira Gandhi a/p Mutho* [2016] 4 MLJ 455 (CA) (hereinafter *Indira Gandhi* (CA)).

60 *Rawalpindi* (n 20) [25] (Saeed J).

61 *Rawalpindi* (n 20) [25] (Saeed J).

62 Ibid [180 (a)–(b)] (Saeed J).

63 Ibid [51] (Khawaja J).

contain language comparable to or nearly as explicit as that of our Constitution," Justice Khawaja emphasized that "[i]n particular, it is important to note that the structural elements of our Constitution and the representative – fiduciary relationship does not find expression in the Indian preamble, nor do we find any commands similar to the express directives from the People which are the hallmark of our Constitution."[64] Thus, "these are very significant differences between the Indian and Pakistani Constitutions which point to inadequate textual support for the basic structure theory in India and which highlight the opposite in Pakistan."[65]

Like its neighboring counterparts in India and Bangladesh,[66] the Pakistan Supreme Court asserted a power to protect core features of the constitution from alteration when confronted with amendments that sought to intrude on the judiciary's institutional turf.[67] Judges on the Pakistan court, though, took pains to underscore how the notion of implicit unamendability was distinct from the Indian "basic structure" doctrine and emphasized the autochthony of the Pakistani Constitution's "salient features" doctrine.[68]

What purpose might constitutional comparativism serve in light of the approaches of the Malaysian and Pakistan courts in the two case studies discussed above? Both apex courts cross-cite to foreign case law – most prominently, in this context, to the Indian Supreme Court's decisions on the basic structure – but in different ways and for what appears to be distinct purposes. The Malaysian Federal Court endorsed the Indian Supreme Court's jurisprudence as well as cases from other Westminster model systems, not as binding case law, but as a helpful comparative source in its own decisions establishing the basic structure doctrine as part of Malaysia's constitutional structure.[69] The Pakistani Supreme Court in *Rawalpindi* also engaged with *Kesavananda*, but the judges rejected any notion that the Indian case law on the basic structure doctrine was applicable to Pakistan, emphasizing the differences between the Indian and Pakistani Constitutions.[70]

The differences in the judicial rhetoric of the Malaysian and Pakistan apex court opinions might point to the role of constitutional identity in adjudication.[71] Judicial

64 Ibid [71] (Khawaja J).

65 Ibid [71] (Khawaja J).

66 See, e.g., *Kesavananda* (n 2); *Anwar Hussain Chowdhury v Bangladesh*, 41 DLR 1989 App Div 165 (Bangladesh).

67 See Yap and Abeyratne (n 19).

68 *Rawalpindi* (n 20) [51] (Khawaja J), [180(a)–(b)] (Saeed J).

69 The Malaysian Federal Court's approach to the Indian basic structure case law in this instance might be characterized as in line with a model of constitutional engagement with transnational sources. See Vicki Jackson, 'Constitutional Comparisons: Convergence, Resistance, Engagement' (2005) 119 Harv L Rev 109, 114 (describing engagement as an approach in which "transnational sources are seen as interlocutors, offering a way of testing one's own traditions and possibilities by examining them in the reflection of others").

70 *Rawalpindi* (n 20) [71] (Khawaja J); see also *Rawalpindi* (n 20) [25] (Saeed J).

71 On constitutional identity, see generally Gary Jacobsohn, *Constitutional Identity* (Harvard University Press 2010) ch 4, 186; Robert Toniatti, 'Sovereignty Lost, Constitutional Identity

appropriation of comparative legal sources, as Gary Jacobsohn observes, "can become part of a judicial strategy to reinforce critical components in the home country's constitutional identity."[72] In describing the use of Indian precedent by the Sri Lankan judiciary, Jacobsohn argues that "constitutional borrowing can be unambiguously opportunistic without being unprincipled," in that "[t]he choices made on the Sri Lankan Court – to borrow and not to borrow – were consistent with the larger judicial effort to secure the constitutional moorings upon which the identity of the Sri Lankan state was tethered."[73]

For the Malaysian Federal Court in *Semenyih Jaya* and *Indira Gandhi*, references to the foreign case law of respected common law counterparts were used in service of strengthening the legitimacy of the Malaysian court's own decision in establishing a doctrine with implications for the judiciary's role that had not previously gained traction.[74] Malaysian courts have looked to the Indian Supreme Court's decisions in other areas; as Deepa Das Acevado observes in this volume, Malaysian appellate courts explicitly looked to the Indian religious freedom jurisprudence in articulating their own version of an essential religious practices doctrine.[75] More broadly, Justice Zainun Ali's judgment in *Indira Gandhi* is significant in how it marshalled judicial engagement with comparative sources in a rhetorically effective manner by locating the Malaysian constitutional system within the broader context of shared principles of judicial power and constitutional supremacy that it views as foundational to Westminster model systems.[76]

In contrast, given the baggage of history between India and Pakistan, it is perhaps unsurprising that the judges on Pakistan's Supreme Court emphatically appealed to local constitutional values in the form of the "salient features" of their own Constitution. The Pakistani judges' insistence on autochthonous account of constitutional unamendability reveals mindfulness of the salience of constitutional

Regained' in Alejandro Saiz Arnaiz and Carina Alcoberro Llivina (eds), *National Constitutional Identity and European Integration* (Intersentia 2013) 49, 63, 67; Leonard F.M. Besselink, 'National and Constitutional Identity before and after Lisbon' (2010) 6(3) Utrecht L Rev 36, 42–44; Pietro Faraguna, 'Taking Constitutional Identities Away from the Courts' (2016) 41(2) Brook J Int'l L 491.

72 Jacobsohn (n 71) ch 4, 186.

73 Ibid ch 4, 187.

74 See Kwai Hang Ng and Brynna Jacobson, 'How Global Is the Common Law? A Comparative Study of Asian Common Law Systems – Hong Kong, Malaysia, and Singapore' (2017) 12(2) AJCL 209, 232 (discussing how foreign cases are sometimes 'cited to bolster the legitimacy of a judge's reasoning as well as to provide new ideas or experiences of other more established jurisdictions' so that it 'becomes an institutionalized mechanism for judges to import new ideas and contents into the domestic law').

75 Deepa Das Acevedo, 'An Inter-Asian Approach to Religion-State Relations?' ch 6 this volume. But see Guari Pillai, 'Reproductive Rights: A South-Asian Re-Imagination' ch 7 this volume.

76 Shukri Shahizam, 'Mediating Contingency: Indira Gandhi' (International Constitutional Law Society 2024 Annual Conference, Madrid, 8 July 2024).

narrative in popular discourse. In *Rawalpindi*, Pakistan's Supreme Court affirmed the judiciary's authority to invalidate amendments that violate core constitutional features that are entirely indigenous and local to Pakistan.

V CONCLUSION

These two case studies from Pakistan and Malaysia show the migration of a doctrine empowering judges to review constitutional amendments for unconstitutionality, famously articulated by the Indian Supreme Court. There is something to be said for these examples illustrating inter-Asian judicial discourse in the form of references to the jurisprudence of a more established Asian court that has successfully managed to develop a judicial power that more fragile courts seek to build, but these examples also highlight the limitations of a static framework for Inter-Asian Law. Judicial engagement with constitutional comparativism, for both the Pakistan and Malaysian courts, employed in distinct ways, ultimately appears to be used in service of building a locally based narrative of their constitution's own identity.

6

An Inter-Asian Approach to Religion–State Relations?

Deepa Das Acevedo

I INTRODUCTION*

Not so very long ago, scholars spoke quite freely of secularism as the defining mode of religion–state relations in Euro-American countries. "Secularism as a political doctrine," wrote Talal Asad, "arose in modern Euro-America."[1] Similarly, Charles Taylor observed that "[i]t is frequently claimed by . . . societies outside the European cultural zone, that secularism is an invention of this civilization," before adding that, "in fact, there is truth in the claim that secularism has Christian roots."[2] Agreement between scholars as distinct in disciplinary orientation and theoretical commitments as Asad and Taylor – even agreement that is a prelude to highly differentiated analysis – bears noting. It underscores the extent to which secularism has been viewed as both reflecting and reinscribing a fundamentally Euro-American ethos. Secularism, in this analysis, is the modern Euro-American approach to religion–state relations.

This chapter asks whether there is a comparable Inter-Asian approach to religion–state relations. Can we identify principles or perspectives in the management of religious life that are shared among Asian[3] countries? Is there evidence of Asian legal actors engaging with one another in a way that produces a shared conceptual vocabulary even if it also produces context-specific arrangements? Regardless of the answers to these questions, the very process of asking them does the important

* My thanks to Ben Schonthal and Jim Whitman for sharing insights and sources, to Justin Huston at the University of Alabama Bounds Law Library for superb research assistance, and to Matthew Erie and Ching-Fu Lin for the invitation to contribute to this volume.

[1] Talal Asad, *Formations of the Secular: Christianity, Islam, Modernity* (Stanford University Press 2003) 1.

[2] Charles Taylor, "Modes of Secularism" in Rajeev Bhargava (ed), *Secularism and Its Critics* (OUP 1999) 31.

[3] This chapter follows the volume editors' approach to conceptualizing "Asia." See generally, Matthew S Erie and Ching-Fu Lin, "Introduction: The Emergence of Inter-Asian Law", this volume.

work of shifting comparative scholarship away from its unspoken but powerful assumption that comparison occurs between Euro-America and its others. Moreover, whereas some areas of comparative scholarship have begun to consider interactions between and among Asian jurisdictions, the study of religion–state relations and secular governance has largely retained an explicit or implicit emphasis on comparing Asian experiences with those of Euro-America.

In the rest of this chapter, I trace the intra-Asia travels of a legal doctrine first developed by the Indian Supreme Court. The Essential Religious Practices (ERP) Doctrine is one of the Indian Supreme Court's most well-known creations and, arguably, *the* most well-known element of its expansive and widely discussed religious freedom jurisprudence. By following the ERP Doctrine into other Asian jurisdictions, I am able to construct the best-case argument for the existence of an Inter-Asian approach to religion–state relations. The chapter uses two jurisdictions where the ERP Doctrine has, arguably, been influential – Malaysia and Sri Lanka – to show that there has indeed been significant conceptual migration within Asia with regard to religious freedom jurisprudence.[4] At the same time, I argue that we should not mistake cross-pollination for convergence because there are important differences in the theoretical networks and sociopolitical contexts within which the ERP Doctrine has traveled.

Sections II–IV provide a primer on the ERP Doctrine. Section II establishes a constitutional context for the Doctrine's articulation by identifying and explaining conflicting impulses in India's national charter. Following this, Section III describes the Doctrine's articulation via an Indian Supreme Court decision issued soon after independence and surveys some of the most prominent instances in which ERP analysis has been used. Finally, Section IV discusses criticism of the ERP Doctrine, which is both long-standing and escalating in intensity. Section V introduces the ERP Doctrine's manifestations in Malaysia and Sri Lanka through a sampling of influential cases. After describing both the Indian origins and intra-Asian movements of the ERP Doctrine, Section VI evaluates the Doctrine's regional influence. As I argue, although the ERP Doctrine does not signal convergence in the form of an Inter-Asian approach to religion–state relations, it does allow us to trace a flow of scholarly and jurisprudential ideas that is Asian in both origin and destination.

II CONFLICTING CONSTITUTIONAL IMPULSES

The ERP Doctrine was first articulated in 1954 by the Indian Supreme Court, just four years after the country's new Constitution took effect. The Doctrine responded to a puzzle set in place by the Constitution's simultaneous espousal of two very

4 Sujit Choudhry, "Migration as a New Metaphor in Comparative Constitutional Law" in Sujit Choudhry (ed), *The Migration of Constitutional Ideas* (CUP 2006) 20–21 (providing several reasons why "migration" is preferable to "borrowing" as a metaphor for the movement of constitutional ideas).

different – indeed, mutually conflicting – attitudes toward citizen–state relations.[5] Any explanation of the ERP Doctrine thus begins not with the decision that announced it, but with the Constitution that necessitated it.

On the one hand, the Indian Constitution enthusiastically endorses an active, even a *transformative*, role for the state vis-à-vis society. For instance, members of the Constituent Assembly worried that "left to itself, religion could permit orthodox men to burn widows alive on the piers [sic] of their deceased husbands ... coerce indulgence in social evils like child marriage or even crimes like human sacrifice ... or relegate large sections of humanity to the sub-human status of untouchability."[6] Accordingly, the Indian Constitution grants immense powers to the state, and particularly to the courts responsible for interpreting the nation's charter, so that they may actively "reshape key structures of the social order."[7] Most relevantly for this chapter, Article 25(2)(a) empowers the state to regulate or restrict "any economic, financial, political, or other secular activity which may be associated with religious practice." This is a vision of Indian democracy founded on an understanding of sovereign authority that is *shared* or *divided* between citizens and the state.[8]

At the same time, India's Constitution espouses traditional liberal protections like "freedom of conscience and [the] free profession, practice and propagation of religion." While the liberalism encoded into the Constitution is undoubtedly overshadowed by the same document's transformative impulses, it is not quite correct to say – as some commentators have done – that this liberalism is "only ... half-hearted."[9] On the contrary, and despite the considerable authority accorded to them, state actors at federal and provincial levels, and belonging to legislative and judicial entities, have regularly held themselves back.[10] Indeed, few things exemplify this so well as the ERP Doctrine itself. This countervailing impulse reflects a conventional vision of democratic governance where sovereignty is wholly vested in citizens and merely exercised on their behalf by their representatives.

Elsewhere, I have described these two understandings of democratic sovereignty – one that accords parity to the state, one that prioritizes the people – as ideally existing in a state of "dynamic equilibrium."[11] Here, however, my focus is on the mechanics of maintaining that equilibrium. How is a court meant to balance the state's prerogative to transform society with, as it were, society's prerogative to remain

5 Deepa Das Acevedo, "Temples, Courts, and Dynamic Equilibrium in the Indian Constitution" (2016) 64 AJCL 555.

6 P N Bhagwati, "Religion and Secularism under the Indian Constitution" in Robert D Baird (ed), *Religion and Law in Independent India* (Manohar Publishers & Distributors 2005) 35, 43.

7 Gary J Jacobsohn, *Constitutional Identity* (Harvard University Press 2010) 216.

8 Das Acevedo (n 5).

9 Anuj Bhuwania, "Directive Principles and India's Statist Transformative Constitutionalism" (draft paper on file with author) 3.

10 Das Acevedo (n 5) 577–578.

11 Ibid 558.

untransformed? The ERP Doctrine represented both an early acknowledgment of the tension between these two constitutionally embedded visions of citizen–state relations and an attempted framework for grappling with it.

III ERP

The opinion responsible for the ERP Doctrine, *Commissioner, Hindu Religious Endowments, Madras v. Sri Lakshmindra Thirtha Swamiar of Sri Shirur Mutt,*[12] was prompted by two relatively recent developments: the Indian Constitution, which went into effect in 1950, and an elaborate and powerful regulatory apparatus created by Madras state for the governance of Hindu institutions. That regulatory infrastructure, the Hindu Religious Endowments Board, was the latest in a long line of efforts to formalize state authority over Hindu institutions in southern India, ostensibly in the interests of better management.[13] The latest version of this regulatory infrastructure (headed by the "Commissioner" named in the case citation) had moved to displace the petitioner, who was the superior, or *matadhipati*, of a Hindu monastic establishment (or *math*, anglicized to "Mutt" in the case citation). The state argued that the *matadhipati* was incapable of responsibly managing his institution's finances, as evidenced by the *math*'s mounting debts, while the *matadhipati* responded that the state's intrusion amounted to a violation of the constitutional rights newly accorded to him and the community he led.

The ERP Doctrine emerged through the Court's discussion of the *matadhipati*'s religious freedom rights under Article 25. The State of Madras emphasized the importance of Article 25(2)(a), which empowered the state to regulate or restrict "any economic, financial, political, or other secular activity which may be associated with religious practice." But this oversimplified matters in the eyes of the Court because, "[i]n the first place, what constitutes the essential part of a religion is primarily to be ascertained with reference to the doctrines of that religion itself."[14] In this original formulation, the ERP Doctrine was a straightforward application of the "divide and choose" principle: society would first determine what was essential, and the state would subsequently choose the rest as constituting its zone of authority. The Doctrine, in other words, was a check on the state's Article 25(2)(a) authority over religion – which, itself, was meant to serve as a check on religion's authority over social life.

The ERP Doctrine was not just a landmark judicial innovation because of the Court's willingness to draw lines – or, more correctly, to allow *others* to draw lines – between essential and nonessential aspects of religion. It also signaled the Indian

[12] AIR 1954 SC 282.
[13] While litigation was pending, the statute and the statutory body in question changed and adopted a slightly different name; in this chapter, I use the original "HRE" nomenclature.
[14] *Shirur Mutt* at ¶ 20.

Court's willingness to break with other Common Law models of religion–state relations. It is true, the Court noted, that in the American and Australian contexts, "the right to freedom of religion has been declared in unrestricted terms without any limitation whatsoever"[15] – but that was not the model chosen by India's Constituent Assembly. Not only had the framers of India's Constitution carved out "economic, financial, political, or other secular activity . . . associated with religious practice" as appropriate zones of state authority, but they had *also* imposed a generalized limitation on the individual right granted by Article 25 by declaring that it was "[s]ubject to public order, morality and health and to the other provisions of this Part." In other words, in India, religious activity was subject to state regulation to the extent that it did not concern anything deemed "essential," and – *even if deemed essential* – religious activity could be curtailed in the name of "public order, morality and health" (POMH) as well as other fundamental rights. Consistent with the idea of sovereignty that is shared between citizens and the state, this constitutional framework made it impossible for the state to avoid playing an authoritative role in religious life.

However, as *Shirur Mutt* also makes clear via its articulation of the ERP Doctrine, the state's role was not without its own limitations. By declaring society's authority over determinations of "essentiality," the Court also acknowledged the idea of *citizen* sovereignty, and of the citizenry's ability to declare zones of autonomy. "If the tenets of any religious sect of the Hindus prescribe that offerings of food should be given to the idol at particular hours of the day, [or] that periodical ceremonies should be performed in a certain way," observed the Court, then "all these would be regarded as parts of religion."[16] Nothing would have been easier than to declare that what was off-limits to state regulation was itself for the state to decide – to articulate, as I have elsewhere called it, a "judicial preferences"[17] doctrine. (Indeed, as Section IV explains, a "judicial preferences doctrine" is what the ERP has largely become.) In its original articulation, however, the Doctrine was meant to express the continued importance of citizen autonomy despite the state's powerful role in shaping religious life, and it did this by granting to citizens the ability to designate a religious practice as "essential."

IV CRITIQUING ESSENTIAL PRACTICES

Since it was handed down, *Shirur Mutt* has been cited and analyzed hundreds of times – not all of them approvingly. In this section, I describe two prominent lines of critique: one concerning the substance of the ERP Doctrine and the other

[15] Ibid ¶ 23.
[16] Ibid ¶ 20.
[17] Deepa Das Acevedo, *The Battle for Sabarimala: Religion, Law, and Gender in Contemporary India* (OUP 2023) 124.

concerning who is responsible for implementing it. Both critiques are justifiable given what the Doctrine has become over the course of its almost seventy-year-long lifespan. However, as I also show, the features that critics find most problematic are not inescapable elements of the Doctrine as originally articulated.

The most common substantive critique of the ERP Doctrine centers on a minor terminological shift with momentous consequences. As originally articulated in *Shirur Mutt*, the Doctrine granted constitutional protection to any practices that were *essentially religious*. Put differently, practices that received this protection were fundamentally religious in character and cohered with POMH and other fundamental rights. Those that remained unprotected concerned "economic, financial, political, or other secular activit[ies] ... associated with religious practice." However, almost immediately after its articulation, beginning in the late 1950s, the ERP Doctrine underwent an important transformation. No longer would it distinguish between religious and nonreligious activities; instead, courts began to use it to distinguish activities that were *essential to* a religion from those that were nonessential. Under this new formulation, it would no longer be enough for a practice to be essentially religious and consonant with POMH and other fundamental rights. Instead, to receive constitutional protection from state regulation and reform, a religious practice would have to be *both* these things *and also* be essential to the religious community in question.

Essentiality, moreover, came to be defined stringently: as that which defines the core of a religion so profoundly that, without it, "a religion will be no religion."[18] Perpetual observation, written documentation, and doctrinal necessity became nonnegotiables for ERP status.[19] These expectations would be difficult to meet within the context of any faith tradition, but they are arguably impossible within Hinduism given its absence of centralized ecclesiastical hierarchy and complicated (not to mention colonially transformed) relationship with written texts. What appeared to be a relatively minor shift from adverb to adjective thus in fact imposed a severely heightened burden on religious persons and communities seeking to retain some autonomy from the state. Furthermore, this substantive shift in the ERP Doctrine was no accident of Common Law jurisprudence, and it was not produced over the course of generations: on the contrary, it is attributable to a small, tightly clustered handful of cases.[20]

The second prominent critique of the ERP Doctrine is centered on the question of *who* makes the determination of essentiality – a core element of the original

[18] *Commissioner of Police v. Acharya Jagdishwarananda Avadhuta*, 12 SCC 770, 783 (2004) (Rajendra Babu, J).

[19] Deepa Das Acevedo, "Just Hindus" (2020) 45 LSI 965.

[20] The dividing line, as Chief Justice D.Y. Chandrachud would note several decades later, was the Supreme Court's unanimous opinion in *Sri Venkataramana Devaru v. State of Mysore*. *Indian Young Lawyers Association v. State of Kerala*, WP(C) No. 373 of 2006, ¶ 209 (Chandrachud, J).

Shirur Mutt formulation. Following *Devaru*, a handful of cases issued by Justice P.B. Gajendragadkar largely established that the Court's role in ERP analysis equaled or rivaled that of the religious community itself. In *Durgah Committee v. Hussain Ali*, Gajendragadkar declared that even practices viewed as religious by the community itself "may have sprung from merely superstitious beliefs and may in that sense be extraneous and unessential accretions to religion itself."[21] Since, obviously, the community could not be depended upon to distinguish between "religious" and "merely superstitious" elements, it went without saying that the Court would have to perform this important function. In *Shri Govindlalji v. State of Rajasthan*, Gajendragadkar acknowledged that "sometimes practices, religious and secular, are inextricably mixed up" but was confident in the Court's ability to separate them.[22] And in *Shastri Yagnapurushdasji* (better known as the *Satsang* Case), Gajendragadkar emphatically dismissed the Satsangis' own assessment of their community as being independent of Hinduism.[23]

The ERP Doctrine has thus gone from being a test to identify *essentially religious* practices using the judgment of believers to being a test that identifies *essential* religious practices using the judgment of the courts. In its original formulation, it was intended to be a check on the state's power to reform and regulate religious life – an acknowledgment of citizen sovereignty in the face of immense state authority. In its current and long-standing format, however, it merely reinforces the state's power over religious life by granting courts functionally unlimited power to define religion.[24]

Notwithstanding persuasive arguments about the logical "impossibility of religious freedom,"[25] wherever the state must define religion in order to keep out of it, the ERP Doctrine as it has been transformed by the Indian Supreme Court renders the very idea of religious freedom laughable. For this reason, the Doctrine has attracted widespread and vehement criticism, with commentators remarking, for instance, that "the problems with the ERP test are so stark and clear,"[26] that "[t]his doctrine has restricted religious freedom, particularly with respect to minority groups and non-mainstream Hindu sects,"[27] and that "judicial adventurism" facilitated by the Doctrine "has resulted in invidious outcomes based on absurd canonical

[21] AIR 1961 SC 1406, ¶ 34.
[22] AIR 1963 SC 1638, ¶ 59.
[23] *Shastri Yagnapurushdasji v. Muldas Bhudardas Vaishya*, AIR 1966 SC 1119, ¶ 55.
[24] Rajeev Dhavan and Fali S Nariman, "The Supreme Court and Group Life: Religious Freedom, Minority Groups, and Disadvantaged Communities" in B N Kirpal (ed), *Supreme But Not Infallible: Essays in Honour of the Supreme Court of India* (OUP 2000) 256, 260.
[25] Winnifred Fallers Sullivan, *The Impossibility of Religious Freedom* (Princeton 2005).
[26] Gautam Bhatia, "The Essential Religious Practices Test and the Inversion of Agency: Notes from the Hijab Hearing" (*ICLP*, February 9, 2022) (on file with author).
[27] Rehan Aindri Abeyratne, "Privileging the Powerful: Religion and Constitutional Law in India" (2018) 13 AsJCL 307, 309–310.

interpretations."[28] Even the most generous observers cannot help but acknowledge that the Doctrine has seemingly come to effectuate the opposite of its stated intent, inasmuch as it represents "the Court's attempt to discipline and cleanse religion or religious practices that are seen as unruly, irrational, and backward by putting the state in charge of places of religious worship."[29]

Despite these justifiable critiques, the ERP Doctrine remains one of India's most well-known jurisprudential innovations – and it is not hard to see why. As originally conceived, the Doctrine sought to balance classically liberal impulses (religious freedom) with recognizably postcolonial concerns (social reform and state-building). Faced with dueling models for religion–state relations, the Doctrine – like the Constitution that inspired it – sought to negotiate a third way that encompassed *both* models in a state of dynamic equilibrium. Additionally, in its original formulation the Doctrine purported to give courts a path to objectively measuring and delimiting a famously subjective area of behavior. While the *Shirur Mutt* articulation perhaps understated the extent to which judicial perspectives would necessarily inform the analysis, it also sought to give preeminence to non-state actors without completely relinquishing state involvement. Small wonder, then, that the creative framework of the ERP Doctrine has traveled beyond India's borders into other Asian courts.

V ERP ELSEWHERE IN ASIA

Malaysia and Sri Lanka share characteristics with India and with one another that are particularly salient in the context of religious freedom jurisprudence.[30] All three declared their independence from British colonial rule in the middle of the twentieth century: India in 1947, Sri Lanka in 1948, and Malaysia in 1957. All three nations became elective constitutional states: India and Sri Lanka transitioned, with varying (and still varying) levels of success, to electoral democracies, while Malaysia adopted an elective monarchical form of government. Demographically, despite considerable differences in size and composition, all three countries have a dominant religious community as well as significant minority communities. Moreover, many of these communities overlap: Hindus form a majority (80 percent) in India and minorities of varying size in Sri Lanka (13 percent) and Malaysia (6 percent), while the same applies to Buddhists in Sri Lanka (70 percent) compared to Malaysia (20

28 Dushyant Kishan Kaul, "The 'Essential Practices' Doctrine: Examining the Constitutional Impact of Inordinate Judicial Intervention on Religious Freedoms" (2022) 29 IJMGR 350, 351.

29 Ronojoy Sen, *Religion, Secularism, and the Indian Supreme Court* (OUP India 2010) 66.

30 The demographic and other statistical information presented throughout this section has been taken from the US Central Intelligence Agency's World Factbook entries for each country; figures have been rounded up or down as appropriate.

percent), and to Muslims in Malaysia (61 percent) compared to India (14 percent) and Sri Lanka (10 percent).

However, these same numbers show that the specifics of majority–minority divisions differ across the three countries. So too do the ways in which religious identity, religious freedom, and religion–state relations are articulated by each country's constitution. Since 1976, India's Constitution has referred to the country as a "secular" state, and there has never been a formally established religion – although Hinduism effectively receives unique treatment and is indisputably dominant. Sri Lanka's 1978 Constitution (its third since independence) explicitly accords "the foremost place" to Buddhism and charges the state with "protect[ing] and foster[ing] the Buddha Sasana"; however, the same Constitution also guarantees freedom of religion and conscience (Article 10) as well as the freedom of religious association (Article 14(1)). Malaysia goes further still, noting that "Islam is the religion of the Federation" (Article 3(1)), which makes it the only one of the three to have an established faith. However, the Malaysian Constitution also guarantees religious freedom to individuals as well as to groups (Article 11(1) and (3)). As the rest of this section shows, these social and legal distinctions ensure that the relatively clear influence of Indian ERP Doctrine within Malaysian and Sri Lankan religious freedom jurisprudence does not quite rise to the level of convergence.

A. *ERP in Malaysia*

Malaysia's ethnic and religious diversity is pronounced. Along religious lines, a Muslim majority of roughly 61 percent exists alongside significant Buddhist (20 percent), Christian (9 percent), and Hindu (6 percent) minorities. Likewise, an ethnic Malay majority of approximately 62 percent exists alongside significant ethnic Chinese (21 percent) and Indian (6 percent) minorities. The presence of more than one sizable religious minority makes the Malaysian context similar to the Indian one, as do the specific religious communities that are most populous in each country. However, religious identity in Malaysia is melded together with ethnicity in a way that does not easily translate to India. Sometimes this conflation of ethnic and religious identity is encoded into law, as with the constitutional definition of what it means to be Malay,[31] while in other circumstances, as with the assumption that all ethnic Indian Malaysians are Hindu, it is largely social practice.[32]

Legally, too, Malaysia both shares strong similarities with India and diverges in meaningful ways. Beyond their rootedness in the Common Law, both countries share certain constitutional commitments – and even some constitutional prose.

[31] Federal Constitution of Malaysia (1957) § 160 (2).

[32] Jaclyn L Neo, "What's in a Name? Malaysia's 'Allah' Controversy and the Judicial Intertwining of Islam with Ethnic Identity" (2014) 12 ICON 751, 754.

Both constitutions envision a religiously plural, non-theocratic nation: Article 25(1) of the Indian Constitution declares that "all persons are equally entitled to freedom of conscience and the right freely to profess, practise and propagate religion," while Article 3(1) of the Malaysian Constitution ensures that all religions "may be practised in peace and harmony in any part of the Federation." Going further, Article 26 of the Indian Constitution empowers every religious denomination or section thereof to "establish and maintain institutions for religious and charitable purposes," to "manage its own affairs in matters of religion," to "own and acquire movable and immovable property," and to "administer such property in accordance with law." Article 11(3) of the Malaysian Constitution, meanwhile, authorizes every religious group to "manage its own religious affairs," to "establish and maintain institutions for religious or charitable purposes," and to "acquire and own property and hold and administer it in accordance with law."

However, there are important differences in the way each document treats religious identity and behavior. The Malaysian Constitution ties Malay ethnicity with Muslim religious identification in a way that the Indian Constitution does not do for any ethnic or language affiliation. Additionally, Article 3(1) of the Malaysian Constitution explicitly envisions a special status for one religion: "Islam is the religion of the Federation."[33] To be sure, there are compelling arguments to be made that the text of India's Constitution exhibits favorable bias toward Hinduism,[34] and there are even more reasons to think that the growing saffronization of Indian politics is finding its way into constitutional interpretation. Nevertheless, it remains the case that the Indian Constitution does not formally identify a state religion and affirmatively embraces a secular system of governance.

The ERP Doctrine made its inaugural appearance in Malaysia via the Court of Appeals' decision in *Meor Atiqulrahman bin Ishak v Fatima binti Sihi* (henceforth, the "*Serban* Case").[35] There, the principal of a government school had expelled three male primary school students who insisted, in violation of school rules, on wearing a turban (*serban*) as part of their religious practice. The students won in the initial round of litigation. In the course of overturning that decision, the Court of Appeals explicitly looked to *Shirur Mutt* and the line of cases it generated – in fact, it even adopted the narrowed post-*Devaru* articulation of the ERP test. The key question, the Court declared, was "whether the wearing of a *serban* is an integral part of the religion of Islam" and, unfortunately, "[t]here was not a shred of evidence

33 Yvonne Tew, "Stealth Theocracy" (2018) 58 Va J Int'l L 31 (arguing that "[c]ourts are the main agents of … the elevation of Islam's constitutional position"). Relatedly, see Tamir Moustafa, "The Politics of Religious Freedom in Malaysia" (2014) 29 Md J Int'l L 481, 482 ("suggest[ing] that far from resolving conflict, the judicial system is itself a primary source of tension").

34 See, e.g., M Mohsin Alam Bhat, "Religious Freedom in Contest: Enforcing Religion through Anti-Conversion Laws in India" (2021) 9 JLRS 178, 183; Pritam Singh, "Hindu Bias in India's 'Secular' Constitution: Probing Flaws in Instruments of Governance" (2005) 26 TWQ 909, 909 (arguing that there is a "Hindu bias in the Constitution of India").

35 *Meor Atiqulrahman bin Ishak & Ors* v Fatimah Sihi & Ors [2000] 5 MLJ 375.

before the learned [lower court] judge confirming that the wearing of a *serban* is mandatory in Islam and is therefore an integral part of Islam."[36]

When the students appealed to Malaysia's apex court, the Federal Court, it also relied on ERP analysis, albeit under the new nomenclature of *integral* practice analysis.[37] However, the Federal Court went much further by stating that the extent of the prohibition (partial versus total) was a relevant consideration in determining its constitutionality. So too was the motivation behind the prohibition: Malaysia, the Federal Court remarked, is "multi-racial, multi-cultural, multi-lingual and multi-religious" and "we cannot ignore the educational system that had helped to mould the minds of Malaysian boys and girls to grow up as Malaysians." The individuals in charge of that educational system "should be given some respect and credit when they formulate some regulations applicable in their schools for the general good of all the students, the society and later the nation."

Although the Federal Court's interpretation of the ERP Doctrine seemingly speaks in the language of secular universalism, commentators have with good reason cautioned against viewing it this way.[38] Subsequent deployments of the Federal Court's modified ERP analysis have worked at cross-purposes with the idea of "multi-racial, multi-cultural, multi-lingual and multi-religious" Malaysia articulated in the *Serban* Case. For instance, in the 2013 "Kalimah Allah" opinion, a Malay-language Catholic newspaper challenged a ministerial order proscribing it from referring to the Christian god using the word "Allah." The Court of Appeal overturned a lower court ruling favoring the Church partly on the grounds that, despite ample evidence of Malay Christians using "Allah" to refer to their god, doing so was not an integral – that is, mandatory – element of their faith.[39] Notably, another line of reasoning that seemed particularly persuasive to the Court was the idea that "the purpose and intention … of the words: 'in peace and harmony' in art[icle] 3(1) is to protect the sanctity of Islam as the religion of the country and also to insulate against any threat faced or any possible and probable threat to the religion of Islam."[40]

As both the Kalimah Allah and *Serban* cases suggest, and as previous commentators have noted,[41] the ERP Doctrine responds to a different tension in Malaysia than it does in India. In the Indian context, ERP analysis was originally intended to

[36] Ibid ¶¶ 10–11.

[37] *Meor Atiqulrahman bin Ishak v Fatimah binti Sihi*, No. 01-3-2005(N) (2006) MYFC 18, (noting that "[t]he Court of Appeal was criticized for relying on Indian authorities" but affirming that "[t]here is no doubt that the integral part of the religion approach has its merits").

[38] Shylashri Shankar, "A Juridical Voyage of "Essential Practices of Religion" From India to Malaysia and Pakistan" (2016) 60 ABS 941, 952–953; Jaclyn L Neo, "Definitional Imbroglios: A Critique of the Definition of Religion and Essential Practice Tests in Religious Freedom Adjudication" (2018) 16 ICON 574, 587.

[39] *Menteri Dalam Negeri & Ors v. Titular Roman Catholic Archbishop of Kuala Lumpur*, (2013) 6 MLJ 468, 496.

[40] *Titular Roman Catholic Archbishop*, 6 MLJ 468, 490.

[41] Shankar (n 38) 952.

balance competing constitutional impulses regarding the relationship between citizens of any faith and the state. Article 25(1) provided a relatively conventional grant of religious freedom, while Articles 25(2)(a) and 25(2)(b) counterbalanced that freedom by empowering the state to intervene in religious life. The ERP Doctrine mediated between the two by empowering non-state actors to delimit the boundaries of state intervention – subject, of course, to the POMH limitation and other rights. In Malaysia, on the other hand, the ERP Doctrine serves to negotiate the relationship between a religion, Islam, that is granted constitutional primacy, and a state that is directed to respect the existence and contours of other faiths. Consequently, while the language and pattern of Malaysian ERP analysis are easily recognizable as Indian in origin, the purpose of engaging in that analysis is decidedly different: inviting – and resisting – an established religion.

B. *ERP in Sri Lanka*

The well-known antagonism between Sri Lanka's Sinhala and Tamil factions has often overshadowed the country's ethnic and religious diversity. In addition to the ethnic Sinhalese who comprise an overwhelming majority of the population (roughly 75 percent) and Tamils, whether Sri Lankan or Indian, who form the largest minority (15 percent), there is also a sizable Sri Lankan Moor population (9 percent). Religious diversity is even more pronounced, with Buddhists constituting a large majority (70 percent) and Hindus the largest minority (13 percent), but with sizable Christian and Muslim populations as well (around 7 percent and 10 percent, respectively). This means that Sri Lanka, like India and Malaysia, has more than one sizable religious minority. At the same time, and somewhat like the Malaysian case, religion and ethno-linguistic identity overlap in Sri Lanka with respect to the majority Sinhala Buddhist community in a way that does not easily translate to the Indian context.

Like Malaysia, Sri Lanka also shares strong legal connections with India. These include a shared Common Law heritage and, in both of Sri Lanka's republican constitutions (1972 and 1978), a shared commitment to a religiously plural, non-theocratic nation. Article 10 of the Sri Lankan Constitution resembles Article 25(1) in the Indian context, inasmuch as it guarantees "freedom of thought, conscience and religion, including the freedom to have or to adopt a religion or belief of his choice." Article 14(1), meanwhile, provides individuals with "the freedom, either by himself or in association with others, and either in public or in private, to manifest his religion or belief in worship, observance, practice and teaching." However, there are meaningful points of divergence. Article 9, the only article in the "Buddhism Chapter" of the 1978 Constitution, declares that "The Republic of Sri Lanka shall give to Buddhism the foremost place and accordingly it shall be the duty of the State to protect and foster the Buddha Sasana." Article 10, meanwhile, differs from its Indian counterpart in that it does not explicitly protect the ability to "profess and propagate" one's religious beliefs, and there is no group right that is comparable to India's Article 26 or Malaysia's Article 11(3).

More relevantly, however, Sri Lankan jurisprudence on the Buddhism Chapter is relatively sparse, unlike the voluminous case law engaging with India's religious freedom provisions that began developing soon after independence. The relative scarcity of Article 9 jurisprudence, which is likely owing to several distinct infrastructural and political factors,[42] means that some of the most frequently discussed cases are not only many decades old, but also involve contestations over the 1972 Constitution rather than the one currently in force. That earlier Constitution also contained a "Buddhism clause" in Article 6, and, with one important exception,[43] the language of the two constitutions is identical. Consequently, these earlier cases are illustrative of the way ERP analysis has been influential in Sri Lanka: far more subtly than in Malaysia, and without direct citation to *Shirur Mutt* or other Indian ERP case law, yet unmistakably present just below the surface.

In an early case decided under the 1972 Constitution, Sri Lanka's apex court[44] was asked to assess the constitutionality of a statute, the *Pirivena Education Bill*, that increased government authority over the schools (*pirivenas*) where most Sri Lankan Buddhist monks were educated. The petitioners included leaders of prominent lay Buddhist organizations as well as senior Buddhist monks and a senior civil servant. They argued that the *Pirivena Bill* ran afoul of Article 6 because it involved an impermissible intrusion of secular state authority into the administration of Buddhist institutions: The state was not protecting Buddhism, the petitioners maintained, but subordinating it to itself. The Court disagreed, holding that "Buddhist schools were not, in fact, part of Buddhism."[45]

In another decision handed down just weeks before the 1978 Constitution would be ratified, the Supreme Court of Sri Lanka was asked to reject the application of a Buddhist monk who had earned a law degree and wished to enroll as an attorney. The petitioners in *Sumana Thero* were many of the same lay Buddhist organizations who had approached the Court in the Pirivena Bill Case. They argued, once again, that the state's constitutional obligation to protect Buddhism required it to remain aloof from the internal workings of Buddhist religious life – but, this time, they were opposed by *other* actors also claiming to speak on behalf of Buddhism, including the monk's own monastic superiors. Again, the Court rejected the petitioners' arguments, declaring that the ultimate arbiters of proper monastic conduct ought to be

[42] For a discussion of these factors, see Benjamin Schonthal, *Buddhism, Politics, and the Limits of Law: The Pyrrhic Constitutionalism of Sri Lanka* (CUP 2016) 169 and 175.

[43] Schonthal (n 42).

[44] As Schonthal notes, the highest court in Sri Lanka at the time was the Constitutional Court rather than the (now-highest) Supreme Court. Ibid 162.

[45] Ibid 165.

the prelates of an individual monk's religious order rather than the state acting through its judicial actors.

The reasoning in *Sumana Thero* and the Pirivena Bill Case both reflected elements of the ERP Doctrine. In the Pirivena Bill Case, the Court declined to invalidate state action regulating religious institutions on the grounds that the regulation of those institutions neither clashed with Article 6's directive to protect Buddhism nor with Article 18 of the 1972 Constitution, which granted individuals the "freedom to have or to adopt a religion or belief of his choice, and the freedom … to manifest his religion or belief in worship, observance, practice and teaching." In the Court's view, the regulation of Buddhist schools neither worked at cross-purposes with the protection of Buddhism nor was connected closely enough with the freedom to "manifest" one's religious beliefs via, among other things, teaching. In *Sumana Thero*, the Court declared that the objections of senior Buddhist prelates, which represented "the only reliable evidence" that a monk could not also be an attorney, could not override the fact that "there is no such rule in the Vinaya [Pitaka]" – namely, the religious code governing monastic life. Put differently, according to the doctrines of the community itself, there was no necessary tension between being an ordained monk and being an attorney.

Although *Shirur Mutt* and the phrase "essential practices" appear nowhere in either majority opinion, their influence, and the influence of Indian constitutional law more generally, is hard to miss. The dissenting judge in *Sumana Thero*, Justice Wanasundara, followed what was, by this time, standard practice at the Indian Court, when he decided to "go to the original source and try to ascertain what the Buddha has actually said on these topics."[46] He concluded, on the basis of this exegetical foray, "[t]hat a monk's life, as ordained by the Buddha, in its pure form, is incompatible with lay life" – adding that this incompatibility "would be apparent to anyone even having a little acquaintance with the Dhamma."[47] Meanwhile, the majority in the Pirivena Bill Case engaged at length with Articles 25 and 26 of the Indian Constitution in order to distinguish them from the provisions of the 1972 Constitution. Not only did the Sri Lankan Constitution contain no protection for the propagation of religion, it also contained no equivalent to Article 26's group rights. Absent such an explicit provision of group rights, the connection between the state's regulation of pirivena schools and the right that *did* exist in the Sri Lankan context – to "manifest" one's religion through "teaching" – was too tenuous to warrant constitutional protection. Other landmark cases involving the Buddhism Chapter of the 1978 Constitution, perhaps most notably *In Re Thirteenth Amendment*,[48] confirm the extent to which Sri Lankan religious freedom jurisprudence is in conversation – if not in agreement – with Indian analogues.

46 *In the Matter of an Application by Rev. Sumana Thero* (1978) 3 Sri LR 365, 387 (Wanasundara, J, dissenting).

47 *Sumana Thero*, 3 Sri LR 365, 388–389.

48 *In Re the Thirteenth Amendment to the Constitution* (1987) 2 Sri LR 312.

If essential practices analysis in India was originally meant to navigate conflicting constitutional impulses – to reform citizens' religious practices and to respect citizens' religious autonomy – the purpose of broadly similar analysis in Sri Lanka seems quite different. Essentiality, in the Sri Lankan context, has been deployed in contestations between a religion, Buddhism, that is granted special protection, and a state whose constitution recognizes no collective religious freedom rights. And, perhaps unsurprisingly given past relations between India and Sri Lanka, "essentiality" has served to demarcate differences in constitutional priorities where the temptation to assume similarity runs strong.

VI CONCLUSION

The ERP Doctrine first articulated by the Indian Supreme Court in *Shirur Mutt* has, unquestionably, migrated to other Asian jurisdictions. This chapter has shown that the apex courts of Malaysia and Sri Lanka have relied on the ERP Doctrine's literal vocabulary or conceptual framework (or both), as well as on the larger corpus Indian religious freedom jurisprudence within which the Doctrine is situated. In fact, the Doctrine's influence within Asia is both broader and deeper than this discussion has suggested: The apex courts of other countries (e.g., Pakistan[49]) have drawn on ERP analysis, while there are also other cases decided by the Malaysian[50] and Sri Lankan[51] courts that show traces of the Doctrine's concepts or terminology.

At the same time, we should not mistake the jurisdictional travels of the ERP Doctrine for a process of harmonization, convergence, or simple transplantation. Indeed, as comparative law scholars have argued for some time, laws "are not merely 'bare propositional statement[s]' … but rather 'an incorporative cultural form … buttressed by important historical and ideological formations.'"[52] They are inextricably informed by and responsive to their contexts of origin.

But comparative law scholars have also cautioned that "we must be careful to not slip into the error of believing that legal practices can be so rooted in their 'cultures' that they can never be transplanted."[53] The ERP Doctrine's travels and transformations cohere with this insight, too. As decades of comparative scholarship suggest – and the ERP Doctrine confirms – laws are neither wholly determined by their bare terms (and hence are not perfectly transferable) nor are they wholly determined by their historical and social contexts (so they are not perfectly *non*-transferable).

[49] Shankar (n 38) discusses ERP analysis in Pakistan.

[50] *Hjh Halimatussaadiah bte Hj Kamaruddin v. Public Services Commission* (1994) 3 MLJ 61 (discussed in Neo (n 38)).

[51] *In Re the Thirteenth Amendment* (n 48).

[52] Pierre Legrand, "What 'Legal Transplants'?" in David Nelken and Johannes Feest (eds), *Adapting Legal Cultures* (Hart 2001) 55, 59.

[53] James Q Whitman, "The Neo-Romantic Turn" in Pierre Legrand and Roderick Munday (eds), *Comparative Legal Studies: Traditions and Transitions* (CUP 2003) 312, 341–342.

What is most evident in the ERP Doctrine's inter-Asian travels is that Asian countries look to one another for conceptual frameworks that can be redirected to and reshaped for domestic use. Apex courts in the region are indeed doing something more than lifting bare terminology, and their actions serve to make "Asia … and not the West … the referent for Asia's own legal modernity."[54] By the same token, however, these courts are doing something less than transplanting legal reasoning or working toward any level of harmonization or convergence. In fact, as both the Malaysian and Sri Lankan examples suggest, they may often be *reaching across* boundaries *juridically* in order to *reaffirm* boundaries that are *political* or *social*.[55]

In the realm of scholarship, there is an even clearer case to be made for the existence of an Inter-Asian approach to religion–state relations. As this volume suggests, scholars of Asian law, even when largely interested in specific country contexts, are extremely amenable to comparative analysis, and especially *collaborative* comparative analysis. They are active in tracing concepts, including the idea of ERP, across jurisdictional lines, and readily use analytic lenses – again, like ERP – developed by one court to explain,[56] and even to critique,[57] the jurisprudence of another court. Scholars of Asian law, in short, have rarely, if ever, proceeded on the misguided notion that nation-state boundaries are impermeable. This may be unsurprising, given the prevalence in Asia of countries that share messily intertwined colonial pasts, but it is also where the evidence, and usefulness, of Inter-Asian Law is most apparent.

54 Introduction: The Emergence of Inter-Asian Law, this volume, 2.

55 For a similar argument, see Gary J Jacobsohn and Shylashri Shankar, "Constitutional Borrowing in South Asia: India, Sri Lanka, and Secular Constitutional Identity" in Sunil Khilnani et al (eds), *Comparative Constitutionalism in South Asia* (OUP 2013) 216.

56 Schonthal (n 42) 166; (n 40).

57 Rehan Abeyratne, Rethinking Judicial Independence in India and Sri Lanka (2015) 10 AsJCL 99, 125–126 (critiquing Chief Justice Silva's opinion in *Kapuwatta Mohideen Jumma Mosque v. OIC Weligama*, SC Application No. 38/2005 (FR) SC Minute of 9/11/2007 on various grounds, including the Chief Justice's failure to recognize that the behavior at issue – using a loudspeaker to broadcast the Muslim call to prayer – is a "regular practice of Mosques," unlike an Indian case on which the Chief Justice had relied, which "involved practices … that are not central to the Christian faith").

7

Imagine to Re-Imagine

Bringing Inter-Asian Law to Abortion

Gauri Pillai

I INTRODUCTION

In this chapter, I make a compelling, yet unique, case for Inter-Asian Law (IAL). I do so not by looking at successful instances of citation of Asian law among Asian jurisdictions. Instead, I take a field from which IAL has been starkly absent – a field dominated by the Global North, in which the Global South, especially South Asia, is a rare participant: reproductive rights, specifically abortion. I illustrate the architecture of the field by surveying India's citation pattern, noting its excessive reliance on the Global North, especially the United States (US) Supreme Court decision in *Roe v Wade*.[1] I understand this pattern as an instantiation of a broader bias within comparative constitutional law.

I then imagine a break from this pattern. The break is necessitated by where the citation of *Roe* has taken, or would take, South Asian abortion jurisprudence. The break is provided by introducing Nepal and India as hypothetical, alternate referents for India and Bangladesh. And the break is justified by the resulting re-imagined legal mandate on abortion. The break, and its implications, thus make my case for Inter-Asian learning and borrowing.

II THE PATTERN: MAPPING AND UNDERSTANDING

Comparative law citation within Indian cases on abortion tracks a clear pattern. Exemplifying *Roe's* "sweeping, global influence,"[2] courts attribute a prominent

[1] *Roe v Wade* 410 U.S. 113 (1973) (*Roe*). Most cases cited in this chapter were decided before *Roe* was overruled by *Thomas Dobbs v Jackson Women's Health Organisation* 142 S. Ct. 2228 (2022) (*Dobbs*). However, in engaging with *Roe* and its critiques, the chapter uses *Roe* as a symbol of the hallowed place consistently offered to US jurisprudence on abortion. That *Roe* has been overruled only makes the argument in this chapter stronger: that Inter-Asian comparisons are likely more generative and ought to be encouraged. The chapter, however, shows that this argument stands not only in a post-*Roe* world but even during *Roe's* heyday.

[2] Rachel Rebouché, "Comparative Pragmatism" (2012) 72 Md L Rev 86.

place to it. Consider *Suchitra Srivastava*, a path-defining Indian Supreme Court decision from 2009, distinctive for its recognition that a "woman's right to make reproductive choices," including the decision to undergo an abortion or give birth to a child, is a "dimension" of her personal liberty under Article 21 of the Indian Constitution.[3] In *Suchitra*, the Court drew on *Roe* to construct limitations to the abortion right on the grounds of women's health and the State's "compelling interest" in preserving the potential life of the fetus.[4] Several High Courts have since endorsed *Suchitra's* reliance on *Roe*.[5] Some go beyond *Roe*, grounding the right to make reproductive decisions within a panoply of US Supreme Court decisions.[6] Others look outside the US to the German Constitutional Court,[7] the Canadian Supreme Court,[8] the House of Lords in the United Kingdom,[9] and the European Court of Human Rights.[10]

Even a cursory glance at the referents identified as relevant by Indian courts reveals the preeminence of the Global North. The Global South – as a whole, not just South Asia – is starkly absent. This is not because there have not been landmark abortion cases from the Global South (or South Asia).[11] Rather, it is part of a wider trend, endemic to comparative constitutional law, or legal modernity more broadly as the editors to this volume note in their introduction. The "grammar" of modern constitutionalism has been defined by the Global North, especially North America

3 *Suchitra Srivastava v Chandigarh Administration* (2009) 9 SCC 1 [11] (*Suchitra*).

4 Ibid.

5 *Ashaben v State of Gujarat* (2015) AIR CC 3387 [8] (*Ashaben*); *R v State of Haryana* 2016 SCC OnLine P&H 7425 [25.20] ("*R v Haryana*"); *Surjibhai Kalasva v State of Gujarat* SCr.A No 585/2018 (Gujarat High Court, January 30, 2018) [19] (*Surjibhai*); *ABC v Chhattisgarh* WP(Cr) No. 454/2020 (Chhattisgarh High Court, October 6, 2020) [28] (*ABC*); *Poornima Devu Mandarkar v Union of India* WP 10835/2018 (Bombay High Court, April 3, 2019) [87] (*Poornima*).

6 *Ranichand Baiga v State of Chhattisgarh* WPPIL No. 27/2017 (Chhattisgarh High Court, December 12, 2018); citing *Carey v Population Services International* 431 US 678 (1977) and *Elsenstadt v R. Baird* 405 US 438 (1972); *V Krishnan v G Rajan* (1994) 2 MWN (Cri) 333 ("*V Krishnan*") [34]–[39] (citing US cases on the "mature minor exception").

7 (1975) 39 B Verf GE cited in *Ashaben* (n 5) [7]; *R v Haryana* (n 5) [25.21]; *Surjibhai* (n 5) [23]; *ABC* (n 5) [27].

8 *R v Morgentaler* [1988] 1 SCR 30 cited in *Ashaben* (n 5) [8.1]; *R v Haryana* (n 5) [25.23]; *Surjibhai* (n 5) [23]; *ABC* (n 5) [29].

9 *V Krishnan* (n 6) [22]–[33] (citing English law on the question of minor's rights to abortion without parental consent); *Paton v United Kingdom* (1980) 3 EHRR 408 and *H v Norway* (1992) 73 DR 155 cited in *Ashaben* (n 5) [8.2]; *R v Haryana* (n 5) [25.22]; *Surjibhai* (n 5) [23]; *ABC* (n 5) [30]; *King v Bourne* [1938] 3 All ER 615 cited in *R v Haryana* (n 5) [25].

10 *RR v Poland* [2011] ECHR 828 cited in *R v Haryana* (n 5) [25]; *Surjibhai* (n 5) [23].

11 Corte Constitutional [C.C.] [Constitutional Court], Sala Plena mayo 10, 2006, Sentencia C-355/2006 (Colombia); *Christian Lawyers' Association v National Minister of Health* 2004 (4) All SA 31 (South Africa); Acción De Inconstitucionalidad, Pleno de la Suprema Corte de Justicia [SCJN] [Supreme Court], Agosto de 2008, 146/2007 (Mexico); *Lakshmi v Office of the Prime Minister* 2067, 52(9) NKP 1551 (2010) (Nepal).

and Western Europe.[12] The Global South plays a minimal role in norm-setting, particularly beyond its "usual suspects" of India, South Africa, and Colombia.[13] This pattern speaks to the "unwritten but firmly entrenched hierarchy" within the politics of constitutional knowledge-building.[14] It is a product of the assumption that the Global North is the "wellspring of universal learning," while the Global South embodies "parochial wisdom ... antiquarian traditions ... exotic ways and means,"[15] or at best a "weak reproduction" of Global North principles,[16] reinforcing the distinction between the "core and the periphery" of constitutional law.[17] This "northern selection bias"[18] is especially conspicuous within constitutional litigation on abortion where a "few influential jurisdictions" like the US and Germany continue to hold the fray.[19] Relying, as India does, on the North as the "gold standard" perpetuates a "soft form of imperialism,"[20] encouraging an "elusive dependence" by former colonies and "awkward condescension" by the colonizers.[21] The resulting body of knowledge "homogenises a reality that is full of shades and hues."[22] It suppresses Southern constitutional experiences,[23] painting them as "divergent and deficient, secondary and subordinate,"[24] a form of

[12] Daniel Bonilla Maldonado, *Toward a Constitutionalism of the Global South* (OUP 2013) 3; Philipp Dann, Michael Riegner and Maxim Bönnemann (eds), *The Global South and Comparative Constitutional Law* (OUP 2020) 1; Zoran Oklopcic, "The South of Western Constitutionalism: A Map Ahead of a Journey" (2016) 37(11) Third World Quarterly 2081; Cheryl Saunders, "Towards a Global Constitutional Gene Pool" (2009) 4 NTU L Rev 3; Sujit Choudhry, "Bridging Comparative Politics and Comparative Constitutional Law: Constitutional Design in Divided Societies" in Sujit Choudhry (ed), *Constitutional Design for Divided Societies: Integration or Accommodation?* (OUP 2008) 3–31; Tom Ginsburg, *Judicial Review in New Democracies: Constitutional Courts in Asian Cases* (CUP 2003) 15; Upendra Baxi, "Constitutionalism as a Site of State Formative Practices" (2000) 21 Cardozo L Rev 1183–1210.

[13] Ran Hirschl, *Comparative Matters* (OUP 2016) 212.

[14] Maldonado (n 12) 4; Oklopcic (n 12) 2083.

[15] Jean Comaroff and John Comaroff, *Theory from the South, or, How Euro-America is Evolving toward Africa* (Routledge 2012) 1.

[16] Maldonado (n 12) 12.

[17] David Law, "Pedagogy and Conceptualisation of the Field" in David Law (ed), *Constitutionalism in Context* (CUP 2022) 11.

[18] Hirschl (n 13) 212.

[19] Reva Siegel, "Constitutionalisation of Abortion" in Michel Rosenfeld and András Sajó (eds), *The Oxford Handbook of Comparative Constitutional Law* (OUP 2012).

[20] Karen Knop, "State Law without Its State" in Austin Sarat et al (eds), *Law Without Nations* (Stanford University Press 2011) 76.

[21] Radhika Coomaraswamy, *Sri Lanka: The Crisis of the Anglo-American Constitutional Traditions in a Developing Society* (Vikas 1984) 1.

[22] Ibid 14.

[23] Saunders (n 12) 3.

[24] Florian Hoffmann, "On the Significance of An/Other Modernity in Comparative Constitutional Law" in Philipp Dann, Michael Riegner and Maxim Bönnemann (eds), *The Global South and Comparative Constitutional Law* (OUP 2020) 62.

"epistemic injustice."[25] Most importantly, it ignores creative constitutional alternatives offered by the Global South to contemporary legal problems.

The idea I propose is, then, "very simple really, although its implications are quite radical."[26] Through an act of imagination, the construction of two hypothetical referents, Nepal for India and India for Bangladesh, I invert the order of things. I look to the referents for their "ingenious, highly imaginative modes of survival,"[27] and create a conceptual space for rethinking key constitutional dilemmas on abortion from the South.

As a method, imagination finds no representation within comparative constitutional law which typically studies contexts where comparative citation (Inter-Asian or otherwise) has already occurred. So, the method of imagination itself requires development. For this, I draw on legal theory. Del Mar understands "imagination" as an act of entering into a "distinctive epistemic frame" where we "selectively suspend certain epistemic norms and commitments" and participate along the simulated spectrum opened up to us in this process.[28] Initiating imagination requires "artefacts," resources putting us on "epistemic alert" and calling upon us to "do things with them".[29] Imagination stimulates inquiry, a mode of experimental, what-if thinking which draws on hypothetical reasoning as a device to think with.[30] For Del Mar, imagination is thus not an "escape from reality"[31] but rather a "form of making, doing, acting, and interacting . . . one [that] proceeds tentatively, trying out different possibilities, generating ever more perspectives, leaving room for and inviting others to suggest alternatives."[32]

In this chapter, I imagine, as proposed by Del Mar. My artifacts are the alternate comparative referents: Nepal for India and India for Bangladesh. "Playing" with them,[33] I suspend the epistemic commitment to *Roe* and instead ask: What if India turned to Nepal and Bangladesh turned to India? Here, I bring to life the central question animating this volume: what if Asia, and not the West, is the referent for Asia's own legal modernity? Imagination allows me to access this hypothetical reality. I then participate in it to tentatively explore the implications of this change in referent.

Reproductive rights drive home the potential of imagination as a method of comparative constitutional law. *Roe's* influence is so dominant that it requires a hypothetical suspension of the norm to create the space for Inter-Asian referents. Imagination enables this, keeping *Roe* aside for a moment to let Asia speak. Yet,

[25] Dann, Riegner and Bönnemann (n 12) 4.
[26] Comaroff and Comaroff (n 15) 1.
[27] Ibid 18.
[28] Maksymilian Del Mar, *Artefacts of Legal Inquiry: The Value of Imagination in Adjudication* (Bloomsbury 2020) 125.
[29] Ibid 78, 115.
[30] Ibid 6.
[31] Ibid 25.
[32] Ibid 60.
[33] Play is an important concept for Del Mar (n 28) 116.

imagination only takes us so far. Legal imagination seeks to persuade us that shifting toward Asian referents is good for reproductive rights.[34] However, comparative citation is rarely motivated by the sole desire to enhance rights-based outcomes. Rather, courts more often engage in comparative citation to locate themselves as members of an "international conversation" on how "modern" countries balance competing rights,[35] part of the "liberal-democratic club of nations."[36] Imagination by itself cannot alter this underlying incentive structure. This requires a broader shift from a unipolar to a multipolar global legal configuration, where belonging to the Inter-Asian "club" is also seen as equally desirable. Initiatives like this volume on IAL lay the necessary groundwork for this shift.

III HYPOTHETICAL REFERENTS: CONSTRUCTION AND COMPARISON

Raghavan, Thiruvengadam, and Khilnani compellingly argue why South Asia can, and should, be a referent for South Asia:

> despite their divergent recent histories and political experiences, South Asian countries in fact display a remarkable degree of constitutional and legal kinship. There are several common elements among the region's constitutions, political structures, and legal systems. These elements are drawn from the region's colonial past and from its many diverse indigenous legal traditions. *The potential for intra-regional borrowing and comparative study is considerable.*[37]

Beyond constitutional and legal similarities, there also exist cultural commonalities, especially the role of gender as a crucial determinant of health influencing the exposure to disease, the risk of poor health, and access to healthcare including abortion.[38] South-Asian comparisons (including hypothetical ones) are therefore methodologically justifiable. Let us now imagine.

A. *Nepal for India*

Earlier I introduced *Suchitra*, a landmark reproductive rights decision in India. While much has been written about how *Suchitra* protected reproductive autonomy

[34] Martti Koskenniemi, *To the Uttermost Parts of the Earth: Legal Imagination and International Power 1300–1870* (CUP 2021) 4, noting that legal imagination is a tool of persuasion.

[35] Rebouché (n 2) 89.

[36] Hirschl (n 13) 9.

[37] Sunil Khilnani, Vikram Raghavan and Arun Thiruvengadam, *Comparative Constitutionalism in South Asia* (OUP 2012) (emphasis added).

[38] Fariyal Fikree and Omrana Pasha, "Role of Gender in Health Disparity: The South Asian Context" (2004) 328 BMJ 823–826; World Health Organisation, "Nepal: Gender and Health", https://iris.who.int/bitstream/handle/10665/344677/GER-Nepal-eng.pdf?sequence=1, accessed May 30, 2025.

as a fundamental right,[39] negligible attention has been paid to how *Suchitra* also led to the growth of the fetus as a prominent figure within abortion law in India.[40] Here, I document this phenomenon, emphasizing *Suchitra's* reliance on *Roe* in initiating this monumental step.

To deduce whether a "cogent rationale" existed for restricting the abortion right,[41] *Suchitra* promptly turned to Justice Blackmunn in *Roe* who held:

> *the State does have an … important and legitimate interest in protecting the potentiality of human life*. These interests are *separate and distinct*. Each grows in substantiality as the woman approaches term and, at a point during pregnancy, each becomes "compelling".[42]

From this starting point of separateness between women's rights and fetal interests, Justice Blackmunn easily obscured the interconnectedness between the two. He failed to recognize that protecting fetal interest incurs costs, just like protecting *any* State interest, whether it be security, welfare, or education, incurs costs. While the distribution of costs is typically accompanied by deliberation – Who *should* bear it? Who *can* bear it? – here, the allocation seemed deceptively simple. The costs fell to women, currently pregnant and those with the ability to become pregnant. These costs are tangible:

> They can't be measured solely in terms of money, although that is certainly at stake. Women also incur costs to their freedom, physical and mental security, identity, and privacy when they are denied jobs because they are fertile, when they are subjected to court ordered medical operations against their will, and when they are given additional civil and criminal penalties for using drugs or alcohol during pregnancy that are never imposed on women who are not pregnant or on men. Women are assigned responsibility for taking care of fetuses without being given the resources they need to do so, and then penalized for falling short.[43]

In artificially severing fetal interests from women's rights, *Roe* sidelined questions about the distribution of costs involved in protecting the fetus. Unfortunately, the *Suchitra* Court followed *Roe* down the same road. Citing *Roe*, it concluded that

39 Dipika Jain and Payal K Shah, "Reimagining Reproductive Rights Jurisprudence in India: Reflections on the Recent Decisions on Privacy and Gender Equality from the Supreme Court of India" (2020) 39(2) Colum J Gender L 1–53.

40 Tracing the evolution of fetal life in India, Gauri Pillai, "Shades of Life in Indian Abortion Law" (2022) 16(1) NLSJ 131–134.

41 *Suchitra* (n 3) [23].

42 *Roe* (n 1) 94 (emphasis added).

43 Rachel Roth, *Making Women Pay: The Hidden Cost of Foetal Rights* (Cornell University Press 2003) 4; See also Faith Agostinone-Wilson, "Abortion through the Lens of Fetal Personhood" in Faith Agostinone-Wilson (ed), *Enough Already! A Socialist Feminist Response to the Re-emergence of Right Wing Populism and Fascism in Media* (Brill 2020); Silja Samerksi, "Pregnancy, Personhood and the Making of the Fetus" in Lisa Disch and Mary Hawkesworth (eds), *The Oxford Handbook of Feminist Theory* (OUP 2016) 700.

there is a "compelling state interest in protecting the life of the prospective child" allowing the State to reasonably restrict abortion.[44] This observation set in motion a paradigm change within abortion law in India.

Before *Suchitra*, the fetal figure had been more or less absent within Indian abortion law. In parliamentary debates on the law in 1971 (and later in 2021), only two members voiced the concern that abortion is "virtually murder"[45] and a "crime against humanity."[46] Others unanimously agreed that "there is no violation of [the right to life] in **any** manner".[47] Indian courts too have rejected pleas that India's law on abortion violates fetal right to life. Courts have repeatedly refused to "enter upon a debate as to when fetus comes to life or the larger question touching upon the ethics of abortion", instead emphasizing that the abortion law preserves women's lives and thus is consistent with the right to life.[48] Some courts have even held that "an unborn foetus is not an entity with human rights … A child when born and takes first breath, is a human entity."[49]

Suchitra's Roe-driven recognition of the State's compelling interest was thus *the* big shift that spurred the steady growth of fetal interests in India. *Suchitra's* rationale was endorsed time and again by the Supreme Court[50] and State High Courts.[51] Some courts even took forward *Suchitra's* framing. While *Suchitra* was silent on the point at which the State's compelling interest to protect the fetus gets activated, in *R v Haryana* the Punjab and Haryana High Court indicated viability, when the fetus is capable of surviving outside the womb of the pregnant woman, as the relevant moment.[52] Once again, *Roe's* strong influence is visible here; viability was a standard initially set by *Roe* as the fetus has the "capability of meaningful life outside the mother's womb" at viability.[53] While the US has now moved past viability,[54] and viability has been extensively critiqued as a temporal threshold,[55] it still holds purchase within Indian law. Taking *Suchitra* even further, some High Courts have

44 *Suchitra* (n 3) [11].

45 Statements regarding Medical Termination of Pregnancy Bill, Lok Sabha (August 2, 1971) (MM Joseph; Muhammad Sheriff).

46 Statements regarding Medical Termination of Pregnancy (Amendment) Bill 2020, Lok Sabha (March 17, 2020) (Dean Kuriakose).

47 Ibid (Dr. Harshvardhan).

48 *Nand Kishore Sharma v Union of India* AIR 2006 Raj 166 [4]; *Cry for Life Society v Union of India* WP(C) No. 10130/2013 (Kerala High Court, June 9, 2020).

49 *High Court on its own Motion v State of Maharashtra* 2017 CriLJ 218 [15], [20].

50 *X v NCT of Delhi* CA No. 5802/2022 (Supreme Court, September 29, 2022) [103] ("*X v NCT*"); *Z v Bihar* (2018) 11 SCC 572 [28].

51 *S v State of Gujarat* SCrA No. 585/2018 (Gujarat High Court, January 30, 2018) [18]; *Surjibhai* (n 5).

52 *R v Haryana* (n 5) [33.4].

53 *Roe* (n 1) 97.

54 *Planned Parenthood of Southeastern Pennsylvania v Casey* 505 US 833 (1992).

55 A Burin, "Beyond Pragmatism: Defending the 'Bright Line' of Birth" (2014) 22(4) Med Law Rev 494–525.

veered dangerously close to recognizing a fetal right to life. In *Suparna Debanath*, the Calcutta High Court observed:

> There is always a difficulty in choosing a precise point when the unborn gets a right to life. *The right answer may lie in accepting that there are degrees of right to life and the foetus gets a stronger right to life as it develops in the mother's womb.* The more it develops, the more difficult it becomes to take a decision to abort the same.[56]

As with Justice Blackmunn in *Roe*, these shifts have led Indian courts too to ignore that women unilaterally bear the costs of the State's interest in protecting fetuses. Take the example of cases of abortion sought on ground that there exists a "substantial risk" that the fetus, if born, would be afflicted by a "serious physical or mental abnormality."[57] Here, the courts' only criterion of assessment is whether the fetus is capable of surviving outside the womb. If the fetus has "grim chances of survival and limited life span,"[58] abortion is allowed. If the prospective child has some future, abortion is denied, "though it would be traumatic for [the woman]."[59] In fact, a High Court once admitted in 2018: "I have observed over a period of time that the Doctors, while expressing their opinion [on termination], do not consider the trauma and the agony, which the [woman] undergoes."[60] Yet, it went on to deny her an abortion.

Beyond outright disregard, some courts minimize the costs borne by women, trivializing them as forms of "self-indulgence."[61] They dismiss anxiety about the outcome of the pregnancy[62] or the concern that being pregnant would compel reconciliation with a violent partner and sustain financial dependence on him.[63] Other courts acknowledge the costs borne:

> I am conscious of the fact that to carry a child in her womb by a woman as a result of conception through an act of rape is not only extremely traumatic for her but humiliating, frightening and psychologically devastating and as a human being, more particularly in the Indian society she becomes an object of scorn and ostracization.[64]

56 *Suparna Debnath v State of West Bengal* AST No 3/2019 (Calcutta High Court, January 29, 2019) (*Suparna*) (emphasis added).

57 The Medical Termination of Pregnancy Act 1971, s 3(b)(ii).

58 *Kulwinder Kaur v Chandigarh* W.P.(C) 1088/2019 (P&H High Court, January 31, 2019); See also *Manga Singh v Chandigarh Administration* W.P.(C) 23222/2019 (P&H High Court, September 2, 2019); *Pallavi Bhoi v State of Chhattisgarh* W.P.(C) 2261/2019 (Chhattisgarh High Court, July 9, 2019).

59 *ABC* (n 5) [34]; *X v Uttarakhand* W.P.(M/S) 1909/2018 (Uttaranchal High Court, July 17, 2018) [13]; See also *Nikhil Datar v Union of India* 2008 (110) BOMLR 3293 (*Nikhil*); *Suparna* (n 56).

60 *Surjibhai* (n 5) [24] (emphasis added).

61 Adrienne Rich, *Of Woman Born: Motherhood as an Experience and Institution* (WW Norton and Company 1976) xvi.

62 *Sheetal Shankar Salvi v Union of India* (2018) 11 SCC 606.

63 *Neelam Choudhary v Union of India* 2019 (1) BomCR 681.

64 *Ashaben* (n 5) [11.5].

Yet they require the pregnant woman, who was kidnapped and gang raped, to "bravely" continue with the pregnancy, reminding her that post-abortion, her grief might only "double" as she had "just ended the life of [her] child."[65] And if a woman refuses to bear the costs, she is publicly shamed, with one court condemning her refusal as "reproductive materialism"![66]

It is here, then, that we must take seriously my call to suspend established epistemic norms and imagine. Let us ask: What if *Suchitra* had not turned to *Roe* to seek direction on fetal interests? What if it had, instead, looked to Asia? Would it have allocated the costs of fetal protection differently?

Just a few months before *Suchitra*, the Nepal Supreme Court decided *Lakshmi Dhikta*.[67] Unlike *Roe*, and despite citing *Roe*,[68] *Lakshmi Dhikta* began by emphasizing the interconnectedness between the woman and the fetus: "A fetus cannot be recognized as a separate personality from that of the mother as it owes its existence to the mother . . . the interests of the mother and that of the fetus are not separate. Instead, it is appropriate to view it in an integrated manner."[69] This crucial recognition functioned as the Court's inflection point, from which it refused to consider the fetus as an entity bearing the right to life *because* the costs on women would be too high:

> If a fetus is to be considered a life in itself and identity of a fetus and that of the mother who carries the fetus through conception is to be considered separate, the existence of fetus's life cannot be endangered even when the physical or mental health of a mother is under threat, and in such a situation, the independence of the fetus shall have to be recognized until the last stage of mother's life. Thus, even if the existence of the mother is endangered, she will have to endure until the last minute for the protection of fetus's life or last measures for the protection of the life of the pregnant mother shall be taken only after ensuring the protection of the independent life of the fetus. In reality, such an argument is not practical.[70]

The Court painstakingly set out the costs incurred by women:

> Women may be forced to become pregnant and to continue pregnancies if their reproductive health rights are not protected in a correct manner, and instead of being respected as rights holders they will be transformed into mere instruments

65 Ibid [12].

66 *Nandini Tushar Rawool v State* W.P.(C) No 8313/2018 (Bombay High Court, August 14, 2018).

67 *Lakshmi* (n 11); India–Nepal comparisons on abortion are not unprecedented and have been justified in light of alignment in their constitutional understandings of gender equality and privacy, and the similarity of their statutory frameworks on abortion: See Mara Malagodi, "Intersectional Inequalities and Reproductive Rights: An India-Nepal Comparison" (2020) 3(2) U OxHRH J 195–201.

68 *Lakshmi* (n 11) [9].

69 Ibid [14].

70 Ibid [13].

> bearing compulsive responsibility of producing human. Although becoming pregnant is a noble human act, no other situation that can be more burdensome and condemnable when the pregnancy is forced. Once the bearer is denied of its right to either carry the pregnancy or not, the outcome cannot be considered to constitute the fulfilment of one's highest duty, and instead of right it becomes a form of slavery.[71]

Such "servitude,"[72] the Court acknowledged, would harm women's physical and mental health, life, dignity, freedom, and participation in society.[73] She may lose her "opportunity of employment or income generation," affecting her chances of "professional development" (a cost which the Court did not trivialize).[74] It would also treat women unequally – "while becoming pregnant is not a consequence of women's act alone; after conception, only women [bear] the direct burden"[75] – and have a heightened adverse impact on vulnerable groups of women, "rural, illiterate, and poor," causing the "feminization of poverty."[76]

This comprehensive cataloguing of costs and their bearers did not mean that the Court denied any role for fetal interests at all stages of pregnancy. The Court concluded that the right to abortion did not vest "the right to oppose pregnancy at all times, therefore, it is necessary to consider the right to abortion within an appropriate limit."[77] While the Court was silent on what this "appropriate limit" might be, the Court's starting point is what is most important: the recognition that the costs incurred by women ought to be central in determining the legal status of the fetus. *Lakshmi Dhikta* could have gone further and offered a re-imagined distribution of costs for fetal welfare. The Court did acknowledge that the "existence and evolution of the human race … is a matter of common public interest."[78] Yet, the costs for it are borne by just one group. A reimagined cost structure would not ignore potential life. Rather it would distribute more fairly the costs of protecting it. That is, to protect fetuses, the State would not restrict abortion, compelling women alone to bear the costs of the *State's* interest. Rather, it would target the incidence of unwanted pregnancy (through better sex education and improved contraceptive provision) and support parents in providing childcare,[79] therein redistributing the

71 Ibid [33].
72 Ibid.
73 Ibid [36].
74 Ibid [37].
75 Ibid [18]; on the vision of transformation equality underlying *Lakshmi*, see Melissa Upreti, "Toward Transformative Equality in Nepal: The Lakshmi Dhikta Decision" in Rebecca Cook, Joanna Erdman and Bernard Dickens (eds), *Abortion in Transnational Perspective* (University of Pennsylvania Press 2014).
76 *Lakshmi* (n 11) [18].
77 Ibid [41].
78 Ibid [32] (emphasis added).
79 Roth (n 43) 12.

costs of fetal welfare among society as a whole. In fact, a "wealth of evidence" shows that fetal interests are also more "effectively" pursued this way.[80]

Lakshmi Dhikta did not go this far. However, it did present the seeds for this radical re-imagination. In taking its cues from *Roe* and its progeny, this re-imagination is what *Suchitra* lost out on. Hypothetically, then, a change in frame of reference – from *Roe* to *Lakshmi* – could have ushered in this fundamental realignment of India's abortion law. There is, of course, no guarantee of such an outcome; judicial decisions are rarely a product of applicable doctrine alone. Yet, it certainly serves to illustrate the central thrust of this chapter: imagination as a method to tap into the immense creative potential of IAL.

B. *India for Bangladesh*

To make my case stronger, I construct a second hypothetical referent: India for Bangladesh. While India is, typically, a "usual suspect" of comparative constitutional study,[81] having received significant attention for its approach to access to justice, socioeconomic rights, and transformative constitutionalism, India remains absent from global deliberations on reproductive rights. This is possibly on account of the existing Northern tilt within constitutionalism on reproductive rights and India's own nascent initial jurisprudence on the theme. However, with time and as shown in the Nepal for India, Indian decision-making on reproductive rights has not only become more robust but also offers innovations demanding to be studied across borders. Here, I focus on two such innovations and their relevance to Bangladesh.

India and Bangladesh have identical criminal prohibitions on abortion, a legacy of colonialism. The Bangladesh Penal Code criminalizes voluntarily causing a woman to miscarry. The only exception is a procedure to save the life of the pregnant woman.[82] Unlike the Indian Medical Termination of Pregnancy Act 1971, Bangladesh, however, does not have a regime of legislative exceptions to criminal law, allowing abortion under a more expansive set of conditions. As a result, abortion law in Bangladesh remains strict and narrow.

During the Liberation War in 1971, many Bangladeshi women were sexually assaulted by members of the Pakistani army. In response, Bangladesh introduced a transitional "waiver" on the criminalization of abortion to preserve national honor.[83] Over time, the object of safeguarding national identity was replaced with a second

80 Sally Sheldon, "The Decriminalisation of Abortion: An Argument for Modernisation" (2016) 36 OJLS 358; Catharine A. MacKinnon, "Reflections on Sex Equality Under Law" (1991) 100(5) Yale Law Journal 1320, 1281–1328.

81 Hirschl (n 13) 212; India-Bangladesh comparisons are also not "unusual", as noted by Psymhe Wahud, "State, Abortion and Women: Bangladesh in Context" (2022) 23(2) Austl J Asian L 116.

82 The Penal Code 1860, s 312.

83 Keertana Kannabiran Tella, *Abortion Rights, Reproductive Justice and the State* (Routledge 2022).

nation-building project: controlling population, for which successive Planning Commissions recommended the liberalization of Bangladesh's abortion laws.[84] To that end, the State crafted a procedure, menstrual regulation (MR), involving vacuum aspiration to regularize the menstrual cycle when it is absent for up to two weeks. MR sat outside the existing criminal framing, proposed as a method of post-contraception (to deal with contraceptive failure) rather than abortion. With the introduction of MR, the State priority of controlling the population was satisfied. Any further attempt at liberalizing Bangladeshi abortion law was abandoned.[85] This is despite clear evidence that the rates of (unsafe and illegal) abortion continue to mirror those of MR,[86] suggesting that the latter alone is not sufficient in meeting women's reproductive needs.

In May 2020, a writ petition was filed before the Supreme Court of Bangladesh challenging the constitutionality of its criminal prohibition on abortion for forcing pregnancy and violating "individuals' rights to life, liberty, freedom of choice and privacy."[87] In foregrounding reproductive self-determination, the petition made strides in an arid constitutional landscape otherwise dominated by concerns about women's health.[88] Reflecting a by-now-familiar script, the petition drew heavily on *Roe's* articulation of privacy.[89] However, *Roe's* privacy-based abortion right has been subject to extensive critique. Privacy, it is argued, typically protects private spaces, like families, homes, and marriages, from State intervention. These spaces may be sources of oppression to vulnerable groups, with privacy serving as an "injury got up as a gift" for members of these groups.[90] Even if privacy protected intimate decisions, *Roe's* construction of privacy envisages only a negative duty of non-intervention on the State rather than a positive duty to assist in accessing abortion.[91] The only beneficiaries of *Roe's* right are, then, privileged groups of women, who do not need State assistance, financial or otherwise. The limitations of *Roe's* framing spill over into the Bangladeshi writ petition. In understanding privacy as protecting

84 This is in line with the global politics of population control, see Kalpana Wilson, "The 'New' Global Population Control Policies: Fuelling India's Sterilisation Atrocities" (2015) 87 Different Takes 4.

85 Wahud (n 81).

86 Susheela Singh et al, "The Incidence of Menstrual Regulation Procedures and Abortion in Bangladesh, 2010" (2012) 38(3) IPSRH 122–132.

87 *Syeda Nasrin v The Government of People's Republic of Bangladesh* WP No. ___/2020 (Supreme Court of Bangladesh) [8] (Writ Petition) (on file with author).

88 Sajeda Amin and Sara Hossain, "Women's Reproductive Rights and the Politics of Fundamentalism: A View from Bangladesh" (1995) 44 Am Univ Law 1324; For critique of health as framing for abortion, see Catherine Albertyn, "Abortion, Reproductive Rights and the Possibilities of Reproductive Justice in South African Courts" (2019) 1 OxHRH J 90–97.

89 Writ Petition (n 87) [10].

90 Catherine MacKinnon, "Privacy v. Equality: Beyond Roe v. Wade" *Feminism Unmodified* (Harvard University Press 1987) 100.

91 *Harris v McRae* 448 U.S. 297 (1980); Loretta Ross, "Understanding Reproductive Justice: Transforming the Pro-Choice Movement" 36(4) Off Our Backs 14–19.

women's personal decisions on abortion, the petition limited itself to challenging State intervention through criminal law. It did not demand State action to ensure equal access to abortion. The overreliance on *Roe* within the petition thus detracted Bangladesh from a "gender transformative outcome."[92]

Now, let us enter the alternate epistemic frame made possible by the act of imagination. Imagine that Bangladesh had looked not to *Roe* but to India to construct its privacy right. India offers an affirmative conception of privacy which moves far past *Roe's* limitations. At the outset, the Indian Supreme Court has rejected privacy's "spatial" account for serving as a "veneer for patriarchal domination and abuse of women."[93] Instead, it understands privacy as "decisional autonomy" to make "intimate decisions ... [about] one's sexual or procreative nature"[94] including "whether to bear a child or abort her pregnancy."[95] The Court also imposes on the State not just negative duties of non-intervention but also positive duties to "remove obstacles for an autonomous shaping of individual identities,"[96] based on the recognition that it is "meaningless to speak of" negative duties "in the absence of" positive duties. The State is therefore required to take "active steps" to improve access to reproductive healthcare, including abortion.[97] A turn to India instead of *Roe* would therefore have significantly altered the nature of the privacy right grounding Bangladesh's right to abortion.

Beyond privacy, a case has also been made for Bangladesh to base the constitutional challenge to its abortion law on the right to sex equality. The argument is that restrictions on abortion reflect and further stereotypical assumptions about women as mothers. They also compel women to do the labor of motherhood, which is undervalued and invisiblized because mothering is seen as natural and inevitable. Further, Bangladesh's law criminalizes a healthcare procedure only women need without altering the structurally unequal social conditions that often prompt abortions. Overall, "women are disadvantaged, for a reason specific to sex, through state-mandated restrictions on abortion."[98] In contrast to privacy, the sex equality argument, the claim goes, would recenter the "women's question," undoing historical oversight and marginalization, to bring "gender-transformative changes in the abortion discourse."[99]

Locating such an argument within Bangladesh's constitutional equality clause is, however, difficult, as the provision currently endorses a formal conception of

[92] Wahud (n 81) 117.

[93] *KS Puttaswamy v Union of India* (2017) 10 SCC 1 [140] (Chandrachud J) (*Puttaswamy*); *Joseph Shine v Union of India* (2019) 3 SCC 39 [50] (Chandrachud J.).

[94] *Puttaswamy* (n 93) [142] (Chandrchud J).

[95] Ibid [229] (Chelameshwar J) and [239] (Nariman J).

[96] Ibid [140] (Chandrachud J).

[97] *X v NCT* (n 50) [130], [133].

[98] Wahud (n 81) 119.

[99] Ibid.

equality.[100] Pregnancy falls outside formal equality's mandate of treating likes alike, as pregnancy renders women unlike, defeating their claim to equality at the threshold.[101] Looking outward, Bangladesh might first, as is common practice, turn back to the US. Here, too, Bangladesh would stumble, as the US Constitution has arguably not yet recognized pregnancy discrimination as a form of sex discrimination, bound as it is to the notion of formal equality. This is best exemplified by the cursory rejection of the sex equality argument in *Dobbs*.[102]

In contrast, India's constitutional conception of equality is substantive, aimed not at offering like treatment to likes but rather at redressing the disadvantage experienced by groups of "citizens who [have] suffered historical disadvantage, whether it be of a political, social, or economic nature".[103] It seeks to eliminate "age-long disabilities and sufferings"[104] and abolish "social inequity, the social stigma and the social disabilities in our society"[105] to achieve "real equality" among groups.[106] In transcending formal equality's sameness–difference paradigm, substantive equality treats pregnancy discrimination as sex discrimination.[107] In denying abortions, restrictive abortion laws thus not only dehumanize individual women but also subordinate women as a group.[108]

While India, too, has been slow to bring a non-discrimination lens to reproductive rights,[109] the first steps have already been taken. In *X v NCT*, the Indian Supreme Court recognized that reproduction is not just "biological" but also "political," with the decision to reproduce being bound up within broader social structures: "[a] woman's role and status in family, and society generally, is often tied to childbearing and ensuring the continuation of successive generations."[110] In *Devika Biswas*, the Court condemned State policies compelling women from marginalized groups to undergo sterilization for mirroring prevailing "systemic discrimination" by denying reproductive freedom to "the most vulnerable groups of society whose economic

[100] Ibid 118.

[101] Jennifer Hendricks, "Body and Soul: Equality, Pregnancy, and the Unitary Right to Abortion" (2009) 45 Harv CR-CLL Rev 26.

[102] *Dobbs* (n 1) 10, 11; See, in contrast, Reva Siegel, Serena Mayeri and Melissa Murray, "Equal Protection in Dobbs and Beyond" (2023) 42 Colum J Gender & L 67–97.

[103] *Navtej Singh Johar v Union of India* AIR 2018 SC 4231 [15] (Malhotra J).

[104] S Nagappa, Constituent Assembly Debates (Volume VII, November 29, 1948) [7.62.99], [7.62.101].

[105] Santanu Kumar Das, Constituent Assembly Debates (Volume XI, November 24, 1949) [7.62.172].

[106] K T Shah, Constituent Assembly Debates (Volume VII, November 29, 1948) [7.62.87].

[107] Sandra Fredman, "Reversing Roles: Bringing Men into the Frame" (2014) 10(4) Int J L in Context 445.

[108] Dorothy Roberts, "Race, Gender and Genetic Technologies: A New Reproductive Dystopia?" (2009) 34(4) Signs 1480.

[109] Gauri Pillai, *Reproductive Rights in India: The Search for a "New" Constitutional Home* (Doctor of Philosophy Thesis, University of Oxford 2022).

[110] *X v NCT* (n 50) [97].

and social conditions leave them with no meaningful choice in the matter."[111] In *Sambara Sabar*, the Orissa High Court recognized that the death of an impoverished, pregnant woman during childbirth violated not only her right to life but was also part of an abiding, historical pattern of disadvantage:

> [her death] is not an isolated instance as far as Odisha is concerned. The number of women in the tribal belts, in the rural and semi-urban areas, who have lost lives during pregnancy and as a result of unsafe deliveries is a matter for deep concern ... The increasing numbers of maternal deaths in Odisha point to a systemic failure of the health care system which appears to have failed the poorest and the weakest at a time when they need it the most.[112]

In recognizing the denial of reproductive rights as discrimination, these cases shine light on the full extent of the constitutional wrong at play, going beyond the severe impact on individual women to locating each instance as part of a systemic structure of disadvantage. This shift in emphasis is of immense relevance in a context where the very decision to grant the transitional waiver and craft the MR policy was made to fulfill State priorities, like "flushing out" Pakistani blood and controlling population, rather than to guarantee women's rights.[113] Resting on this shaky foundation, Bangladesh's MR policy and access to this service are inevitably mediated by gender and class. The policy mandates the consent of husband (or legal guardian) to obtain MR.[114] Unmarried women are, then, turned away, and sometimes accused of being sex workers. Providers hold negative perceptions even about married women seeking MR, who are pestered to keep the child and accused of infidelity, leaving them guilty and ashamed. Providers also scold and shout at women, especially illiterate and impoverished women, and demand extra fees if they cry in pain. They also blame later miscarriages on women having undergone MR previously.[115] Within these "structural and social inequalities ... shaping decision-making surrounding pregnancy terminations" in Bangladesh,[116] the criminalization of abortion not only denies women privacy but also entrenches their inequality.

Turning away from *Roe*, Bangladesh could learn from India by reading its privacy clause affirmatively and equality clause substantively. The strengthened

[111] *Devika Biswas v Union of India* (2016) 10 SCC 733 [87] (emphasis added).

[112] *Sambara Sabar v State of Odisha* 135 (2023) CLT 85 [36] (emphasis added).

[113] Wahud (n 81) 113; Shireen Huq, "Bodies as Sites of Struggle: Naripokkho and the Movement for Women's Rights in Bangladesh" (2003) 29 BDS 47.

[114] Wahud (n 81) 115.

[115] Meda Chesnay-Lind and Syeda Hadi, "Patriarchy, Abortion, and the Criminal System: Policing Female Bodies" (2017) 27(1) Women & Crim Just 73–88; Sabina Rashid et al, "Experiences of Abortion in Nepal and Menstrual Regulation in Bangladesh: A Gender Analysis" (2008) 16(2) Gender & Development 252–272.

[116] Sabina Rashid, "Quality of Care and Pregnancy Terminations for Adolescent Women in Urban Slums, Bangladesh" in Andrea Whittaker (ed), *Abortion in Asia: Local Dilemmas, Global Politics* (Berghahn Books 2010) 103.

constitutional framework could then be used as a lever to challenge Bangladesh's criminal abortion laws, in turn reconfiguring its approach to abortion. This possibility is brought to life by the act of imagination, helping us see that the "Asian region is a dynamic field of legal modernization and experiment."[117]

IV CONCLUSION

This chapter, in its title, invites readers to imagine bringing IAL to abortion so as to re-imagine key constitutional dilemmas. I have attempted such imagination by invoking two artifacts (the hypothetical referents), suspending *Roe's* dominance, and traveling along the simulated reality to explore its implications. The exercise revealed how IAL inherits from the North, here, *Roe's* legacy, but experiments, modifies, and innovates to rethink the law. The act of imagination allowed us to access this re-imagined law and, at the very least, posit it as a referent for Asia. The chapter also inaugurated imagination as a method of comparative constitutional law, of relevance beyond the immediate confines of abortion litigation. The potentiality of both the imaginative method *and* the substantive shifts to abortion law made possible by it cements the place of IAL.

[117] See generally, Introduction: The Emergence of Inter-Asian Law, this volume 4.

8

Withstanding the Rise of Illiberalism

Lessons from the COVID-19 Pandemic Responses in Taiwan, South Korea, and Singapore

Yi-Li Lee and Wen-Chen Chang

I INTRODUCTION

Globally, the rise of illiberal democracy and authoritarianism continues even post-COVID-19 pandemic, during which many governments were given blank checks to combat the virulent disease.[1] Asian countries are no exception. From Japan to the Philippines and from Mongolia to India, emergency decrees were declared, and laws were enacted to concentrate political power, curtail individual freedoms, and even disrupt periodic elections. Autocratic leaders capitalized on gains in popularity and regained the people's support.[2] Interestingly, however, against such democratic backsliding, some countries seem to have withstood the challenges posed by the pandemic and sustained their liberal and democratic governance to varying degrees. For example, in Taiwan and South Korea, democratic competition continued unabated during the pandemic, and rights assertions by affected individuals and human rights groups became even stronger.[3] In Singapore, albeit usually seen as an authoritarian constitutional polity, the government proactively sought community engagement and social support for undertaking pandemic measures, which were surprisingly less restrictive and far more transparent.[4]

1 Gábor Halmai, "The Pandemic and Illiberal Constitutional Theories" in Matthias C Kettemann and Konrad Lachmayer (eds), *Pandemocracy in Europe: Power, Parliaments and People in Times of COVID-19* (Bloomsbury 2021).

2 Joelle Grogan, "States of Emergency" (2020) 4 EJLR 338.

3 Sunghee Chung and Sujin Lee, "South Korea: Democracy, Innovation, and Surveillance" in Victor V Ramraj (ed), *COVID-19 in Asia: Law and Policy Contexts* (OUP 2021) 243; Wen-Chen Chang (張文貞) and Chun-Yuan Lin (林春元), "COVID 19 in Taiwan: Democracy, Technology and Civil Society" in Victor V Ramraj (ed), *COVID-19 in Asia: Law and Policy Contexts* (OUP 2021) 53; Wen-Chen Chang (張文貞) and Chun-Yuan Lin (林春元), "Taiwan's Effective Pandemic Control with Dialogic Constitutionalism" in Joelle Grogan and Alice Donald (eds), *Routledge Handbook of Law and the COVID-19 Pandemic* (Routledge 2022) 321–322.

4 Shirin Chua and Jaclyn L Neo, "COVID-19 as an Opportunity for Democratic Consolidation?" (*Verfassungsblog*, February 24, 2020), https://verfassungsblog.de/covid-19-as-an-opportunity-for-democratic-consolidation/, accessed August 19, 2024.

This chapter aims to investigate the respective constitutional foundations, jurisprudential developments, and democratic processes in Taiwan, South Korea, and Singapore that have enabled the varying degree of resistance against the rise of illiberal and authoritarian governance during the pandemic. While South Korea and Taiwan are strong democracies and Singapore is usually characterized as an illiberal and soft authoritarian polity, their experiences in combating the spread of COVID-19 have revealed three common features. First, by learning from one another's experiences with severe acute respiratory syndrome (SARS) and Middle East respiratory syndrome (MERS), as well as those of other Asian countries,[5] the pandemic responses in these three countries were not given blank checks but subjected to democratic oversight and political accountability. The incorporation of openness, trust, and transparency into government policies and practices in combating the pandemic helped the three countries avoid pathologies usually associated with democratic backsliding. Second, unlike other authoritarian governments in the region,[6] these three countries have adopted a relatively democratic approach. Not only was civil society oversight involved, but also institutional checks and balances both vertically and horizontally remained strong and effective. Third, judicial deference was generally provided by the courts of the three countries if the government measures did not seriously or repeatedly violate basic rights and fundamental principles. Meanwhile, a harder look would be given if rights protection was in stronger demand with less harm to public health safety.

As this chapter argues, the combating pandemic experiences of Taiwan, South Korea, and Singapore have demonstrated that adhering to democratic checks and balances within the framework of constitutional separation of powers was effective in managing the pandemic crisis. Democratic processes and institutions could continue to function within the established legal frameworks to ensure due process, civic participation, and political accountability during the pandemic. In addition, non-governmental organizations (NGOs) and courts in these three countries have played counterbalancing roles and acted as intermediaries between the government and affected individuals challenging government policies and pandemic measures. These experiences demonstrate that tensions between effectively combating the pandemic and preserving rule of law and human rights can be mitigated democratically. Additionally, Taiwan, South Korea, and Singapore share several common characteristics in their responses to the COVID-19 pandemic. Given that COVID-19 was a transboundary problem, these countries' experiences highlighted considerable

5 Jaewan Kim et al, "Why Have the Republic of Korea, Taiwan, and Singapore Coped Well with COVID-19 and What Are the Lessons Learned from Their Experiences?" (2022) 63(3) YMJ 297–300.

6 Paul Krugman, "How China Lost the Covid War" (*New York Times*, November 28, 2022), www.nytimes.com/2022/11/28/opinion/china-covid-autocracy-democracy.html, accessed August 19, 2024.

cross-jurisdictional learning and adaptation. Notably, they borrowed from each other's strategies in pandemic legal frameworks, multi-level coordination between central and local governments, and the active role of NGOs. Together, these elements contributed to the effective management of the pandemic across all three countries. This insight that pandemic governance presents no excuse for democratic backsliding in these three Asian countries may enrich pandemic governance studies and shed light on the discussion of Inter-Asian Law.

II COVID-19 PANDEMIC RESPONSES IN TAIWAN, SOUTH KOREA, AND SINGAPORE

A. *Pandemic Legislation: Lessons from SARS and MERS Experiences*

To mitigate the impact of the COVID-19 pandemic, many governments implemented extraordinary measures such as declaring emergency decrees that easily raised concerns about grave human rights violations and government powers aggrandizement. Learning from their experiences of SARS and MERS,[7] the governments of South Korea, Taiwan, and Singapore, however, did not issue any emergency decrees but instead relied on existing laws or enacted new laws to manage the pandemic crisis.

In 2015, South Korea experienced the largest MERS outbreak outside the Middle East.[8] To prevent the previous mistakes of poor risk communication and government secrecy, the National Assembly revised the Infectious Disease Control and Prevention Act (IDCPA),[9] effectively preparing the government to combat COVID-19. Key revisions include providing a wide scope for administrative orders enabling the Minister of Health and Welfare and local governments to take necessary measures.[10] For instance, Article 34-2(1) allows public health authorities to disclose information on confirmed cases to the public. Article 40 authorizes the authority to shut down contaminated locations.[11] Article 76-2(1) authorizes the Minister of Health and Welfare to collect personal data to track confirmed patients without a court warrant during infectious disease emergencies.[12] Article 76-2(2) allows public

7 Kim et al (n 5); Brian Y An and Shui-Yan Tang, "Lessons from COVID-19 Responses in East Asia: Institutional Infrastructure and Enduring Policy Instruments" (2020) 50(6–7) ARPA 792–793.

8 Gyooho Lee, "Legitimacy and Constitutionality of Contact Tracing in Pandemic in the Republic of Korea" (2020) SSRN Electronic Journal 3–4.

9 June Park and Eunbin Chung, "Learning from Past Pandemic Governance: Early Response and Public-Private Partnerships in Testing of COVID-19 in South Korea" (2021) 137 WD 105198.

10 Younsik Kim, "Uncertain Future of Privacy Protection under the Korean Public Health Emergency Preparedness Governance amid the COVID-19 Pandemic" (2022) 8(1) CSS 3.

11 Article 34-2 (1) of the IDCPA.

12 Article 76-2 (1) of the IDCPA.

health authorities to require medical institutions to provide information on patients and those feared to be infected.[13]

To enhance the government's response to the COVID-19 crisis, the Korean National Assembly revised the IDCPA, the Quarantine Act, and the Medical Services Act, which the President promulgated on March 4, 2020.[14] The revised IDCPA aimed to enhance responses to those exposed, regulate medical supply flows abroad, and strengthen epidemiological investigation capacity. For example, Article 40-3 of the revised IDCPA enables public health authorities to ban exports of drugs and medical supplies, such as face masks and hand sanitizers, when shortages are expected.[15] The Act provides a wide-ranging list of measures under provisions stating that public health authorities "shall take all or some of the following measures." To balance the protection of human rights, Article 34-2 of the IDCPA states that "personal information determined to be irrelevant to the prevention of infectious diseases by Presidential Decree, such as sex, age, and so on, shall be excluded."[16] The revised Quarantine Act clarifies the legal basis for requests not to allow anyone infected or suspected of being infected with COVID-19 to enter or leave South Korea, excluding South Korean nationals.[17] Finally, the revised Medical Service Act aims to establish and implement more effective monitoring of infections within healthcare facilities, obligating heads of medical institutions and medical personnel to voluntarily report to the Minister of Health and Welfare if an infection is detected within the institution.[18] These revisions formed the legal basis for the Korean government to implement administrative countermeasures against COVID-19.

However, some legal provisions raised concerns regarding privacy and surveillance.[19] Article 76-2 of the revised IDCPA allows national public health authorities or local governments to request information from various governmental and non-governmental institutions, potentially enabling infringements of human rights and rendering the protection of personal information ineffective.[20] Additionally, the ban

[13] Article 76-2 (2) of the IDCPA.

[14] "South Korea: Parliament Responded Quickly to COVID-19 by Amending Three Acts" (*LIBRARY*, June 4, 2020), www.loc.gov/item/global-legal-monitor/2020-06-04/south-korea-parliament-responded-quickly-to-covid-19-by-amending-three-acts/, accessed August 19, 2024.

[15] Gyooho Lee, "Legislative and Administrative Responses to COVID-19 Virus in the Republic of Korea" (April 28, 2020), https://ssrn.com/abstract=3587595, accessed August 19, 2024.

[16] Jeong-In Yun, "Law-Making and Accountability in Responding to COVID-19: The Case of South Korea", https://law.unimelb.edu.au/__data/assets/pdf_file/0010/3476809/MF20-Web2-SouthKorea-FINAL.pdf, accessed August 19, 2024.

[17] Lee (n 8).

[18] Ibid.

[19] Woosung Hwang, "COVID-19 in South Korea: Privacy and Discrimination Concerns" (*Bill of Health*, June 9, 2020), https://blog.petrieflom.law.harvard.edu/2020/06/09/south-korea-global-responses-covid19/, accessed August 19 2024.

[20] Seokmin Lee and Tae-Ho Kim, "South Korea's Combating COVID-19 under the Rule of Law" (*Verfassungsblog*, April 8, 2021), https://verfassungsblog.de/south-koreas-combating-covid-19-under-the-rule-of-law/, accessed August 19 2024.

on gatherings in the IDCPA, among the most commonly used administrative public health measures by the Korean government to restrict viral spread, may infringe constitutional rights. These gathering restrictions have also been used against protests, religious events, and gatherings at certain businesses.[21]

Taiwan has learned hard lessons from the 2003 SARS outbreak, which resulted in the loss of medical personnel and individual lives.[22] In response, the Communicable Disease Control Act (CDC Act) was substantially amended. The CDC Act now serves as the framework for government action on communicable disease control and public health emergencies. It authorizes the creation of a centralized command system with clear power divisions between national and local governments. The Central Epidemic Command Center (CECC) or Central Command represents the central government, setting standards and providing regulatory measures such as inspection, contact tracing, quarantine, isolation, travel restrictions, requisition, expropriation, and compensation.[23] For example, Article 20 of the CDC Act requires the government to stock sufficient quantities of pharmaceuticals, devices, and protective equipment for disease control. It also includes provisions against discrimination and human rights infringement in the name of disease control. Local governments are primarily tasked with case-by-case enforcement.

Three key provisions in the CDC Act balance human rights and individual freedoms.[24] Article 10 prohibits the disclosure of information related to patients or suspected patients with communicable diseases, imposing fines for violations.[25] Article 11 guarantees the dignity and legal rights of those with communicable diseases, medical personnel, patients under quarantine, and their families, ensuring they are respected and protected without discrimination. Article 12 obliges public and private persons and institutions not to deny patients with communicable diseases their rights to education, employment, nursing care, or housing, nor to provide any unfair treatment.[26]

To supplement the CDC Act, Taiwan's Legislative Yuan passed the Special Act for Prevention, Relief, and Revitalization Measures for Severe Pneumonia with Novel Pathogens ("Special Covid-19 Act") on February 25, 2020. This Act authorized a special budget of TWD 60 billion (approximately US$2.15 billion)[27] and set a term from January 15, 2020, to June 30, 2021, with the possibility of extension by the Legislative Yuan. Since the CDC Act had already equipped the government with

[21] Ibid.

[22] Chang and Lin (n 3, 2021).

[23] Chuanranbing Fanjhih Fa, *[Communicable Disease Control Act]*, amended June 19, 2019, Articles 36, 37, 38, 44, 45, 48, 58, https://perma.cc/NV4N-KMCN, accessed August 19, 2024.

[24] Chang and Lin (n 3, 2021).

[25] Fines from TWD 90,000 up to TWD 450,000 can be imposed in case of violation, according to Article 64 of the CDC Act.

[26] In case of violating Articles 11 and 12, fines from TWD 10,000 up to TWD 150,000 can be imposed, according to Article 69 of the CDC Act.

[27] Chang and Lin (n 3, 2021).

significant power against the pandemic, most provisions of the Special COVID-19 Act focused on relief, compensation, and stimulus. However, two provisions of the Special COVID-19 Act caused concern. Article 7 was criticized for granting the Central Command exclusive power to implement necessary measures for pandemic control, potentially violating the principle of proportionality and infringing on freedom of movement.[28] Additionally, Article 8 gave the Central Command the power to release personal data if an individual violated a quarantine or isolation order, raising concerns about possible violations of privacy protection and proportionality.[29]

Singapore, along with South Korea and Taiwan, utilized the Infectious Diseases Act (IDA) instead of emergency measures to address the COVID-19 crisis.[30] The Act, reinforced after the 2003 SARS outbreak, involves protocols to identify and isolate infected individuals for two weeks.[31] On April 7, 2020, the Parliament of Singapore passed the COVID-19 (Temporary Measures) Act (CTMA), authorizing the Ministry of Health to implement necessary public health measures if COVID-19 poses a serious threat. The CTMA includes provisions to restrict activities to prevent virus spread, compensate distressed parties, facilitate in-person meetings, maintain court functions through remote technology, and suspend contractual obligations. To enforce the IDA,[32] the Ministry of Health implemented subsidiary legislation, such as the COVID-19 (Temporary Measures) (Control Order) Regulations 2020, regulating corporate meetings, charities, trade unions, and societies, reducing rent, and providing temporary relief for unfulfilled contracts.[33]

In May 2020, the Parliament of Singapore revised Article 64 of its Constitution, allowing members to meet remotely if it is difficult or unsafe to assemble in one place.[34] This revision designates a temporary alternative parliamentary meeting location, valid for six months with a possible six-month extension.[35] After the

28 Ching-Fu Lin (林勤富), "Taiwan: Legal Response to Covid-19" in Jeff King and Octávio L M Ferraz (eds), *The Oxford Compendium of National Legal Responses to Covid-19* (Oxford Constitutional Law, July 2021), https://oxcon.ouplaw.com/view/10.1093/law-occ19/law-occ19-e18, accessed August 19, 2024.

29 Ibid.

30 Chua and Neo (n 4).

31 Catherine Tay Swee Kian and Fatimah Lateef, "Infectious Diseases Law and Severe Acute Respiratory Syndrome – Medical and Legal Responses and Implications: The Singapore experience" 7(2) (2004) PJR 123.

32 Jaclyn L Neo and Darius Lee, "Singapore's Legislative Approach to the COVID-19 Public Health 'Emergency'" (*Verfassungsblog*, April 18, 2020), https://verfassungsblog.de/singapores-legislative-approach-to-the-covid-19-public-health-emergency/, accessed August 19, 2024.

33 Ibid.

34 Constitution of the Republic of Singapore (Amendment) Act 2020. https://sso.agc.gov.sg/Acts-Supp/22-2020/Published/20200520, accessed August 19, 2024.

35 Shirin Chua and Jaclyn L Neo, "Democracy in the Time of COVID-19: Pandemic Management, Public Trust and Democratic Consolidation in Singapore" in Joelle Grogan and Alice Donald (eds), *Routledge Handbook of Law and the COVID-19 Pandemic* (Routledge 2022) 84–95.

July 2020 parliamentary elections, this framework was implemented for the first time during the State Opening of Parliament.[36]

In terms of legal frameworks, as discussed above, each country not only adapted its legislative responses by learning from others' experiences with SARS and MERS but also demonstrated significant cross-jurisdictional learning and borrowing to manage the pandemic crisis effectively. For example, inspired by South Korea's amendments to its IDCPA after MERS, Taiwan's CDC Act empowered the CECC to coordinate with local governments on contact tracing and data collection, establishing a real-time, centralized system.[37] Another example is Singapore's IDA, which included public health data management provisions. Drawing inspiration from Taiwan's CECC, Singapore used digital platforms to gather public policy feedback, enabling local districts to tailor responses to community needs while aligning with central guidelines.[38]

B. *Pandemic Central and Local Politics*

The global experiences of the COVID-19 pandemic have shown that tensions can easily arise between national and local governments, particularly when there is uncertainty about the division of competences. To address the rapid spread of the pandemic, intergovernmental dialogue and political coordination between national and local governments are crucial.[39] Different levels of government embody different merits and limits. One advantage of centralized power is that it can provide more consistent policies and mobilize resources on a large scale, yet it may be incapable of dealing with a sudden outbreak. In contrast, local governments are on the frontlines of the crisis and can respond immediately but also require greater discretion in their swift responses.[40] Local delegation may better cope with local variations and mobilize resources, and yet fragmented implementation may result in unequal treatment and inconsistency. In the face of the pandemic, neither central nor local government alone guaranteed the best policy.

To strengthen collaboration within multi-level governance on pandemic management, South Korea and Taiwan restructured and centralized their respective public health approaches and institutions after the SARS outbreak in Taiwan in 2003 and the MERS outbreak in South Korea in 2015. These reforms have enhanced the ability of multiple-level governments to respond effectively. For example, after 2015, South Korea's reforms placed primary responsibility for epidemics in the hands

36 Ibid.

37 Joseph Wong, "Combating COVID-19 in Democratic Taiwan and South Korea" (2020) 119(818) CH 211–212.

38 Kim et al (n 5).

39 Joelle Grogan, "COVID-19, Rule of Law and Democracy: Analysis of Legal Responses to a Global Health Crisis" (2022) 14 HJRL 349.

40 Ibid.

of the Korean Centers for Disease Control and Prevention.[41] In Taiwan, the Central Command, a rapid-response agency, was created within the Ministry of Health and Welfare.[42]

During the pandemic, the relations between national and local governments in both South Korea and Taiwan were often characterized by tension. For instance, when South Korea faced shortages of COVID-19 vaccines, Mayor Kwon Young-jin of Daegu City announced that Daegu would purchase the Pfizer vaccine through a foreign trading company. The city submitted its import proposal to the central government. However, the Ministry of Health and Welfare rejected this action as untrustworthy,[43] and Pfizer also raised concerns about the foreign trading company, noting that its vaccines are not provided through intermediaries. Consequently, the mayor apologized to the citizens and the entire nation in a news conference and withdrew the proposal.[44]

Another dispute between national and local governments in South Korea concerns privacy issues. With the need for real-time tracing, the IDCPA was amended to include provisions for pandemic surveillance.[45] These provisions authorized national health authorities to access information that was previously exclusive to law enforcement authorities. This significantly enhanced their capacity to focus testing and quarantine efforts on individuals at greater risk of infection.[46] Hence, the central government of South Korea employed two apps to trace and isolate those infected or suspected of being infected. One app is used for contact tracing, notifying individuals if they may have crossed paths with a confirmed case. The other app is used to monitor self-quarantine compliance.[47] However, these measures were criticized for infringing on the privacy of infected individuals, who did not consent to them and who faced social stigma. Some local governments also expressed concerns over excessive collection and disclosure of personal data in the process of epidemiological investigation and through the use of contact tracing devices.[48] They were worried that the use of those digital tracing apps might infringe

41 Lee (n 15).

42 Chang and Lin (n 3, 2021).

43 Jun Ji-hye, "Daegu-arranged Pfizer Vaccine Offer Improper: Gov't" (*Korea Times*, June 3, 2021), www.koreatimes.co.kr/www/nation/2021/06/119_309867.html, accessed August 19, 2024.

44 Yoo Cheong-mo, "Daegu Mayor Apologizes for Controversial Bid to Import Pfizer Vaccines" (*Yonhap News Agency*, June 8, 2021), https://en.yna.co.kr/view/AEN20210608006300315, accessed August 19, 2024.

45 Myungji Yang, "Behind South Korea's Success in Containing Covid-19: Surveillance Technology Infrastructures" (*Social Science Research Council*, June 21, 2021), https://items.ssrc.org/covid-19-and-the-social-sciences/covid-19-in-east-asia/behind-south-koreas-success-in-containing-covid-19-surveillance-technology-infrastructures, accessed August 19, 2024.

46 Lee (n 15).

47 Hwang (n 19).

48 Sunghee Chung and Sujin Lee, "South Korea: Democracy, Innovation, and Surveillance" in Victor V Ramraj (eds), *COVID-19 in Asia: Law and Policy Contexts* (OUP 2021) 243.

on individuals' privacy and human rights through excessive collection and release of personal information.[49]

In Taiwan, significant executive power has been vested in the Central Command. Under Article 37(3) of the CDC Act, the Command was the ultimate authority in coordinating the anti-pandemic efforts. Some disputes have arisen when the Central Command has opposed the introduction of stricter disease control measures by local governments. For example, in August 2020, Chang Hua County decided to test all outside visitors for COVID-19, regardless of whether they had symptoms. Even if some epidemiologists supported the measure, it raised ethical concerns that the testing was not properly reviewed as part of a government-funded research project and that the proper review process had not been followed.[50] Accordingly, the testing was suspended because it violated the Human Subjects Research Act of 2016. Concerned that false positives might overwhelm the country's medical system and undermine COVID-19 prevention measures, the CECC overruled the initiative.

Furthermore, local governments expressed their discontent with the Central Command. Some demanded more discretion and resources, while others demanded more precise rules and procedures. The dissenting voices prompted the Central Command to adjust its measures and coordinate with local authorities. Upon the declaration of level 3, the Central Command held a National Epidemic Prevention Meeting with city and county governments to coordinate regulatory measures and distribute testing resources.[51] Another example is Kinmen County's policy of requiring all passengers entering the island to be tested for COVID-19. Citing Article 37 of the CDC Act, the Central Command revoked the order. Due to the limited medical resources of this outlying island, the Central Command then agreed to test all passengers in Taiwan's main airports before they visited Kinmen.[52]

During the COVID-19 pandemic, multi-level governance frameworks that enhanced coordination between central and local governments in pandemic management[53] were not only implemented in Taiwan, South Korea, and Singapore, but also evolved as part of a learning process among these three countries. In South

[49] Cheol Kang and Ilhak Lee, "COVID-19 Pandemic, Transparency, and 'Polidemic' in the Republic of Korea" (2021) 13 Asian BRev 213.

[50] "Taiwan's Changhua Conducted Undisclosed Coronavirus Tests for Six Months: CECC" (*Taiwan News*, August 20, 2020), www.taiwannews.com.tw/en/news/3991295, accessed August 19, 2024.

[51] "National Epidemic Prevention Meeting Report at Morning Press Conference on 21 May" (*Centers for Disease Control*, May 21, 2021), www.cdc.gov.tw/En/Bulletin/Detail/V5_1p7SPS5FJ9vt9WzmXRA?typeid=158, accessed August 19, 2024.

[52] Matthew Strong, "Compulsory COVID Tests at Airports on Taiwan's Outlying Islands are Illegal: CECC" (*Taiwan News*, June 1, 2021), www.taiwannews.com.tw/en/news/4214233, accessed August 19, 2024.

[53] Grogan (n 39).

Korea, for instance, amendments to the IDCPA included data-sharing practices that local governments adopted.[54] These centralized data were accessible by local jurisdictions, mirroring Taiwan's integration model,[55] and facilitated rapid, localized responses while maintaining alignment with national health regulations. Singapore implemented a similar approach by utilizing digital platforms to collect public feedback on pandemic measures, inspired by Taiwan's responsive CECC model. Local districts used these platforms to address specific community concerns while ensuring consistency with central guidelines.[56] Through shared experiences and mutual adaptations, each country drew insights from the others, refining governance frameworks to manage public health crises more effectively.

C. *Elections, Recalls, and Referendum*

The COVID-19 pandemic has put democracy and elections at risk across the world. A number of scheduled elections were either postponed or canceled to protect electoral integrity. In addition, despite the ongoing pandemic, a number of countries adopted various voting procedures in their electoral processes. Some countries decided to hold elections in person despite the high infection risks and practical difficulties of holding elections. Other countries opted for remote voting procedures, such as postal voting.[57]

In contrast to other countries, South Korea, Taiwan, and Singapore still held their elections as scheduled. On April 15, 2020, South Korea was one of the first countries to hold parliamentary elections following the pandemic outbreak. On March 9, 2022, it also held its presidential election. In addition, new voting procedures were adopted in elections during the pandemic.[58] For example, in February 2022, the lawmakers of South Korea revised their election laws to allow infected voters to vote in the presidential election from quarantine or healthcare centers and to allow early voting in parliamentary and presidential elections.[59]

54 Shin Ae Hong, "Toward Better Pandemic Governance and Preparedness: South Korea's Whole-of-Nation Approach to COVID-19" (2024) 24 BMCPH 2126.

55 Chang and Lin (n 3, 2022).

56 Bryan W K Chow et al, "Use of a Digital Contact Tracing System in Singapore to Mitigate COVID-19 Spread" (2023) 23 BMCPH 2253.

57 International IDEA, "Global Overview of COVID-19: Impact on Elections" (*International IDEA*, December 1, 2022), www.idea.int/news-media/multimedia-reports/global-overview-covid-19-impact-elections, accessed August 19, 2024.

58 Yun (n 16).

59 Antonio Spinelli and Luke Butcher, "Managing Elections During Covid-19: The Republic of Korea's First Crucial Test" (*International IDEA*, May 24, 2022), www.idea.int/sites/default/files/news/news-images/managing-elections-during-covid-19-the-republic-of-koreas-first-crucial-test-en.pdf, accessed August 19, 2024.

In addition, the National Election Commission of South Korea provided comprehensive plans to regulate elections.[60]

In Taiwan, all 2020 elections were held as scheduled despite the pandemic. After the Central Command was established to address the pandemic crisis on January 20, 2020, several elections including the reelection for the mayor of Kaohsiung.[61] In addition, Taiwan also held a referendum on December 18, 2021. The election for local officials and councilors was also held on November 26, 2022.[62] The National Election Commission of Taiwan also provided comprehensive plans to regulate elections and referendums.[63]

On May 4, 2020, Singapore's lawmakers passed the Parliamentary Elections (COVID-19 Special Arrangements) Act, which established a special statutory regulation for holding parliamentary elections during the ongoing pandemic. The Act allows quarantined voters to vote in places of mass isolation, such as hotels or student dormitories,[64] and candidates who are ill to miss the nomination process and to make special arrangements for polling and counting. Following the dissolution of Parliament on June 23, 2020, Singapore, like South Korea and Taiwan, held its 2020 general election despite the high public health risks and economic crisis brought on by the pandemic.[65]

D. *Judicial Response*

A pandemic presents a compelling challenge for courts – strong or weak – to provide oversight when the government fails to meet its legal obligations to protect its citizens. In backsliding democracies, judicial oversight is typically limited, ineffective, or nonexistent due to lack of independence, authority, and/or capacity.[66] In contrast, courts in South Korea, Taiwan, and Singapore continue to operate smoothly during the pandemic. Pandemic-related lawsuits are categorized as follows:

[60] Sung Lee, "Democracy in the Time of COVID-19: Lessons from South Korea" (*USGLC*, April 24, 2020), www.usglc.org/blog/democracy-in-the-time-of-covid-19-lessons-from-south-korea, accessed August 19, 2024.

[61] Lin (n 28).

[62] Lev Nachman, "How Taiwan's Midterm Elections Work" (*The Diplomat*, November 7, 2022), https://thediplomat.com/2022/11/how-taiwans-midterm-elections-work, accessed August 19, 2024.

[63] National Election Commission of Taiwan, "Prevention Measures on the Coronavirus Disease during Local by-Elections" (*National Election Commission of Taiwan*, March 24, 2020), https://web.cec.gov.tw/english/cms/newseng/32821 accessed August 19, 2024.

[64] Jaclyn Neo and Shirin Chua, "Singapore: Legal Response to Covid-19" (*Oxford Constitutional Law*, May 2022), https://oxcon.ouplaw.com/display/10.1093/law-occ19/law-occ19-e30, accessed August 19, 2024.

[65] Charmaine Ng, "Singapore GE2020: High Court Dismisses Constitutional Challenge Against Holding Election Now; Appeal Set for Tuesday" (*Straits Times*, June 30, 2020), www.straitstimes.com/politics/singapore-ge2020-high-court-dismisses-constitutional-challenge-against-holding-election-now?close = true, accessed August 19, 2024.

[66] Grogan (n 39).

Habeas Corpus Lawsuits

The implementation of regulatory measures for pandemic control, including inspections, contact tracings, quarantines, and inbound and outbound travel restrictions, undoubtedly raised human rights concerns. In Taiwan, several judicial challenges against quarantine orders and civil penalties were mostly rejected by the courts. For instance, the Taiwan High Court approved a petition concerning quarantine orders and due process under Article 8 of Taiwan's Constitution and the 2014 Habeas Corpus Act that the district court had dismissed.[67] Another argument claimed that strict discharge requirements for repeated negative laboratory tests resulted in an unjustified and unconstitutional extension of quarantine, but this petition was also rejected.[68] Concerns also arose regarding the deportation of foreign nationals. *J.Y. Interpretation No. 708* of the Taiwanese Constitutional Court granted legal remedies to foreign nationals facing deportation or temporary detention.[69] However, in May 2020, a migrant worker's appeal against his temporary detention due to the pandemic was denied, considering the detention facility's hygiene measures. After considering all relevant factors, including the detention facility's hygiene measures, the court eventually denied his request.[70]

Lawsuits against Other Government Measures

In Singapore, political activist Han Hui Hui and others had their appeal against vaccine-related regulations denied by the High Court, which found the petition lacking legal merit.[71] Courts also jailed individuals who refused to wear masks for violating COVID-19 regulations.[72] In South Korea, bans on mass gatherings were challenged but mostly upheld by the courts due to the pandemic's severity.[73] The Korean government's vaccine pass programs also faced legal challenges. For example, one constitutional petition challenged this vaccine pass system as violating the fundamental rights of unvaccinated people. The Constitutional Court, however, dismissed the petition on procedural grounds.[74] However, the Seoul Administrative

[67] Chang and Lin (n 3, 2022).

[68] Ibid.

[69] *JY Interpretation No. 708*, Judicial Yuan, ROC.

[70] Hsinchu Difang Fayuan [Taiwan Hsinchu District Court] May 13, 2020, Minguo 109 (Yi) No. 3 Ruling.

[71] Lakeisha Leo, "High Court Dismisses Bid by Activist Han Hui Hui and Others to Declare Vaccine-Related Measures as Unlawful, Irrational" (*News Asia*, June 16, 2022), www.channelnewsasia.com/singapore/high-court-dismiss-han-hui-hui-bid-covid-19-vaccination-measures-unlawful-irrational-2751291, accessed August 19, 2024.

[72] David Sun, "'Sovereign' Briton Who Refused to Wear Mask on MRT Deported" (*Straits Times*, August 21, 2021), www.straitstimes.com/singapore/courts-crime/sovereign-briton-who-refused-to-wear-mask-on-train-deported, accessed August 19, 2024.

[73] Lee and Kim (n 20).

[74] "헌법재판소 2022. 1. 11.자 2021헌마1485 결정 [방역패스 위헌확인]" (*CaseNote*, January 11, 2022), https://casenote.kr/%ED%97%8C%EB%B2%95%EC%9E%AC%ED%8C%90%EC%86%8C/2021%ED%97%8C%EB%A7%881485, accessed August 19, 2024.

Court temporarily excluded private educational facilities from vaccine pass mandates and suspended the vaccine pass plan for children at all seventeen types of facilities.[75] In Taiwan, after the May 2021 wave of infection, opposition politicians filed a lawsuit arguing that the Central Command was legally obligated to provide the public with sufficient vaccines. The plaintiffs' claim was rejected since the court held that there was no legal basis for requiring such an obligation.[76]

Compensation Lawsuits

In Korea, the Seoul District Court awarded compensation to a man harmed by the COVID-19 vaccine.[77] The Disease Control and Prevention Agency had previously rejected his application, but the Seoul Administrative Court admitted his petition, recognizing a causal relationship between the vaccine and his condition.[78] The court also recognized victim status and compensation to a paralyzed nursing assistant post-vaccination.[79] Additionally, the Seoul Central District Court ordered the Ministry of Education to compensate individuals barred from the national qualification exam due to COVID-19 symptoms.[80]

Election Lawsuit

In Taiwan, the quarantine order banning COVID-19-positive individuals from voting was criticized for violating fair election principles. Despite requests for policy revision, the National Election Commission defended the ban's constitutionality,[81] and the Taipei High Administrative Court dismissed an injunction petition, prioritizing public health.[82] In Singapore, a petition argued that COVID-19 measures

[75] Han-soo Lee, "Court Blocks Covid-19 Vaccine Rule Partially" (*Korea Biomed*, January 14, 2022), www.koreabiomed.com/news/articleView.html?idxno = 12965, accessed August 19, 2024.

[76] Taipei High Administrative Court, Szuzi 110, No. 623 Ruling.

[77] For the first time, a Korean court in Seoul awarded compensation to a man claiming to suffer from injury due to COVID-19 vaccine (*COVID-19 Litigation*, September 28, 2022), www.covid19litigation.org/news/2022/09/south-korea-court-orders-compensation-side-effects-covid-19-vaccine, accessed August 19, 2024.

[78] "법원 '백신 부작용 국가가 보상' 첫 판결, 줄소송 예고" (September 20, 2022), http://weekly.chosun.com/news/articleView.html?idxno = 22142, accessed August 19 2024.

[79] "South Korea to Compensate Nurse Paralyzed after COVID-19 Shot" (*Reuters*, August 6, 2021), www.reuters.com/world/asia-pacific/skorea-nurse-eligible-govt-benefit-after-covid-19-vaccine-reaction-2021-08-06/, accessed August 19, 2024.

[80] Yonhap, "Govt. Ordered to Compensate COVID-19 Patients Barred from Teacher Qualification Test" (*Korea Herald*, December 9, 2021), www.koreaherald.com/view.php?ud = 20211209000403, accessed August 19, 2024.

[81] "Election Body Says COVID-19 Ban Not Unconstitutional" (*Taipei Times*, November 22, 2022), www.taipeitimes.com/News/taiwan/archives/2022/10/22/2003787519, accessed August 19, 2024.

[82] Central News Agency, "The Taipei High Administrative Court Dismissed This Injunction Petition by Infected People" *The Central News Agency (中央通訊社)* (November 25, 2022), https://tw.news.yahoo.com/%E7%A2%BA%E8%A8%BA%E8%80%85%E7%84%A1%E6%B3%95%E6%8A%95%E7%A5%A8-%E6%B0%91%E7%9C%BE%E5%90%91%E6%B3%95%E9%99%A2%E8%81%B2%E8%AB%8B%E5%81%87%E8%99%95%E5%88%86%E9%81%AD%E9%A7%81-092058353.html (in Chinese), accessed August 19, 2024.

deprived voters of free and fair elections. The Court of Appeal rejected this, finding no evidence that the measures violated voting rights, stating that health concerns should be addressed separately.[83]

Misinformation

Governments in all three countries have strengthened laws against spreading misinformation about infectious diseases. Taiwan's Special Covid-19 Act and CDC Act impose criminal penalties for disseminating false information.[84] South Korea's law includes severe penalties for spreading fake news online.[85] Criminal sanctions against misinformation raise concerns about free speech infringement. In Taiwan, a local prosecutor charged an individual for sharing false COVID-19 information on Facebook. Initially acquitted, the case was appealed, and the Taipei High Court sentenced the accused to three months in jail under the Special COVID-19 Act.[86]

NGOs

During the COVID-19 pandemic, human rights groups in South Korea, Taiwan, and Singapore actively voiced concerns regarding legislative and regulatory measures that could serve to aggrandize government powers. South Korea and Taiwan feature a fairly robust civil society that has played a crucial role in shaping democratic constitutionalism and human rights discourse.[87] These entities are alert to potential compromises of fundamental freedoms or civil liberties. For example, human rights NGOs in Taiwan were the first to oppose the passage of the Special COVID-19 Act due to its expansive delegation of power.[88] When the digital tracking program was launched, concerns regarding privacy violations were raised.[89] One

83 Daniel De Costa Augustin v. Attorney-General [2020] SGCA 60, www.elitigation.sg/gd/s/2020_SGCA_60, accessed August 19, 2024.

84 To supplement the CDC Act of Taiwan, the Legislative Yuan of Taiwan passed the Special Act for Prevention, Relief, and Revitalization Measures for Severe Pneumonia with Novel Pathogens (Special Covid-19 Act) on February 25, 2020.

85 "Gov't to Clamp down on Coronavirus Fake News" (*Korea Times*, August 25, 2022), www.koreatimes.co.kr/www/nation/2020/08/356_294917.html, accessed August 19, 2024.

86 Covid-19 Litigation, "Taiwan – Taipei Court Condemns Facebook User for Spreading Incorrect Information on COVID-19" (*COVID-19 Litigation*, May 16, 2022), www.covid19litigation.org/news/2022/05/taiwan-taipei-court-condemns-facebook-user-spreading-incorrect-information-covid-19, accessed August 19, 2024.

87 Jiunn-rong Yeh (葉俊榮), "Marching Towards Civic Constitutionalism with Sunflowers" in Brian Jones (ed), *Law and Politics of the Taiwan Sunflower and Hong Kong Umbrella Movements* (Routledge 2017) 52–53; Tae-Ung Baik, "Public Interest Litigation in South Korea" in Po Jen Yap and Holning Lau (eds), *Public Interest Litigation in Asia* (Routledge 2010) 115–135.

88 Chang and Lin (n 3, 2022).

89 Ching-Fu Lin (林勤富), Chien-Huei Wu (吳建輝) and Chuan-Feng Wu (吳全峰), "Reimagining the Administrative State in Times of Global Health Crisis: An Anatomy of Taiwan's Regulatory Actions in Response to the COVID-19 Pandemic" (2020) 11(2) EJRR 256.

well-known NGO, the Taiwan Association for Human Rights, expressed worry that the vast amount of personal data collected by such digital systems may be misused by the government. It was due to these NGOs' persistence that the deletion of relevant personal data and security of data transmissions were promised and eventually written into the Special COVID-19 Act.[90] Another, more recent, example arose when the CECC required all inbound passengers, including Taiwanese nationals, to provide a test report before arriving at an airport in Taiwan. Human rights NGOs and lawyers – citing the fundamental right to return home – successfully pushed the CECC to make changes and accommodations overnight.[91]

In South Korea, the Human Rights Commission and NGOs have expressed similar concerns with respect to the excessive collection and disclosure of personal data in the process of epidemiological investigations and contact-tracing devices.[92] They were concerned that such digital tracing apps would infringe on privacy and human rights due to the excessive collection and use of personal information. In response to their concerns and after taking advice from the Human Rights Commission, the South Korean government narrowed the scope of information collected on confirmed COVID-19 cases that could be released to government agencies or the public.[93]

Non-governmental organizations in Singapore also criticized the pandemic measures of the Singapore government, particularly on the issues of migrant workers.[94] For example, NGOs expressed their deep concerns about the implementation of the revised Employment of Foreign Manpower Regulations, which allows employers to confine migrant workers in their accommodation.[95]

During the COVID-19 pandemic, NGOs in Taiwan, South Korea, and Singapore also played key roles in cross-jurisdictional learning, borrowing, and collaboration. They hosted numerous virtual workshops and training sessions to enhance public health awareness, promoting educational campaigns on hygiene, vaccination, and social distancing.[96] Taiwanese NGOs, for example, organized webinars to share their experience with effective contact tracing and community health initiatives,

[90] Yi-Li Lee (李怡俐) and Wen-Chen Chang (張文貞), "Mixed Constitutions in East Asia: South Korea and Taiwan as Examples" (2022) 16(2) LEHR 273–294.

[91] Chang and Lin (n 3, 2022).

[92] Chung and Lee (n 48).

[93] Yang (n 45).

[94] "Only Fifteen Covid-19 Cases among Dorm Residents in April, May and June 2021; Workers Still Largely Locked Down" (*Transient Workers Count Too*, July 2, 2021), https://twc2.org.sg/2021/07/02/only-fifteen-covid-19-cases-among-dorm-residents-in-april-may-and-june-2021-workers-still-largely-locked-down/, accessed August 19, 2024.

[95] "Post-Covid Law Makes Migrant Workers Prisoners of Employers" (*Transient Workers Count Too*, June 29, 2022), https://twc2.org.sg/2020/06/29/post-covid-law-makes-migrant-workers-prisoners-of-employers/, accessed August 19, 2024.

[96] Taiwan-Asia Exchange Foundation, "Taiwan NGOs' International Assistance under COVID-19 Pandemic", www.taef.org/doc/913, accessed November 7, 2024.

attended by participants from South Korea and other countries.[97] Additionally, NGOs in three countries engaged in cross-jurisdictional dialogues to enhance policy advocacy efforts. A notable example is their focus on the impact of preexisting migration policies and COVID-19 public health measures on migrant workers.[98] By sharing experiences in lobbying for governmental support, housing rights, and employment protections, these NGOs strengthened legal support mechanisms within their respective countries.[99]

III FEATURES OF DEMOCRATIC RESILIENCE IN COMBATING THE PANDEMIC CRISIS

A. *Democratic Values Reflecting from Past Experiences*

Democracy and the rule of law were tested during the COVID-19 pandemic when governments took the opportunity to expand their powers by enacting emergency laws or undertaking strict administrative measures that violated fundamental legal principles and infringed on human rights. South Korea, Taiwan, and Singapore were no exceptions to this tendency.

Although Taiwan and South Korea have authoritarian histories, they have evolved into strong Asian democracies, holding periodic elections to ensure that the representative governments are accountable to the people.[100] In contrast with authoritarian China and other countries, the responses of South Korea and Taiwan governments were based on democratic oversight and accountability. Their political leaders, having learned from their experiences during the SARS and MERS outbreaks in 2003 and 2015, respectively, as well as from one another's responses, framed the pandemic in democratic terms, showing strong commitment to the democratic values of their societies.[101] For example, when asked if Taiwan took advantage of emergency measures against COVID-19, President Tsai Ing-wen stressed that democratic institutions and processes could function within existing legal frameworks to

97 Taiwan International Cooperation and Development Fund, "Taiwan ICDF Is Collaborating with Korea-Based Good Neighbors and US-Based Dimagi Inc. to Co-Host the Webinar on Strengthening the Public Health System for Maintaining Essential Health Services during the COVID-19 Pandemic", www.icdf.org.tw/wSite/ct?xItem=62733&ctNode=31572&mp=2, accessed November 7, 2024.

98 Sasakawa Peace Foundation, "Repression and Resilience: COVID-19 Response Measures and Migrant Workers' Rights in Major East and Southeast Asian Destinations" (2020) 89–164.

99 Ibid.

100 Lee and Chang (n 90).

101 Caroline Tynan, "State Responses to COVID-19: South Korea, Taiwan, and the Power of Strong Democracies" (*Global Policy*, June 4, 2020), www.globalpolicyjournal.com/blog/04/06/2020/state-responses-covid-19-south-korea-taiwan-and-power-strong-democracies, accessed August 19, 2024.

ensure transparency, accountability, public participation, and due process.[102] Likewise, in South Korea, President Jae-in publicly emphasized that Korea's response to COVID-19 demonstrated democratic solidarity and cooperation.[103]

Recognizing the importance of maintaining public trust and democratic accountability during a pandemic, top health officials in South Korea and Taiwan incorporated openness and transparency as core values in their relevant policies and regulatory measures.[104] For example, Taiwan's Central Command held daily live-broadcast press conferences to update the public regarding the pandemic and government policy for dispelling fake news and misinformation.[105] Similarly, in South Korea, the Korean Disease Control and Prevention Agency, led by top scientists and health experts, held daily public briefings since the start of the outbreak.[106]

Furthermore, to manage the pandemic effectively, the presidents of Taiwan and South Korea allowed public health officials to control the communication of pandemic guidelines and showed high respect for their professional expertise and decision-making. To maintain administrative efficiency, the decisions of Taiwan's Central Command were substantially followed, with President Tsai Ing-wen and Premier Su Tseng-chang refraining from interference. Similarly, in South Korea, President Moon Jae-in allowed public health officials to take the lead in initiating government responses.[107]

Further, elections and referendums during the pandemic exemplified democratic resilience in South Korea and Taiwan.[108] Democratic values such as openness, accountability, and transparency helped these countries avoid issues commonly found in undemocratic societies. Similarly, Singapore, traditionally regarded as a hybrid authoritarian regime, demonstrated stronger democratic governance during the pandemic. For instance, the government maintained parliamentary functions and held a general election on July 10, 2020, months before the parliament's term ended. The largest opposition party won ten seats, the highest number in Singapore's post-independence history.[109] Additionally, increased political activity

[102] Office of the President Republic of China, "President Tsai Addresses Copenhagen Democracy Summit Via Video" (*Office of the President Republic of China*, June 19, 2020), https://english.president.gov.tw/News/6010, accessed August 19, 2024.

[103] 김민지, "문 대통령 "우리가 만든 민주주의, 대한민국을 코로나 방역모범국 만들어" (June 10, 2020), www.kocis.go.kr/koreanet/view.do?seq = 1035308, accessed August 19, 2024.

[104] Lee and Chang (n 90).

[105] Chang and Lin (n 3, 2022).

[106] Lee and Chang (n 90).

[107] Ibid.

[108] Ibid.

[109] Chua and Neo (n 4). Jin Yao Kwan, "'Democracy and Active Citizenship Are Not Just about the Elections': Youth Civic and Political Participation during and beyond Singapore's Nine-Day Pandemic Election (GE2020)" (2022) 30(3) YOUNG 247.

and criticism during the pandemic also led to policy changes in the areas of immigration and asylum.[110]

B. *Political Discourse in Vertical and Horizontal Dimensions*

As China or other authoritarian countries demonstrate, the pandemic has strengthened a preexisting techno-authoritarian project aimed at maintaining public health and public order, which violates fundamental human rights. Even worse, several weak democracies have also exhibited democratic erosion or pandemic autocracy.[111] Contrary to countries that exhibit authoritarianism or illiberal democracy, the experiences of these three Asian countries show that civil society oversight and institutional checks and balances between central and local governments remain effective in managing and adjusting pandemic responses through a democratic approach.[112]

For example, unlike NGOs in illiberal democracies that may encounter legal obstacles or political retaliation when opposing government actions, NGOs in these three countries were able to operate as mediating forces to regulate the exercise of government powers during pandemic crises. In addition, people were willing to assert their individual rights and may resort to judicial remedies if they were not satisfied with the government's decisions. More importantly, even though the governments in the three countries were provided with more leeway and greater deference by the people, the NGOs continued to serve as a counterbalance, questioning government policies and decisions that were not reasonably balanced and diminishing the tendency of power concentration that has been observed in other countries where democratic backsliding or authoritarian governance was gradually revived.[113] The dialectical processes between various levels of government offer an alternative approach for establishing accountability and fostering healthy competition for better coordination.[114] In Taiwan, local governments voiced disagreements with the Central Command, pushing it to coordinate with local authorities and adjust measures for greater effectiveness. This process also prevented local governments from abusing power. For instance, when the Miaoli County government prohibited all migrant workers from leaving their dormitories, the Central Command intervened, urging adherence to level 3 alert rules and facilitating testing to lift the ban.[115] Additionally, competition among local governments served as a

[110] Chua and Neo (n 4).

[111] Stephen Thomson and Eric C Ip, "COVID-19 Emergency Measures and the Impending Authoritarian Pandemic" (2020) 7(1) JLB 1–33.

[112] Chung and Lee (n 3, 2022).

[113] Lee and Chang (n 90).

[114] Chang and Lin (n 3, 2022).

[115] Centers for Disease Control, "In Response to Cluster Infections in Electronics Factories in Miaoli County, CECC Provides Details about COVID-19 Control Measures Adopted by

check on each other's power. The sincere efforts of local governments, such as hotspot testing in New Taipei City, created a feedback loop that encouraged the central government and other local governments to expand testing. This competition for more efficient vaccination also initiated a process of mutual learning among local governments.[116]

C. *Responsive Judiciary*

In response to the severity of the pandemic, the courts in South Korea, Taiwan, and Singapore used various legal tools and strategies to find a balance between the guarantee of human rights and government actions. These decisions demonstrate that the courts of the three countries generally presented a great deal of deference to the administrative discretion provided that the exercise of their power did not gravely or excessively violate basic rights and fundamental principles.[117] The lawsuits involving the habeas corpus, vaccination pass programs, elections, and regulating misinformation are obvious examples. However, in some rights-oriented cases, the courts may become less deferential and rule against the government. As the vaccine compensation cases demonstrate, the Korean court recognized victims as eligible for government benefits and compensation if the vaccination and the victims' illness are directly connected. In conclusion, in the majority of cases, the courts in the three countries deferred discretion to the competent authorities. In the COVID-19 context, this judicial deference is understandable; however, the courts should carefully examine each case and explain their underlying reasoning to the relevant agencies and the general public.

IV CONCLUSION

The COVID-19 pandemic has provided governments with an excuse to expand their powers, for better or worse, through the use or creation of emergency laws and tough administrative measures. However, governments' dangerous expansion of power increases the risks of democratic backsliding and exacerbation of existing human rights violations, if no effective legislative or judicial checks are put in place. As China and other countries show, the pandemic has reinforced a preexisting techno-authoritarian project aimed at protecting public health and public order, thus infringing fundamental human rights. Even worse, some weak democracies also have exhibited democracy erosion or pandemic autocracy.

Incident Command Post" (*Centers for Disease Control*, June 6, 2021), www.cdc.gov.tw/En/Bulletin/Detail/SQeL9I-JHXpfZRWt1haipg?typeid=158, accessed August 19, 2024.

[116] Chang and Lin (n 3, 2022).

[117] Lee and Chang (n 90).

However, unlike those countries, South Korea, Taiwan, and Singapore have demonstrated their strength and success in combating the spread of COVID-19. For example, in South Korea and Taiwan, democratic processes and institutions continued to function within the established legal framework, ensuring accountability, civic participation, and due process during the pandemic. Even in Singapore, often seen as an illiberal and authoritarian regime, legal and political institutions have shown resilience, fostering political consciousness and encouraging greater citizen participation. Such an achievement demonstrates that a stronger democracy is still the most effective approach to combat COVID-19. Meanwhile, their successful experiences show how the conflicts or tension between preserving democracy and human rights and regulating the drastic impacts of COVID-19 might be reduced or mitigated. Moreover, as COVID-19 was a transboundary issue, the experiences of these three countries demonstrated substantial cross-jurisdictional learning and adaptation in pandemic legal frameworks, multi-level governance between central and local authorities, and the active role of NGOs. Together, these factors enabled effective pandemic management across all three countries, highlighting key features of Inter-Asian Law in the realm of pandemic governance.

PART III

Law's Movements

Transnational Networks, Religious Donors, and Institutional Co-Learners

9

The Travels and Travails of Chinese Law in Inter-Asia

Matthew S. Erie

I INTRODUCTION

How does law travel in Inter-Asia? This chapter focuses on traveling law as an empirical event, but it also reflects on prevailing theories in comparative law that explain how law moves from one jurisdiction to another. These include inter alia colonialism and imperialism, law and development, regional integration, and regulatory competition and convergence. Perhaps the dominant paradigm in comparative law for traveling law is the legal transplant, a concept that has generated a sprawling literature.[1] The point of this chapter is not to say that Inter-Asia is aberrational, for to do so is to commit another act of legal orientalism; instead, the perspective is to use the Inter-Asian Law (IAL) material, and specifically the fraught movements of Chinese law in Inter-Asia, to critically reflect on comparative law conventions.

The approach I take in this chapter is to bring the comparative law theories into conversation with the literature on Inter-Asia and related inquiries from diverse fields including legal history, anthropology, and socio-legal studies. These studies suggest that, first, Inter-Asia is a space marked particularly by a long history of mobility, and one that continues to animate contemporary international

[1] See, e.g., Alan Watson, *Legal Transplants: An Approach to Comparative Law* (University of Georgia Press 1993); Ralf Michaels, "'One Size Can Fit All' – On the Mass Production of Legal Transplants" in Günter Frankenberg (ed), *Order from Transfer: Comparative Constitutional Design and Legal Culture Law* (Edward Elgar 2013); Jonathan M Miller, "A Typology of Legal Transplants: Using Sociology, Legal History and the Argentine Example to Explain the Transplant Process" (2003) 51(4) AJCL 839–885; Richard Zajac Sannerholm, "'Cut-and-Past'? Rule of Law Promotion and Legal Transplants in War to Peace Transitions" in Antonina Bakardjieva Engelbrekt and Joakim Nergelius (eds), *New Directions in Comparative Law* (Edward Elgar 2003) 56–80; Daniel Berkowitz, Katharina Pistor and Jean-Francois Richard, "The Transplant Effect" (2003) 51 AJCL 163–204; William Ewald, "Comparative Jurisprudence (II): The Logic of Legal Transplants" (1995) 43(4) AJCL 489.

commerce.[2] Mobility may refer to remits, commodities, religions, philosophies, technologies, and pathogens; it may equally apply to law.[3] Further, whereas Inter-Asia is embedded – historically and contemporaneously – within global trade and migration routes, it has also been populated by outsiders – whether pirates or jihadis – whose participation within those circuits creates contrast and distance, elements that are prerequisites to critical reflection on norms.[4] Chinese law may also be such an outsider that permits reflecting on taken-for-granted paths.[5]

By bringing together comparative law theories and Inter-Asian concepts, this chapter suggests two corrections to previous ways of thinking about how or why law moves from one jurisdiction to another, and the legal transplant in particular. First, to speak of transplants is to abstract a process from its origins in human labor. Transplants have become fetishized in the comparative law literature in Marx's original sense as appearing to have a disembodied "objective" character instead of a "social" one, rooted in the intellectual work of people as members of national, regional, or transnational societies.[6] Second, transplants have come to be conceptualized, for the most part, as the unilateral movement of one state's law to a recipient, who exists in a dyadic relationship. Such a conceptualization is a stylized ideal, like transplants' objectification, and removed from reality.

The Chinese law experience in Inter-Asia shows less a hegemon exporting its law and more host states weighing options to be adapted into their legal system, many of which are themselves accretions of laws from multiple systems, including laws originally from Western or colonial powers and Asian neighbors. For its part, the Party-State makes its standards, laws, and institutions available to nondemocratic regimes against the backdrop of their economic dependence on the People's

[2] Engseng Ho, "Inter-Asian Concepts for Mobile Societies" (2017) 76(4) J Asian Stud 917.

[3] Fahad Ahmad Bishara, *A Sea of Debt: Law and Economic Life in the Western Indian Ocean, 1780–1950* (CUP 2017); Iza Hussin, "Circulations of Law: Cosmopolitan Elites, Global Repertoires, Local Vernaculars" (2014) 32(4) Law & His Rev 773–795; Nurfadzilah Yahaya, *Fluid Jurisdictions: Colonial Law and Arabs in Southeast Asia* (Cornell University Press 2022).

[4] Jatin Dua, *Captured at Sea: Piracy and Protection in the Indian Ocean* (University of California Press 2019); Darryl Li, *The Universal Enemy: Jihad, Empire, and the Challenge of Solidarity* (Stanford University Press 2020); For a mind-altering account that spotlights mushrooms (rather than humans) as such agents of reflection, see Anna Lowenhaupt Tsing, *The Mushroom at the End of the World: On the Possibility of Life in Capitalist Ruins* (Princeton University Press 2017).

[5] Chinese law has been denied status as "law," and rather, associated with "sham" law, "non-legality," and "mandates." See Mark Jia, "Illiberal Law in American Courts" (2020) 168 U Pa L Rev 173; Xin He, "(Non)legality as Governmentality in China" (May 28, 2020) University of Hong Kong Faculty of Law Research Paper No. 2020/035, https://ssrn.com/abstract=3612483 or http://dx.doi.org/10.2139/ssrn.3612483, accessed May 27, 2025; Mayling Birney, "Decentralization and Veiled Corruption under China's 'Rule of Mandates'" (2014) 53 World Dev 55–67. See also Donald C Clarke, "Order and Law in China" (2022) U Ill L Rev No. 2, 541.

[6] Karl Marx, "Capital" in Robert C Tucker (ed), *The Marx-Engels Reader* (WW Norton & Co. 1978) 319–320.

Republic of China (China or PRC).[7] Hence, there are both "push" and "pull" factors which shape law's movements. In short, the corrections to transplants suggest, one, mobility happens because of people and, two, those people engage in law shopping, as an expression of both the diversity of options and their own agency.

Recentering human agency helps shed light on motives of moving law and may explain why and how traveling law reaches its destination or fails to do so. More broadly, Inter-Asia may have its own distinct features, including alt-colonial histories, diaspora, megaregional integration (e.g., the "ASEAN way" and the Belt and Road Initiative's "win–win"), "legal cooperation," transnational networks, and law-in-policy diffusion. This chapter endeavors to strike a balance between observing continuities in the methods and mechanisms of traveling law between different legal donors (Anglo-American, Western European, Japanese, etc.) and the particularities, novelties, and autochthonous development patterns of China's current moment, that is, between commonalities (if not universals) and differences.

A number of secondary questions follow: One, does Chinese law need to travel in Inter-Asia, instead of Chinese businesses relying on, for example, English or American law? If it does, then why, how, and to where? What are the arguments for and against Chinese law's travels? Two, does the movement of Chinese law in Inter-Asia require a rethinking of established theories of comparative law? Three, what are the implications for Chinese law and for host jurisdictions?

To preview the findings and evidence of this chapter, Chinese law is moving (albeit slowly and hesitantly) to other jurisdictions, and the way it does so both evinces long-standing theories but also requires some degree of re-tooling. There are a range of factors that determine why Chinese law travels and whether it does so smoothly: who does the work of moving Chinese law, why and how; the relationship between the PRC and the recipient state (i.e., historical, commercial, and cultural ties); the needs and interests of both donor and host; and the inter-systemic compatibility between the two sides (i.e., legal systems, economic systems, political systems). This chapter applies this range to several case studies: Cambodia, Uzbekistan, and Vietnam. The case studies draw on the emerging literature of "Chinese, Law and Development," including original fieldwork and studies to date, as well as related literatures, to take stock of the field.

The picture that emerges from these case studies is that the PRC, a non-traditional donor, provides normative resources for developing states, especially in emerging areas of law where the PRC may have a first-comer advantage. Yet despite the centrality of "development" (*fazhan*) and the notion of "Chinese-style modernization" (*Zhongguoshi xiandaihua*), in the Party-State's foreign policy, China may

7 To clarify my use of terms. "China" or "the PRC" refer to the nation-state; "Party-State" is the integration of the Chinese Communist Party with the PRC Government, a combination that has become more inextricable in recent years under the leadership of Xi Jinping; "Chinese Government" refers to the state side of the Party-State.

be less a whole model of and for development and more an assemblage of laws, policies, and practices that may be borrowed, repurposed, and adapted. To be clear, law is only one aspect of China's normative appeal, and regulatory regimes, political campaigns, and technical and digital standards may have more "pull" than law in the long run.[8] Ultimately, Chinese law may be fragile and uncertain in its extraterritorial travels, and a focus on the transnational networks that support the movement of law demonstrates its contingency.

II CHINA AS NON-TRADITIONAL LEGAL DONOR

Whereas the PRC has emerged as one regional power in Asia, a threshold question is whether the Party-State needs or wants its law to travel to other jurisdictions. The argument for traveling Chinese law is that such movement may confer commercial, geostrategic, and symbolic advantages. Commercially, in addition to the increasing use of PRC law in international business transactions as well as PRC courts and arbitration to resolve disputes that arise in the course thereof, Chinese companies (and their lawyers) may have greater familiarity with such sources and institutions of law.

Further, to the extent that the Party-State can supply the raw materials for legal development in developing countries, such accomplishments are a "win" for the PRC and give some credence to its promotion of its own conception of development overseas. Geostrategically, whether China can truly become a legal hub for resolving commercial disputes, a center for legal education, and a jurisdiction for addressing not just national, but also intra-regional, and transnational legal problems would significantly boost the country's economic, diplomatic, and potentially military relations with other states.

In addition to material benefits and facilitation of foreign policy, building a market for one's law can raise the profile of a donor state on the world stage and communicate its sophistication and attractiveness to global audiences. Hence, there are signaling effects to China's would-be law exportation.

The argument against exporting Chinese law is that China is not a legal superpower in the sense of the United States (US) or the United Kingdom (UK) and does

[8] See, e.g., Trang (Mae) Nguyen, State-Owned Enterprises in Vietnam's 2013 Constitution (draft on file with the author) (comparing Vietnam's Commission for Management of State Capital with China's State-Owned Assets Supervision and Administration Commission, suggesting that the former may have been inspired, in part, by the latter); Ministry of Foreign Affairs of the PRC, "China and the UAE Hold the First Meeting of the Consultation Mechanism on Counterterrorism and Deradicalization Cooperation" (September 18, 2022), www.fmprc.gov.cn/mfa_eng/wjbxw/202209/t20220919_10767793.html, accessed May 27, 2025 (providing a platform for "China-UAE cooperation on counterterrorism and deradicalization"); Matthew S Erie and Thomas Streinz, "The Beijing Effect: China's 'Digital Silk Road' as Transnational Data Governance" (2021) NYU J Int'l Law & Pol 1, 12 (discussing the relevance of non-binding technical standards in China's "Digital Silk Road").

not need to be. It can rely on preexisting legal infrastructures (e.g., English law as governing law of its contracts or International Criminal Court (ICC) arbitration for dispute resolution), rather than establish its own alternatives. While there is merit to the con argument, that argument has largely been abandoned in the age of Chinese hyper-nationalism, wherein the promotion of Chinese law overseas has become a building block of foreign policy.[9] This is particularly so under the current "foreign-related 'rule of law'" (*shewai fazhi*) campaign.[10]

Another threshold question, beyond the subjective aims of Chinese nationalism, is whether Chinese law is objectively different from the law of other jurisdictions. While there are numerous examples of China borrowing from other legal systems, for example, Chinese company law has increasingly assumed features familiar to US corporate law scholars and Chinese criminal law borrows from German law,[11] demonstrating the palimpsestic nature of Chinese law,[12] there are undoubtedly distinct features of the Chinese legal system that warrant attention. A few of the more noteworthy ones include: its role in encoding aspects of the Chinese "socialist market" economy,[13] the centrality of the administrative state (and corresponding inversion of norms between, on the one hand, the non-justiciable PRC Constitution and, on the other hand, local administrative regulations having considerable influence in the everyday lives of PRC citizens),[14] and, perhaps most glaringly, the predominant position of the Chinese Communist Party (CCP) as either formally reflected in the law or as occupying a status above the law.[15]

For most of its modern history, China has been a recipient of traveling law from other jurisdictions, and while such trajectories continue to this day, China has in recent years started showcasing its own laws, policies, and regulations to countries in the Global South. Historically, the centers of European civil law, namely, France,

9 See Matthew S Erie, "The Soft Power of Chinese Law" (2023) 61 Colum J Transnat'l L 1.

10 See Matthew S Erie, "Foreign Policy Implications for China's 'Foreign-Related 'Rule of Law'" (2023) 67 Orbis 565.

11 See Wang Jiangyu, China's Corporate Law Reform: Legal/Technical Convergence, Political Divergence, The State of Asian Legal Studies: Past, Present, and Future (Tenth Anniversary of the Centre for Asian Legal Studies), National University of Singapore Law Faculty (November 11, 2022); Michael Bohlander, "Drafting a Commentary on the Chinese Criminal Code – German Reflections on a Chinese Desideratum" (2021) 9(1) Peking U L J 1–21.

12 Matthew S Erie and Do Hai Ha, "Law and Development Minus Legal Transplants: The Example of China in Vietnam" (2021) 8(2) Asian JLS 380.

13 An example is the 2021 Chinese Civil Code's category of "special legal persons" (*tebie faren*) such as "rural collective economic organizations" (*nongcun jiti jingji zuzhi*). See Mariana Timoteo, "China Codifies. The First Book of the Civil Code between Western Models to Chinese Characteristics" (2019) 1 Opinio Juris in Comparatione: Studies in Comparative and National Law 23–44.

14 Perry Keller, "Sources of Order in Chinese Law" (1994) 42(4) AJCL 712.

15 For instance, the most recent amendments to the 2005 Company Law (Article 19) legalize the presence of CCP units in all companies. See 2022 Zhonghua renmin gongheguo gongsifa (quanwen) (中华人民共和国公司法（全文）) [2022 PRC Company Law (Entire Text)] Art. 19, www.maxlaw.cn/changshi/gszlgsf/28.html, accessed May 27, 2025.

Germany, and the common law metropoles, the UK and the US, actively engaged in different types of law promotion beyond their borders. These types run the gamut from colonialism, the most violent imposition of foreign law, to a range of projects born out of the foreign policy needs of advanced economies (e.g., law and development, legal development assistance, "rule of law" advocacy, etc.) to more potentially innocuous versions pursuant to the emergence of regional and megaregional regulations, as well as international law.[16] China has experienced most all of these law exports as a recipient country; it is only recently, however, that it has begun initiatives to offer its own experience in law and development for audiences outside of China, and principally, Inter-Asia.

As with Japan's approach to providing legal development assistance mainly to its own former colonial possessions in Southeast Asia, China's entry into the legal donation market is relatively "light-touch" compared to the European or Anglo-American versions. Whereas Western promoters of law and development have sought to introduce constitutional, legislative, and regulatory reform in host states, including designing new legal institutions, whether courts or law schools, the Chinese approach is much more muted. On the supply side, and pursuant to the "foreign-related 'rule of law' campaign," the main institutions involved in what in the Chinese lexicon is called "legal cooperation" (*falü hezuo* or *falü jiaoliu*) are the Supreme People's Court, Ministry of Justice, All China Lawyers' Association, China Law Society, law schools, law firms, arbitration commissions, and other members of the legal industry. These legal and judicial experts build platforms for learning and exchange with counterparts from other countries in Asia and beyond. Often such platforms take the form of international conferences or symposia organized around themes like "risk mitigation for foreign investment" or "commercial dispute resolution." These platforms further build transnational networks that continue legal exchanges.

At the same time, China has sought to bring more foreign lawyers, judges, and arbitrators from host states to China for training, workshops, and continuing education. The main goals from the Chinese perspective are both practical and geostrategic. As to the former, the Chinese judiciary is concerned about the enforceability of PRC courts' judgments overseas and so is actively working with judiciaries in host states to agree to mechanisms, including soft and hard law, to address that concern. As to the latter, the CCP and the legal and judicial organs of the state have an interest in "good-telling the story of Chinese rule of law" (*jianghao Zhongguo fazhi gushi*),[17] to increase the understanding of the Chinese

[16] One example is the General Data Protection Regulation, a EU piece of legislation, which has served as a model for non-EU jurisdictions throughout the world.

[17] Zhonggong Zhongyang (中共中央) [Central Committee of the CCP], Fazhi Zhongguo jianshe jihua (2020–2025) (法治中国建设计划 (2020–2025年)) [Plan for the Construction of China under the Rule of Law (2020–2025)], https://perma.cc/9MSR-VGVH, accessed May 27, 2025.

legal system to foreign lawyers, judges, and arbitrators to suggest that Chinese law has generated solutions to socioeconomic problems that other developing states can consult for their own developmental needs. Throughout its engagement with other states, Chinese representatives are mindful to avoid ethnocentric positions and statements, and while they may not always be successful in practice, their cultural sensitivity (at least at the elite level) suggests an awareness that may not have characterized past legal donors.[18]

In addition to its bilateral and multilateral efforts vis-à-vis host states, China has become an active member of international law organizations as part of its broader effort to shape international law. On the public international law side, China is a vocal participant in the UN system and has sought to introduce its own definitions of human rights, including the "right to development" into UN resolutions. On the private international law side, including trade and investment, China has embraced a number of international organizations, including the World Trade Organization and the United Nations Commission on International Trade Law as well as the United Nations Conference on Trade and Development. China has sought to master the procedural rules of these organizations and to promote its developmental approach through them. Whereas in many cases, the Party-State was not one of the original designers of these organizations, it has studied them as an insider and is thus positioned to shape norms from within.[19] In summary, China has adapted tools of sending law and policy used by previous legal donors and has also innovated in its outreach to host states and international organizations.

III CHINESE LAW AS A MIRROR TO COMPARATIVE LAW THEORY

Does the movement of Chinese law require rethinking conventional comparative law theories and the categories they employ? There are grounds to suggest that given the nature of China's relationships with other states in Inter-Asia and the international legal order, some aspects of China's legal interactions require new or at least partially revised explanatory models. First and foremost, while the idealized "tributary system"[20] has since undergone revision by historians, and it is generally agreed that imperial China exercised military domination in border zones, Chinese

[18] Matthew S Erie, "Chinese Law and Development: Implications for US Rule of Law Programs" in Lucas Meyers (ed), *2022–2023 Wilson China Fellowship: Understanding China amid Change and Competition* (Wilson Center 2023) 38.

[19] Gregory Shaffer and Henry S Gao, "China's Rise: How It Took on the U.S. at the WTO" (2017) U Ill L Rev No. 1, 115–184.

[20] To be fair, the historian most often cited as supporting the idea of the tributary system acknowledged it as a Chinese theoretical concept and not an actual system of administration. John K Fairbank, "A Preliminary Framework" in John King Fairbank (ed), *The Chinese World Order: Traditional China's Foreign Relations* (Harvard University Press 1968) 12.

rulers did not engage in the kind of the colonization of distant territories that characterized the age of imperialism.[21]

Second and subsequently, contemporary China is not a (neo)colonial and military power as traditionally understood, at least based on the familiar examples of Euro-American empires, although based on imperial China's long interactions with bordering states, such relationships are contentious and may touch on sensitive issues involving territorial and judicial sovereignty. As a result, China's relationships with recipient states may present a different paradigm. The PRC may be closer to what historians have called "informal empire"[22] through its trade imbalances and lending practices. The implications for traveling Chinese law are that its movements are perhaps bargained for but they are not forced, that is, the home state cannot coerce the recipient to adopt its law at least through traditional military force. To date, the Party-State couples the building of regional and global frameworks (e.g., Shanghai Cooperation Organization (SCO), Belt and Road Initiative, Asian Infrastructure and Investment Bank, Global Development Initiative, Global Security Initiative, etc.) with government-to-government relations that sometimes show severe asymmetries.

Hence, different types of Chinese actors, whether governmental, corporate, private, or semi-private, are engaged in different types of Chinese law promotion. Multilaterally, within its new frameworks, the Party-State may supply its own laws and standards for novel legal infrastructures. *Consensus* (or its appearance) may be the chief aim of such efforts. Bilaterally, through international investment agreements and diplomacy, the Party-State may bring its weight as investor-lender to bear on transactional issues. State-owned enterprises (SOEs) may, in particular, benefit from the Party-State's resources. These relationships are characterized by *economic coercion*. At a more granular level, counterparties may be attracted to the Chinese approach to development, including questions of law and policy, as it presents an "alternative" to familiar ones, including those of the International Monetary Fund (IMF) and World Bank. Such interactions are characterized by *inducement*. While the Party-State may not be the originator of these strategies for law promotion, it deploys them in ways that differ from Anglo-American predecessors.

While recognizing that China – as the donor – may exercise pressure on its trade partners, its "softer" strategies to date to promote its law, including legal and judicial education, training, and networks, open the door to balancing the Party-State's incentives and aims with those of its partners. "Law's Crossings" will provide a series

[21] Peter Perdue, "The Tenacious Tributary System" (2015) 24 J Contemporary China 1002–1014; James A Millward, "The Qing and Twentieth-Century Chinese Diversity Regimes" in Andrew Phillips and Christian Reus-smit (eds), *Culture and Order in World Politics* (CUP 2019) 71–92; John E Wills Jr, "Tribute, Defensiveness, and Dependency: Uses and Limits of Some Basic Ideas about Mid-Qing Dynasty Foreign Relations" (1988) 48 Am Neptune 225–229.

[22] John Gallagher and Ronald Robinson, "The Imperialism of Free Trade" (1953) 6 Econ His Rev 1–15.

of examples where Chinese law or regulation traveled to another jurisdiction with varying degrees of success. In particular, the analysis points to transnational networks that may function to migrate law from China to host states, but not always unproblematically.

IV LAW'S CROSSINGS

Instances of the mobility of Chinese law are not common. The reasons for this have to do with both China's foreign policies (which, historically, were "non-interventionist" although China's commitment to non-intervention appears to be eroding in the course of its increasing economic integration in host states) and inherent qualities of the law (i.e., Chinese law may not offer optimal modeling, although, depending on the area of law, Chinese law may offer host states relatively low-cost solutions to emerging problems). Nonetheless, there have been a number of cases where Chinese law has traveled, to varying degrees, in Inter-Asia, including to Cambodia, Uzbekistan, and Vietnam. For each case, I explain how and why Chinese law was adopted by another jurisdiction, with particular attention to law shopping and the movers of law and suggest reasons as to why outcomes differ.

A. *Cambodia*

Among the countries that are the most economically dependent on China, Cambodia stands out. That was not always the case. In the early 1990s, Cambodia was the poster child for post-conflict state building. The United Nations Transitional Authority in Cambodia helped the country write its 1993 Constitution, considered "one of the most extraordinary chapters in the efforts of the international community to promote democratic transitions in the post-Cold War era."[23] However, contrary to expectations, the government, led by Hun Sen's Cambodian People's Party (CPP), did not promote democratization. Instead, the CPP cracked down on opposition parties starting in 2013 and ushered in a period of democratic decline. As a result, Western aid and investment in the country plummeted. While Cambodia still looks to France, its former colonizer for law, that relationship has thinned. Since these changes, China has emerged as the dominant trade and investment partner of the country.[24]

There is, of course, a long history between China and Cambodia meditated by diaspora, much of it from southern China. Cambodian families up and down the class spectrum have deep ties to China. Many Cambodians speak Chinese, and

[23] See Bui Ngoc Son, "Constitutional Amendment and Democracy" (2021) 30 Minnesota J Int L 75, 138 (citing Stephen P Marks, "The New Cambodian Constitution: From Civil War to a Fragile Democracy" (1994) 26 Colum Hum Rts L Rev 45–46).

[24] Sokphea Young, "Constitutional Democracy around the Globe: Challenges & Future Directions" (2022) Georgetown Center for Transnational Legal Studies, London, July 11, 2022.

sometimes as well as Khmer. Transactional life in Cambodia shares affinities, as well, with Chinese preferences for doing business. This old diaspora is encountering a newer Chinese diaspora. The new diaspora is both geographically more diffuse than the old one (i.e., it is not necessarily limited to southern China) and more diverse socioeconomically. The new diaspora includes both high-net-worth individuals who find ways to purchase real estate in Cambodia (by law, non-Cambodians are prohibited from doing so) and also members of the criminal underworld, who have caused high rates of crime in the country.[25] As a result, there are different views in Cambodia about the increasing Chinese presence, so while the China–Cambodian relationship cannot be called uniform, it is certainly robust.

Against this backdrop of economic coupling and social ties, it is perhaps little wonder that the government-to-government, or, more specifically, party-to-party relationship is as strong as it is.[26] Cambodian judges, political elite, and, especially, members of the CPP are active participants in China-led networks, some of which are bilateral and others multilateral.[27] As a result of this back-and-forth, ideas on law and governance also travel between the two countries. Benjamin Lawrence has identified two examples of ideas migrating from China to Cambodia through such

[25] Pál Nyíri, "Investors, Managers, Brokers, and Culture Workers: How Migrants from China Are Changing the Meaning of Chineseness in Cambodia" in Pál Nyíri and Danielle Tan (eds), *Chinese Encounters in Southeast Asia: How People, Money, and Ideas from China are Changing a Region* (University of Washington Press 2017); Ivan Franceschini, "As Far Apart as Earth and Sky: A Survey of Chinese and Cambodian Construction Workers in Sihanoukville" (2020) 52(4) Critical Asian Studies 512–529.

[26] For the longer history of the CCP's engagement with Cambodian political regimes, and specifically, the Democratic Kampuchea, see Andrew Mertha, *Brothers in Arms: Chinese Aid to the Khmer Rouge, 1975–1979* (Cornell University Press 2014).

[27] As to multilateral political engagement, the literature on China and ASEAN is extensive. See, e.g., Saw Swee-Hock, Sheng Lijun and Chin Kin Wah (eds), *ASEAN-China Relations: Realities and Prospects* (ISEAS Publishing 2005); Zhao Hong, *China and ASEAN: Energy Security, Cooperation and Competition* (ISEAS Publishing 2015). There are also bilateral ties for intergovernmental exchange; see, e.g., Zhongjian zhengfu jian xietiao weiyuanhui juxing di liu ci huiyi (中柬政府间协调委员会举行第六次会议) [China-Cambodia Intergovernmental Coordination Committee Holds Sixth Meeting], Yazhou xiongfeng (亚洲雄风) [Asian Glory] (July 15, 2022), https://m.thepaper.cn/baijiahao_19029019, accessed May 27, 2025. In terms of judicial exchange specifically, see, e.g., Zuigao renmin fayuan (最高人民法院) [Supreme People's Court], Di san jie Zhongguo-Dongmeng da faguan luntan Nanning shengming (第三节中国东盟大法官论坛南宁声明) [The Third China-ASEAN Justice Forum Nanning Statement], Renmin fayuanbao (人民法院报) [People's Courts News] (July 1, 2022), www.court.gov.cn/zixun-xiangqing-366561.html, accessed May 27, 2025; 2022 nian Zhongguo-Dongmeng falv yanjiu zhongxin yu Jianpuzhai sifa bu hezuo xieyi xiangmu tuijin gongzuo zuotan hui shunli zhaokai (2022年中国 – 东盟法律研究中心与柬埔寨司法部合作协议项目推进工作座谈会顺利召开) [The 2022 China-ASEAN Legal Research Center and the Cambodian Ministry of Justice Cooperation Agreement Project Promotion Symposium was successfully held], Zhongguo Dongmeng falv yanjiu zhongxin (中国东盟法律研究中心) [China-ASEAN Legal Research Center] (January 7, 2022), https://mp.weixin.qq.com/s?__biz=MzA5MjUyODY2Ng==&mid=2650462250&idx=1&sn=eb0ade1ede44da619ed498381cd823dd&chksm=8865b15fbf1238498aab03a753e804fdc75964f0f8ae648d56d307256c7f5ed1565d4b954f66&scene=27, accessed May 27, 2025.

elite networks including constitutional reform and representative politics.[28] As to the former, Lawrence noted the strong similarity between Article 49 of the Cambodian Constitution, as amended in 2018, and Article 54 of the Chinese Constitution.[29] Specifically, Article 49 has been amended to read: "Every Khmer citizen shall put the national interest first and shall not perform any activities, either directly or indirectly, which would affect the interests of the Kingdom of Cambodia and Khmer citizens."[30] Article 54 of the Chinese Constitution reads, "Citizens of the People's Republic of China shall have the obligation to safeguard the security, honor and interests of the motherland; they must not behave in any way that endangers the motherland's security, honor or interests."[31]

As a result of the amendment, Cambodia joins China as one of only two countries in the world to include a specific prohibition against actions by citizens that can be construed as having a negative impact on the interests of the state. Lawrence is cautious in his conclusion about direct causation, stating, "while it is difficult to empirically demonstrate that this convergence resulted from an intentional act of borrowing from China, such convergence between the two articles is indicative of a concerted act of borrowing by Cambodia, particularly given the context of the increasingly close relationship between the two countries."[32] However, the probability of a direct borrowing becomes more likely in the second congruence observed by Lawrence.

In addition to the constitutional amendment, another change introduced in 2018 was the Supreme Council for Consultation and Recommendation (SCCR). Prime Minister Hun Sen created the SCCR by way of royal decree to establish a body to represent members of opposition political parties. As a consultative body, the SCCR convenes twice a year and submits reports to the prime minister on pressing issues requiring legislative attention, including land disputes, corruption, and environmental pollution. By 2019, the SCCR had thirty members representing fifteen political parties.[33] While the SCCR provides an appearance of multi-party representation, critics have argued that it is largely illusory as Hun Sen dominates the mandate of the SCCR.[34] Further, Hun Sen had disbanded the major opposition

[28] Benjamin Lawrence, "Authoritarian Constitutional Borrowing and Convergence in Cambodia" (2021) 43(2) Contemporary Southeast Asia 320–343.

[29] Ibid 331–333.

[30] Ibid 332.

[31] Zhonghua renmin gongheguo xianfa (中华人民共和国宪法) [Constitution of the People's Republic of China], adopted at the Second Session of the Tenth National People's Congress on March 14, 2004, with amendments made at the First Session of the Thirteenth National People's Congress on March 11, 2018.

[32] See Lawrence (n 28) 333.

[33] Cambodian People's Party, "PM Chairs Meeting of Supreme Council for Consultation and Recommendations" (August 28, 2019), www.cpp.org.kh/details/150922, accessed March 1, 2023.

[34] Long Kimmarita, "PM Places Boundaries on Supreme Council's Work" (*The Phnom Penh Post*, May 17, 2020), www.phnompenhpost.com/national/pm-places-boundaries-supreme-councils-work, accessed May 27, 2025.

party and thereby denied formal opposition in the National Assembly, the main legislative body. Lawrence notes that the SCCR is the functional equivalent to China's People's Political Consultative Conference (CPPCC), also a consultative body that purports to represent those from political parties other than the CCP including religious and ethnic minority leaders.[35] The CPPCC, like the SCCR, provides recommendations for legislative and policy attention. However, critics have attacked the CPPCC as nothing more than an ornament of the ruling party.[36]

In terms of the issue of causality, members of the SCCR have made the explicit comparison between their representative body and the CPPCC. In particular, two leading members of the SCCR made the connection explicit in interviews with Lawrence in 2019.[37] Additionally, Chinese state media quoted a SCCR delegate who stated, "the CPPCC and the SCCR have similar roles," and further represented that the SCCR Secretariat Chhim Phal Virun embraced any cooperation with the CPPCC, stating that the SCCR "want[s] to learn about the CPPCC's contributions to supporting China's anti-corruption drive."[38] While statements about functional equivalence or even of intent of one body to emulate another are not dispositive, circumstantial evidence suggests an ongoing back-and-forth between CPP and CCP leaders on questions of squaring representative politics with authoritarian rule.

It is important to underscore that Cambodia, like many developing states, is eclectic and non-discriminatory in its borrowing of law from other states. Cambodia, for example, has adapted law from France, Japan, Singapore, Thailand, and elsewhere. China, thus, is far from being the sole inspiration. Reflecting some of the insight from the literature on Inter-Asia, mobility is usually not unidirectional but, rather, has multiple origins and trajectories. Cambodia's recent incorporation of Chinese law and institutions into its own framework occurs in this context of competing legal donors. While it is true at a general level that the star of France, as the former colonial power in Cambodia, is waning, and that China's profile is rising, this is not necessarily an inevitable or linear process.

B. *Uzbekistan*

Uzbekistan, like other lower-middle-income countries, seeks ties with multiple trade and security partners, rather than becoming dependent on any one country; still, China's influence in the country – as it is in the Central Asian region, more

35 See Lawrence (n 28) 335.

36 Robert Barnett, "Mimetic Re-Enchantment: The Contemporary Chinese State and Tibetan Religious Leadership" in Nils Bubandt and Martijn van Beek (eds), *Varieties of Secularism in Asia: Anthropological Explorations of Religion, Politics and the Spiritual* (Routledge 2012) 36.

37 See Lawrence (n 28) 336.

38 See Lawrence (n 28) 335 (citing Mao Pengfei and Nguon Sovan, "China's Top Political Advisory Body Vital in Promoting Multiparty Cooperation – Cambodian Politicians" (*Xinhua*, March 4, 2019), www.xinhuanet.com/english/2019-03/04/c_137868401.htm, accessed May 27, 2025).

generally – is growing.[39] Given the history of the region, the dominant influence on legal development in the region has been Russia.[40] Nonetheless, just as Uzbekistan has looked to China as a counterweight to overreliance on Russia and has sought out economic cooperation with the PRC since 1991, so too is it starting to esteem the PRC legal system as a source for legal development, particularly in emerging areas such as data governance and cyber security. In this regard, Chinese law has traveled to Uzbekistan through China's own brand of "legal cooperation." In turn, and evincing some of the recursivity of Inter-Asian mobility, Uzbekistan has been an active member of the Chinese-led SCO, which is proposing an alternate body of international law.[41]

Uzbekistan, like its neighbors, has sought to cultivate positive relationships with China as a counterweight to overdependence on Russia. This strategy is reflected both in Uzbekistan's bilateral and multilateral relationships with the PRC. During the presidency of Islam Karimov, the first President of the Republic of Uzbekistan, from 1991 to 2016, the country sought a cautious opening to Chinese trade, while limiting the inflow of Chinese laborers and migrants. The focus during that period was more on Uzbekistan's domestic economic modernization than anything else.[42] Starting in 2001, with the establishment of the SCO, Uzbekistan's role became more diversified as the region sought cooperation on, first, security, and, subsequently, economic integration. The second most resource-rich country in the region after Kazakhstan, Uzbekistan's role in the SCO was important to Chinese policymakers, and the composition of the SCO, given the country's rich reserves of oil and gas.[43] As an example of China and its allies, including Uzbekistan, working to shape international law, in 2011, the SCO, plus Uzbekistan, Russia, and Tajikistan submitted a draft International Code of Conduct for Information Security to the United Nations to formalize new cyber governance rules. Whereas the proposal failed, in 2015, those same countries, joined by Kazakhstan and Kyrgyzstan proposed a revised version that the UN approved in the form of a cybercrime resolution entitled "Countering the Use of Information and Communication Technologies for Criminal Purposes."[44]

In 2019, the PRC hosted officials from thirty-six countries along the BRI for large-scale training and seminars on cyberspace, big data, and media management.

39 Raffaello Pantucci and Alexandros Petersen, *Sinostan: China's Inadvertent Empire* (OUP 2022).

40 Scott Newton, *The Constitutional Systems of the Independent Central Asian States: A Contextual Analysis* (Bloomsbury 2017).

41 Tom Ginsburg, "Authoritarian International Law" (2020) 114(2) AJIL 221–260.

42 Dina Rome Spechler and Martin C Spechler, "The Foreign Policy of Uzbekistan: Sources, Objectives and Outcomes: 1991–2009" (2010) 29(2) Central Asian Survey 159–170.

43 Ralph Wrobel, "China's New Energy Geopolitics: The Shanghai Cooperation Organization and Central Asia" (2014) 133(October) ASIEN 25.

44 Roza Nurgozhaeva, "Rule-Making, Rule-Taking or Rule-Rejecting under the Belt and Road Initiative; A Central Asian Perspective" (2020) 8(1) Chinese J Comp L 253.

Later that year, Uzbekistan introduced its Data Protection Law and a set of executive bylaws such as Presidential decrees 4452 on IT control and protection, and 117 on development of IT communication technologies. Whereas Uzbekistan relies on several foreign partners for legal assistance on cybersecurity law, the Ministry of Justice has highlighted the role of legal cooperation with China on cyber issues as one of its most effective partnerships.[45] Although very little is written in Uzbek, Russian, Chinese, or English on the topic of Sino-Uzbek legal cooperation in cyber, interviews with Uzbek legal practitioners and scholars suggest that Uzbekistan's special inter-ministerial working groups, created for legislative drafting, indeed borrow explicitly from China's relevant laws for their conceptual frameworks.[46]

Data governance law is one area where China has a first-cover advantage, an advantage that has not gone unnoticed by China's international business partners. China's growing body of law on data governance, including its 2017 Cybersecurity Law, 2021 Data Security Law, and 2021 Personal Information Protection Law, are generally deemed to be more comprehensive than any analogous legislation in the US, for example, and a regime that may provide an alternative to the European Union (EU)'s General Data Protection Regulation. Generally, experts view three competing regimes, that of China, the US, and the EU, each providing a different model of data governance, even if there is overlap and borrowing between the regimes.[47] China's version of "data sovereignty" is particularly attractive to middle-income countries that are shopping for legal material, yet the relationship is less one of direct transplantation than receptivity to underlying data governance principles of governmental and territorial control over data that materialize in highly different and context-dependent domestic data laws.[48] Like the CPP members in the first example, the Uzbek officials look to the Chinese laws not out of a kind of obeyance, but rather because they want to optimize their own digital development. The networks that facilitate such exchange are also not unilateral as some of those ties overlap with those of the SCO, meaning that multiple inputs generate legal and regulatory changes for both the multilateral organization and its member states.

[45] Ministry of Justice [in Russian], www.minjust.uz/ru/press-center/news/95835/, accessed July 2, 2024.

[46] Interviews conducted with Uzbek scholars by researchers associated with the China, Law and Development project (August 26, 2021). See also Dentons, "Uzbekistan Enacts First Data Protection Law" (July 16, 2019), www.dentons.com/en/insights/articles/2019/july/16/uzbekistan-enacts-first-data-protection-law, accessed July 2, 2023.

[47] Anu Bradford, *The Brussels Effect: How the European Union Rules the World* (New York 2020) 153; Emmanuel Pernot-Leplay, "China's Approach on Data Privacy Law: A Third Way between the U.S. and the EU?" (2020) 8(1) Penn State J L & Int Aff 50–117; Susan Ariel Aaronson, *A Future Built on Data: Data Strategies, Competitive Advantage and Trust* (CIGI Paper No. 266, June 9, 2022).

[48] See Erie and Streinz (n 8) 23.

C. *Vietnam*

A complex set of historical, foreign policy, and geo-economic factors shape Vietnam's relationship with China, a relationship that, in turn, affects the movement of law between the two economies. On the one hand, Vietnam and China share a long history of mutual exchange given their geographic, cultural, and commercial proximity. In addition to their both belonging to, broadly speaking, the greater Sinosphere and the long interpenetration of their markets, they both adopted versions of socialism in the second half of the twentieth century. As a result of these commonalities, Vietnam has a long history of borrowing legal ideas from China. On the other hand, due to both imperial China's wars with Vietnam and more recent border conflicts, Vietnamese appreciation for Chinese cultural innovation is tempered by distrust and even periodic animosity toward Chinese. The relationship is multifaceted and defies simple characterizations. Hence, the adoption of Chinese law is not frictionless and has occasionally been thwarted by widely held beliefs that deepened engagement with China may erode Vietnam's sovereignty. In short, Vietnam likes to keep China close, but not too close, and this affects the movement of law.

Vietnam and its relationship with China shows some of the complexity in using conventional categories of "empire" and "colonialism" to describe China's engagement with neighboring countries. The Sino-Vietnamese relationship is, first, noteworthy for its duration and the extent of the thick exchange between the countries through trade and cross-border commerce. This exchange has included the sharing of ideas about law, justice, and order. Scholars, officials, and traders brought Neo-Confucian ideas about law and legality from China to Vietnam as early as the fifteenth century.[49] Fast forwarding to the planned economy era in the mid twentieth century, the Union of Soviet Socialist Republics (USSR) and not China was the main model for modern Vietnam's legal development.[50] Specifically, the Democratic Republic of Vietnam (DRV) and later the Socialist Republic of Vietnam (SRV) looked to the USSR for structuring its public law.[51] Yet even during this time, the PRC played a role as an intermediary or source of "second-order" legal borrowing as evinced by the DRV's 1953 Law on Land Reforms, which was written with the instruction of Chinese advisors.[52] Hence, even during this formative period, the DRV looked to different models for optimal sources of legal design.

[49] Ngoc Huy Nguyen and Van Tai Ta, *The Lê Code* (Ohio University Press 1987) 18.

[50] Penelope (Pip) Nicholson, *Borrowing Court Systems: The Experience of Socialist Vietnam* (Martinus Nijhoff Publishers 2007) 67.

[51] Pham Duy Nghia and Do Hai Ha, "The Soviet Legacy and Its Impact on Contemporary Vietnam" in Hualing Fu et al (eds), *Socialist Law in Socialist East Asia* (CUP 2018) 103–106.

[52] William J Duiker, *Ho Chi Minh: A Life* (Allen & Unwin 2006) 437.

The long history of "looking over the border" at the other country's legal and political reforms serves as precedent to two more recent examples of Chinese law and policy traveling from China to Vietnam: the 2018 Special Economic Zone (SEZ) bill and the 2018 Cybersecurity Law.[53] These examples show that the adaptation of Chinese law and policy to Vietnam is complicated by a range of factors, including popular distrust of China in Vietnam and the SRV's efforts to build its own models that diverge from China's. The outcomes of the two examples differ: The SEZ bill eventually failed, and the Cybersecurity Law passed but in such a way that demonstrates both congruence with but also differentiation from Chinese law. A constant in studying these two examples (a constant that may be applied to the study of China's legal exchanges more generally) is that data on these law crossings are extremely hard to collect as information is generally not made public and insiders for the most part are not willing to share information with researchers.

The first example stems from emulation of China's industrial policy of establishing SEZs to concentrate capital and boost domestic growth. Although China did not invent the SEZ, China's SEZs, most famously, Shenzhen, have become the exemplar of such pro-business sub-national jurisdictions, throughout the world.[54] China began assisting other developing countries build their own SEZs in the 2000s, and today there are an untold number of SEZs, as well as free trade zones, industrial parks, and other variants, that the Chinese have built throughout Southeast Asia, Africa, and elsewhere.[55] Along with the Chinese-invested hard infrastructure of the zones and parks, there is also the soft infrastructure of the regulatory framework for such areas. This soft infrastructure includes the legislative and regulatory design for tariffs, customs, tax, corporate, labor rules, and other trade and investment rules that facilitate the entry of foreign direct investment and outbound capital.[56] China is perhaps less well known for this soft infrastructure, and yet it has also caught the attention of other states and been the source for emulation.

The SRV had floated the idea of SEZs since at least the late 1990s but only gained full backing from the Politburo, the nerve center of the Communist Party of Vietnam (CPV), from 2012 to 2013.[57] As a result, the government started drafting the SEZ Bill in 2014 and it was forwarded to the National Assembly for deliberation in 2017. The drafters studied examples from a number of other jurisdictions but

[53] Cybersecurity Law adopted June 12, 2018, and effective January 1, 2019 (Act No. 24/2018/HQ14) (Viet).

[54] Man Sun et al, "Rejuvenating SEZs through Internationalization: A Case Study of Chinese Domestic and International SEZs" (2022) 11 Land 1–13.

[55] Xiangming Chen, "Change and Continuity in Special Economic Zones: A Reassessment and Lessons from China" (2019) 26(2) Transnat'l Corp 49–74.

[56] Douglas Z Zeng, "The Past, Present, and Future of Special Economic Zones and Their Impact" (2021) 24(2) J Int Econ L 259–275.

[57] Government (2017) Submission Paper No. 411/TTr-CP regarding the Bill on Special Administrative-Economic Units (10 October) 6. For a more detailed legislative history of the 2018 SEZ bill, see Erie and Ha (n 12).

learned in particular from the example of China.[58] Furthermore, Chinese experts from the China Centre for Special Economic Zones Research, based at Shenzhen University, provide technical advice and consultation. This took the form of several events including multi-day visits, fieldwork activities, two-week training programs, workshops, and at least one international conference.[59] The Chinese provided technical assistance, including on the legal framework for the Vietnamese SEZs, with Chinese experts from multiple institutions providing different types and levels of support throughout the process of drafting the legislation.[60]

The SEZ Bill, however, generated a tempest of criticism in the public sphere in Vietnam. Although the criticisms varied and were voiced by different constituencies, an underlying concern was that the SEZ Bill gave preferential treatment to Chinese investors, threatened Vietnam's national security, and provided "negative lessons" from China to Vietnam across a range of important policy areas, from labor to land use management.[61] Objections spilled out of legislative halls to the streets and there were public demonstrations aimed against Chinese investors and their influence.[62] The SEZ Bill thus fell afoul of latent anti-Chinese sentiment in the Vietnamese public, and the cascading protest ultimately sank the bill.[63]

Whereas the SEZ Bill shows how traveling Chinese law and policy may not always reach its destination, the 2018 Cybersecurity Law, which also borrowed from the Chinese template, shows more success. As mentioned in the case of Uzbekistan, China has developed its own framework for data governance laws and cybersecurity laws and one that is viewed broadly as an alternative to those of the US and EU. This framework has attracted the attention of other nondemocratic regimes, including the CPV. Vietnam enjoys an advanced ecosystem of digital infrastructure including 5G and a high penetration of both internet and mobile phone use throughout the population. The Vietnamese Government argued that the Cybersecurity Law was essential to safeguard "national security, social order and safety, or the lawful rights and interests of agencies, organizations, and individuals."[64] As shown by Bui Ngoc Son and Jye-An Lee, the Cybersecurity Law was controversial; however, as critics believed, it essentially copied China's Cybersecurity Law and would infringe individual freedom and commercial confidentiality.[65] Ultimately, the law was passed over objections.

58 Drafting Committee, Report on the Review of the International Experience in Constructing, Developing and Managing SEZs and Similar Models, October 9, 2010.
59 See Erie and Ha (n 12) 386.
60 Ibid.
61 Ibid 388.
62 Atsushi Tomiyama, "Vietnam's Economic Zones Derailed by Anti-China Protests" (*Nikkei Asian Review*, September 3, 2018), https://asia.nikkei.com/Politics/International-relations/Vietnam-s-economic-zones-derailedby-anti-China-Protests, accessed April 19, 2020.
63 See Erie and Ha (n 12) 389.
64 Law on Cybersecurity, 2018 (No 24/2018/QH14) (Viet.), Art. 2.
65 Ngoc Son Bui and Jyh-An Lee, "Comparative Cybersecurity Law in Socialist Asia" (2022) 55 Vand J Transnat'l L 634.

To begin with the differences between the Vietnamese and Chinese digital ecosystems, whereas both the Vietnamese and Chinese governments tightly regulate the Internet, social media platforms, and e-commerce in their respective jurisdictions, there is nonetheless generally a higher level of user freedom in Vietnam. Vietnam, for instance, does not (yet) feature a "great firewall" as does China.[66] Perhaps more fundamentally, as Bui and Lee argue, the Chinese regulatory regime valorizes cyber sovereignty and which has transmorphed into "data sovereignty" in its most recent legislation, whereas the Vietnamese cyber authorities privilege a much more universalist understanding of data control that does not prioritize data sovereignty over integration into a global network.[67] Consequently, the two laws show convergence, and likely Vietnamese borrowing across a set of important issues, including the regulation of banned acts, network operators, critical infrastructure, data localization, and personal data.[68] However, the two laws differ in terms of both their technological architecture and their privileging data sovereignty versus more open versions of data management.[69]

Importantly, the doers of law's movement in the case of the Chinese Cybersecurity Law's influence on the Vietnamese Cybersecurity Law are difficult to identify with any degree of certainty. This is perhaps not surprising given that the Cybersecurity Law directly involves national security in a way that the SEZ bill may not. The most exhaustive comparative study of the two laws to date, written by Bui and Lee, does not address this point. There are some impressions available via public petitions. Vietnamese bloggers for example have claimed that "the Vietnamese cybersecurity police are trained in China ... We cannot rule out that China has helped Vietnam to design and equip its cybersecurity infrastructure."[70] Still, without more authoritative sources, it is hard to distinguish facts from conspiracy theories. Nonetheless, in part fueled by concerns of Chinese influence, protests against the Cybersecurity Law dovetailed with those against the SEZ Bill, and in fact, protestors rallied against the two proposed pieces of legislation together. Ultimately, the Cybersecurity Law was passed – overwhelmingly so – despite the protests, unlike the SEZ Bill. The diverging result is perhaps explained by the fact that the Vietnamese government regards the Internet and social media as, simply, too important and could not make concessions.[71]

66 Ibid 636.

67 Ibid 636; Erie and Streinz (n 8) 4.

68 Bui and Lee (n 65) 637. See also Justin Sherman, "Vietnam's Internet Control: Following in China's Footprints?" (*The Diplomat*, December 11, 2019), https://thediplomat.com/2019/12/vietnams-internet-control-following-in-chinas-footsteps/, accessed May 27, 2025.

69 Bui and Lee (n 65) 675–676.

70 Reporters without Borders, "RSF Calls for Repeal of Vietnam's New Cybersecurity Law" (*RSF News*, June 14, 2018), https://rsf.org/en/rsf-calls-repeal-vietnam-s-new-cybersecurity-law, accessed May 27, 2025.

71 Giang Nguyen-Thu, "Vietnamese Media Going Social: Connectivism, Collectivism, and Conservatism" (2018) 77(4) J Asian Stud 895–808.

V CONCLUSION: EXPLAINING OUTCOMES

The Party-State is building transnational networks of legal experts, lawyers, and consultants throughout Inter-Asia. Chinese law, as a result, is becoming integrated into the domestic and transnational law of the region. China is both sending its legal technicians out to recipient countries to provide advice on legislative drafting and institutional design and judicial and legal elites from host states to attend trainings and workshops in China to study Chinese legislation and associated regulations. The Party-State did not invent transnational networks; the Americans, British, French, German, and Japanese, have all been building their own versions for decades. These networks consist of law schools and continuing legal education, inter-judicial dialogue, international law firms, trainings led by judicial officials and civil society members, alumni organizations, and other platforms. The Chinese approach borrows from these preceding ones; for example, Chinese law schools recruit overseas students. Notably, at least up until the COVID-19 pandemic, such programs saw an increase in the proportion of foreign students from developing countries throughout Asia, Africa, and even Latin American relative to students from the West, a reflection of the geopolitics of education.

Nonetheless, there are historical and structural reasons that suggest that the Chinese approach to developing transnational networks through "legal cooperation" is different. Notably, China lacks the military power that was formative of colonial relationships and which has undergirded much of the modern geography of transnational mobility, whether in the fields of education, industry, or trade. Rather, China's attraction lies in its economic model. China has, at times, struggled to tell the story of Chinese law in its economic development. The current emphasis on "foreign-related 'rule of law'," part of which mandates the "good-telling the story of Chinese rule of law" is meant to address this gap, although time will tell whether it can gain traction with foreign audiences.[72]

Along these lines, Chinese law may be significantly modified in transit or not always reach its destination altogether. The above cases of Cambodia, Uzbekistan, and Vietnam have different outcomes which require explanation. The Cambodian government has begun looking to China for constitutional law reform and legal institutions without noticeable problems. Yet doing so is more a reflection of Cambodia's utilitarianism and ecumenism than any Chinese hegemony. Weak states in Inter-Asia attempt to balance the interests of competing powers, including legal donors.[73] Such optionality benefits their legal development as they may reap

[72] See Matthew S Erie, "Turning Legal Systems Inside Out: American Legal Exceptionalism and China's Dream of Legal Cosmopolitanism" (2023) 44 U Penn J Int L 731.

[73] See Stephen M Walt, *The Origins of Alliances* (Cornell University Press 1987) 5 (arguing that with the proliferation of donors, their individual leverage decreases). See also Trang (Mae) Nguyen, "International Law as Hedging: Perspectives from Secondary Authoritarian States"

the rewards of a competitive market in traveling laws, although optionality may not always lead to optimality.

Cambodia is perhaps the best example of this. A (French) civil law system, Cambodia has also borrowed heavily from both Anglo-American common law and Japanese civil law. It further looks to Singapore, Thailand, and other Southeast Asian states. Chinese law is the most recent entrant to its legal eclecticism. Political and legal elites in Cambodia are content shopping around for laws including those of the PRC. Popular views toward China vary, and yet concerns are, to date, insufficient to thwart Chinese-inspired law-making.

Likewise, Uzbekistan, a country with a stronger economy than Cambodia, also seeks to straddle the Russia–China divide, borrowing the most optimal attributes from both systems. Under the current Uzbek leadership, China's approach to data governance benefits the regime and, as with Cambodia, civil society cannot provide a check to governmental action, especially in the field of cybersecurity. Uzbekistan may continue to absorb Russian law for certain legal fields and look to China as an innovator in others. While doing so, it will endeavor not to appear too close to either, although China still lags Russia in its influence in Central Asia.

For Vietnam, a country with a booming export-led economy, it must balance its ties to China with its strategic links with the US and, as such, walks a fine line between its economic interdependence with China and popular perceptions that it is ceding Vietnamese sovereignty toward the Chinese. The SEZ Bill and Cybersecurity Law fall on opposite sides of this divide, the former failing to pass through popular and formal vetting and the latter ultimately attaining passage. The public's concerns about Chinese influence were enough to thwart the SEZ Bill, but given that governing cyberspace is an existential concern for the regime, the government would brook no challenge to the law's passing. It is conceivable that the government gave up the SEZ Bill, as a concession, to get the Cybersecurity Law through the National Assembly.

The three cases afford an opportunity to reasses some of the conventional thinking about how and why law moves from one jurisdiction to another. Specifically, the Chinese preference for or tendency toward networks spotlights the human actors who push and pull law. In all three cases, politicians, lawyers, and judges travel to China to study Chinese experience in law and development. In the Vietnam case, not only is training held in China, but also Chinese legal technicians travel to Vietnam to provide onsite consultation. It is possible that Chinese experts have also traveled to Cambodia and Uzbekistan, as well. Amid this traveling to and from, legal and judicial elite are not just transporting ideas about legal reform and innovation, but they are molding them to their respective agendas, ideologies, and cognitive frames. Traveling is, after all, motion, and motion is

(2020) 114 AJIL Unbound 144, 237–241 (applying the concept of hedging to small states' approaches to using international law).

synonymous with change. As legal precepts, constitutional provisions, grounding principles, and representative institutions travel, they are also being modified and tailored to individual contexts through the specific lenses of laws' travelers. More focus on the aspirations, motives, and incentives of the doers of traveling law, perhaps through micro-histories or ethnographies, may explain how and why adaptations happen and under what conditions they work or fail to do so, or, in other words, why transplants fail.[74]

In terms of the study of China-beyond-China, the case studies suggest that Inter-Asia features several crisscrossing legal circuits that inform any number of law's movements, whether for legal development assistance or international commerce, collective security, and related questions of regional importance. China does not act on a blank slate. Proponents of Chinese law's popularization abroad must grapple with not only domestic legal environments of host states but also regional and even global dynamics, and both the domestic and regional are shaped, in part, by other competing legal traditions.[75] Inter-Asia is not necessarily unique in the matrices of competing legal traditions that shape domestic and regional legal reforms.[76] Yet, given its colonial and imperial legacies, informal and formal empires, and rising economic superpowers, Inter-Asia may be a site of particularly intense legal interaction. Whether it's leave-no-stone-unturned Cambodian law, Uzbek law at the Eurasian cross-roads of Russian and Chinese law, or Vietnamese law, with its equal parts French civil law and Soviet law, and which must respond to US–China tensions, host countries are simultaneously constrained by and potentially enabled developmentally by the multiple legal influences in which they are embedded.

The multiple sourcing of law by low-income and middle-income states in Inter-Asia has further implications for political developments in the region. The fact that China supplies legal and regulatory tools that nondemocratic states can adopt into their own frameworks suggests that such offerings may embolden such regimes leading to further repression of the population. The nature of China's offerings, whether personal data law, cybersecurity, or constitutional provisions, which prohibit alleged "anti-state" acts, all point to such an outcome. Such possibilities have generated concerns about "authoritarian international law" or China's "making the world safe for autocracy."[77] These are valid concerns, yet such thinking occasionally elides the fact that Chinese law can be a poor traveler and miss its landing. The SEZ

[74] See Berkowitz, Pistor and Richard (n 1). See also Ahmad A Alshorbaby, "On the Failure of a Legal Transplant: The Case of Egyptian Takeover Law" (2012) 22 Ind Int'l & Comp L Rev 237, 227; Helen Xanthaki, "Legal Transplants in Legislation: Defusing the Trap" (2008) 57 ICLQ 659, 659; Mathias Siems, "Malicious Legal Transplants" (2018) 38 LS 103, 103.

[75] See Bishara (n 3); see also Yahaya (n 3).

[76] See, e.g., Jeppe Mulich, *In a Sea of Empires: Networks and Crossings in the Revolutionary Caribbean* (CUP 2020).

[77] See Ginsburg (n 41). See also Jessica Chen Weiss, "A World Safe for Autocracy? China's Rise and the Future of Global Politics" (*Foreign Affairs*, June 11, 2019) 92.

Bill in Vietnam is one such casualty.[78] There is real fragility in Chinese law's portability into other states, both on the China side and the host state side. Most recently, the November 2022 "white paper" protests led by Chinese college students clamoring for "*fazhi*" (rule of law) and "*minzhu*" (democracy) illustrate the former, although the regime's ability to clamp down on such protests suggests the opposite – its resilience. Similarly, contentious politics in would-be host states evince uncertainty on that side. While the spread of Chinese law calls for diligence, it equally requires calibrated analysis.

Further, enhancing repression in host states and those states' being beholden to China are two different outcomes and should not be conflated. While China may be deepening the economic dependencies of weaker states throughout Inter-Asia, such states may also continue to source law from other donor states, including China's competitors. One traveling Chinese law does not a tributary state make. Nonetheless, the fact that China has entered the competitive field of law and development should make the more traditional donors, including the US, take notice. While China may borrow from previous approaches, its methods and ends may also show degrees of difference, even novelty. While these may struggle in the short term, and their viability depends on a number of variables, including the extent to which China can remain attractive as an exemplar of development to other states in the region, it is plausible they will gain in popularity in the long term, particularly in Inter-Asia.

[78] See Erie (n 9) (explaining why the China-Africa Joint Arbitration Center has, to date, largely been a failure).

10

Decolonization, Inter-Regionalism, and Islam

Indonesia's New Criminal Code as Inter-Asian Law

Theodora Putri and Veronica L. Taylor

I INTRODUCTION

Indonesia gained independence in 1945 and transitioned from decades of postwar autocratic rule to democratic political and legal reforms in 1998 ("the *reformasi* period"). Nearly thirty years later, the Indonesian Parliament passed a new Criminal Code (Law No. 1 of 2023 or the new *Kitab Undang-Undang Hukum Pidana* (KUHP)) on December 6, 2023. Creating a new Code in any civil law system is a historic milestone. For Indonesia, it also marks a further divestiture from its colonial legacy. The new KUHP, which comes into effect in 2026, replaces the colonial Penal Code (the existing KUHP), which has been in effect in Indonesia since 1918.

Criminal law in any society is profoundly normative: It defines and imposes sanctions on the most socially unacceptable and harmful behaviors. Social norms, however, are neither static nor homogeneous. This is particularly true for Indonesia, where profoundly diverse ethnic, linguistic, and geographic differences are governed by a highly pluralist legal system in which state secular, Islamic, and customary sources of law overlap and collide.[1] What has been less well analyzed is how the norms informing Indonesia's legal system are influenced by actors within and beyond Asia.[2] This chapter examines the morality provisions in Indonesia's new Criminal Code (the new KUHP) as an arena of contestation among state, secular, and religious reform actors.

[1] Ratno Lukito, *Legal Pluralism in Indonesia: Bridging the Unbridgeable* (Routledge 2013).

[2] For the political history of transregional influence on Indonesia, see Joshua Snyder, "'Arabisation' Death of a Concept?: Gulf States, the Malay-Indonesian World, and the Quest for Post-Sectarian Engagement" (2023) 19(1) JIOR 72–87. For a discussion of external influences on legal education in Indonesia, see Veronica L Taylor, "Asian Legal Education's Engagement with Policy" in Bryant Garth and Gregory Shaffer (eds), *The Globalization of Legal Education* (OUP 2022) 213–237.

In an early and excellent analysis of the new KUHP, Simon Butt argued that:

> Some have suggested the morality provisions [in the new KUHP] reflect Indonesia's recent conservative (mostly Islamic) turn. There may be some truth to this. But equally likely is that national legislators enacted the Code for more pragmatic reasons. These include that they expected that the morality provisions and the democratisation and decolonisation rhetoric would be publicly popular in the leadup to the 2024 elections.[3]

We do not dismiss the political self-interest argument, but in this chapter, we seek to surface some of the sources of influence in this and other legal reform processes in Indonesia that originate in the Middle East, most visibly from Saudi Arabia.[4] These are foreign state projections of soft power[5] that compete with interventions in Indonesia by donors from the Global North as well as newer international development actors, which we discuss below. Using the KUHP reform as an Indonesian case study, we highlight an understudied dimension of Inter-Asian Law (IAL): the transnational and transregional nature of Islamic law, legal institutions, actors, and networks; how these become conduits for transmitting legal norms (whether independent of or in the service of foreign states); and the tension between the global heterogeneity of Islamic law and the efforts of foreign Islamic states to project more absolutist interpretations of Islamic norms into pluralist states such as Indonesia through a range of proxies.

Taking this perspective adds some nuance to the intense and confusing domestic debates about significant legal reforms in Indonesia and critique of these by Western commentators. We argue that inter-regional influences traversing the Middle East–Southeast Asia nexus are already well-established and likely to continue in Indonesia. This invites consideration of IAL as being not only the product of mobile legal concepts and practices conveyed through epistemic communities or processes of harmonization with regional or global standards, but also as a project animated by political and religious ideologies in the service of geopolitical competition.

3 Simon Butt, "Indonesia's New Criminal Code: Indigenising and Democratising Indonesian Criminal Law?" (2023) 32(2) GLR 190, 208–209.

4 In an otherwise excellent piece of scholarship on the reform of the KUHP, Butt (n 3) dismisses this argument in favor of analysis such as: Tito Ambyo, "Indonesia's New Criminal Code: Scaling Up Conservatism and Watering Down Protections for Critics and Minorities" (Australian Institute of International Affairs, January 11, 2023), www.internationalaffairs.org.au/australianoutlook/indonesias-new-criminal-code-scaling-up-conservatism-and-watering-down-protections-for-critics-and-minorities/, accessed May 26, 2025.

5 For some of the historical background to this, see, for example, Jonathan Benthall, "The Rise and Decline of Saudi Overseas Humanitarian Charities" (CIRS Occasional Paper No. 20, September 12, 2018), https://ssrn.com/abstract=3248344, accessed May 26, 2025.

II INDONESIA'S EXISTING CRIMINAL CODE

Before considering which external actors compete to influence legal reform in Indonesia, we should define the competition. At the heart of this case study in contestation is the Indonesian Criminal Code, the existing KUHP, which originated with the Dutch Penal Code (*Wetboek van Strafrecht* or WvS) of 1881.[6] Upon independence in 1945, the Indonesian government retained that Code,[7] the *Wetboek van Strafrecht voor Nederlandsch-Indie (WvS NI)*.[8] A year later, it was officially restated as Indonesia's Criminal Code.[9] However, it remained in Dutch with no official Indonesian translation until the Code reform of 2023.[10] This was a full twenty-five years after the intense constitutional and legal reforms that followed Indonesia's democratization in 1998 and nearly eighty years after its independence.

It is important to note that neither the existing nor the new KUHP represents the totality of criminal law in Indonesia. As with other codified civil law systems, the general provisions in the KUHP apply to criminal acts in the Code and to separate statutes that supplement the Code by covering specific crimes, such as money laundering, corruption, terrorism, and sexual violence. A significant number of administrative statutes also contain criminal sanctions, such as the laws on education, natural resources, broadcasting, and intellectual property.[11]

The new KUHP has been designed to resolve inconsistencies and ambiguities in the language of the Code, while achieving three fundamental policy goals: decolonization, democratization, and harmonization.[12] Decolonization signifies a move away from the Code's Dutch colonial roots. Democratization expresses the aspiration that the new KUHP will reflect democratic principles and the will of Indonesia's people. Harmonization stands for the alignment of the new KUHP with other Indonesian laws and international standards. Looking at continuities between the existing and the new KUHP, Butt argues persuasively that none of these policy goals was fully achieved.[13] While the new KUHP is a milestone for Indonesia as a

6 The Dutch used the principle of "*concordance*" to adapt and apply the Dutch law, including the Penal Code, to their colony: Topo Santoso, *Principles of Indonesian Criminal Law* (Bloomsbury 2023) 23.

7 1945 Constitution Transitional Rules, Article II.

8 Through Staatsblaad 1915 No 732.

9 Law No. 1 of 1946 on Criminal Law Regulations, with some wording from the WvS NI adjusted and updated. Initially, the KUHP only applied to Java and Madura. In 1958, the Indonesian government issued Law No. 73 of 1958, stating that Law No. 1 of 1946 (as amended) would apply to all regions of Indonesia.

10 In the meantime, legal practitioners have relied on unofficial translations by prominent law scholars like R. Soesilo and Prof. Moeljatno. While widely used, these translations have differences that sometimes lead to confusion and uncertainty.

11 Books 1 and 2 of the existing KUHP are the main references for Indonesian criminal law. Book 1 is general provisions; Book 2 regulates acts categorized as crimes (Articles 104 to 488); and Book 3 covers minor offenses (historic content which is rarely used).

12 Law No. 1 of 2023, Elucidation 1.

13 Butt (n 3).

new industrialized economy in Asia and marks a new level of maturity for its political and legal systems, it has been the focus of criticism nationally and internationally.[14]

III "DECOLONIZING" AND "DEMOCRATIZING" THE CRIMINAL CODE

The KUHP has always been accused of being a colonial legacy – neither aligning with Indonesian society's values nor conforming to international norms, including the many international conventions that Indonesia has ratified. Between 1946 and 2022, the KUHP was partially amended more than ten times. As early as 1961, Indonesian scholars started initiatives to fully replace the "colonial" KUHP with a "national" KUHP.[15] However, the Code's complexity, the pluralist nature of Indonesian society and a lack of political will stymied progress.

The sixty years that it took to draft the new KUHP was an extended time frame, even for Code reform in a civil law system. The new KUHP emerged from at least fifteen drafts, led by teams under five prominent criminal law professors who served under thirteen Ministers of Law and Human Rights and six Presidents. The product of those efforts, Law No. 1 of 2023 on the Criminal Code, comes into force in 2026.[16]

The reform process initially focused on decolonization. Many Indonesians saw the existing KUHP as inconsistent with Indonesia's sovereignty, full of articles designed to create public order for the colonists, and not reflecting Indonesian values. Indonesia is a multiethnic, multicultural archipelago of over 17,500 islands with over 1,300 recognized ethnic groups and more than 700 living languages. Legal pluralism is an inevitable consequence: *adat* (or customary law), Islamic law, and state law are intertwined in Indonesia,[17] although the political and cultural dominance of central Java is also a constant thread in Indonesian political and social history.

Although it gained its independence in 1945, Indonesia was an authoritarian state until the democratic reforms that followed President Suharto's fall in 1998. In the period that followed independence, an unspoken dimension of "Indonesian values" was their relationship to religion. Indonesia is a majority Muslim country with 275 million people, 87 percent of whom comprise the world's largest Muslim population. Within Indonesian Islam, 99 percent of those who identify as Muslim

[14] Ibid.

[15] Muladi, "Beberapa Catatan Berkaitan Dengan RUU KUHP Baru" ["Several Notes Relating to the New Criminal Code Bill"] (National Seminar on the Draft Criminal Code at Universitas Internasional Batam, January 17, 2004).

[16] Law No. 1 of 2023, Article 622, which repeals the existing KUHP and its amending laws and criminal provisions in twenty-nine other laws and recodifies several sectoral laws containing criminal provisions.

[17] Lukito (n 1).

are Sunni, with the balance being Shi'a or belonging to other smaller groups such as Ahmadi Muslims (or *Ahmahdiyah*). Post-1945 nation-building efforts by Presidents Sukarno (1945–1967) and Suharto (1968–1998) were avowedly secular – pro-development, pro-modernization, and anti-competing normative forces such as Islam and communism. This was expressed in the nationalist philosophy of *Pancasila* (which recognizes six formal religions), the outlawing of Marxism and communism and the subordination of Islamic law and Islamic courts to state law. The new Criminal Code (KUHP) retains provisions prohibiting the public "spread or development" through any media, of communist and Marxist-Leninist teachings or "other understandings that conflict with Pancasila" (Article 188(1)).[18]

Indonesia today is not an Islamic state; Islamic law covers family relations for Muslims and Islamic banking, finance, and dispute resolution for those who choose them.[19] Only the province of Aceh has an Islamic criminal jurisdiction.[20] Islamic family law in Indonesia is codified as state law and generally interpreted through the lens of Shafi'i jurisprudence.

A. *The Changing Islamic Landscape in Post-Democracy Indonesia*

Despite the secular nature of the state, Islamic political parties and mass organizations within Indonesia are diverse and have played an important role in Indonesian political history and contemporary politics. A full analysis is beyond the scope of this chapter, but political and legal scholars of Indonesia agree that the post-1998 democratic reforms opened the door for a range of Islamic – and Islamist – political actors, as well as progressive democratic, political forces in Indonesia.[21]

Indonesia's two largest mass Islamic organizations, Nahdlatul Ulama (NU) and Muhammadiyah, together account for about 60 percent of Indonesian Muslims and operate extensive social welfare and education networks, including leading Islamic universities. Both have been characterized as moderate and socially progressive, but this view has been challenged.[22]

[18] Butt (n 3) 197.

[19] Islamic family law is itself codified as state law. See, e.g., M B Hooker, *Indonesian Syariah: Defining a National School of Islamic Law* (Institute of Southeast Asian Studies, 2008); Kerstin Steiner, "Branding Islam: Islam, Law, and Bureaucracies in Southeast Asia" (2018) 37(1) J Curr SEAsia Aff 27.

[20] As part of the quasi-autonomy under a Special Autonomy Law of 2001, replaced with the 2006 Law on Aceh that was the basis for settlement of a long-running secessionist conflict.

[21] Suzanne Brenner, "Private Moralities in the Public Sphere: Democratization, Islam, and Gender in Indonesia" (2011) 113(3) American Anthropologist 478, 480. On the backlash against that opening up, see, e.g., Greg Fealy, "Jokowi's Repressive Pluralism" (*East Asia Forum*, September 27, 2020), https://eastasiaforum.org/2020/09/27/jokowis-repressive-pluralism/, accessed May 26, 2025.

[22] Marcus Mietzner and Burhanuddin Muhtadi, "The Myth of Pluralism: Nahdlatul Ulama and the Politics of Religious Tolerance in Indonesia" (2020) 42(1) Contemp SEAsia 58–84.

Other Islamic organizations occupy opposite (and controversial) ends of the political and religious spectrum: The Islam Liberal Network, for example, aims to promote a pluralist and liberal interpretation of Islamic thinking, while other groups openly advocate for disruption of the current legal order and the transformation of Indonesia into an Islamic state. Hizut Tahrir Indonesia, for example, advocates for a pan-Islamic caliphate and the full implementation of *shari'a*, the Indonesian Mujahadeen Council advocates for full implementation of *shari'a* as a precursor to an Islamic state, and the Islamic Defenders Front (*Forum Pembela Islam*, FPI) advocated violent persecution of non-Muslims until it was banned as a terrorist organization in 2020.[23] Closer to the middle of the spectrum is the Muslim Brotherhood-inspired Prosperous Justice Party (*Partai Keadilan Sejahtera*, PKS), which has been registered as a political party since 1998 and has frequently been part of governing coalitions since the *reformasi* period.

Significantly, many of these institutions receive financial support from the Middle East on a scale that has now displaced the official development assistance that donors in the Global North provided as post-1998 rule of law and democratization support to Indonesian government agencies and liberal legal reform non-governmental organizations.

Two of the most prominent conduits are the Indonesian Islamic Propagation Institute (LDII) and the Islamic and Arabic College of Indonesia (LIPIA), which are both Saudi-funded. LDII is an evangelical organization that, to date, has built more than 750 Saudi-oriented mosques in Indonesia. It also provides university-level *shari'a* education and training for preachers in Saudi orthodoxy. LIPIA is a branch of the Imam Muhammad ibn Saud Islamic University in Riyadh and one of the largest Saudi-funded universities in Indonesia. It is a major center for Saudi proselytization and teaches Wahhabi Islamic jurisprudence, exclusively in Arabic. The normative position of both LDII and LIPIA is anti-Shi'a, anti-Christian, anti-Ahmadiyah coupled with a "scripturally rigid" position on Islamic jurisprudence.[24] This is significant because Islamic law in Indonesia has to date been interpreted through a Shafi'i jurisprudential lens which – unlike Middle Eastern Hanbali or Wahabi schools of jurisprudence – recognizes judicial interpretation and community norms as legitimate bases from which to derive Islamic law and thus adapt it to local and contemporary circumstances.

At the same time, Iran is an ideological and financial supporter of the Shi'a minority in Indonesia, primarily through the Jakarta Islamic Center, a hub for translations of Iranian texts and other religious studies, and a provider of scholarships for Indonesian Shi'a to study in Iran.

[23] See, e.g., Fred R von der Mehden, "Saudi Religious Influence in Indonesia" (*Middle East Institute*, December 1, 2014), www.mei.edu/publications/saudi-religious-influence-indonesia, accessed May 26, 2025.

[24] Theodore Friend, *Indonesian Destinies* (Harvard University Press 2009) 383.

Institutions such as these overtly seek to more fully Islamicize all aspects of Indonesian life, including the legal system and so are in direct conflict with progressive Indonesian Muslims for whom a secular legal system that allows for legal pluralism (including the rights of indigenous groups) is inextricably linked to democracy. Political scientists now generally concur that secular democracy in Indonesia declined precipitously during the decade of President Joko Widodo's ("Jokowi") administration (2014–2024).[25] Although Jokowi was wary of political Islamists and sought to shore up statist *Pancasila* ideology, he also strengthened ties with Saudi Arabia in a bid to attract increased Saudi investment.[26] This included historic reciprocal visits by each head of state and agreements on policing and security exchanges, military and counter-terrorism cooperation, and trade agreements that[27] enhanced existing ties through migrant labor from Indonesia and Saudi control of quotas for Indonesians making different kinds of pilgrimages to Mecca and Medina.[28]

At the same time, Saudi-financed institutions in Indonesia sought to place supporters in influential institutional positions. As Varagur puts it:

> "Saudi alumni" are now visible in many arenas of Indonesian public life, holding positions in Muhammadiyah, the Prosperous Justice Party, and the Cabinet. Some have also become preachers and religious teachers, spreading Salafism across the archipelago.[29]

As we discuss below, the final stages of the long road to reforming the Criminal Code in Indonesia were marked by intense competition between progressives seeking to align criminal law with international human rights standards and help make Indonesia's criminal justice system more transparent and responsive and those seeking to entrench moral and sexual norms grounded in conservative Islam within the legal framework.

[25] Tom Power and Eve Warburton (eds), *Democracy in Indonesia: From Stagnation to Regression?* (ISEAS-Yusof Ishak Institute 2020); Edward Aspinall, and Marcus Mietzner, "Southeast Asia's Troubling Elections: Nondemocratic Pluralism in Indonesia" (2019) 30(4) J Democracy 104–118.

[26] Haeril Halim, "Jokowi to welcome Saudi Arabia's King Salman, investment" (*The Jakarta Post*, February 22, 2017), www.thejakartapost.com/news/2017/02/22/jokowi-welcome-saudi-arabia-s-king-salman-investment.html, accessed May 26, 2025.

[27] Ibid.

[28] For a pre-Jokowi synopsis of Saudi–Indonesia relations, see Timothy J Bettis, "Inter-Arab Competition in Southeast Asia: A comparative Analysis of Gulf State Foreign Policies" (*Naval Postgraduate School*, September 2021), https://calhoun.nps.edu/server/api/core/bitstreams/a4e00120-c487-443e-ba51-1e257a5b20a0/content, accessed May 26, 2025.

[29] Kritika Varagur, "Saudi Arabia Quietly Spreads Its Brand of Puritanical Islam in Indonesia" (*Voice of America*, January 17, 2017), www.voanews.com/a/saudi-arabia-quietly-spreads-its-brand-of-puritanical-islam-in-indonesia-/3679287.html, accessed May 26, 2025.

B. *The Long Road to a Final Draft*

Indonesia officially agreed to create a "national" Criminal Code at the First National Law Seminar in 1963. A drafting team of Indonesian legal experts, led by prominent criminal law professors, was formed under the National Legal Development Institute in 1964. The team submitted the first draft of the new KUHP to the Minister of Justice in 1993. However, it was not until 1998, under President Habibie, that the new KUHP was sent to the House of Representatives. In 2004, the new KUHP became part of the national legislation priority program (the legislative agenda, *Prolegnas*), but the intensive review of the draft in the House did not start until 2013 and then not until the end of the parliamentary term.

In 2015, Joko Widodo became the first president to commit to finishing the new KUHP. He released a Presidential Letter outlining the government's commitment to discussing the new KUHP. This was followed by the agreement between the government and the House of Representatives to complete the discussion by the end of 2017. However, that discussion was postponed, extended, and delayed throughout 2018–2019. The delays largely flowed from the complete lack of consensus about the substantive content of the Code provisions.

In 2018, a coalition of Indonesian civil society organizations (CSOs)[30] tried to slow down the process by filing a lawsuit in the Jakarta Pusat District Court against the government for failing to create an official KUHP translation. They aimed to force the government to step back from completing the new KUHP because of the lack of consensus on its content. The court rejected the case, and the Minister of Law characterized it as "a joke."[31]

In September 2019, tensions rose in the final month of the 2014–2019 House of Representatives term. Rumors spread that Members had agreed to a bill, except for articles related to decency. This led to protests in over twelve Indonesian cities, with students and organizations opposing specific articles in the draft Code and demanding revisions. They criticized the government and Parliament for prioritizing politics over public interest and the lack of transparency and public participation in the KUHP reform discussions.[32]

Eventually, Jokowi intervened, asking the House of Representatives to postpone the Bill's passage and instructing the Minister of Law and Human Rights to gather input from community groups to complete the Bill. The President acknowledged

[30] The organizations that filed the lawsuit include the Institute for Criminal Justice Reform, the Jakarta Legal Aid Institute (LBH Jakarta), and the Indonesian Legal Aid Foundation (YLBHI).

[31] Zulfikar Fazli, "Yasonna Anggap Gugatan KUHP Lucu-lucuan" [Yasonna Considers the KUHP Lawsuit a Joke] (*Medcom.id*, June 8, 2018), www.medcom.id/nasional/politik/RkjZeAWk-yasonna-anggap-gugatan-kuhp-lucu-lucuan, accessed June 18, 2024.

[32] Callistasia Wijaya, "RKUHP: Masih ada pasal 'ngawur' yang 'memperparah' nasib korban perkosaan yang hamil" [RKUHP: "Confusing" Articles That "Worsen" the Fate of Rape Victims Who Become Pregnant] (*BBC.com*, September 17, 2019), www.bbc.com/indonesia/indonesia-49712137, accessed June 19, 2024.

that at least fourteen topics in the Bill needed further in-depth study and public hearings. Those related to:

1. living law
2. the death penalty
3. defamation of the President and Vice President
4. possessing supernatural powers
5. damage from poultry and livestock
6. contempt of court
7. blasphemy
8. animal abuse
9. homelessness
10. preventing pregnancy and abortion
11. abortion
12. adultery
13. cohabitation
14. rape

By contrast, the National Alliance for Criminal Code Reform (*Aliansi Nasional Reformasi KUHP*), a coalition of at least forty CSOs that had followed and engaged with the new KUHP process since 2005, stressed that the problems with the Bill extended to at least twenty-four topics.[33]

IV REGULATING MORALITY UNDER INDONESIAN LAW

The new KUHP was not the first post-democratic legal reform in Indonesia in which Islamic morality, gender equality, and democratization have been contested: The 2008 Pornography Law and the 2022 Sexual Violence Law were also arenas in which transregional influences – particularly through proxies for Saudi Arabia – were visible.

In Indonesia, marriage between men and women to have children and build a family is widely understood to be the only proper concept of sexuality.[34] Both state and community see this as a "traditional value,"[35] despite the lived reality of other

[33] See https://reformasikuhp.org and Pemetaan Analisis Aliansi Nasional Reformasi KUHP Terhadap Draft RKUHP Full September 2019 [Mapping and Analysis by the National Alliance for Criminal Code Reform on the Full Draft of RKUHP as of September 2019] (*Reformasi KUHP*, November 7, 2020), https://reformasikuhp.org/pemetaan-dan-analisis-aliansi-nasional-reformasi-kuhp-terhadap-draft-rkuhp-full-september-2019-sebelum-penundaan-oleh-presiden/, accessed May 26, 2025.

[34] Evelyn Blackwood, "Regulation of Sexuality in Indonesian Discourse: Normative Gender, Criminal Law and Shifting Strategies of Control" (2007) 9(3) Cult Health Sex 293, 296; Tom Boellstorff, "The Emergence of Political Homophobia in Indonesia: Masculinity and National Belonging" (2004) 69(4) Ethnos 465, 470.

[35] Ibid 296.

expressions of sexual identity among Indonesians.[36] It also reflects the Islamic approach of regulating life through marriage and the belief that a good family is the foundation of a good society.[37] Women are idealized as mothers and faithful wives and "belong" to the family and household; men are the breadwinners and "belong" to the state and community.[38]

The Suharto regime (1968–1998) used these beliefs to promote its preferred view of national development. Gender and family ideology blurred the boundaries between public and private, strengthened state power, and allowed the state to assert the right to govern the family.[39] This helped to combat competing forces within society, such as religion or ethnic allegiances.[40] When Suharto fell in May 1998, political actors were newly able to assert moral authority that did not originate with the state.[41]

The *reformasi* period following Suharto was an intense decade of replacing authoritarian laws and institutions with democratic ones, including human rights. At the same time, new social freedoms allowed Indonesian Muslims to express their piety publicly[42] – part of the "Islamic revival" in Southeast Asia.[43] Many who believed in Suharto's prescriptive ideals saw social norms weakening.[44] They demanded that the state enforce Islamic morality more actively, giving Islamic groups and parties an increased voice in Indonesian politics,[45] including opportunist politicians, who used Islamic narratives to gain votes.[46]

36 Boellstorff (n 34).

37 Sayyid Muhammad, *Fiqih Keluarga: Seni Berkeluarga Islami* [Family Fiqh and the Art of the Islamic Family] (Bina Media, Yogyakarta 2005) 10.

38 Blackwood (n 34) 295; Kathy Robinson, "Masculinity, Sexuality and Islam: The Gender Politics of Regime Change in Indonesia" in Linda Rae Bennett and Sharyn Graham Davies (eds), *Sex and Sexualities in Contemporary Indonesia* (Taylor & Francis 2015) 55. See also Law No. 1 of 1974 on Marriage, Chap IV Art 31 Para (3).

39 Brenner (n 21) 480.

40 Ibid.

41 Ibid.

42 David M Bourchier, "Two Decades of Ideological Contestation in Indonesia: From Democratic Cosmopolitanism to Religious Nationalism" (2019) 49(5) J Contemp Asia 713.

43 Vincent J H Houben, "Southeast Asia and Islam" (2003) 588(1) Annals Am Acad Pol & Soc Sci 149.

44 Sharyn Graham Davies, "How a Populist Morality Movement is Blocking a Law against Sexual Violence in Indonesia" (*The Conversation*, September 19, 2019), https://theconversation.com/how-a-populist-morality-movement-is-blocking-a-law-against-sexual-violence-in-indonesia-analysis-123448, accessed June 16, 2024.

45 Bourchier (n 25); Maria Platt, Sharyn Graham Davies and Linda Rae Bennett, "Contestations of Gender, Sexuality and Morality in Contemporary Indonesia" (2018) 42(1) Asian Stud Rev 1.

46 Qurrata A'yun, "Politicising Blasphemy in Indonesia: How Islamic Alliances Are Established" (2020) 4 Melbourne Asia Review, https://minerva-access.unimelb.edu.au/items/7a2901bf-96aa-548d-9459-1c86ac6277fa, accessed May 26, 2025; Michael Buehler, *The Politics of Shari'a Law: Islamist Activists and the State in Democratizing Indonesia* (CUP 2016).

A. *The 2008 Pornography Law*

Law Number 44 of 2008 on Pornography was passed in October 2008, having started as an Anti-pornography Bill in 2003.[47] The catalyst was the relaxation of strict censorship and new press freedoms under Law No. 40 of 1999, which saw a mushrooming of magazines and tabloids with pictures of scantily dressed women.[48]

In 2004 the word "pornoaction" (*pornoaksi*) was coined, defined as "an action in public that exploits sex, obscenity and/or erotica." The title of the Bill was changed to the Draft Law on Anti-pornography and Pornoaction (*Rancangan Undang-Undang Anti Pornografi dan Pornoaksi*, RUU APP). The impetus was concerns about popular entertainers (*dangdut* singers) dancing "erotically."[49] New provisions in the Bill prohibited, among other things, revealing certain sensual body parts (defined as genitals, thighs, buttocks, navel, and any part of a woman's breasts)[50] and engaging in erotic dancing in public areas.[51] Protest erupted in response, particularly from women activists, who saw it as a state restriction on women's appearance in public.[52] Saudi-supported organizations in Indonesia, by contrast, particularly those adhering to what the Indonesian Ministry of Religious Affairs calls "puritanical Islam," teach that women should be fully veiled, with face and body completely covered.

The debate heated up again in 2006 when Playboy, the American men's adult magazine, published an Indonesian version.[53] Playboy Indonesia folded, and its Editor-in-Chief Erwin Arnada was prosecuted under Article 282 KUHP for disseminating content or portraits that offend decency.[54] Although acquitted by the District Court, the Supreme Court found Arnada guilty, and he was jailed for two years.

47 Law No. 44 of 2008 defined pornography as "pictures, sketches, illustrations, photos, writing, sounds, moving images, animations, cartoons, conversations, gestures, or other forms of messages through various forms of communication media and/or public performances, which contain obscenity or exploitation sexual activity that violates the norms of decency in the society."

48 Stephen Sherlock, "Parties and Decision-Making in the Indonesian Parliament: A Case Study of RUU APP, the Anti-Pornography Bill" (2009) 10(2) Austl J Asian L 159, 163.

49 Inul Iri Obral Bokong [Inul is Jealous of Discounted Buttocks] (*Detik Hot*, December 8, 2005), https://hot.detik.com/music/d-494264/inul-iri-obral-bokong, accessed May 26, 2025.

50 Draft law on Anti-pornography and Pornoaction (RUU APP) Article 4.

51 Ibid Article 28.

52 Pam Allen, "Women, Gendered Activism and Indonesia's Anti-Pornography Bill" (February 2009) (19) in *Intersections: Gender and Sexuality in Asia and the Pacific*, http://intersections.anu.edu.au/issue19/allen.htm, accessed June 16, 2024.

53 "Playboy Indonesia 'not pornography,'" (*Al Jazeera*, April 5, 2007), www.aljazeera.com/news/2007/4/5/playboy-indonesia-not-pornography, accessed May 26, 2025.

54 See interviews with a number of important national figures in "Kasus Playboy Indonesia Dari Terbit Hingga Tutup Kontroversial" [The Case of Playboy Indonesia from Publication to Close is Controversial] (*Tempo*, August 27, 2010), https://nasional.tempo.co/read/274387/kasus-playboy-indonesia-dari-terbit-hingga-tutup-kontroversial, accessed May 26, 2025.

Many commentators speculate that this decision was made under pressure from mobilized protests, particularly from the FPI, which at the time was led by Muhammad Rizieq Shihab.[55] The FPI was founded as a hardline Islamist organization in 1998 and grew to a membership of millions that undertook mass protests and rallies against ethnic Chinese and Christian minority figures and liberal and reformist politicians. These included the Chinese-Indonesian Governor of Jakarta, Basuki Tjahaja Purnama (or "Ahok"),[56] resulting in him losing his 2017 re-election bid, being prosecuted for blasphemy on flimsy grounds and jailed, while FPI was banned by the Indonesian government in 2020. Its former leader, Rizieq Shihab, fled to Saudi Arabia, where he had long-standing ties.[57]

The Indonesian Council of Ulema (*Majelis Ulama Indonesia* or MUI) also emerged as one of the strongest supporters of the draft law. The MUI is a peak body of Islamic groups in Indonesia, including Saudi-supported institutions such as the LDII. In this debate, despite public protest, MUI was adamant in its efforts, urging the Parliament to pass the Bill.[58] The Saudi-funded pressure group, National Movement to Safeguard the Fatwas of the Indonesian Ulemas Council (not a subset of the MUI as such), was also vocal,[59] and one MUI member representative argued that, "People's culture is contaminated with Western culture that knows no boundaries of porn, so people live immoral and undignified lives."[60] Contamination by the decadent (non-Muslim) West is a common trope in Islamist discourse in Indonesia, but it is at odds with the MUI's stated collective claim to represent "moderate Islam."[61]

Islamic parties and Islamist organizations were not the only groups in Parliament pushing for the Bill. It was heavily supported by nationalist parties, such as *Golkar*

[55] Institute for Criminal Justice Reform, "Putusan MA soal 'Playboy' Diprotes" [The Supreme Court Decision on Playboy was protested] (January 20, 2011), https://icjr.or.id/putusan-ma-soal-playboy-diprotes/, accessed May 26, 2025.

[56] Russell Dunn, "Ahok, the FOE and PilPres2029" (*New Mandala*, November 16, 2016), www.newmandala.org/ahok-fpi-pilpres-2019/, accessed May 26, 2025.

[57] Krithika Varagur, "The World's Largest Muslim-Majority Country Was Long Considered a Tolerant Place. But Thanks to Saudi Money and Influence, It Has Taken a Sharply Conservative Turn" (*The Guardian*, April 16, 2020), www.theguardian.com/news/2020/apr/16/how-saudi-arabia-religious-project-transformed-indonesia-islam, accessed May 26, 2025.

[58] Kabupaten Sumenep [Regency of Sumenep, Madura], "MUI akan Gelar Demo Besar-Besaran Jika RUU APP Tidak Disahkan" [MUI will hold a massive demonstration if the RUU-APP (Anti-Pornography and Pornographic Acts Bill) is not ratified] (April 11, 2006), www.sumenepkab.go.id/berita/baca/mui-akan-gelar-demo-besar-besaran-jika-ruu-app-tidak-disahkan, accessed May 26, 2025.

[59] Syafiq Hasyim, "Indonesia's MUI Today: Truly Moderate or Merely Pragmatic?" (*ISEAS Perspective*, January 20, 2021), www.iseas.edu.sg/articles-commentaries/iseas-perspective/iseas-perspective-2020-3-indonesias-mui-today-truly-moderate-or-merely-pragmatic-by-syafiq-hasyim/, accessed May 26, 2025.

[60] Statement by Prof Dr KH Umar Shihab, the head of Ukhuwah Islamiyah (Islamic Brotherhood) Commission MUI for 1998–2015, before he became a Member of Parliament of the Golkar Party in Sumenep (n 58).

[61] Hasyim (n 59).

(Functional Groups Party) and the Democratic Party. They used the Bill to improve ties with Islamic organizations.[62] Eventually, an agreement between eight of ten factions in the Parliament (*Dewan Perwakilan Rakyat*, DPR)[63] allowed it to pass without the pornoaction content.

The MUI as Legal Reform Actor

The role of the MUI as a political and legal actor in Indonesia is beyond the scope of this chapter, but it is significant that the (then) MUI chairman, Ma'ruf Amin, was recruited by Jokowi to serve as his Vice-Presidential running mate after the FPI succeeded in running Jakarta Governor Ahok out of office on blasphemy charges. Ma'ruf became Vice President in the second Jokowi administration (2019–2024).

MUI was established as a peak body of Islamic scholars to advise the government and issue *fatawa* (advisory opinions) about the conformity of laws, regulations, and social practices with Islamic law and to interface between government and mass Islamic organizations. In 2001, MUI issued *fatwa* No 287/2001, stating that depicting erotic behavior that can arouse lust through print and electronic media is *haram* (forbidden), as are cohabitation and wearing revealing, tight-fitting, or see-through clothing.[64] Hasyim argues that, although not gender specific, the real target of the *fatwa* is women.[65] MUI's view is that to maintain public morality in Indonesia requires limiting the flow of immorality in Muslims' bodies and minds, particularly those of women, as the source of *fitna* (immorality).[66] These negative perceptions originate from the concept that Eve was a follower of the Devil and that women's bodies are the abode of Satan. This is reinforced by the famous depiction of women in Prophet Muhammad's words: "Whenever a man and a woman meet together, the third party is Satan."[67]

MUI works against a background of deepening institutional and interpersonal ties between Saudi Arabia and Indonesia and what some commentators have in the past pointed to as the "Arabisation" of Indonesian society.[68] Some scholars now argue that Indonesia is in a "post-Arabisation" period, where Saudi-inspired expressions of

[62] Sherlock (n 48).

[63] The Indonesian Democratic Party of Struggle (PDI Perjuangan) and Prosperous Peace Party (Partai Damai Sejahtera) continue to reject this law as vague and endangering the public; see "RUU Pornografi Disahkan Dalam Suasana Kontroversial" [Pornography Law Passed in Controversial Atmosphere] (*Hukumonline*, October 3, 2008), www.hukumonline.com/berita/a/ruu-pornografi-disahkan-dalam-suasana-kontroversial-hol20405, accessed May 26, 2025.

[64] Ibid.

[65] Syafiq Hasyim, *The Shariatisation of Indonesia: The Politics of the Council of Indonesian Ulama (Majelis Ulama Indonesia, MUI)* (Brill 2023) 310.

[66] Ibid 307.

[67] Hasyim (n 65) 308, citing the work of the renowned Islamic feminist, Nawal El Saadawi, *The Hidden Face of Eve: Women in the Arab World* (Zed Books 2007) 203.

[68] Asmiati Malik and Scott Edwards, "Saudi Arabia's Influence in Southeast Asia: Too Embedded to Be Disrupted?" (*The Conversation*, November 9, 2018), theconversation.com/saudi-arabias-influence-in-southeast-asia-too-embedded-to-be-disrupted-106543, accessed May 26, 2025.

piety have become mainstream.[69] In the 1990s, few urban women in Indonesia wore *hijab* (headscarves). The estimate is that 75 percent do so today,[70] and more than fifty local administrative decrees compel this, in apparent violation of national human rights guarantees.[71] An increasingly visible minority of women wear full veils or black *chador*, previously unknown in Indonesia.[72] Another important indicator is the mainstreaming of Saudi-supported television, radio, and social media content, including YouTube channels and the rise of young, urban Salafist influencers.[73]

B. *The 2022 Sexual Violence Law*

The Indonesian Parliament passed Law Number 12 of 2022 on Sexual Violence (*Undang-Undang Tindak Pidana Kekerasan Seksual* or UUTPKS) after it was first proposed by the National Commission on Violence against Women (*Komnas Perempuan*) in 2012. In 2016, the (then) Draft Law of the Elimination of Sexual Violence (*Rancangan Undang-Undang Penghapusan Kekerasan Seksual* or RUU PKS) was submitted to Parliament, and in 2020 the Parliament adopted the Bill, before finally passing it in 2022.

The reform was prompted by dissatisfaction with how criminal justice handled sexual violence. The KUHP had a very limited definition of sexual violence, and existing laws, including the Code of Criminal Procedure and Law No. 31 of 2014 on Victim and Witness Protection, failed to provide necessary protection and services for victims. In the KUHP, sexual violence was categorized under "crimes against decency" (*tindak pidana kesusilaan*) and limited to adultery (Article 284); rape (Article 285 – defined as a man who uses physical force or threat of force toward a woman to have penetration of the penis into the vagina – outside marriage); aggravated rape (Articles 286-289); intercourse with underage women; indecent activities with minors; and obscene acts (Article 290). Locating sexually related crimes under "crimes against decency" contributes to the view of many Indonesians that sexual violence is a matter of morality in which the victim is blameworthy rather than a form of criminal violence.

69 Joshua Snyder, "'Arabisation' Death of a Concept?: Gulf States, the Malay-Indonesian World, and the Quest for Post-Sectarian Engagement"(2023) 19(1) J Indian Ocean Region 72–87.

70 See also Diego Fossati and Yew-Foong Hui, "The Indonesia National Survey Project: Economy, Society and Politics" in Diego Fossati, Yew-Foong Hui and Siwage Dharma Negara (eds), *The Indonesia National Survey Project: Economy, Society and Politics* (ISEAS Publishing 2017) 19–20.

71 Ambyo (n 4).

72 Yuyun Sunesti, "Riset Ungkap 3 Hal Baru tentang Perempuan Muda Bercadar di Indonesia" [Research Reveals 3 New Things about Young Women with Veils in Indonesia], (*The Conversation*, December 17, 2020), https://theconversation.com/riset-ungkap-3-hal-baru-tentang-perempuan-muda-bercadar-di-indonesia-152006, accessed May 26, 2025.

73 Fachri Aidulsyah, "The Rise of Urban Salafism in Indonesia: The Social-Media and Pop Culture of New Indonesian Islamic Youth" (2023) 51 AJSS 252–259.

Formalizing the RUU PKS took a decade due to resistance from political parties and the community but mainly from conservative Islamic groups and from within the Parliament itself. The PKS openly rejected the Bill until the end.[74] In their view, it conflicted with Islamic values, promoted sex outside marriage, and supported LGBT relationships. PKS also objected to the Bill using "sexual consent" – in their view, consensual sexual relations are strictly prohibited for those not officially married. They feared that a broader concept of consent would condone *zina* (illegal sexual intercourse in Islamic law). A nuanced debate about this is difficult in a climate where conservative religious views have become populist. Commentators suggest that the PKS rejected the Bill not only based on Islamic values, but also to gain votes in the 2019 election.[75] In response, the Draft Law on Sexual Violence Crimes (*Rancangan Undang-Undang Tindak Pidana Kekerasan Seksual*, RUU TPKS)[76] working committee revised the Bill to exclude the phrase "sexual consent."[77]

The Family Love Alliance (*Aliansi Cinta Keluarga*, or AILA) also consistently opposed the RUU TPKS. AILA is an inter-institutional alliance concerned with strengthening the family by following Islamic teachings. They saw the Bill as a Western product that did not reflect Indonesian values or *Pancasila* and ignored the real sexual crimes – free sex and deviant sexual behavior. AILA argued, "The philosophy of the RUU TPKS is 'sexual freedom' under the guise of protecting victims."[78]

Law No. 12 of 2022 on Sexual Violence represents a decade of sustained advocacy by the National Commission on Violence against Women in collaboration with a coalition of women's crisis center organizations and law reform and women's rights CSOs throughout Indonesia. It also secured the full support of the Ministry of

[74] UU TPKS was approved by eight factions in the House of Representatives: The Indonesian Democratic Party of Struggle (PDI Perjuangan), Functional Groups (Golkar), the Great Indonesia Movement Party (Gerindra), the National Democratic Party (NasDem), the National Awakening Party (Partai Kebangkitan Bangsa, PKB), the National Mandate Party (Partai Amanat National, PAN), the Democratic Party (Party Demokrat), and the United Development Party (Partai Persatuan Pembangunan, PPP). The PKS rejected it.

[75] Balawyn Jones and Max Walden, "Conservative Rejection of Indonesia's Anti-Sexual Violence Bill Misplaced" (*The Conversation*, February 26, 2019), https://theconversation.com/conservative-rejection-of-indonesias-anti-sexual-violence-bill-misplaced-111683, accessed May 26, 2025.

[76] Note that there are no authorized official translations of Indonesian draft or final legislation, so this Bill has also been translated as "the Bill on Sexual Violence Eradication" and the "Sexual Violence Bill."

[77] "Panja Klaim RUU TPKS Tak Muat Frasa Sexual Consent" [Panja Claims RUU TPKS Does Not Include the Phrase Sexual Consent] (CNN *Indonesia*, November 17, 2021), https://www.cnnindonesia.com/nasional/20211117130747-32-722365/panja-klaim-ruu-tpks-tak-muat-frasa-sexual-consent, accessed May 26, 2025.

[78] Fida A, "AILA Indonesia Kembali Suarakan Penolakan terhadap RUU TPKS" [AILA Indonesia Voices Opposition against the RUU TPKS] (*Hidayatullah*, April 12, 2022), https://hidayatullah.com/berita/nasional/2022/04/12/228580/jelang-disahkan-aila-indonesia-kembali-suarakan-penolakan-terhadap-ruu-tpks.html, accessed May 26, 2025.

Women and Children, the Ministry of Law and Human Rights, and the DPR, including moderate Islamic parties, most notably Indonesia's National Awakening Party (*Partai Kebangkitan Bangsa*, PKB) and its main constituent organization, Nahdlatul Ulama (NU), which is Indonesia's largest Islamic organization.[79]

AILA as a Legal Reform Actor

AILA's rejection of the Sexual Violence Law was also part of a long-standing campaign. In 2016–2017, it challenged provisions of the KUHP in the Constitutional Court based on non-conformity with (their view of) Islamic values. They asked the Court, among other things, to expand the definition of adultery (Article 284, currently defined as unfaithfulness to one's marriage partner) and expand the definition of indecent acts in Article 292 to include the same sex.[80]

By a narrow majority of five to four, the Constitutional Court rejected the petition.[81] The majority held that the Court should exercise judicial restraint and avoid being a "positive legislator" by extending the scope of acts in the Code.[82] The dissenters argued that the Constitution should not allow absolute freedom for each person to act merely according to their own will and that this applies more so if that behavior confines and contradicts religious values and Divine light, as well as the living law which lives and develops among Indonesian people.[83] That argument was carried into the debate about the new KUHP.

V PASSAGE OF LAW NO. 1 OF 2023 ON THE CRIMINAL CODE (THE NEW KUHP)

The new KUHP was passed by Parliament in December 2022 and promulgated as Law No. 1 of 2023 with some controversial articles intact. Those attracting the most concern related to "living law," freedom of expression (including provisions related to demonstrations, insults to the President, Vice President and the government), and the articles related to *zina* and cohabitation.

[79] M Iqbal Machmudi, "NU dan Muhammadiyah Dukung RUU PKS dengan Catatan" [NU and Muhammadiyah Support the PKS Bill with Notes] (*Media Indonesia*, March 6, 2020), https://mediaindonesia.com/humaniora/294764/nu-dan-muhammadiyah-dukung-ruu-pks-dengan-catatan#google_vignette, accessed May 26, 2025; Kristian Erdianto and Inggried Dwi Wedhaswary, "Fraksi PKB Dukung RUU Penghapusan Kekerasan Seksual Segera Disahkan" [PKB Faction Supports the Elimination of Sexual Violence Bill Will Be Passed Immediately] (*Kompas*, February 8, 2019), https://nasional.kompas.com/read/2019/02/08/18095021/fraksi-pkb-dukung-ruu-penghapusan-kekerasan-seksual-segera-disahkan, accessed May 26, 2025.

[80] Constitutional Court of the Republic of Indonesia, Case 46/PUU-XIV/2016, 6–7, https://www.mkri.id/index.php?page=web.Putusan&id=1&kat=1&cari=81, accessed June 18, 2024.

[81] The Court's decision is analyzed in detail by Butt (n 3) 204. See also Simon Butt, "Religious Conservatism, Islamic Criminal Law and the Judiciary in Indonesia: A Tale of Three Courts" (2018) 50(3) J Leg Plur Unoff Law 402.

[82] Ibid 453.

[83] Ibid 465.

Critique of the new KUHP came predominantly from the community, law reform actors and human rights organizations rather than religious organizations. In the months preceding its passage, the Criminal Code Drafting Team, particularly the Deputy Minister of Law and Human Rights, approached stakeholders to discuss and build support for the Bill. Those consulted ranged from the MUI and Islamic organizations to academics, CSOs, and activists. The result was several changes to the draft of the new KUHP often referred to as a "middle way" or compromise among the diversity of views, which had emerged over the long period of its drafting.

A. *The Drafting History of the New Criminal Code*

Between 1981 and 1993, a drafting team led by Mardjono Reskodiputro[84] used the term "recodification" to describe revising the KUHP. The team reviewed the existing KUHP and reformulated it into a more understandable Indonesian language. It took twelve years to finalize a complete draft, which was submitted in 1993. However, the draft remained stuck in the Ministry of Justice for years. The discussion resumed in 1998 when Muladi became Justice Minister, and continued under the next Minister of Justice, Yusril Izha Mahendra, who formed a new drafting team, appointing Muladi and Barda Nawawi to lead it.

The new team worked for another ten years before they handed a refreshed draft to (then) President Yudhoyono, who submitted it to the House of Representatives in 2012. The Muladi team used a "total codification" approach, inserting criminal acts from various laws not covered by the KUHP[85] to prevent "dualism" (criminal offenses being regulated within and outside the KUHP). They built on the reform ideas in the 1993 draft, as did the next drafting team, led by Harkristuti Harkrisnowo.[86] The new features included in the final draft of Law No. 1 of 2023 were:[87]

[84] Mardjono Reksodiputro chaired the third Drafting Committee for the new KUHP (1987–1993). The first Committee chair was Prof. Soedarto (1963–1986) followed by Prof. Roeslan Saleh (1986–1987). Under Mardjono's leadership, on March 13, 1993, the new KUHP was first submitted to the Minister of Justice, Ismail Saleh: "Setengah Abad Lebih Melahirkan RKUHP" [More than half a century of giving birth to the RKUHP] (*Tempo*, February 6, 2018), https://hukum.tempo.co/read/1057807/setengah-abad-lebih-melahirkan-rkuhp, accessed May 26, 2025.

[85] Bernhard Ruben Fritz Sumigar, "Kodifikasi dalam RKUHP dan Implikasi terhadap Hukum Pidana Indonesia" [The Codification of the Draft of KUHP and its implications for Indonesia's Criminal Law] (Institute for Criminal Justice Reform, 2015), https://icjr.or.id/wp-content/uploads/2015/09/Implikasi-kodifikasi-dalam-R-KUHP_Final.pdf, accessed May 26, 2025.

[86] Prof. Harkristuti Harkrisnowo led the Drafting Committee after Professor Muladi passed away in 2020. She successfully steered the RKUHP to become Law No. 1 of 2023.

[87] Mardjono Reksodiputro, "Meletakkan (kembali) Proses Pembaruan Hukum Pidana Dalam Konteks Pembangunan Hukum Nasional" [(Re)laying the Criminal Law Reform Process In the Context of National Legal Development] (the National Consultation Meeting ELSAM Initiative and National Alliance R-KUHP in Jakarta, May 2–3, 2018), https://reformasikuhp.org/merancang-arah-pembaruan-hukum-pidana-indonesia/, accessed June 18, 2024.

- An updated approach to qualifying crimes no longer distinguishes between crimes (Book 2) and violations (Book 3) and is now linked to types of penalties, including principal penalties, additional penalties, and special penalties (such as the death penalty);[88]
- The principal penalties include new penalties, such as supervision and community service. These serve as alternatives to short-term imprisonment, allowing judges to choose the appropriate punishment based on the purpose of sentencing;[89]
- The type of fine penalty is formulated using fine categories;[90]
- *sentencing guidelines for judges;*[91]
- Acknowledgement of the role of customary law in defining offenses and imposing criminal sanctions, while maintaining the principle of legality;[92] and
- Expanding criminal liability beyond individuals to include corporate criminal liability.[93]

The attitude to the normative content of the Code evolved with the design and mechanics of the drafting process. Mardjono comments that from about 2000, the drafting team sought to create a law that truly reflected Indonesian culture and Islamic teaching.[94] The addition of "Islamic teaching" as a drafting criterion is difficult to substantiate, but it coincides with the post-*reformasi* rise in public discourse about Islamic morality and an uptick in local government regulations on women's dress and personal conduct.[95]

The scholars leading and participating in the drafting team over different periods of its history were highly educated and globally connected, with extensive experience in serving government and balancing competing interests. Without an empirical study, we do not know how they considered and filtered influences from abroad. We do know what those vectors of influence were likely to have been. We have considered influences from the Middle East earlier in this chapter and the debates across political and popular Islam that played out in the lead-up to the introduction of the new KUHP.

88 Law No. 1 of 2023, Article 64.
89 Ibid Article 65 and its elucidation, Article 51.
90 Ibid Article 79.
91 Ibid Articles 53–54.
92 Ibid Article 2.
93 Ibid Articles 45–50.
94 Mardjono Reksodiputro, "Sejarah Singkat Konsep KUHP Nasional" [A Brief History of the Concept of the National Criminal Code] (paper presented at the National Seminar on the Draft Criminal Code, Faculty of Law, University of Indonesia, June 12, 2014), https://mardjonoreksodiputro.blogspot.com/2013/12/sejarah-singkat-konsep-kuhp-nasional.html, accessed May 26, 2025.
95 Luviana, "Women's Bodies Are Controlled through Discriminatory Local Regulations" (*Konde*, July 25, 2022), www.konde.co/2022/07/busana-dan-tubuh-perempuan-dikontrol-lewat-perda-diskriminatif-38-tahun-peringatan-cedaw.html/, accessed May 26, 2025.

Western legal reform influence tends to be less overt and less well-funded than it was in the immediate post-1998 *reformasi* period. It includes long-standing personal and institutional ties with the legal systems in which many Indonesian legal elites are educated: the Netherlands, the United States, and Australia. Each of these countries maintains official development assistance-funded legal reform projects in Indonesia of many decades' standing that directly or indirectly connect to criminal justice reform. Although the strategic priorities and projects have changed over time, in the aggregate these tend to promote practices that enhance rule of law and build Indonesian capacity to participate in bilateral and multilateral agreements.[96] In the case of Australia, the approach is to fund Indonesian CSOs to engage with and persuade government and parliamentary actors.

From Asia, influential legal systems tend to be those of economies that Indonesia aspires to emulate, including Singapore, South Korea, and Taiwan. Singapore and Indonesia are linked through their mutual membership of ASEAN and Singapore's role as a de facto commercial dispute and arbitration hub for Indonesia. They concluded an extradition treaty in 2024.[97] South Korea has been particularly active in providing advice on regulatory reform and modernizing legislative capacity,[98] which is an important indirect support to South Korean foreign investment in Indonesia. Neighboring Malaysia is deliberately omitted from this list, even though it is an ASEAN member, a diverse and majority Muslim country, a neighbor that shares a border with Indonesia, and a more highly ranked economy.[99] Indonesian policymakers are generally allergic to the suggestion the Malaysia is a helpful model, for complex historical and cultural reasons and for the legitimate (but also convenient) reason that Malaysia's common law heritage and constitutional monarchy make its legal institutions unlike Indonesia's.

96 See, for example, the Australian Indonesia Partnership for Justice (AIPJ), which has "Implementing Justice Reforms in Law Enforcement, Courts, and Corrections Institutions that Support the Rule of Law" as one of its strategic priorities: www.aipj.or.id. USAID, which indirectly influences criminal justice through programming on governance and anti-corruption: www.usaid.gov/indonesia/democracy-human-rights-and-governance, and the Netherlands through its universities and Centre for International Legal Development, which have been actively engaged in criminal justice reform support, including the adoption of restorative justice approaches through alternative sanction, e.g.: www.cilc.nl/indonesia-is-restorative-justice-the-solution-for-overcrowding-in-indonesias-prisons/#:~:text=Indonesia%20and%20the%20Netherlands%20share,support%20legal%20and%20judicial%20reforms, accessed November 1, 2024.

97 "Indonesia-Singapore extradition agreement is progressive: Minister" (*Antara*, March 29, 2024), https://en.antaranews.com/news/309582/indonesia-singapore-extradition-agreement-is-progressive-minister, accessed May 26, 2025.

98 Cabinet Secretariat, Republic of Indonesia, "Cabinet Secretariat South Korea's MOLEG Holds Seminar on Statutory Interpretation" (May 28, 2021), https://setkab.go.id/en/cabinet-secretariat-south-koreas-moleg-holds-seminar-on-statutory-interpretation/, accessed May 26, 2025.

99 Although Indonesia's is the larger economy by size, Malaysia's income per capita is three times larger than Indonesia's. See current World Bank data comparisons: https://data.worldbank.org/?locations=TH-MY-ID-SG-PH-VN, accessed November 1, 2024.

B. *Adultery in the New KUHP*

Conservative Islamic critics were active in pressing for reframing adultery as a more broadly defined crime under the existing KUHP. Article 284 hinges on the definition of marriage in Article 27 of the Civil Code, which states that a man can only be married to one woman and a woman to only one man, and prosecution relies on a complaint (*delik aduan*) from the respective spouse. The concept of *zina* in Islam refers to illegal sexual intercourse and encompasses both adultery and fornication, including unmarried sex.[100] The PKS Party demanded that the new KUHP use this expanded definition. The MUI also strongly supported this expansion. The (then) Minister of Law and Human Rights, Patrialis Akbar, who came from the National Mandate Party (Partai Amanat Nasional or PAN), an Islamic nationalist party, promised to ensure that the expanded article was included in the new KUHP.[101]

Around this time, the sensational results of a survey of university students were publicly reported in Indonesia. The authors claimed that 97.05 percent of 1,660 respondents from sixteen universities in Yogyakarta were losing their virginity in consensual sexual relations during their time at university. While the authors and results lacked credibility,[102] the results were widely quoted, reinforcing perceptions of moral decline.

During the Yudhoyono administration (2004–2008), two significant provisions were added to the 2005 draft. However, as the debate progressed, these provisions were scaled back. The 2005 draft covered *zina* (adultery) in Article 484, paragraphs 1 (a) to (d), reproducing the existing definition of adultery. It also included paragraph 1(e) to criminalize sexual intercourse between unmarried men and women. This draft also expanded the range of third parties who could file a complaint to initiate criminal prosecution and increased the maximum penalty from nine months (as per Law No. 1 of 1946) to five years.[103] The 2008[104] and 2012[105] versions retained this *zina*

[100] Ziba Mir-Hosseini, "Criminalising Sexuality: Zina Laws as Violence against Women in Muslim Contexts" (2011) 8(15) SUR International Journal on Human Rights 7, accessed May 26, 2025.

[101] Ali, "Definisi Zina dalam KUHP Akan Direvisi" [Definition of Adultery in the Criminal Code to be Revised] (*Hukumonline*, July 5, 2011), www.hukumonline.com/berita/a/definisi-zina-dalam-kuhp-akan-direvisi-lt4e11c8adcccd4/, accessed May 26, 2025.

[102] The survey was conducted by the Institute for Love and Humanitarian Studies (Lembaga Studi Cinta dan Kemanusiaan) and the Center for Business and Humanities Training (Pusat Pelatihan Bisnis dan Humaniora, LSCK PUSBIH). Neither has any Internet presence beyond the survey results and the citations of their survey results. See Winanti Praptiningsih, "Tes Keperawanan dan Isu Moralitas Publik" [Virginity Testing and Public Morality Issues] (*Jurnal Perempuan*, January 2, 2015), www.jurnalperempuan.org/wacana-feminis/tes-keperawanan-dan-isu-moralitas-publik?locale=en, accessed May 26, 2025.

[103] Draft Penal Code 2005, Article 484.

[104] Draft Penal Code 2008, Article 485.

[105] Draft Penal Code 2012, Article 483.

definition and higher penalty, perhaps for the deterrent effect and to symbolize the moral intention rooted in Islamic teachings.

In 2019 version,[106] the criminal sanction for adultery was reduced to a maximum imprisonment of one year or a fine, which is still heavier than the penalty in the existing KUHP. Additionally, the parties able to make a criminal complaint about adultery were narrowed from "harmed third party" to parents or children. In the 2022 version,[107] eligibility to file a criminal complaint about adultery was further restricted to only the husband or wife for married individuals and parents or children for unmarried individuals. The drafters also modified the scope of *zina* by moving the provision about sexual intercourse between unmarried men and women from the main body of the article to the elucidation section. This move appeared to address objections from those opposing the broader definition of zina while still accommodating those advocating for its expansion. This wider scope of zina beyond marital relationships was finalized in Article 411 of Law No. 1 of 2023.

C. *Cohabitation in the New Criminal Code*

Provisions on cohabitation were also adjusted while drafting the new KUHP. The cohabitation provision in the 2005 version stated: "Any person who lives together as husband and wife outside of *legal marriage* shall be imprisoned for a maximum of 5 (five) years or a maximum fine of Category IV."[108]

This made cohabitation per se illegal, not an offense triggered by a complaint. The 2019 draft[109] revised this to require a complaint by the husband, wife, parents, or children, or by the village head in the absence of complaints from the husband, wife, parents, or children. Moreover, in the 2022 version,[110] the part about the village head making a complaint was eventually removed. The complaints were narrowed to apply only to a spouse for married individuals and to parents or their children for unmarried individuals, making cohabitation an "absolute complaint" offense, like adultery.

The next issue was the "legal marriage" element, criticized as being Java-centric. Outside Java, many people do not have access to government services or the resources to conduct a legal marriage, or they mark their married status based on *adat* law or religious rites. In the draft 2019 of the Code, the word "legal" was removed to acknowledge this plurality. This was a prudent choice but may be difficult to implement in practice. For the sanctioned, a maximum of five years' imprisonment was reduced to one year, and the draft 2019 until Law No. 1 of 2023,

[106] Draft Penal Code 2019, Article 417.
[107] Draft Penal Code 2022, Article 411.
[108] Draft Penal Code 2005, Article 486.
[109] Draft Penal Code 2019, Article 418.
[110] Draft Penal Code 2022, Article 412.

it's agreed on a maximum of six months' imprisonment or a fine of up to 10 million IDR (equal to 650 USD).

VI IMPLICATIONS OF THE NEW CRIMINAL CODE'S TREATMENT OF MORALITY

The new Criminal Code broadened the definition of adultery to include unmarried individuals and allowed parents or children over sixteen to file complaints about adultery. It also criminalized the offense of cohabitation while acknowledging that marriage exists in various customary and religious forms, though it does not recognize de facto or same-sex relationships. The lengthy drafting process for the new KUHP reflects a government trying to navigate between the expectations of very different parties and interests.

Some people see the criminalization of sexual relations between consenting adults as government interference with both individual privacy and individual rights and freedoms.[111] The secular nationalist parties with a majority in the legislature were against stricter laws on morality but did not want to openly oppose the idea because it could lead to them being painted as supportive of adultery and free sex in a climate of increasing social and Islamic conservatism. Using the limiting techniques in the drafting kept them safe from that accusation.

One technique the government used to steer to the middle ground was "absolute complaints." Both the *zina* (adultery) and cohabitation provisions are absolute criminal complaints: Prosecution requires a complaint from the parties named in the law. This is intended to prevent moral policing by unrelated individuals or groups. It tries to balance state interference in private matters by limiting prosecution to instances where people who are harmed (the husband, wife, parents, or their children) make a complaint to the police.

On the other hand, groups such as the MUI and conservative Islamic parties saw these provisions as bulwarks against moral decline. Although Islamic conservatives were not satisfied with the light sentences in the final version of the Code, they succeeded in shaping provisions reflecting Indonesia's values and identity in more Islamic rather than pluralist terms. The advantage for the government was that Law No. 1 of 2023, as national law, eliminates the possibility of regulating these offenses at the regional level (beyond Aceh) and so is a structural barrier to vigilantism and arbitrary actions.[112]

[111] Because it contravenes Article 17 of the International Convention on Civil and Political Rights which Indonesia ratified in 2005.

[112] Normand Edwin Elnizar, "Seminar KUHP Baru, Kohabitasi Hingga Hukuman Mati" [Seminar to Review New Criminal Code, Cohabitation to Death Penalty] (*Hukumonline*, February 22, 2023), www.hukumonline.com/berita/a/immh-ui-gelar-seminar-mengkaji-kuhp-baru–bahas-kohabitasi-hingga-hukuman-mati-lt63f5e94f6128a/?page = 2, accessed May 26, 2025.

The new KUHP also has unresolved challenges. One is realizing gender equality. On their face, the *zina* and cohabitation provisions suggest that two persons commit the crime. This means both the man and woman involved should be prosecuted, but it relies on the *morality* articles not being manipulated to punish women.

Another challenge is the social reality of underage sexual activity and child marriage in Indonesia. Parents often address the "problem" of sexually active children by using religious celebrants or local officials to perform early marriages.[113] This avoids *zina* and upholds religious and social norms, although economic pressure and other motives also play a role. Because a parent can file a complaint and withdraw it at any time before trial, there is a risk that parents might use this to coerce their children into marriage, even though this is an offense under the Sexual Violence Law.

VII CONCLUSION

These compromises are unlikely to satisfy international critics of the new KUHP (including the Western providers of legal technical assistance through official development assistance), who see it as part of the slippage in Indonesia's commitment to the rule of law and international human rights obligations post-*reformasi*. However, they represent the political reality of a secular democracy in which religion (particularly Islam) remains an important factor in the foundation and politics of the state[114] and where legal reform is a domestic and international battleground for conflicting worldviews. Until the law is implemented in 2026 and until the Code of Criminal Procedure is revised, it will be difficult to ascertain with confidence whether the new KUHP is simply a symbolic marker of Islamic virtue or has the intended effect of shaping Indonesian behavior in practice, and how justice actors such as the police, prosecutors, and courts will enforce and interpret it.

[113] AIPJ2, "Analysis of Marriage Dispensation Decision in Indonesia" (November 19, 2019), https://aipj.or.id/pages/publication/analisis-putusan-dispensasi-kawin-di-indonesia, accessed May 26, 2025.

[114] Nadirsyah Hosen, "The Politics of Shari'a Law: Islamist Activists and the State in Democratizing Indonesia" (2018) 91 Pacific Affairs 428.

11

Lay Participation in Legal Decision-Making in Asia in a Global Context

Valerie P. Hans

I INTRODUCTION

Taiwan became the latest country to adopt lay legal decision-making when it passed the Taiwan's Citizen Judges Act in 2020 and began holding lay judge trials in January of 2023.[1] It joined several other Asian countries in reforming its legal system to include citizens as decision-makers. In contemporary times, it might be surprising that many jurisdictions continue to rely on untrained citizens to decide criminal and civil cases.[2] With a few exceptions, most countries have a ready supply of professionally trained judges to decide the outcomes of legal cases. In fact, some countries have either abolished or severely restricted the scope of lay participation in their legal systems.[3] So why have so many others turned to the citizenry to resolve legal

[1] Citizen Judges Act (Act on Criminal Trials with the participation of Citizen Judge [Guomin Faguan]) (August 28, 2020), https://law.moj.gov.tw/ENG/LawClass/LawAll.aspx?pcode=A0030320 (TW), accessed May 29, 2025. See also Sophia Yang, "35,000 Taiwanese Citizens Tapped for Jury Duty as Lay Judge System Starts in 2023" (*Taiwan News*, December 3, 2022), www.taiwannews.com.tw/news/4739408, accessed May 29, 2025. For analysis, see commentary by leading Taiwanese scholars and lawyers in "Taiwan Citizen Judges Act: Part I" (October 10, 2022) 3(4) US-Asia Law Institute, https://usali.org/usali-perspectives-blog/taiwans-citizen-judges-act-part-1, accessed May 29, 2025; "Taiwan Citizen Judges Act: Part II" (October 10, 2022) 3(5) US-Asia Law Institute, https://usali.org/usali-perspectives-blog/taiwans-citizen-judges-act-part-2, accessed May 29, 2025.

[2] Sanja Kutnjak Ivković and Valerie P Hans, "A Worldwide Perspective on Lay Participation" in Sanja Kutnjak Ivković et al (eds), *Juries, Lay Judges, and Mixed Courts: A Global Perspective* (CUP 2021) (describing global use of lay participation in criminal cases); Valerie P Hans, "The Landscape of Lay Participation in Civil Litigation" in Margaret Woo and Remco van Rhee (eds), *Comparative Civil Procedure: Power, Authority and Culture in Dispute Resolution* (Elgar 2025) 356 (describing global extent of lay participation in civil cases).

[3] See, for example, Claire M Germain, "Trials by Peers: The Ebb and Flow of the Criminal Jury in France and Belgium" in Sanja Kutnjak Ivković et al (eds), *Juries, Lay Judges, and Mixed Courts: A Global Perspective* (CUP 2021) 218; Anna Offit, "Dismissing the Jury: Mixed Courts and Lay Participation in Norway" in Sanja Kutnjak Ivković et al (eds), *Juries, Lay Judges, and Mixed Courts: A Global Perspective* (CUP 2021) 197.

disputes? The example of Taiwan shows that even some countries with no history of lay legal decision-making are adopting new systems that incorporate lay citizens in contemporary times. Why do so?

Studies of lay legal decision-making have identified a host of values that lay participants bring to the task of legal decision-making.[4] Most obviously, citizen decision-makers are able to incorporate contemporary community values into their fact-finding. A group of individuals drawn from a cross section of the population is in a much better position to know the community's sentiments and to consider them as they decide on the responsibilities and evaluate the behavior of the parties. Citizens also offer a measure of protection against legal professionals who may have become inattentive, jaded, or biased because of their earlier experiences with legal cases. Citizen participation has the potential to generate broader societal benefits as well, in that it can contribute to the transparency and legitimacy of the legal system and foster the spirit of civic engagement in those who take part.[5]

Considering these benefits, perhaps it is no longer surprising that close to two-thirds of the world's countries use lay citizens in some decision-making capacity in the resolution of criminal cases.[6] In a recent analysis of 195 countries (193 United Nations countries, combined with two additional jurisdictions, Hong Kong and Taiwan), Sanja Kutnjak Ivković and I found that 64 percent of the world's countries, a total of 125 countries, used some form of lay citizen decision-making in legal cases.[7]

The most common form is a mixed court of lay judges and professionally trained judges, the form that Taiwan has adopted, with seventy-one countries, including

4 For summaries of the arguments, see Sanja Kutnjak Ivković, *Lay Participation in Criminal Trials: The Case of Croatia* (Austin & Winfield 1999); Neil Vidmar, *World Jury Systems* (OUP 2000); Neil Vidmar and Valerie P Hans, *American Juries: The Verdict* (Prometheus 2007); Valerie P Hans, "Jury Systems Around the World" (2008) 4 Annual Rev of L & Social Science 257.

5 John Gastil et al, *The Jury and Democracy: How Jury Deliberation Promotes Civic Engagement and Political Participation* (OUP 2010) 46–47 (finding that low-frequency voters jurors in criminal cases were more likely to vote in later elections); John Gastil et al, "Civic Awakening in the Jury Room: A Test of the Connection between Jury Deliberation and Political Participation" (2002) 64 J Politics 585, 586 (examining whether jurors deliberating and reaching a verdict affected the likelihood of voting in subsequent elections); John Gastil et al, "Jury Service and Electoral Participation: A Test of the Participation Hypothesis" (2008) 70 J Politics 351, 358–360 (analyzing the effect of jury deliberation on jurors' likelihood of voting in subsequent elections). See also Shari Seidman Diamond, "What Jurors Think: Expectations and Reactions of Citizens Who Serve as Jurors" in Robert E Litan (ed), *Verdict: Assessing the Civil Jury* (Brookings Institution Press 1993) 282 (documenting positive responses among those who served as jurors); Valerie P Hans et al, "Deliberative Democracy and the American Civil Jury" (2014) 11 JELS 697, 710–712 (finding that jurors who sat on twelve-person civil juries required to be unanimous were more likely to vote after serving).

6 Kutnjak Ivković and Hans, "A Worldwide Perspective" (n 2); Sanja Kutnjak Ivković and Valerie P Hans, "Beacons of Democracy? A Worldwide Exploration of the Relationship between Democracy and Lay Participation in Criminal Cases" (2023) 98 Chicago-Kent L Rev 131–161.

7 Kutnjak Ivković and Hans, "A Worldwide Perspective" (n 2) 336 tbl 16.3.

Taiwan, using this form of lay participation.[8] Next most common is trial by jury, in which the jury deliberates on its own to arrive at a verdict, practiced by close to fifty countries.[9] Two less common methods are lay courts, which operate outside the formal legal system, found in twenty countries, and lay magistrates, who decide cases either individually or in groups, in thirteen countries.[10]

We discovered that the frequency and type of lay citizen involvement in legal decision-making differ across the continents.[11] It is highest in the continents of Australia and Oceania (93%), North America (78%), Africa (72%), and Europe (70%), and markedly lower in South America (33%) and in Asia (41%). The forms of lay participation are also notably different. In most continents, mixed courts are more common than juries.

That pattern is true in Asian countries. Twelve Asian countries use mixed courts: China, Japan, Kazakhstan, Lebanon, Malaysia, Mongolia, North Korea, Taiwan, Tajikistan, Turkmenistan, Uzbekistan, and Vietnam, whereas juries are used in the six countries of Hong Kong, Iran (in media cases), Myanmar, the Russian Federation, South Korea, and Sri Lanka.[12]

Not surprisingly, mixed courts are more common in countries that follow a civil law tradition, while countries with a common law tradition are more apt to rely on jury systems.[13] Most of these systems of lay participation have been in use for some time. However, it is useful to examine the newly introduced systems of lay participation in Asia. They offer important lessons to us about the inter-Asian and global influences at work in the transplanting of legal institutions.

II NEW SYSTEMS OF LAY PARTICIPATION IN ASIA

Four Asian countries have introduced new systems of lay participation in the last several decades: Russia,[14] Japan, South Korea, and, most recently, Taiwan. This chapter explores the context and motives for introducing lay participation, and how each country debated and decided upon a specific form of citizen involvement in legal decision-making. The chapter also reviews research on the experiences with lay participation in these countries.

[8] Ibid 338 tbl 16.5.
[9] Ibid.
[10] Ibid.
[11] Ibid 339. We relied on the online source *World Atlas* (2019) to classify countries by continents. Kutnjak Ivković and Hans, "A Worldwide Perspective" (n 2) 330–331.
[12] Sanja Kutnjak Ivković and Valerie P Hans, "Database of Lay Participation in Legal Decision Making" (2022) Unpublished Database, Michigan State University and Cornell University. The Philippines uses lay courts; Iran relies on both the jury (in media cases) and lay courts; and Mongolia uses mixed courts and lay courts.
[13] Kutnjak Ivković and Hans, "A Worldwide Perspective" (n 2) 340–341.
[14] Russia might be classified as being on the European continent and the Asian continent; however, the World Atlas assigns each country to only one continent and Russia is listed as a country in the Asian continent. *World Atlas* (n 11).

III MOTIVATION TO INTRODUCE NEW SYSTEMS OF LAY PARTICIPATION

In each of the four countries, the adoption of new systems of lay participation occurred during a period of political democratization. Those who pressed for citizen decision-making in law emphasized how citizen involvement would promote democratic self-governance, create connections between the citizenry and the government, and improve public confidence in the courts.

Russia and former countries within the Union of Soviet Socialist Republics (USSR) provide a clear example of political upheaval leading to democratization and legal reform. Trial by jury has a long history in Russia, where it was first introduced in the 1860s. However, it was effectively abolished during the Bolshevik Revolution and eventually replaced by a mixed court of lay and professional judges, which prevailed during the Soviet period.[15] Jury trials were resurrected in Russia in 1993, after the collapse of the Soviet Union led to significant judicial and other reforms.[16] International organizations interested in promoting democracy in former Soviet countries provided advisors and external funding, which contributed to the development and launching of Russia's modern jury system.[17]

In Japan, during the same period of the 1990s, there was growing interest in reforming the legal system. The business community was frustrated by the slow pace of the country's judicial process, inadequate numbers of individuals in the legal profession, and minimal alternative dispute resolution options. Rieko Kage writes that the Japanese business community was not especially interested in citizen participation, but they did constitute a powerful force demanding general judicial reforms.[18] The business community's interest in reform converged with that of other groups. Japan's remarkably high conviction rate of 99 percent had led one scholar to identify it as a "prosecutor's paradise,"[19] raising concerns about whether professional judges were overly inclined to accept prosecution arguments even in cases with strong defense claims.[20] Reinforcing these concerns, reports surfaced

[15] Nikolai Kovalev and Sergei Nasanov, "The Russian Jury Trial: An Ongoing Legal and Political Experiment" in Sanja Kutnjak Ivković et al (eds), *Juries, Lay Judges, and Mixed Courts: A Global Perspective* (CUP 2021) 237.

[16] Ibid 248.

[17] For fuller discussion of the political and other forces at work in justice reform in the former countries of the USSR, see Nikolai Kovalev, *Criminal Justice Reform in Russia, Ukraine, and the Former Republics of the Soviet Union* (Edwin Mellen Press 2010).

[18] Rieko Kage, *Who Judges? Designing Jury Systems in Japan, East Asia, and Europe* (CUP 2017).

[19] David T Johnson, *The Japanese Way of Justice: Prosecuting Crime in Japan* (OUP 2002).

[20] Dimitri Vanoverbeke and Hiroshi Fukurai, "Lay Participation in the Criminal Trial in Japan: A Decade of Activity and Its Sociopolitical Consequences" in Sanja Kutnjak Ivković et al (eds), *Juries, Lay Judges, and Mixed Courts: A Global Perspective* (CUP 2021) 69, 71.

about notable cases of wrongful conviction.[21] The Japan Federation of Bar Associations, which represents lawyers in private practice across the country, also pressed for reform, including the introduction of a jury system in Japan, as did members of the Research Group on Jury Trial, who had been encouraging a return to Japan's jury system for years.[22] The Justice System Reform Council was thus created in 1999 to analyze and recommend legal reforms for the purposes of "clarifying the role to be played by justice in Japanese society in the 21st century and examining and deliberating fundamental measures necessary for the realization of a justice system that is easy for the people to utilize, participation by the people in the justice system … and other reforms of the justice system …"[23] After protracted and intense debate, it ultimately recommended that Japan adopt a mixed court system, *Saiban-in seido*. After a five-year period of preparation, the first trial was held in 2019. The intent of the legislation enacting *Saiban-in seido* was "to contribute to the promotion of the public's understanding of the judicial system and thereby raise their confidence in it."[24]

In his summary of South Korea's jury system, Park noted the "significant strides toward the democratization of the country" in the 1980s after political successes in challenging its oppressive military government; changes included direct election of government leaders by citizens and greater independence of judges.[25] By the 1990s, policymakers and activists urged the introduction of judicial reforms, including citizen participation in legal decision-making, "to enhance the democratic legitimacy of and public confidence in the trial processes."[26]

Finally, the debates over the form of Taiwan's lay participation system tracked political divisions, as Kage explains, with the conservative KMT party inclined toward a mixed court system that would keep professional judges in control, whereas the opposition DPP endorsed a jury system in which jurors would deliberate independently of professional judges.[27] Ultimately, a mixed court system similar to that of Japan's *Saiban-in seido* was decided upon. Interestingly, Taiwan's Citizen Judge Act begins with the following language imbued with democratic concepts of popular sovereignty and transparency: "This Act is enacted to facilitate the participation in the criminal trial by both citizens and judges, enhance the transparency of

21 Ibid 71.

22 Hiroshi Fukurai, "The Rebirth of Japan's Petit Quasi-Jury and Grand Jury Systems: Cross National Analysis of Legal Consciousness and Lay Participatory Experience in Japan and the US" (2007) 40 Cornell Int'l LJ 315.

23 Takuya Katsuta, "Japan's Rejection of the American Criminal Jury" (2010) 58 AJCL 497 (citing Justice System Reform Council [2001]).

24 Vanoverbeke and Fukurai (n 20) 69 (summarizing legislative intent reflected in Jury Law, Article 1).

25 Jaihyun Park, "The Korean Jury System: The First Decade" in Sanja Kutnjak Ivković et al (eds), *Juries, Lay Judges, and Mixed Courts: A Global Perspective* (CUP 2021) 88, 90.

26 Ibid 90.

27 Kage (n 18) 152.

the judiciary, account for the public's opinions towards the law, promote the public's confidence in the judiciary, and provide the public with a better understanding of the judiciary, so as to honor the ideal of popular sovereignty."[28]

Although the political, social, and legal circumstances differed, policymakers in all four countries were motivated by the potential benefits of a more democratically responsive legal process. An interesting question is whether democratizing the legal system by incorporating lay citizen decision-makers strengthens democracy more generally. Using a global database that included information about countries' lay participation systems and their political characteristics, Sanja Kutnjak Ivković and I calculated the statistical associations between the presence of citizen participation in a country and country-level democracy indicators.[29] We discovered that countries with lay participation systems had significantly higher democracy scores.[30] The relationships between lay participation democracy measures were strongest and most consistent for countries with jury systems; the relationships were less consistent for countries with mixed courts as their form of lay participation. Of course, we cannot say from the statistical analysis alone that lay participation *causes* greater democratization. The causal arrow may go the other way; countries with strong democracies may provide the conditions for lay participation to flourish.[31]

IV INTER-ASIAN AND GLOBAL INFLUENCES

What is notable about these introductions of lay participation is the way in which judges, lawyers, and policymakers actively engaged in exploring different international models for lay participation. Of course, with two-thirds of global countries having some form of lay participation, there were multiple models to examine. We can also observe the operation of inter-Asian influence, as experts from Asian countries advised policymakers in other Asian countries about the advantages and disadvantages of different approaches.

In South Korea, a Judicial Reform Committee was established in 2003 to consider judicial reforms; its report recommended an "advisory jury" in part because of concerns about the constitutionality of a criminal verdict decided by non-law-trained judges.[32] Although Japan had not yet settled on its lay participation system, members of Korea's Judicial Reform Committee were "well aware of the debates over justice system reform in neighboring Japan."[33] South Korea introduced its advisory jury system in 2008; it reflects diverse global influences in that it includes features of both the United States (US) jury system (independent deliberation) and

28 Citizen Judges Act (n 1) art 1.

29 Kutnjak Ivković and Hans, "Beacons of Democracy?" (n 6).

30 Ibid 147 tbl 1.

31 Ibid 159–160 (discussing the issue of causation and suggesting the possibility of bidirectional causality).

32 Kage (n 18) 165–168.

33 Ibid 166.

the German lay assessor system (opportunities to consult with the professional judge during deliberation).[34] Defendants must request a jury trial and a professional judge must approve the request, which over time has limited the number of jury trials.

In Japan, in advance of introducing the *Saiban-in seido* system, the Japanese Supreme Court engaged in a "study tour" of jury and lay judge systems around the world.[35] Furthermore, the Ministry of Justice established a Study Group on the Saiban-in System to review the implementation of the new system; members of the Study Group referenced a variety of global sources in their discussions. Rieko Kage analyzed the minutes of the Study Group's eighteen meetings from September 2009 through June 2013; she found that their discussions included periodic references to practices in other countries.[36] The most frequent references – a total of 41 – were to practices in the US. Second in frequency were eleven references to the advisory jury system in South Korea.[37] Third most frequent were six references to the United Kingdom. Fewer than five references were made to the practices in Italy, Germany, France, Sweden, and Europe more generally. It is interesting to observe that the most common references were to countries with jury systems, rather than to countries with other mixed court systems like Japan's. Kage found that study group members referenced the outside world on a variety of topics, including lay judge selection, the eligibility of cases to be decided by the lay judge system, the appeals process, and lay jurors' psychological stress.[38]

Taiwan began examining different models of lay participation as early as 1988. The Judicial Yuan sent officials on fact-finding trips to multiple countries around the globe, including France, Switzerland, and Austria.[39] Despite intensive study and discussion, no proposals were successfully launched in this early period.

Reinvigorating the debates in 2011, a committee chaired by Judicial Yuan Vice President Su included legal scholars who had obtained doctorates in different countries: two from the US, one from Germany, and one from Japan. The committee also invited scholars from Germany, Japan, and Korea to give lectures on their countries' lay participation systems.[40] The "trial observer" system that emerged from the committee's deliberations, however, met with strong objections.[41] The trial

[34] Jae-Hyup Lee, "Korean Jury Trial: Has the New System Brought About Changes?" (2010) 12(1) Asian-Pacific L & Policy J 58.

[35] Kage (n 18) 133.

[36] Rieko Kage, Discussant Comments for Professor Hiroshi Fukurai, East Asian Lay Participation Roundtable (May 24, 2024) Clarke Program in East Asian Law & Culture, Cornell Law School, Ithaca NY.

[37] Ibid.

[38] Ibid.

[39] Kage (n 18) 144.

[40] Ibid 146–147.

[41] See discussion in Mong-Hwa Chin, *A Social Psychological Perspective on the Decision-Making Processes of Trial Judges in Taiwan* (Dissertation, Duke University School of Law, 2014) 86–118. See also Kuo-Chang Huang and Chang-Ching Lin, "Mock Jury Trial in Taiwan – Paving the Ground for Introducing Lay Participation" (2014) 38(4) Law & Hum Behav 367.

observer system created a mixed court of lay and professional judges; however, the votes of the lay judges were to be nonbinding, leading eventually to rejection of that model.

As Taiwan's policymakers continued to debate the appropriate lay participation model for the country, policymakers drew on the experiences of both Japan's mixed court system and South Korea's advisory jury system, again revealing the role of inter-Asian communication in legal reform.[42] The Japanese lawyer Satoru Shinomiya, for example, visited Taiwan to lecture and consult with legal and policy experts about Japan's *Saiban-in seido*. Based on Japan's experience with a mixed court, Shinomiya proffered advice about how to create and maintain a successful lay participation system.[43]

The lay participation reform process in South Korea, Japan, and Taiwan thus drew on models and practices from around the globe, as well as from other Asian countries. Through visits to other countries' courts to observe trials with lay judges or juries, consultations with legal officials in other countries, and participation in international conferences and working groups, these legal actors and policymakers were engaged in the business of legal transplantation.

A "legal transplant" refers to the common occurrence of one country incorporating into its own legal system another country's law, legal procedure, or legal institution, or even entire legal system.[44] Some scholars of comparative law object that the term "legal transplant" conveys the mistaken idea that a transplanted law or legal procedure will operate in the same way in a new country as it did in the country of origin. They suggest that referring to the process as "legal translation" more accurately captures the ways in which countries adopt but also modify laws and legal procedures from other countries to suit their own needs.[45] Because the four countries I discuss modified the approaches used elsewhere to create new institutions that fit within their own legal systems, these activities certainly qualify as exercises in legal translation.

V A COMMON AND DISTINCTIVE FEATURE OF ASIAN LAY PARTICIPATION SYSTEMS: A STRONG ROLE FOR PROFESSIONAL JUDGES

One noteworthy feature of the four systems of lay participation in Asia is that each of them preserves a strong role for the professional judges. In Russia, the trial judge has a great deal of power to shape the jury's experience and responses. Rather than

42 Kage (n 36).
43 Valerie P Hans, "Ardent Advocate for Citizens' Voices: Satoru Shinomiya and the Development of Japan's *Saiban-in seido*" in Mari Hirayama (ed), *The Festschrift for Professor Satoru Shinomiya* (Nippon Hyoronsha 2022) 582, 589.
44 Valerie P Hans, "Trial by Jury: Story of a Legal Transplant" (2017) 51 L & Soc'y Rev 471.
45 Ibid 472.

obtaining a jury's general verdict of guilty or not guilty, the trial judge provides the jury with a list of specific questions about the evidence in the case. If there are apparent inconsistencies or errors in the jury's responses, the judge can set aside the jury's factual conclusions. During a jury trial, the judge may halt the proceeding and return the case to the prosecutor for further development of the facts and more investigation. In addition, appeals courts can overturn not only jury convictions but also jury acquittals. All these features create a relatively weak jury system that is vulnerable to political pressures.[46] In other reforms, the Russian government restricted the types of cases that juries may hear, in particular political crimes in which an independent jury might be considered to be most valuable (or most threatening, from a governmental perspective).[47]

In Japan's mixed courts, the most serious crimes must be tried by the mixed court; lay judges participate in both guilt and sentencing decisions; and (unlike South Korea) their votes are binding. These requirements suggest a robust presence for citizens. However, a mixed court system in which lay citizens and professionally trained judges decide the case together is likely to privilege professional judges' voices. Sanja Kutnjak Ivković has written extensively about the advantages that professional judges hold in a mixed tribunal based on their legal expertise and previous experiences.[48] Research on agreement rates between lay and professional judges in mixed tribunals finds them to be extraordinarily high, suggestive of strong professional judge influence. Ironically, the vitality of lay judge input in mixed courts may depend on the willingness of professional judges to cede some of their advantages.

These four countries follow civil law traditions. I have previously written about the way in which some countries with civil law traditions and the institution of the jury trial shifted from independent jury systems to mixed tribunals:

> In time, however, a number of civil law countries abandoned trial by jury, shifting to the mixed court approach in which lay judges and professional judges decide cases jointly. The dominant role of the presiding judge was seen as more compatible with the inquisitorial approach of civil law legal systems. Cynically, however, one must also note that a mixed tribunal offers an easier method of controlling unruly lay fact finders.[49]

Finally, in South Korea, the jury system is "advisory" only.[50] The three professional judges presiding over the jury trial may set aside the jury's recommended

46 Kovalev (n 17); Stephen C Thaman, "The Nullification of the Russian Jury: Lessons for Jury-Inspired Reform in Eurasia and Beyond" (2007) 40 Cornell Int'l LJ 357.

47 Kovalev and Nasanov (n 15).

48 Sanja Kutnjak Ivković, "Exploring Lay Participation in Legal Decision Making: Lessons from Mixed Tribunals" (2007) 40 Cornell Int'l LJ 429; Sanja Kutnjak Ivković, "Ears of the Deaf: The Theory and Reality of Lay Judges in Mixed Tribunals" (2015) 90 Chicago-Kent L Rev 1031.

49 Hans (n 44) 482.

50 Park (n 25) 237; Valerie P Hans, "Reflections on the Korean Jury Trial" (2014) 14 J Korean L 81.

verdict and substitute their own judgment. In addition, under certain conditions, the presiding judge may enter the deliberation room to offer advice. If the jury is not unanimous, the judge must join the deliberation; and even when the jury is unanimous, the jurors may still invite the judge to join the deliberation if a majority of jurors agree to it. Research on the South Korean advisory jury has found extraordinarily high agreement rates between the jury and the judge, which is not surprising given the required intervention of the judge when the jury is not unanimous.[51]

The robust role for professional judges in these new Asian systems of lay participation contrasts with the judge's role in other countries that have recently adopted lay participation systems. Argentina's new jury systems provide the strongest contrast. After one province introduced a mixed court system in 2004,[52] other provinces that later adopted lay participation chose a classic jury model rather than a mixed court.[53]

VI IMPACT OF NEW SYSTEMS OF LAY PARTICIPATION

The introduction of new systems of lay participation is a scholar's dream. The structures and operation of existing jury systems were created and reified over many decades and even centuries, so that it is difficult as a scientific matter to identify the effects of the characteristics of lay participation systems. By comparing before and after the advent of a lay participation system, these new introductions allow us to examine how lay participation affects other aspects of the legal system, the outcomes of trials, the public's support for the courts, and more.

The East Asian countries have facilitated scholarly assessment by providing data and information for regular evaluations of the introductions of their lay participation systems. Russia also collected data early on, but according to some researchers, it has become more difficult to track developments over time.

In Japan, there were numerous pre-implementation studies, including a remarkable 640 mock *Saiban-in* trials held in front of public audiences between 2004 and 2009.[54] In some of the mock trials, the mixed court's deliberations were videotaped and became the subject of scholarly study. Since the introduction of *Saiban-in seido*, the Japanese Supreme Court has regularly surveyed the *Saiban-in* and makes reports of case outcomes publicly available on its website. Likewise, in South Korea, a series of surveys of the public, criminal defendants, and legal elites explored

[51] Sangoon Kim et al, "Judge-Jury Agreement in Criminal Cases: The First Three Years of the Korean Jury System" (2013) 10 JELS 35; Park (n 25).

[52] María Inés Bergoglio, "Twelve Years of Mixed Tribunals in Argentina" in Sanja Kutnjak Ivković et al (eds), *Juries, Lay Judges, and Mixed Courts: A Global Perspective* (CUP 2021) 47.

[53] Vanina Almeida et al, "The Rise of the Jury in Argentina: Evolution in Real Time" in Sanja Kutnjak Ivković et al (eds), *Juries, Lay Judges, and Mixed Courts: A Global Perspective* (CUP 2021) 25.

[54] Kage (n 18) 208.

attitudes and views about lay participation.[55] In addition, the Korean Supreme Court's Committee for Citizen Participation in Law has engaged in extensive reviews of jury trials, and the National Court Administration of South Korea has released information about the types of crimes heard by juries, the conviction rates, and judge–jury agreement rates.[56]

Taiwan's Citizen Judges Act includes an article specifically requiring systematic research on the new mixed court system.[57] Chapter 6 is devoted to the creation of a fifteen-person assessment committee and its required activities. For example, Article 105 provides:

> The Judicial Yuan shall promptly constitute the Committee for the Assessment of System of Civil Participation in Criminal Trials (hereinafter referred to as "the Assessment Committee") after the entry into force of this Act. The Assessment Committee shall conduct necessary research and submit an annual assessment report on the implementation of the system of civil participation in criminal trials in the previous year. The Assessment Committee shall submit its final report within a year after the completion of assessment period. The final report shall contain a holistic assessment of the implementation of the system of civil participation in criminal trials, and recommendations for possible amendment of the law or for relevant complementary measures.

Setting aside Russia, where it has been difficult to assess the contemporary operation of its jury system, the extensive collection of data by Japan and South Korea allows us to get a sense of the experiences and impact of these new systems of lay participation. Overall, both Japan and South Korea consider their implementations to have been successful.

Vanoverbeke and Fukurai, taking advantage of the extensive data that the Japanese Supreme Court has published on its website, show that there was a remarkable degree of stability in trial outcomes over the first ten years of *Saiban-in seido*.[58] Perhaps surprisingly, trial conviction rates have remained close to 99 percent, dipping a bit to 98 percent in the few years prior to the pandemic.[59] Mari Hirayama has identified some small declines in indictment rates (which one might expect if prosecutors are more selective in bringing cases before mixed tribunals) and some increases in criminal sentences, particularly in sex offense cases.[60]

[55] Kwangbai Park et al, "Preparing the Ground: The Case of Korea," Paper presented at the Annual Meeting of the Law & Society Association, Baltimore, MD (July 7, 2007) (describing the research conducted by members of the president's reform committee). The survey data were published in Korean in: *Presidential Committee on Judicial Reform, Republic of Korea, Reform for the Judicial Advancement: White Book* (2007).

[56] Park (n 25).

[57] Citizen Judges Act (n 1) ch 6.

[58] Vanoverbeke and Fukurai (n 20).

[59] Ibid.

[60] Mari Hirayama, "The First Ten Years of the Lay Judge System: Now, Do We Have "Hope" for Criminal Trials in Japan?" (2020) 1(3) Hastings J Crime & Punishment 267.

In contrast, Japanese lawyers have reported dramatic effects on criminal investigation and trial procedures, such as increases in court-appointed lawyers, recording of interrogations, more evidence disclosures, and greater overall transparency from the oral trial.[61] In addition, several researchers have reported positive effects of lay judge service on the *Saiban-in*.[62] The lay judges are more positive about the courts following their lay judge service, which is in line with the greater positivity following jury service in the US and Argentina.[63] Vanoverbeke and Fukurai also report post-service political activity among former *Saiban-in*, consistent with the civic engagement effects found elsewhere for jury service.[64]

The South Korean jury experiment has also continued, although the number of jury trials is low in part because of defendant choices and professional judges' ability to veto a jury trial in specific cases.[65] As noted earlier, the advisory jury and the trial judges agree at extremely high rates, perhaps attributable to the interjection of the trial judge into nonunanimous jury deliberations. As Park explains, there continue to be concerns about the nonbinding nature of the advisory jury's verdicts. Yet, surveys suggest that this feature of the jury system is well-supported by the public and legal actors. The majority of the public, former jurors, and judges expressed support for the nonbinding nature of the advisory jury's verdict and do not favor a change. The sole exception: criminal defendants.[66] Prosecutors often appeal South Korean jury verdicts; however, higher courts have upheld the vast majority, and at higher percentages than bench trial case decisions.[67]

VII CONCLUSION

It is an exciting time to be examining lay participation in law. Taiwan's incorporation of systematic study of the implementation and operation of the Citizen Judges Act in its first years deserves applause. That information will be valuable not only for improving Taiwan's new system, but also to provide documentation about how legal

61 Makoto Ibusuki, "'Quo Vadis?' First Year Inspection to Japanese Mixed Jury Trial" (2010) 12 Asian-Pacific L & Policy J 25; Takeshi Nishimura, "Effects of Saiban-in Trial on the Criminal Proceedings and Legal Profession," Paper presented at the Annual Meeting of the Asian L & Society Association (2019).

62 Takayuki and Atsuko Sawada, "Effects of Saiban-in Trial on the Citizen," Paper presented at the Annual Meeting of the Asian L & Society Association (2019); Vanoverbeke and Fukurai (n 20); Kage (n 18) 203–204 (describing positive responses by *Saiban-in* about their experiences).

63 Almeida et al (n 53); Diamond (n 5) 285–286.

64 Vanoverbeke and Fukurai (n 20) 78–82 (discussing lay judge civic engagement). For a summary of civic engagement effects related to jury service, see Gastil et al, *The Jury and Democracy* (n 5) and other sources collected in note 5.

65 Yoori Seong, "Citizen Participant Trial in South Korea: Empirical Research," Paper presented at the East Asian Lay Participation Roundtable (Clarke Program in East Asian Law & Culture, Cornell Law School, Ithaca NY, May 24, 2024).

66 Park (n 25) 100.

67 Ibid 101–103.

systems adapt to the presence of community members as legal decision-makers. Armed with information about how similar systems in Asian countries are working, Taiwan can anticipate some of the challenges it will face to ensure a vibrant system of lay participation that provides a robust voice to the community in the resolution of criminal cases. Fortuitously, this volume on Inter-Asian Law (IAL) provides an opportunity to consider how citizen participation in law and other law reforms affect legal processes, decision-makers, and society at large in Asia and elsewhere in the world.

PART IV

Emerging Problems

Between Technology and Authoritarianism

12

AI Governance in East Asia

Mapping the Contexts and Dynamics of Interaction

*Ching-Fu Lin**

I INTRODUCTION

Given the rapid development of data analytics, computational power, machine/deep learning, and other advances in information and communications technology (ICT), a wide range of artificial intelligence (AI) applications and systems have penetrated every sphere of society, with significant economic, legal, ethical, and political ramifications. A term first coined by John McCarthy and his collaborators at the Dartmouth Summer Research Project in 1955, AI has experienced both booms (AI summers) and busts (AI winters) for seven decades, but now readily promises a new wave of industrial and technological revolution.[1] Artificial intelligence has reemerged as an umbrella term covering machine/deep learning algorithms, robotics, autonomous systems, and natural language processing, among others, as well as an enabling technology that promises to transform the world through self-driving vehicles, digital assistants, robo-advisors, automated mortgage approval, legal services, law enforcement, and court proceedings, all driving significant changes and disruptions across jurisdictions and sectors.[2]

* The author would like to thank the National Science and Technology Council of Taiwan for supporting this research (111-2628-H-007-001) as well as the organization of the workshop (111-2916-I-007-013-A1). The author is also grateful to Kuan-Lin Ho, Yun-Sheng Lin, Hui-Hsuan Yang, and Zhijian Wang for their research assistance. Usual disclaimers apply.

1 See generally John McCarthy and others, "A Proposal for the Dartmouth Summer Research Project on Artificial Intelligence, August 31, 1955" (2006) 27 AI Mag 12 (reproducing the proposal).

2 See generally AI Now Institute, "AI Now Report 2019" (2019), https://ainowinstitute.org/AI_Now_2019_Report.pdf, accessed March 20, 2024; Hannah Bloch-Wehba, "Access to Algorithms" (2020) 88 Fordham L Rev 1265, 1267; Ching-Fu Lin, "Public Morals, Trade Secrets, and the Dilemma of Regulating Automated Driving Systems" in Shin-yi Peng and Ching-Fu Lin and Thomas Streinz (eds), *Artificial Intelligence and International Economic Law: Disruption, Regulation, and Reconfiguration* (CUP 2021) 237.

The rise of AI technologies has also raised concerns and controversies. Algorithmically powered tools have been widely adopted in contemporary workplaces to forge business practices for the purposes of efficiency, productivity, and management.[3] Camera surveillance, data analysis, and ranking and scoring systems are algorithmic tools that have given employers enormous power over their employees, yet their use also triggers serious controversies surrounding privacy, ethics, labor rights, and due process protections.[4] Apart from businesses, governments are among the primary users of AI-powered tools to surveil, sort, profile, and rate their citizens, creating a data-driven infrastructure of preferences that condition people's behaviors and opinions.[5] China's social credit system, Australia's robo-debt program, and the welfare distribution platform of the United States (US) are prime examples of how governments employ automated decision-making to allocate resources and provide public services.[6] The use of algorithmic risk assessment tools to support judges' sentencing decisions has been particularly problematic.[7]

A growing body of literature has explored critical dimensions of the promises and perils of AI and the need for regulatory responses. Some have pointed to rule of law deficits in the automation of government functions, especially through the use of preprogrammed rules such as expert systems, as well as predictive inferencing systems trained with historic big data.[8] Others have emphasized how such technologies systematically fuel inequalities due to the typically unintentional bias against and harm to underrepresented populations.[9] Still others have argued that a society constantly being scored, profiled, and predicted generally threatens due process,

3 See, e.g., Anne Fisher, "An Algorithm May Decide Your Next Pay Raise" (*World Economic Forum*, 2019), www.weforum.org/agenda/2019/07/pay-raises-could-be-decided-by-ai/, accessed March 20, 2024.

4 See Saul Levmore and Frank Fagan, "Competing Algorithms for Law: Sentencing, Admissions, and Employment" (2021) 88 U Chi L Rev 367.

5 See Ching-Fu Lin, "Sorting Teachers Out: Automated Performance Scoring and the Limit of Algorithmic Governance in the Education Sector" in Zofia Bednarz and Monika Zalnieriute (eds), *Money, Power and AI: From Automated Banks to Automated States* (CUP 2023).

6 See generally Yu-Jie Chen and Ching-Fu Lin and Han-Wei Liu, "Rule of Trust": Powers and Perils of China's Social Credit Megaproject" (2018) 32 Colum J Asian L 1; Karen Yeung and Martin Lodge, "Algorithmic Regulation: An Introduction" in Karen Yeung and Martin Lodge (eds), *Algorithmic Regulation* (OUP 2019) 1.

7 See Frank Pasquale, "Secret algorithms Threaten the Rule of Law" (*MIT Technology Review*, June 2017), www.technologyreview.com/2017/06/01/151447/secret-algorithms-threaten-the-rule-of-law/, accessed March 20, 2024; Han-Wei Liu and Ching-Fu Lin and Yu-Jie Chen, "Beyond State v. Loomis: Artificial Intelligence, Government Algorithmization, and Accountability" (2019) 29 Intl J L & Info Tech 1.

8 See Monika Zalnieriute and Lyria Bennett Moses and George Williams, "The Rule of Law and Automation of Government Decision-Making" (2019) 82 MLR 425.

9 See Virginia Eubanks, *Automating Inequality: How High-Tech Tools Profile, Police, and Punish the Poor* (St. Martin's Press 2018); Anupam Chander, "The Racist Algorithm?" (2017) 115 Mich L Rev 1023.

justice, and human rights.[10] While much ink has been spilled on the imminent and critical issue areas of AI law and policy,[11] given the nature of AI as an enabling, infrastructural technology situated in an evolving socio-techno complex, according to Carrillo, systematic and comprehensive research on AI remains "relatively limited," if not impossible.[12] Some of the existing scholarship focuses on a specific issue area, such as autonomous vehicles, smart cities, or algorithmic healthcare, and provides an in-depth analysis of legal, policy, and ethical ramifications, paving the way for regulatory reconfiguration.[13] Other research explores the regulatory trajectories, preferences, and (proposed) models of the industrialized jurisdictions, such as the European Union (EU) and the US, alluding to their potential for global reference or normative diffusion.[14] While some portions of existing scholarship discuss global or comparative perspectives, few touch upon issue areas that directly resonate with the diverse context and dynamics of the non-Western world.[15] Worse, despite the considerable impact of AI on most Asian countries,[16] there is a significant gap in the literature on AI governance in Asia. The current AI governance literature could benefit from a contextual discussion of how Asian jurisdictions perceive and respond to the challenges posed by AI, as well as how they interact with each other through regulatory cross-referencing, learning, and competition.

This chapter therefore aims to explore various contexts and dynamics of interactions among (East) Asian countries – including China, Japan, Korea, Taiwan, and Singapore – and to examine whether, when, and how the paths of their legal and

[10] See Danielle K Citron and Frank Pasquale, "The Scored Society: Due Process for Automated Predictions" (2014) 89 Wa L Rev 1; Steven Livingston and Mathias Risse, "The Future Impact of Artificial Intelligence on Humans and Human Rights" (2019) 33 Ethics & Intl Affairs 141.

[11] Anja Folberth and others, "Tackling Problems, Harvesting Benefits – A Systematic Review of the Regulatory Debate around AI" (2022) KIT Scientific Working Papers No 197, https://papers.ssrn.com/sol3/papers.cfm?abstract_id=4212447, accessed March 20, 2024.

[12] Margarita Robles Carrillo, "Artificial Intelligence: From Ethics to Law" (2020) 44 Telecomm Pol'y 1, 2.

[13] See, e.g., Robert Brauneis and Ellen P Goodman, "Algorithmic Transparency for the Smart City" (2018) 20 Yale J L & Tech 103; Alan L Schuller, "At the Crossroads of Control: The Intersection of Artificial Intelligence in Autonomous Weapons Systems with International Humanitarian Law" (2017) 8 Harv Nat'l Security J 379.

[14] See, e.g., Nicole Scicluna and Stefan Auer, "From the Rule of Law to the Rule of Rules: Technocracy and the Crisis of EU Governance" (2019) 42 West Eur Pol 1420; Michael Veale and Frederik Zuiderveen Borgesius, "Demystifying the Draft EU Artificial Intelligence Act" (2021) Comput L Rev Intl 97, 106; Robert A Smith and Pierre R Desrochers, "Algorithms Be Regulated by Government?" (2020) 63 Can Pub Admin 563, 579; Anupam Chander, "Future-Proofing Law" (2017) 51 UC Davis L Rev 1; Matthew U Scherer, "Regulating Artificial Intelligence Systems: Risks, Challenges, Competences, and Strategies" (2016) 29 Harv J L & Tech 353.

[15] Folberth and others (n 11).

[16] See, e.g., Babu Ram Aryal, "Governance for Artificial Intelligence in Asia Pacific 2018," www.intgovforum.org/multilingual/sites/default/files/webform/articifial_intelligence_apsig_article_1.pdf, accessed March 20, 2024; Janet Pau and Jill Baker and Nina Houston, "Artificial Intelligence in Asia: Preparedness and Resilience" (2017) Asia Business Council, https://asiabusinesscouncil.org/wp-content/uploads/2020/07/AI_briefing.pdf, accessed March 20, 2024.

policy actions cross each other. The diverse legal systems and practices in East Asian countries may affect how governance models are designed to harness AI. How are governments in East Asia (re)shaping their regulatory approaches and institutional designs in response to the multifaceted challenges of AI? Have any normative interactions (or convergences and divergences) emerged in the region, and if so, why? This chapter hopefully offers a clearer picture of the origins and trajectories of various AI governance models in (East) Asia, as well as a contextual understanding of the dynamic interactions between key countries in the region.

II THE RISE OF AI GOVERNANCE: KEY PLAYERS AND INITIATIVES IN ASIA

As AI systems are increasingly deployed in common and consequential contexts, society is according greater attention to how to govern them. Many governance initiatives – adopted by governments, industry sectors, and hybrid organizations at domestic, regional, and transitional levels – are being deliberated and implemented with the aim of responding to the challenges posed by AI. This section will identify the key players in AI governance in East Asia and their legal and policy initiatives.

A. *First Movers in AI Governance in Asia: China, Japan, and Singapore's Agile Approaches*

In Asia, more and more jurisdictions are developing or experimenting with ways of governance in response to AI's promises and challenges. Among them, the governments of China, Japan, and Singapore are the most active and agile nodes of governance in the region, as they have acted relatively early, contemplated or tested multiple versions and models of governance, and attempted to influence the law and policy landscape beyond their domestic contexts. In terms of Korea and Taiwan, while their industries and academia are generally vibrant in the issue area of AI, these governments have demonstrated less regulatory entrepreneurialism, due to their preference for hard(er) law and their pro-innovation orientation, in effect embracing a *wait-until-the-time-is-ripe* approach. This chapter examines and characterizes these countries' respective governance initiatives below.

Viewed by many as a "global leader in AI,"[17] China not only has taken the lead in AI-related research but has also developed a rigorous set of instruments for AI policy and standards, with the broader aim of shaping global rules and securing the

[17] Daitian Li, Tony W Tong and Yangao Xiao, "Is China Emerging as the Global Leader in AI?" (*Harvard Business Review*, February 18, 2021), https://hbr.org/2021/02/is-china-emerging-as-the-global-leader-in-ai, accessed March 20, 2024.

dominance of Chinese AI industries.[18] As early as 2017, China's State Council announced the "New Generation Artificial Intelligence Development Plan," which marks 2025 as the year for China to establish a comprehensive system of AI law, policy, and ethics[19] and which highlights the need for market trust, innovation, and *ex ante* regulation.[20] In the same year, China's Ministry of Science and Technology created the Office of the Development and Advancement of the New Generation of Artificial Intelligence, which serves as a coordinating body for fifteen other relevant agencies.

The first white paper on AI standardization, highlighting the gaps in AI safety and ethical norms and the need for standards harmonization, was published in January 2018 by the China Electronics Standardization Institute.[21] In 2019, the National New Generation Artificial Intelligence Governance Expert Committee released "Governance Principles for a New Generation of Artificial Intelligence: Develop Responsible Artificial Intelligence,"[22] which sets out eight responsible AI principles with "Chinese characteristics" (which may differ from "AI ethics developed in the Western contexts that emphasize more on individual rights and do not always put the collective at the forefront")[23] but simultaneously emphasizes the importance of cross-border dialogue and collaboration.[24] A number of other AI governance policy

18 Bernard Marr, "China Poised to Dominate the Artificial Intelligence (AI) Market" (*Forbes*, March 15, 2021), www.forbes.com/sites/bernardmarr/2021/03/15/china-poised-to-dominate-the-artificial-intelligence-ai-market/?sh = 64b23b1b389e, accessed March 20, 2024.

19 Guowuyuan (国务院) [The State Council of the People's Republic of China], "Guowuyuan Guanyu Yinfa Xinyidai Rengong Zhihui Fazhan Guihua de Tongzhi (国务院关于印发新一代人工智慧发展规划的通知) [State Council Notice on the Issuance of the New Generation Artificial Intelligence Development Plan]" (July 20, 2017), https://perma.cc/N3LJ-JAGJ (CN), accessed March 20, 2024.

20 Julia Chen, "Chinese AI Governance in Transition: Past, Present and Future of Chinese AI Regulation" in Urvashi Aneja (ed), *Reframing AI Governance: Perspectives from Asia* (Digital Futures Lab 2022) 72, 75.

21 Zhongguo Dianzi Jishu Biaozhunhua Yanjiuyuan (中国电子技术标准化研究院) [China Electronics Standardization Institute], "Rengong Zhineng Biaozhunhua Baipishu 2018 (人工智能标准化白皮书2018) [Artificial Intelligence Standardization White Paper 2018]" (2018), https://perma.cc/RP8S-V4FL (CN), accessed March 20, 2024.

22 Zhongguo Guojia Xinyidai Rengong Zhiheng Zhili Zhuanye Weiyuanhui (中國国家新一代人工智能治理专业委员会) [National New Generation Artificial Intelligence Governance Expert Committee], "Xinyidai Rengong Zhiheng Zhili Yuanze Fazhan – Fuzeren de Rengong Zhiheng (新一代人工智能治理原则 – 发展负责任的人工智能) [Governance Principles for a New Generation of Artificial Intelligence: Develop Responsible Artificial Intelligence]" (2019), https://perma.cc/XH4E-RE9V (CN), accessed March 20, 2024.

23 Guangyu Qiao-Franco, "Approaches to Ethical Artificial Intelligence: An Analysis of Chinese Awareness, Discourses and Practice" (European International Studies Association 2021 Conference, September 13, 2021) 18–19, https://portal.findresearcher.sdu.dk/en/publications/approaches-to-ethical-artificial-intelligence-an-analysis-of-chin, accessed March 20, 2024.

24 Zhongguo Dianzi Jishu Biaozhunhua Yanjiuyuan (中国电子技术标准化研究院) [China Electronics Standardization Institute], "Rengong Zhineng Biaozhunhua Baipishu 2021 (人工智能标准化白皮书2021) [Artificial Intelligence Standardization White Paper 2021]" (2021), https://perma.cc/5WNM-DTFG (CN), accessed March 20, 2024.

papers and initiatives were also adopted or revised from 2019 to 2021. In April 2022, the China Academy of Information and Communications Technology (affiliated with the Ministry of Industry and Information Technology) published the "2022 White Paper on Artificial Intelligence."[25] This 2022 White Paper stands out from previous governance instruments because it explicitly points out the imminent risks of AI, such as an algorithmic black box, bias, and discrimination, and makes references to international practices, including those in the US, the EU, Japan, G20, Organisation for Economic Co-operation and Development (OECD), and the G7.[26] In July 2023, the Cyberspace Administration of China released the "Interim Measures for the Administration of Generative Artificial Intelligence Services," which regulates generative AI's development and application considering its social and political implications.[27]

The trajectory of China's development in AI governance indicates a gradual shift toward clearer, stricter, harder, and more centralized rules for AI governance, with the involvement of all relevant agencies.[28] Having said that, China has yet to enact a unified, comprehensive AI law nationwide,[29] although many have been proposed.[30] According to Weixing Shen and Yun Liu, given that certain pressing issues surrounding AI governance have been addressed by specific laws and regulations (such as data-driven price discrimination),[31] the soft-law policy papers, principles, and guidelines appear to be adequate at this moment in striking a balance between technological innovation, economic growth, and social governance in a practical sense.[32]

[25] Zhongguo Xinxi Tongxin Yanjiuyuan (中国信息通信研究院) [China Academy of Information and Communications Technology], "Rengong Zhineng Baipishu (人工智能白皮书) [White Paper on Artificial Intelligence]" (2022), https://perma.cc/5HMD-Y48A (CN), accessed March 20, 2024.

[26] Ibid.

[27] Shengchengshi Rengong Zhineng Fuwu Guanli Zhanxing Banfa (生成式人工智能服务管理暂行办法) [Interim Measures for the Administration of Generative Artificial Intelligence Services] (promulgated by Cyberspace Administration Office July 23, 2023, effective August 15, 2023), https://perma.cc/8U7R-3TJ4 (CN), accessed March 20, 2024.

[28] See Chen (n 20) 74–75, 91.

[29] Some local/pilot laws or laws and regulations targeting a specific sub-area of AI application. See the discussion in Weixing Shen and Yun Liu, "China's Normative Systems for Responsible AI from Soft Law to Hard Law" in Silja Voeneky and others (eds), *The Cambridge Handbook of Responsible Artificial Intelligence: Interdisciplinary Perspectives* (CUP 2022) 150, 156.

[30] Shen and Liu (n 29) 155. See, e.g., Guowuyuan (国务院) [The State Council of The People's Republic of China], "Guowuyuan Bangongting Guanyu Yinfa Guowuyuan 2023 Nian Lifa Gongzuo Jihua De Tongzhi (国务院办公厅关于印发国务院2023年度立法工作计划的通知) [Notice by the General Office of the State Council of Issuing the Legislative Work Plan of the State Council for the Year 2023]" (published June 6, 2023), https://perma.cc/8NGT-9PA9 (CN), accessed March 20, 2024; Zhongguo Shehui Kexueyuan (中国社会科学院) [Chinese Academy of Social Sciences], "Rengong Zhineng Shifanfa 1.1 (Zhuanjia Jianyi Gao) (人工智能示范法1.1（专家建议稿）) [Artificial Intelligence Law, Model Law v 1.1 (Expert Suggestion Draft)]" (2023), https://perma.cc/BBX8-A2CD (CN), accessed March 20, 2024.

[31] Shen and Liu (n 29) 156.

[32] Shen and Liu (n 29) 152.

Japan is among the earliest movers in AI and has been keen to leverage industry expertise and resources in shaping the country's AI governance. Beginning in 2016, the Ministry of Internal Affairs and Communications (MIC) initiated the "Conference toward AI Network Society" to engage with industry, academia, and civil society and foster a multi-stakeholder dialogue.[33] From 2017 to 2022, the outcomes of the deliberations of this Society were published annually as a report that consolidated developments in AI governance in Japan and internationally.[34] While such reports do not carry legal force, they hold fairly strong reference power and serve as the nationwide public–private forum and the common basis for policymaking in AI governance. Notably, this Conference helped the Japanese government prepare the "Draft AI R&D Guidelines for International Discussions" as early as 2017 – which propose nine principles for AI research and development, including collaboration, transparency, controllability, safety, security, privacy, ethics, user assistance, and accountability – to serve as the anchor for deliberations in the G7 and the OECD.[35] On this basis, in 2019, the MIC further developed and issued the "AI Utilization Guidelines: Practical Reference for AI Utilization,"[36] and the Cabinet Secretariat's Integrated Innovation Strategy Promotion Council further announced the important "Social Principles of Human-centric AI," which enumerates fundamental principles on human-centeredness, education, privacy, security, fair competition, fairness, accountability, transparency, and innovation.[37] Both instruments served as important inputs toward the OECD's normative activities,[38] as Japan has been the leader in the AI expert group at the OECD and the OECD Council on Artificial Intelligence that drafted the OECD AI Principles, which are fairly similar to Japan's principles.[39]

33 "The Conference toward AI Network Society" (*STIP COMPASS*), https://perma.cc/WME9-DS4R, accessed March 20, 2024.

34 See, e.g., Ministry of Internal Affairs and Communication, *AI nettowāku shakai suishin kaigi hōkokusho* 2022 (AIネットワーク社会推進会議報告書) [Report of the Conference Toward AI Network Society 2022] (2022), www.soumu.go.jp/main_content/000826564.pdf (JP), accessed March 20, 2024.

35 The Conference toward AI Network Society, "*AI nettowāku ka nikansuru kokusai tekina giron no suishin ni mukete* (報告書2017-AIネットワーク化に関する国際的な議論の推進に向けて) [Draft AI R&D Guidelines for International Discussions]" (2017), www.soumu.go.jp/main_content/000499624.pdf (JP), accessed March 20, 2024; See Souichirou Kozuka, "Japan's Response to New Technologies" (2018) 46 J JP L 1, 13.

36 The Conference Toward AI Network Society, "AI Utilization Guidelines: Practical Reference for AI Utilization" (2019), www.soumu.go.jp/main_content/000658284.pdf, accessed March 20, 2024.

37 Cabinet Secretariat, "Ningen chūshin no AI shakai gensoku (人間中心のAI 社会原則)," (2019) 3, www.cas.go.jp/jp/seisaku/jinkouchinou/pdf/humancentricai.pdf (JP), accessed March 20, 2024.

38 See AI Utilization Guidelines (n 36), preface, 2–3.

39 See Osamu Sudoh, "Japan's AI Utilization Guidelines: An Initiative for Implementing the OECD AI Principles" (*OECD.AI*, June 10, 2020), https://oecd.ai/en/wonk/japans-ai-utilization-guidelines-an-initiative-for-implementing-the-oecd-ai-principles, accessed March 20, 2024.

The Ministry of Economy, Trade and Industry (METI) has also issued a few instruments aiming to address specific AI challenges. In 2018, it released the "Contract Guidelines on Utilization of AI and Data Released," which can serve as a practical template for business transactions and collaboration on AI and big data.[40] Given AI's trade, economic, and industrial implications, the METI also adopted a general policy paper in 2021, which was then updated in the same year, taking into account relevant international practices (such as the EU, Singapore, the US, International Organization for Standardization (ISO), and Institute of Electrical and Electronics Engineers (IEEE)).[41] The METI's policy paper noted that "[b]ased on the opinions of industries and the direction of improvement of literacy . . . legally-binding horizontal requirements for AI systems are deemed unnecessary at the moment."[42] The METI later issued its first comprehensive "Governance Guidelines for Implementation of AI Principles"[43] in 2021, based on a consolidated understanding of existing key codes of conduct, guidelines, and policies to offer concrete albeit voluntary action targets for the "Social Principles of Human-centric AI," and again updated the Guidelines in 2022.[44] In 2024, the METI and the MIC integrated and updated the existing guidelines, compiled expert deliberations, and jointly released the "AI Guidelines for Business Ver1.0."[45] Overall, perhaps due to the "techno-animistic tradition," a relatively open attitude toward technology, robotics, and AI in society,[46] and more trust placed in industry self-regulation, Japan's AI governance strategies have largely been on the soft side, highlighting the need for

40 METI, AI dēta no riyō nikansuru keiyaku gaidorain (AI・データの利用に関する契約ガイドライン) [Contract Guidelines on Utilization of AI and Data Released] (2018), www.meti.go.jp/press/2019/04/20190404001/20190404001-1.pdf (JP), accessed March 20, 2024. The Contract Guidelines were further updated in December 2019 after the amendment of the Unfair Competition Prevention Act. METI, AI dēta no riyō nikansuru keiyaku gaidorain 1.1 (AI・データの利用に関する契約ガイドライン 1.1版) [Contract Guidelines on Utilization of AI and Data Version 1.1] (2019), www.meti.go.jp/press/2019/04/20190404001/20190404001-1.pdf (JP), accessed March 20, 2024.

41 METI, "AI Governance in Japan Ver 1.0, Report from the Expert Group on How AI Principles Should Be Implemented" (2021), www.meti.go.jp/press/2020/01/20210115003/20210115003-3.pdf, accessed March 20, 2024; METI, "AI Governance in Japan Ver 1.1" (2021), www.meti.go.jp/shingikai/mono_info_service/ai_shakai_jisso/pdf/20210709_8.pdf, accessed March 20, 2024.

42 See AI Governance in Japan Ver 1.1 (n 41) 28–29. It was also mentioned that many other OECD member states are still in the stage of softer law approach.

43 METI, AI gensoku jissen no tame no gabanansu gaidorain (AI原則実践のためのガバナンス・ガイドライン) [Governance Guidelines for Implementation of AI Principles], Ver 1.0 (2021), www.meti.go.jp/shingikai/mono_info_service/ai_shakai_jisso/pdf/20210709_9.pdf (JP), accessed March 20, 2024.

44 METI, "Governance Guidelines for Implementation of AI Principles Ver 1.1" (2022), www.meti.go.jp/shingikai/mono_info_service/ai_shakai_jisso/pdf/20210709_9.pdf, accessed March 20, 2024.

45 METI, "AI Guidelines for Business Ver 1.0 Compiled" (2024), https://perma.cc/QGQ7-XMFV, accessed March 20, 2024.

46 Danit Gal, "Perspectives and Approaches in AI Ethics: East Asia" in Markus D. Dubber and Frank Pasquale and Sunit Das (eds), *Oxford Handbook of Ethics of Artificial Intelligence* (OUP 2020) 607, 618.

promoting innovation in the context of certain fundamental principles rather than establishing binding rules.

Singapore has been able to act quickly on AI governance by building on the existing international normative benchmarks. At the World Economic Forum in Davos in 2019, Singapore's Personal Data Protection Commission (PDPC) released the first edition of the "Model AI Governance Framework" with the Infocomm Media Development Authority (IMDA), providing specific implementation guidance for the private sector worldwide and aiming to garner broader adoption and feedback.[47] A revision of this Governance Framework was issued in 2020, together with the "Companion to the Model AI Governance Framework: Implementation and Self-Assessment Guide for Organisations,"[48] the latter of which resulted from a partnership between PDPC, IMDA, and the World Economic Forum Centre for the Fourth Industrial Revolution.[49] Both of these instruments are closely aligned with their international counterparts (in particular, with those adopted by the European Commission's High-Level Expert Group, the OECD Expert Group on AI, the IEEE, and the Software and Information Industry Association) in upholding core principles that AI-based decisions should be transparent, explainable, and fair, and that AI-based systems should be "human-centric."[50] The Governance Framework also includes recommendations involving internal governance structures and measures, the human role in AI-augmented decision-making, operations management, and stakeholder involvement.[51] A Compendium of Use Cases was further published by IMDA and PDPC, featuring real-world examples of how various entities have implemented or aligned their practices with Singapore's Model AI Governance Framework.[52] The IMDA and

47 IMDA and PDPC, "Model Artificial Intelligence Governance Framework" (First Edition, 2019), https://ai.bsa.org/wp-content/uploads/2019/09/Model-AI-Framework-First-Edition.pdf, accessed March 20, 2024.

48 IMDA and PDPC, "Model Artificial Intelligence Governance Framework" (Second Edition, 2020), https://perma.cc/2HRU-3GUX, accessed March 20, 2024; World Economic Forum Centre for the Fourth Industrial Revolution, IMDA and PDPC, "Companion to the Model AI Governance Framework: Implementation and Self-Assessment Guide for Organisations" (*World Econ. Forum*, 2020), www.pdpc.gov.sg/-/media/files/pdpc/pdf-files/resource-for-organisation/ai/sgisago.ashx, accessed March 20, 2024.

49 See also Companion to Model AI Governance Framework (n 48).

50 PDPC, "Singapore's Approach to AI Governance," www.pdpc.gov.sg/Help-and-Resources/2020/01/Model-AI-Governance-Framework, accessed March 20, 2024; see also Model AI Governance Framework (n 48) 11.

51 Model AI Governance Framework (n 48) 10.

52 IMDA and PDPC, "Volume 1: Compendium of Use Cases: Practical Illustrations of the Model AI Governance Framework" (2020), www.pdpc.gov.sg/-/media/files/pdpc/pdf-files/resource-for-organisation/ai/sgaigovusecases.ashx, accessed March 20, 2024; IMDA and PDPC, "Volume 2: Compendium of Use Cases: Practical Illustrations of the Model AI Governance Framework" (2020), https://file.go.gov.sg/ai-gov-use-cases-2.pdf, accessed March 20, 2024. See also Model AI Governance Framework (n 48) 8.

PDPC then launched the AI Governance Testing Framework and Toolkit "A.I. Verify" for businesses, which aim to align with the Model Framework in a verifiable manner. The Model Framework has already garnered initial support from companies such as Google, Microsoft, and DBS Bank.[53] In May 2022, AI Verify was released as a minimum viable product for an international pilot.[54] Singapore cooperated with the US on the interoperation on their AI governance framework.[55] All in all, it seems clear that Singapore has been moving swiftly to embrace international instruments in a rather aggressive manner, and in converting them into implementable practices. The primary focus of Singapore's AI governance seems to remain closely connected to international benchmarks, to help the private sector identify practical and operational rules, and to provide regulatory clarity to the business environment.

B. *Korea and Taiwan's Hard-Law Incrementalism*

The Asian Business Council regarded Korea and Taiwan as the "more resilient economies to AI-induced changes," along with Singapore and Japan, based on their preparedness in the areas of data openness, AI-related tax credits and subsidies, government funding for AI development, policies targeted at job displacement, social safety nets, and the legal responsibilities of AI systems.[56] Yet, both countries have been relatively incrementalist in AI governance, implementing few initiatives, partly due to both countries' preference for a hard-law approach backed by the legislature rather than administrative entrepreneurialism.

Korea moved early in adopting a hard-law framework in AI governance at the general level. In 2020, Korea adopted the "Framework Act on Intelligent Informatization,"[57] a comprehensive amendment that renames and replaces the

[53] PDPC (n 50).

[54] "What is AI Verify" (*AI Verify Foundation*), https://aiverifyfoundation.sg/what-is-ai-verify/, accessed March 20, 2024; see Josh Lee Kok Thong, "AI Verify: Singapore's AI Governance Testing Initiative Explained" (*Future of Privacy Forum*, 2023), https://fpf.org/blog/ai-verify-singapores-ai-governance-testing-initiative-explained/, accessed March 20, 2024.

[55] Cheryl Seah, "Round Up of Significant Legal Developments in AI for 2023" (*Law Gazette*, December 2023), https://lawgazette.com.sg/feature/round-up-significant-legal-developments-ai/ , accessed March 20, 2024; Ministry of Communications and Information, "Singapore and the US to Deepen Cooperation in AI" (2023), www.mci.gov.sg/media-centre/press-releases/singapore-and-the-us-to-deepen-cooperation-in-ai/ (SG), accessed March 20, 2024; The White House, "U.S.-Singapore Critical and Emerging Technology Dialogue: 'Joint Vision Statement'" (October 12, 2023), www.whitehouse.gov/briefing-room/statements-releases/2023/10/12/u-s-singapore-critical-and-emerging-technology-dialogue-joint-vision-statement/, accessed March 20, 2024.

[56] Pau and Baker and Houston (n 16) 5.

[57] Framework Act on Intelligent Informatization (KR), *translated in* Korea Law Translation Center of the Korea Legislation Research Institute, https://perma.cc/C6RH-B6L5 (search required), accessed March 20, 2024.

old "Framework Act on National Informatization of 2009"[58] (formerly the "Framework Act on Informatization Promotion," which sought to establish the policy foundation for promoting the ICT industry).[59] The purpose of the Framework Act on Intelligent Informatization is to realize a smart, well-informed society, to ensure national competitiveness, and to promote the well-being of the population under the fundamental principles of freedom and openness, human dignity and values, safety, privacy protection, and public–private collaboration, among others.[60] The Act also authorizes the Ministry of Science and the ICT to promulgate AI-related policies,[61] pursuant to which the Ministry and the Presidential Committee on the Fourth Industrial Revolution announced the "Draft of the National AI Ethical Guidelines,"[62] with three principles (human dignity, public good in society, and fitness for the purpose of technology) and ten general goals in November 2020 and the "Strategy to Realize Trustworthy Artificial Intelligence"[63] in May 2021. While the Framework Act on Intelligent Informatization is more legalized, it does not include specific implementable requirements. Additionally, the softer governance instruments that have been adopted under the framework seem to remain high-level, general, and abstract. More recently, the Science, ICT, Broadcasting and Communications Committee of the Korean National Assembly proposed the "Act on Promotion of AI Industry and Framework for Establishing Trustworthy AI" in February 2023,[64] which aims at ensuring the safety of and trust in high-risk AI technologies.[65] While the proposed Act has not been finalized, it is known to take the "adopting technology first

[58] Framework Act on National Informatization (2010) (KR), *translated in* Korea Law Translation Center of the Korea Legislation Research Institute, https://perma.cc/5LTZ-MF2F (search required), accessed March 20, 2024.

[59] See generally Jonggu Jeong, "Introduction to the First AI Impact Assessment and Future Tasks: South Korea Discussion" (2022) 11 Laws 1; see also Minbyun and others, "Input for Report on Right to Privacy in the Digital Age: Opinions of Korean Civil Society Organizations for the Upcoming Report by the United Nations High Commissioner for Human Rights on the Right to Privacy in the Digital Age" (*OHOHR*, 2021), www.ohchr.org/sites/default/files/Documents/Issues/DigitalAge/Submissions/CSOs/ROK-CSOs.pdf, accessed March 20, 2024.

[60] Framework Act on Intelligent Informatization, Article 1.

[61] Framework Act on Intelligent Informatization, Articles 4 and 69.

[62] Ministry of Science and ICT, "The Draft of the National AI Ethical Standards" (2020), https://perma.cc/RD2F-LL3U (KR), accessed March 20, 2024.

[63] Ministry of Science and ICT, "Strategy to Realize Trustworthy Artificial Intelligence" (2021), https://perma.cc/PSD8-FPDA (KR), accessed March 20, 2024.

[64] Somang Yang, "Spurred by ChatGPT, South Korea Pushes World's First AI Bill" (*PS-Engage*, March 16, 2023), https://ps-engage.com/spurred-by-chatgpt-south-korea-pushes-worlds-first-ai-bill/, accessed March 20, 2024; Digital Today, "AI 기본법" 올해는 빛볼까...과기정통부 "21대 국회 종료 전 통과 목표" (January 2, 2024), www.digitaltoday.co.kr/news/articleView.html?idxno=499842, accessed March 20, 2024.

[65] Law Times, "「AI (인공지능)산업 육성 및 신뢰 기반 조성에 관한 법률」 제정 동향 및 사업자가 주의해야 할 사항" (April 20, 2023), www.lawtimes.co.kr/news/187090, accessed March 20, 2024.

and regulating later" approach, so as to promote AI innovation and economic development.[66]

In 2017, Taiwan's Ministry of Science and Technology (reorganized as the National Science and Technology Council) began to pour significant research funding into various fields of AI research and development, including the law and policy groundwork.[67] Taiwan is also regarded as "a good example for other countries in East Asia," scoring high in innovation capacity and "having established an R&D framework based on co-innovation between Taiwanese and international companies."[68] In some specific issue areas, Taiwan has adopted a hard-law approach to strike a balance between technological innovation and regulatory stability, albeit with a limited scope of application. Noting the disruptions posed by AI, especially when some autonomous vehicles may have been introduced in the market, the "Unmanned Vehicles Technology Innovative Experimentation Act" was enacted in 2018.[69] It authorizes the Ministry of Economic Affairs to set up a sandbox to regulate the development and testing of autonomous vehicles.[70] Similar developments appear in the financial sector, such as the enactment of the Financial Technology Development and Innovative Experimentation Act in 2018.[71] In September 2019, after consulting with experts in AI, the Ministry of Science and Technology announced the "AI Technology R&D Guidelines," which incorporate three core values – human-centric, sustainable, and inclusive AI – as well as eight guidelines.[72] The AI Technology R&D Guidelines emphasize the importance of being aligned with relevant international benchmarks and make explicit reference to the "Ethics Guidelines for Trustworthy AI" prepared by the EU's High-Level Expert Group on Artificial Intelligence, Japan's "Social Principles of Human-centric AI," the OECD

66 Hwan Kyoung Ko, "Analysis of AI regulatory frameworks in South Korea" (Asia Business L J, April 15, 2024) https://law.asia/ai-regulatory-frameworks-south-korea/, accessed March 20, 2024.

67 See, e.g., AI on Chips Taiwan Alliance, "About AITI", www.aita.org.tw/Eng, accessed March 20, 2024; Zhang Yu-lin, "The Executive Yuan Plans to Invest 40 bn in 4 Years to Boost AI Development" (*China Times*, January 19, 2018), www.chinatimes.com/newspapers/20180119000251-260202?chdtv, accessed March 20, 2024; Executive Yuan, "AI Taiwan Action Plan" (2019), https://perma.cc/6TKX-M87N (TW), accessed March 20, 2024.

68 Oxford Insights, "Government AI Readiness Index" (2021) 55, https://perma.cc/34C2-VRKK, accessed March 20, 2024.

69 Wuren zaiju keji chuangxin shiyan tiaoli (無人載具科技創新實驗條例) [Unmanned Vehicles Technology Innovative Experimentation Act] (enacted December 19, 2018, effective January 1, 2019), https://law.moj.gov.tw/ENG/LawClass/LawAll.aspx?pcode=J0030147 (TW), accessed March 20, 2024.

70 Ibid. See also Chang-hsien Tsai and Ching-Fu Lin and Han-Wei Liu, "The Diffusion of the Sandbox Approach to Disruptive Innovation and Its Limitations" (2020) 53 Cornell ILJ 261, 264–264, 273.

71 Financial Technology Development and Innovative Experimentation 2018 (TW).

72 Keji Bu (科技部) [Ministry of Science and Technology (Taiwan)], "Ren Gong Zhi Hui Keyan Fazhan Zhiyin (人工智慧科研發展指引) [AI Technology R&D Guidelines]" (*AI Taiwan*, 2019), https://ai.taiwan.gov.tw/news/ministry-releases-guidelines-for-ai-research/ (alternatively: www.nstc.gov.tw/nstc/attachments/53491881-eb0d-443f-9169-1f434f7d33c7) (TW), accessed March 20, 2024.

AI Principles, and the IEEE's Ethically Aligned Design.[73] Nevertheless, the AI Technology R&D Guidelines contain only high-level, concise guidelines (comprising only three pages for eight guidelines) and do not seem to be operable or implementable in practice.

In 2019 and 2020, a proposal on the "Basic Act for Artificial Intelligence Development" was introduced in the Legislative Yuan, referencing models and practices found in the US, the EU, the United Kingdom (UK), China, and Japan, but this proposal went no further.[74] In 2023, the Executive Yuan again postponed the proposal of the Basic Act, considering the changing technological landscape and the need to align with the other regulatory frameworks worldwide.[75] Nevertheless, faced with the acute challenges posed by the sudden rise of generative AI, the Executive Yuan issued "Guidelines for the Use of Generative AI by the Executive Yuan and its Subordinate Agencies" in late 2023.[76] In the same year, the Financial Supervisory Commission issued "Core Principles and Policies for AI Applications in the Financial Industry" to strengthen risk management in financial AI technologies.[77] Overall, Taiwan, like Korea, has a strong focus on technological and economic development and a modest preference for a hard(er) law approach,[78] which has

[73] Keji Bu (科技部) [Ministry of Science and Technology (Taiwan)], "KejiBu Dingding 'Ren Gong Zhi Hui Ke Yan Fa Zhan Zhi Yin' wanshan woguo ai keyan fazhan huanjing (科技部訂定「人工智慧科研發展指引」 完善我國AI科研發展環境) [MOST Released the AI Technology R&D Guidelines to Improve the Environment for AI Research and Development]" (*NSTC*, 2019), www.nstc.gov.tw/folksonomy/detail/dbf8da09-22be-4ef1-8294-8832fc6e8a26?l = ch (TW), accessed March 20, 2024.

[74] See Rengong Zhihui Fazhan Jiben Fa Cao'an (人工智慧發展基本法草案) [Basic Act for Artificial Intelligence Development (no official translation)] (9th Legislative Yuan Sessions 7, No. 1021-23371, 2019), https://lis.ly.gov.tw/lygazettec/mtcdoc?DN090714:LCEWA01_090714_00037 (TW), accessed March 20, 2024; Rengong Zhihui Fazhan Jiben Fa Cao'an (人工智慧發展基本法草案) [Basic Act for Artificial Intelligence Development (no official translation)], (10th Legislative Yuan Sessions 2, No. 1021-24953, 2020), https://lci.ly.gov.tw/LyLCEW/agenda1/02/pdf/10/02/01/LCEWA01_100201_00025.pdf (TW), accessed March 20, 2024.

[75] Xu Zi Lin (徐子苓), "Ren gong zhi hui fazhan taikuai Zheng Wen Can: AI Jiben Fa yanhou tuichu (人工智慧發展太快 鄭文燦:AI基本法延後推出)" (*The Liberty Times*, August 1, 2023), https://ec.ltn.com.tw/article/breakingnews/4382694 (TW), accessed March 20, 2024.

[76] Xing Zheng Yuan (行政院) [Executive Yuan], "Xingzhengyuan Ji Suoshu Jiguan(gou) Shiyong Shengchengshi AI Cankao Zhiyin (行政院及所屬機關(構)使用生成式AI參考指引) [Guidelines for the Use of Generative AI by the Executive Yuan and its Subordinate Agencies (Institutions)]" (August 31, 2023), https://perma.cc/WDU3-CTH8 (TW), accessed March 20, 2024.

[77] Jinrong Jiandu Guanli Weiyuan Hui (金融監督管理委員會) [Financial Supervisory Commission], Jinrongye Yunyong Rengong Zhihui Zhi Hexin Yuanze Yu Xiangguan Tuidong Zhengce (金融業運用人工智慧(AI)之核心原則與相關推動政策) [Core Principles and Policies for AI Applications in the Financial Industry] (October 10, 2023), https://perma.cc/3THG-QADD (TW), accessed March 20, 2024.

[78] The preference over hard law, from a rather premature and oversimplified perspective, may be partly attributable to both countries' experiences of an authoritarian history, and as young democracies of civil law tradition weighted heavily by the concept of the rule of law (recurrently resulting in an obsession with promoting "law-based administration" in Taiwan).

resulted in its *wait-until-the-time-is-ripe* approach to AI governance. While there are some guidelines adopted by sector-specific regulatory agencies for certain issue areas with a narrow and concrete scope of application, a hard-law incrementalism seems preferred.

III *INTER-ASIAN* AI GOVERNANCE? NORMATIVE TRAJECTORIES AND INTERACTIONS

Interactions in shaping AI governance across East Asian countries have merit and should play a role in the development of AI governance. Some interactions can be encouraged through channels of cross-reference – the laws, frameworks, guidelines, principles, and use cases – while others may be facilitated by informal mutual dialogue, the exchange of best practices, and regulatory learning. Regular, dynamic interactions will likely result in constructive normative outcomes across jurisdictions, together contributing to global AI governance. Moving forward, two dimensions are worth noting in terms of Inter-Asian Law (IAL) and AI governance, as this chapter unfolds below.

A. *Promoting Interactions in the Context of Divergent Regulatory Preferences and Technological Competition*

Depending on issue areas – climate change, healthcare, financial services, ICT, food safety, and the pandemic – countries with different historical and socioeconomic underpinnings, as well as varying constitutional, administrative, and political environments, tend to diverge in their preferences in regulatory approaches.[79] This cannot be more evidently demonstrated than the case of genetically modified organisms regulation and the two regulatory extremes of the EU and the US.[80] Increasingly, regulatory preferences can amass and result in a path-dependent effect in a given issue area, leading to regulatory divergence and even cross-border conflicts.[81] In some cases,

[79] See, e.g., Dennis Kolcava and Lukas Rudolphet and Thomas Bernauer, "Citizen Preferences on Private-Public Co-Regulation in Environmental Governance: Evidence from Switzerland" (2021) 68 GEC 1; OECD, "Policy Brief on Measuring Regulatory Quality" (*OECD*, April 2018), https://perma.cc/K2CG-NJYZ, accessed March 20, 2024; Sophia Kalantzakos, *The EU, US and China Tackling Climate Change: Policies and Alliances for the Anthropocene* (Routledge 2017).

[80] See generally Mark A Pollack and Gregory C Shaffer, *When Cooperation Fails: The International Law and Politics of Genetically Modified Foods* (OUP 2009).

[81] See generally Oona A Hathaway, "Path Dependence in the Law: The Course and Pattern of Legal Change in a Common Law System" (2001) 86 Iowa LR 101; Sungjoon Cho and Jürgen Kurtz, "Convergence and Divergence in International Economic Law and Politics" (2018) 29 EJIL 169; and Iulianna Romanchyshyna, "Mutual Recognition as a Method to Deal with Regulatory Divergence: What Is Its Reach in EU FTAs?" (2020) 15 GTCJ 6.

jurisdictional competition in an issue area shapes and reshapes countries' regulatory preferences and strategies.[82]

In the area of AI governance, while there are numerous voluntary guidelines and principles, divergences in regulatory practices prevail on the ground,[83] making normative interactions dynamic. For many Asian countries, AI has been regarded as a necessary area for socioeconomic development over the coming decades, and the primary objective of governance is therefore to "create an enabling environment for AI development and deployment."[84] Apart from the practical value of incorporating and influencing international benchmarks (such as saving costs in contemplating new rules, seeking legitimacy, or competing for leadership in global AI governance), there is a need for Asian countries to examine each other's governance initiatives, given the differences underlying their respective political systems, legal traditions, and social contexts,[85] to secure better competitiveness. Having said that, the established regulatory preferences, legal practices, institutional arrangements, and government–business relationships mean that there are transaction costs whenever a path change takes place,[86] but more interactions promote mutual understanding and regulatory learning, paving the way for cooperation.

Some East Asian countries have interacted with, and learned from, each other when developing their AI governance frameworks, in addition to referencing relevant international guidelines and principles. Due to the competition among China, Japan, Korea, and Taiwan in the global technology supply chain,[87] it is crucial for

82 See, e.g., Bruce G Carruthers and Naomi R Lamoreaux, "Regulatory Races: The Effects of Jurisdictional Competition on Regulatory Standards" (2016) 54 J Econ Literature 52.

83 See Lewin Schmitt, "Mapping Global AI Governance: A Nascent Regime in a Fragmented Landscape" (2022) 2 AI and Ethics 303; Panel for the Future of Science and Technology, "Regulatory Divergences in the Draft AI Act: Differences in Public and Private Sector Obligations" (2022) European Parliamentary Research Service PE 729.507, www.europarl.europa.eu/RegData/etudes/STUD/2022/729507/EPRS_STU(2022)729507_EN.pdf, accessed March 20, 2024.

84 Urvashi Aneja and others, "Reframing AI Governance: Perspectives from Asia" (*Digital Futures Lab and Konrad Adenauer Stiftung*, 2022) 13–14, https://perma.cc/H9B3-2NKZ, accessed March 20, 2024.

85 But see Edmond Awad and others, "The Moral Machine Experiment" (2018) 563 Nature 59. According to the MIT Media Lab's global experiment (MIT Media Lab, "The Moral Machine," http://moralmachine.mit.edu/, accessed March 20, 2024), East Asian countries seem to be in the same cluster with similar preferences (and few differences) in terms of AI ethics regarding the governance of autonomous vehicles.

86 See, e.g., Van Alstine, "The Costs of Legal Change" (2002) 49 UCLA LR 789, 793.

87 See, e.g., Jiji, "50 years on, Japan-China Ties Shift from Cooperation to Competition" (*The Japan Times*, September 27, 2022), www.japantimes.co.jp/news/2022/09/27/business/economy-business/jp-china-competition/, accessed March 20, 2024; Mia Nulimaimaiti, "China Lags behind the US, South Korea, Japan and Singapore in 'Talent Competitiveness', Report Says" (*South China Morning Post*, November 11, 2022), www.scmp.com/economy/china-economy/article/3199153/china-lags-behind-us-south-korea-japan-and-singapore-talent-competitiveness-report-says, accessed March 20, 2024; Dwight H Perkins and John P Tang, "East Asian Industrial Pioneers: Japan, Korea, and Taiwan" in Kevin Hjortshøj O'Rourke and Jeffrey Gale Williamson (eds), *The Spread of Modern Industry to the Periphery Since 1871* (Oxford

them to stay tuned to each other's regulatory moves and connected to the international governance vibes. In their eyes, aligning with common standards at both IAL and global levels helps promote industry competitiveness, technology development, and an export-oriented economy, contributing to the maintenance of an enabling environment for AI.[88] For instance, China's "2022 White Paper on Artificial Intelligence" explicitly refers to international normative instruments adopted in the G20, the OECD, the G7, the EU, the US, and Japan. Japan's METI policy paper on "AI Governance in Japan" takes into account international practices of the EU, the US, the ISO, the IEEE, and Singapore. Additionally, Singapore ensures that its practical guidelines closely align with their international counterparts, particularly those adopted by the EU, the OECD, and the IEEE. Taiwan, in turn, looked to most of the above countries in setting its "AI Technology R&D Guidelines" and its proposal on the "Basic Act for Artificial Intelligence Development" – the EU, the US, the UK, France, the IEEE, the OECD, Japan, and China. While the inter-Asian cross-reference activities in AI governance have not been full-fledged, there has been a growing practice of inter-Asian learning. Practically speaking, some of the development and application of AI touches upon sensitive social and ethical values, as well as on public morals, and countries may in the end need to resort to shared standards in the region if not globally.

B. *Supporting Inter-Asian Institutions as Forums for Governance Dialogue*

There is also a need to support regional institutional settings for Asian countries to actively engage with each other (and the world), to forge consensus and collectively invest in substantive norm-making. For instance, the Asia-Pacific Economic Cooperation (APEC) has actively engaged in many AI-related policy activities. In December 2020, China, Chile, Mexico, and New Zealand cohosted the Learning Workshop in Artificial Intelligence: Experiences of APEC Economies to exchange views on various AI governance issues.[89] Also in 2020, the APEC Business Advisory Council (ABAC) released a report on AI adoption in APEC economies, which noted that APEC members have yet to forge a consensus surrounding critical AI issues, but pointed to the need for greater cooperation on coherent regulatory compliance requirements.[90] More recently, APEC published two case study policy

University Press 2017); James W Cortada, "IT Tigers of Asia: South Korea, Taiwan, and Singapore" in James W Cortada (ed), *The Digital Flood: The Diffusion of Information Technology across the U.S., Europe, and Asia* (OUP 2012).

88 Aneja and others (n 84).

89 APEC, Telecommunications and Information Working Group, "Learning Workshop in Artificial Intelligence: Experiences of APEC Economies" (*APEC*, June 2022) 6, https://perma.cc/EZ2R-TCVZ, accessed March 20, 2024.

90 ABAC, "Artificial Intelligence in APEC: Overview of the State of AI in APEC Economies and the Enabling Initiatives That Will further Drive Adoption" (*ABAC*, 2020) 7 and 21, https://ncapec.org/wp-content/uploads/2020/11/ABAC-AI-Report.pdf, accessed March 20, 2024.

reports, "Artificial Intelligence in Economic Policymaking"[91] and "Artificial Intelligence (AI) Policy Recommendation on Digital Transformation for Healthcare Ecosystem – Case Study Report,"[92] to contribute to regional and global dialogues. Also, in the area of data privacy, Japan, Korea, Singapore, and Taiwan, together with Canada, the Philippines, and the US, jointly adopted the Global Cross-Border Privacy Rules Declaration in late 2022 to ensure the free and secure flow of data.[93]

In addition to APEC, which serves as a forum for inter-Asian AI governance dialogue, it is desirable to foster institutional venues and platforms for Asian countries to exchange best practices, forge a consensus, or draft substantive rules and guidelines. This resonates with the fact that Japan, Singapore, and China have been actively participating and sometimes playing leadership roles in both regional and international platforms. Notably, Japan hosted in November 2022 the Global Partnership on Artificial Intelligence (GPAI) Tokyo Summit, attended by member governments in Asia and beyond, which together adopted the "GPAI 2022 Ministers' Declaration," which confirms key commitments, including "protecting and promoting human-centred values and democracy that underpin an inclusive, development-oriented, sustainable and peaceful society," "[opposing] unlawful and irresponsible use of artificial intelligence," and is also committed to "[upholding the] multistakeholder approach and … stronger cooperation between public and private actors."[94]

One potential institutional setting for inter-Asian AI governance dialogue is the Digital Economy Partnership Agreement (DEPA), a module-based collaborative framework initiated by Singapore, Chile, and New Zealand in 2020 to forge common standards and practices that will promote data-driven trade and commerce, emerging technologies, and digital inclusion.[95] The DEPA includes provisions for Parties to cooperate in "developing ethical and governance frameworks for the trusted, safe and responsible use of AI technologies,"[96] and calls on its Parties to "promote the adoption of ethical and governance frameworks that support the trusted, safe and responsible use of AI technologies (AI Governance

[91] Andre Wirjo and others, "Artificial Intelligence in Economic Policymaking" (APEC, November 2022), www.apec.org/apecapi/publication/getfile?publicationId=e27e9c92-dfb4-48ec-bbca-b54fbd68d67f, accessed March 20, 2024.

[92] APEC Policy Partnership on Science, Technology and Innovation, "Artificial Intelligence (AI) Policy Recommendation on Digital Transformation for Healthcare Ecosystem – Case Study Report" (APEC, December 2021), www.apec.org/apecapi/publication/getfile?publicationId=653613d3-0624-49ce-8fbe-ea113258266ed, accessed March 20, 2024.

[93] US Department of Commerce, "Global Cross-Border Privacy Rules Declaration," www.commerce.gov/global-cross-border-privacy-rules-declaration, accessed March 20, 2024.

[94] GPAI, "GPAI 2022 Ministers' Declaration" (November 22, 2022), www.gpai.ai/events/tokyo-2022/ ministerial-declaration/, accessed March 20, 2024.

[95] Digital Economy Partnership Agreement (DEPA) (Chile–New Zealand–Singapore) (signed June 12, 2020).

[96] Ibid Article 8.2.2.

Frameworks)."[97] Despite its "best efforts" wording, DEPA moves well beyond the Comprehensive and Progressive Agreement for Trans-Pacific Partnership's and Regional Comprehensive Economic Partnership's e-commerce (or data flow) chapters in providing a concrete direction, key values, and a template for AI governance.[98] These are promising first steps toward institutionalized cooperation in inter-Asian AI governance, especially when considering that both China and Korea have applied to join DEPA.[99] Given its flexible institutional design and inclusive setting, in the long run, DEPA may serve as an important institutional forum for dialogue, the exchange of best practices, the establishment of a common playbook of general principles, and cooperation among (Asian) countries in AI governance.

IV CONCLUSION

As AI continues to develop and permeate various aspects of society, the need for robust, contextually aware governance frameworks becomes ever more critical. This chapter has examined the dynamic interactions among key East Asian countries, highlighting their diverse regulatory approaches and the importance of normative interactions such as mutual learning, exchange of best practices, and institutionalized cooperation. While China, Japan, Singapore, Korea, and Taiwan each exhibit their own strategies in addressing AI governance, shaped by respective political, legal, and socioeconomic contexts, the evolving nature of AI technology necessitates continuous adaptation and alignment with shared norms and standards, at both the IAL and global levels. The increasing practice of inter-Asian regulatory cross-referencing, joint efforts, and cooperation through international forums underscores the region's recognition of the benefits of shared standards and collaborative governance. In particular, initiatives like DEPA offer promising platforms for fostering dialogue, best practices exchanges, and the development of AI governance. As East Asian countries navigate the complexities of AI governance and continue with regulatory experiments, leveraging regional institutions and facilitating normative interactions remain crucial to develop collective insights and frameworks that serve as vital references for global AI governance discourse.

97 Ibid Articles 8.2.3 and 8.2.4.

98 Dan Ciuriak, "Digital Economy Agreements: Where Do We Stand and Where Are We Going?" (*SSRN*, September 22, 2022) 2–3, https://papers.ssrn.com/sol3/papers.cfm?abstract_id=4217903, accessed March 20, 2024. For more discussion, see also chapters in Shin-yi Peng and Ching-Fu Lin and Thomas Streinz (eds), *Artificial Intelligence and International Economic Law: Disruption, Regulation, and Reconfiguration* (CUP 2021).

99 Bloomberg, "China to Apply to Join Digital Economy Partnership Agreement" (October 31, 2021), https://perma.cc/7WMD-GXRG, accessed March 20, 2024; Rei Kurohi, "South Korea Seeking to Join Digital Economy Pact between Singapore, New Zealand and Chile" (*Straits Times*, October 5, 2021), https://perma.cc/5K88-PBDX, accessed March 20, 2024.

13

The "Smart City" Debate

Exploring Asian Models of Smart Cities through Japan–ASEAN Cooperation

Yoshiko Naiki

I INTRODUCTION

Various cities worldwide are engaged in smart city projects, seeking effective solutions to urban issues (e.g., traffic congestion, waste management, and housing) and global ones (e.g., climate change, energy consumption, and population growth). With the onset of the 2019 coronavirus disease (COVID-19) pandemic, smart city projects began to receive increasing attention. While smart city policies are linked to specific urban policies (e.g., smart mobility and smart grids), smart cities are currently understood as a more "holistic" solution to various urban issues. Moreover, smart cities cannot be discussed without mentioning big data or artificial intelligence (AI) technologies.

This chapter is inspired by the "smart city" debate that started in the 2000s, led by scholars in the fields of geography and sociology engaged in urban research. On the one hand, a vast body of literature exists on smart cities against the backdrop of the proliferation of "corporate-oriented smart cities."[1] The scholarship criticizes "technology-driven, market-led, and top-down" smart city projects led by big information and communications technology (ICT) corporations[2] because they usually propose "one-size-fits-all" solutions for urban development.[3] On the other hand, instead of such an ICT-centric approach, the smart city scholarship suggests "inclusive," "participatory," and "citizen-centric/people-centric" approaches.[4]

[1] See, e.g., Robert G Hollands, "Critical Interventions into the Corporate Smart City" (2015) 8(1) Camb J Reg Econ Soc 61, 62; Alan Wiig, "IBM's Smart City as Techno-Utopian Policy Mobility" (2015) 19(2–3) City 258, 270; Ola Söderström et al, "Smart Cities as Corporate Storytelling" (2014) 18(3) City 307, 318.

[2] Luca Mora and Mark Deakin, *Untangling Smart Cities* (Elsevier 2019) 119.

[3] Rob Kitchin, "Making Sense of Smart Cities: Addressing Present Shortcomings" (2015) 8(1) Camb J Reg Econ Soc 131, 132–133.

[4] See, e.g., Andrew Karvonen et al, "Introduction: Situating Smart Cities" in Andrew Karvonen et al (eds), *Inside Smart Cities: Place, Politics, and Urban Innovation* (Routledge 2018) 6; Robert Cowley et al, "The Smart City and Its Publics: Insights from across Six UK Cities"

However, such debates have largely occurred in the context of European and North American smart city projects. It has been argued: "there are no clear answers as to what a smart city is – anywhere in the world... Most smart city definitions and, thereby its scope, are all western."[5] This chapter builds on this core observation and asks whether Asian smart cities provide an alternative to those of the West and, related, what patterns and relationships are observable between Asian approaches?[6] While the purpose of this chapter is not to provide a comprehensive comparison between Western and Asian smart cities, it suggests that there may be important differences and that these are most fruitfully explored in inter-Asian contexts.

In this regard, the literature on Asian smart cities is growing; scholarly work includes not only case studies (e.g., Singapore, India, China, and South Korea) but also wider comparative studies among Asian countries.[7] Following this emerging literature, this chapter provides a basis for Asian models by analyzing how Japan, and competitors including South Korea and China, engage with member states of the Association of Southeast Asian Nations (ASEAN) on smart city projects. In particular, it highlights the role of Japan in shaping the ideas and norms of smart cities by exporting smart solutions. Exporting the ideas of smart cities can eventually affect urban governance, including legal infrastructures that local governments adopt. With this analysis, this chapter contributes to the study of Inter-Asian Law (IAL).

The remainder of the chapter is organized as follows. It begins by explaining the complexities embedded in smart city research, including the hard and soft law dimensions in smart cities. Next, it provides an overview of Asian smart cities and explains some of their features. Then, this chapter examines smart city cooperation between Japan and ASEAN countries. Discussion section considers the potential diffusion of the smart city concept and urban governance through Japan–ASEAN smart city cooperation, while simultaneously examining possible regulatory

(2018) 11(1) Urban Research & Practice 53; Paolo Cardullo and Rob Kitchin, "Being a 'Citizen' in the Smart City: Up and down the Scaffold of Smart Citizen Participation in Dublin, Ireland" (2019) 84 GeoJournal 1.

5 Goutam Das and Manu Kaushik, "The Quest to Build 100 Smart Cities and Problems on the Way" (*Business Today*, March 15, 2015), www.businesstoday.in/magazine/cover-story/story/challenges-the-govt-faces-in-building-100-smart-cities-india-142884-2015-02-25, accessed June 12, 2024.

6 For literature discussing divergence between the Global North and Global South, see Byron Miller, "Worlding and Provincialising Smart Cities: From Individual Case Studies to a Global Comparative Research Agenda" (2021) 58(3) Urban Studies 655, 658.

7 For the literature on smart cities in Asia, see Federico Caprotti and Li Yu (eds), *Sustainable Cities in Asia* (Routledge 2018); Yu-Min Joo and Teck-Boon Tan (eds), *Smart Cities in Asia: Governing Development in the Era of Hyper-Connectivity* (Edward Elgar Publishing 2020); Thanh Phan and Daniela Damian (eds), *Smart Cities in Asia: Regulations, Problems, and Development* (Springer 2022); National University of Singapore, "Workshop: Smart Cities in Global Comparative Perspective: Worlding and Provincializing Relationships" (2022), https://ari.nus.edu.sg/events/smart-cities/, accessed June 12, 2024.

competition among Japan, South Korea, and China to export smart city projects into ASEAN countries.

II COMPLEXITIES OF SMART CITIES

In the smart city literature, there has been a long scholarly debate on the definition and concept of smart cities. Since this chapter's purpose is not a full analysis of the scholarly debate, the chapter provides the Organisation for Economic Co-operation and Development (OECD)'s concept of smart cities as a baseline definition: "initiatives or approaches that effectively leverage digitalization to boost citizen well-being and deliver more efficient, sustainable and inclusive urban services and environments as part of a collaborative, multi-stakeholder process."[8] While this definition includes several elements of smart cities which are helpful for understanding developments in Asia, this chapter underscores that defining the contours of smart cities remains contested in the region.

Apart from the debate on the concept and definition, smart cities are complex and dynamic infrastructures in light of the following two dimensions.

A. *The Smart City as a Layered System*

The first complexity pertains to the fact that a smart city is not itself a technology but rather a system. Smart cities generally have a three-layered structure. First, the bottom level consists of city infrastructure and utilities (e.g., energy management systems, water and waste management systems, and public transportation controls), which are linked to digital equipment (e.g., cameras, GPS, sensors). Second, the middle level consists of data gathered from citizens and public administration bodies that are connected and analyzed using software and applications on a data platform. Finally, at the top level, data-based urban services can be offered in a comprehensive manner, covering multiple sectors such as energy, transportation, waste, education, health, and safety.

Thus, a smart city is a system. However, "smart technologies" play an important role within the system. Smart technologies refer to three elements of technology to deliver urban services: a collection of data, data processing, and automation of decision-making.[9] On this point, AI technologies are core smart technologies.

[8] OECD, *Enhancing the Contribution of Digitalisation to the Smart Cities of the Future* (OECD 2019) 7. For the discussion of international definitions of smart cities, see Yoshiko Naiki, "Smart Cities and International Trade Law" (2024) 23(3) World TR 363, 365–366.

[9] Astrid Voorwinden, "The Privatised City: Technology and Public-Private Partnerships in the Smart City" (2021) 13(2) Law, Innovation and Technology 439, 440 (referring toMireille Hildebrandt, *Smart Technologies and the End(s) of Law: Novel Entanglements of Law and Technology* (Edward Elgar Publishing 2015)). See also Alan Smart and Dean Curran, "Prospects and Social Impact of Big Data-Driven Urban Governance in China: Provincializing Smart City Research" in Weiping Wu and Qin Gao (eds), *China Urbanizing: Impacts and*

Accordingly, there are both promises and challenges associated with smart city projects: AI and big data can bring improvements in efficiency and decision-making when providing services while there are increased privacy and security risks.[10]

B. *Hard and Soft Laws of Smart Cities*

The second complexity relates to soft and hard laws of smart cities with the former mostly preceding the latter.[11] State action on smart cities typically begins with "soft" instruments – the adoption of national policies and strategies. Smart city policies should be included in the wider policy and planning measures for science and technology of the country. At this initial stage, there will be considerable discussion on the vision, concepts, and ideas of smart cities in the context of each country.

While soft law prevails initially in the design of the foregoing, after the adoption of national policies, legislation related to smart cities (i.e., "hard law") may come into effect. Various existing laws are relevant to smart city projects such as the laws of the environment, transportation, energy, and education. Apart from these existing laws, new legislation for smart cities may concern "special economic zones" (SEZs). The law for SEZs creates experimental sites for new policies and strategies, including a "regulatory sandbox,"[12] a concept that invites experimentation in regulatory design, including deregulation for the purpose of demonstrating new technologies. Deregulation aims, fundamentally, to promote new activities rather than to regulate them. Thus, smart city projects are often subject to the laws of SEZs.

For instance, in 2020, Japan amended the law of national strategic special zones to promote smart cities, known as the "law of super cities."[13] The amended law has undergone two main revisions.[14] First, as a "data

Transitions (University of Pennsylvania Press 2022) 210 ("Smart urbanism and data-driven (urban) governance involve three key aspects that differentiate them, at least discursively, from previous forms of governance: the collection of big data, the use of proprietary algorithms to analyze the data, and the real-time use of data to manage the urban environment.").

[10] The literature on AI/big data and smart cities is vast. See, e.g., AI & Society, "Special Issue on Urban AI" (vol 38 issue 3, June 2023); Rob Kitchin, "Data-Driven Urbanism" in Rob Kitchin et al (eds), *Data and the City* (Routledge 2018); Robert Brauneis and Ellen P Goodman, "Algorithmic Transparency for the Smart City" (2018) 20 Yale J L and Technology 103; Janine S Hiller and Jordan M Blanke, "Smart Cities, Big Data, and the Resilience of Privacy" (2017) 68 Hastings L.J. 309; Ibrahim Abaker Targio Hashem et al, "The Role of Big Data in Smart City" (2016) 36 Int J Inf Manag 748.

[11] Astrid Voorwinden and Sofia Ranchordás, "Soft Law in City Regulation and Governance" in Mariolina Eliantonio (ed), *Handbook on Soft Law* (Edward Elgar 2023) 337–352.

[12] I am grateful to Veronica Taylor for bringing this point of "special economic zones" to my attention. For a discussion of "special economic zones" in the Japanese context, see Mayu Terada, "The Influences of the Law of Super City on Local Governments" (2020) 730 Monthly Jichiken 10, 11–12 (in Japanese).

[13] The Law of National Strategic Special Zones, Amended on May 27, 2020.

[14] For a detailed discussion, see Osamu Nishigami, "The Amendment of the Law of National Strategic Special Zones" (2020) 482 Hougaku Kyoushitsu 49, 51–52 (in Japanese).

platform"[15] is necessary for smart cities, the revision promotes activities such as setting up the data platform and collecting and providing data to relevant business actors. Second, the revision requires responding to the views and concerns expressed by citizens and relevant stakeholders.

Additionally, one of the important existing laws relevant to many regions and cities around the world is the law of data protection and privacy, as smart city projects involve data collection and processing. A core issue is whether the existing laws can function appropriately in the context of data collection and processing in smart cities. In other words, it is important to assure whether existing privacy frameworks can address unique privacy challenges of data collection and processing in the context of smart cities where multiple public and private actors may have access to and share datasets.[16]

III FEATURES OF ASIAN SMART CITIES

Building on the foregoing discussion on the complex system and role of law in smart cities, I argue that Asian smart cities demonstrate both similarities to and divergences from Western smart cities. In this section, I suggest that there are three features of Asian smart cities that are unique. While contested within the region, these features distinguish Asian smart cities from Western equivalents.

A. *"Problem-Oriented" Projects*

A notable feature of Asian smart cities is "problem-oriented" smart projects. In other words, smart cities are tools used to solve specific urban problems in Asia. On this point, the expression "green experimentation" has grown out of low-carbon urban experiences around the world.[17] Smart city projects are often referred to as "experiments"; therefore, experimental aspects are not a particularly distinctive feature in Asian smart cities.[18] However, Asian smart cities' experimentation tends to focus more on environmental protection compared to Western smart cities.

[15] A city itself may serve as a data platform by "absorbing data from the urban environment . . . and then centralizing and repackaging it in accessible, usable interfaces for developers." Kelsey Finch and Omer Tene, "Smart Cities: Privacy, Transparency, and Community" in E Selinger, J Polonetsky and O Tene (eds), *The Cambridge Handbook of Consumer Privacy* (CUP 2018) 125, 135.

[16] Trevor Braun et al, "Security and Privacy Challenges of Smart Cities" (2018) 39 Sustainable Cities and Society 499, 501. For the challenges in the context of smart cities and EU's General Data Protection Regulation, see Laurens Vandercruysse et al, "Data Control in Smart City Services: Pitfalls and How to Resolve Them" (2019) 5(4) EDPL 554.

[17] The term "green experimentation" is borrowed from Peter Drahos, *Survival Governance: Energy and Climate in the Chinese Century* (OUP 2021) 166.

[18] See, e.g., James Evans et al (eds), *The Experimental City* (Routledge 2017); Robert Cowley and Federico Caprotti, "Smart City as Anti-Planning in the UK" (2019) 37(3) Environ Plann D Soc Space 428–448.

Asian smart cities' "green" experimentation has been promoted with particular consideration given to Asia's urban demographic features, that is, its large urban populations, and associated environmental concerns. Scholars have noted that features of urbanization in Asia are distinct from those in other regions.[19] According to UN-Habitat, "Asia has the highest number of urban dwellers worldwide."[20] Furthermore, as of early 2023, "[t]here were a total of 28 megacities with a population of over 10 million inhabitants in the Asia-Pacific region."[21] This feature of urban density raises concerns; "High population densities in megacities can often lead to environmental problems. A dense population, and thus heavier reliance on road network infrastructures, causes increased traffic. This in turn can create significant burdens on the environment."[22] This explains why Asian smart cities have had a "green" experimentation factor compared to Western smart cities. Related to this point, experts have noted that the initial policy demand for Chinese smart cities was based on the need to combat air pollution.[23]

B. *The Role of State-Led Initiatives*

In Western smart city projects, the role of local city governments in building and designing smart cities has been pronounced; as for the famous cases of Amsterdam, Barcelona, Helsinki, and Vienna, experts have noted that city governments play a similarly important role, setting up "a strategic framework" and "a collaborative environment" to promote smart cities.[24] By contrast, Asian smart city projects are more based on national government-driven strategies. Whereas Western smart city projects are also supported by national-level policies in terms of funding and coordination (e.g., the Smart City Challenge[25] of the United States (US) or the European Union (EU) Horizon 2020 program),[26] there is a greater degree of central

19 Li Yu and Federico Caprotti, "Introduction" in Federico Caprotti and Li Yu (eds), *Sustainable Cities in Asia* (Routledge 2018) 1.

20 UN-Habitat, *World Cities Report 2020: The Value of Sustainable Urbanization* (UN-Habitat 2020) 12 (with the region accounting for "54 per cent of the world's urban population").

21 Statista, *Number of Inhabitants in Megacities in the Asia-Pacific Region in 2023* (April 20, 2023), www.statista.com/statistics/910856/asia-pacific-population-in-megacities/, accessed June 12, 2024.

22 Statista Research Department, *Megacities in the Asia-Pacific Region: Statistics & Facts* (February 27, 2024), www.statista.com/topics/4855/megacities-in-asia-pacific/#topicOverview, accessed June 12, 2024.

23 Wenxuan Yu and Chengwei Xu, "Developing Smart Cities in China: An Empirical Analysis" (2018) 5(3) IJPADA 1–16.

24 Mora and Deakin (n 2) 150–151.

25 US Department of Transportation, *Smart City Challenge* (2015), www.transportation.gov/smartcity, accessed June 12, 2024.

26 The European Commission provides the funding under the Horizon 2020 research and innovation program for European smart city projects. European Commission, Horizon 2020, Smart Cities and Communities, https://ec.europa.eu/inea/en/horizon-2020/smart-cities-communities, accessed June 12, 2024; Smart Cities Marketplace, Projects and Sites Overview, https://smartcities-marketplace.ec.europa.eu/, accessed June 12, 2024.

government engagement in Asia. This suggests that "the state's central role in smart city development is undeniable and has been highlighted for countries with strong state planning centrality."[27] The "developmentalist smart city concept" in Asia is, "hardware-driven projects developed by governments and big businesses who are keen to apply the most cutting-edge technologies."[28]

Asian smart cities thus demonstrate tighter linkages between entrepreneurs, big tech, and central governments. Ayona Datta, a smart city researcher focused on India, observed that smart cities in Asia have been promoted through "state-centric entrepreneurial intervention."[29] Datta argues that the framing of "development," "modernity," and "economic growth" in smart cities supports state-driven urban development. For instance, since 2015, India has been making plans to transform 100 cities into smart cities.[30]

Similarly, in 2017, Indonesia launched the "Toward 100 Smart Cities" movement.[31] After the engagement of national governments, the role of ICT corporations became more prominent. Asian smart cities have been described as "techno-centric"[32] and "high-tech."[33] Datta has pointed out the high degree of "technocratic nationalism" through which smart cities are promoted by a group of people "[believing] in the power of technology."[34]

At the same time, as Yu-Min Joo argues, there are several variations of Asian state-led smart city projects.[35] For instance, even China and Singapore, which have been seen as typical developmentalist smart city cases in Asia, have very different pathways when we look at their development and progress. Chinese smart cities, led by a powerful party-state regime, are a distinctive case.[36] Chinese domestic smart cities

[27] Yu-Min Joo, "Developmentalist Smart Cities? The Cases of Singapore and Seoul" (2023) 27(Suppl 1) Int J Urban Sci 164, 167.

[28] Ibid.

[29] Ayona Datta, "Introduction: Fast Cities in an Urban Age" in Ayona Datta and Abdul Shaban (eds), *Mega-Urbanization in the Global South: Fast Cities and New Urban Utopias of the Postcolonial State* (Routledge 2017) 14–15 (referring to Mariana Mazzucato, *The Entrepreneurial State: Debunking Public vs. Private Sector Myths* (Anthem Press 2013)). See also Ayona Datta, "New Urban Utopias of Postcolonial India: 'Entrepreneurial Urbanization' in Dholera Smart City, Gujarat" (2015) 5(1) Dialogues in Human Geography 3–22.

[30] Government of India, "About Smart Cities," https://smartcities.gov.in/about-the-mission, accessed June 12, 2024.

[31] Jonathan Davy, "What Lies ahead of Indonesia's 100 Smart Cities Movement?" (*The Jakarta Post*, December 5, 2019), www.thejakartapost.com/life/2019/12/05/what-lies-ahead-of-indonesias-100-smart-cities-movement.html, accessed June 12, 2024.

[32] See, e.g., Seungho Yoo, "Songdo: The Hype and Decline of World's First Smart City" in Federico Caprotti and Li Yu (eds), *Sustainable Cities in Asia* (Routledge 2018) 146.

[33] See, e.g., Tim Bunnell, "Smart City Returns" (2015) 5(1) Dialogues in Human Geography 45.

[34] Ayona Datta, "A 100 Smart Cities, A 100 Utopias" (2015) 5(1) Dialogues in Human Geography 49, 50.

[35] Joo (n 27) 178 ("I highlighted how the existing developmentalist smart city concept as a state-led and hardware-driven project is far from adequate in explaining what is taking place in Asia's global cities today").

[36] Dean Curran and Alan Smart, "Data-Driven Governance, Smart Urbanism and Risk-Class Inequalities: Security and Social Credit in China" (2021) 58(3) Urban Studies 487, 494.

are related to "green experimentation" but are primarily concerned with "green growth" and "green development," thus seeking an alternative development pathway from the conventional economic growth-centric approach.[37] This is particularly seen in China's "eco-city"[38] projects.[39] These eco-cities were developed against the background of the Chinese government's announcement of the nation's 11th and 12th five-year plans (in the 11th plan [2006–2010], there was a shift from "growth first" to "sustainable development," and in the 12th plan [2011–2016], to "green development and climate change").[40] The first eco-city, in Dongtan near Shanghai (launched in 2006), is a well-known example, although the project did not proceed as planned due to several problems such as the land quota allocation and corruption.[41] Another well-researched Chinese eco-city case is the Tianjin project, which began under the 2007 China–Singapore framework agreement[42] and is generally regarded as a greener and sustainable case.[43]

However, such a domestic image of smart cities in China has also changed. China exports smart technologies through the "Digital Silk Road" under China's "Belt and Road Initiative."[44] Notably, some Asian smart city projects have been led by Chinese big-tech corporations, such as the Alibaba Group[45] and Huawei.[46] For instance, Huawei has engaged in smart city projects in Malaysia,[47]

37 Frans Sengers et al, "Experimenting in the City: Unpacking Notion of Experimentation for Sustainability" in James Evans (ed), *The Experimental City* (Routledge 2016) 19.

38 Eco-cities are defined by their ecological considerations, such as low-carbon initiatives. See, Drahos (n 17) 164; Fulong Wu, "China's Eco-Cities" (2012) 43(2) Geoforum 169.

39 However, this is not to deny that there have been a number of existing European eco-city projects. See, Drahos (n 17) 164 ("By 2009, one survey had identified some 79 practical eco-city initiatives around the world, ranging from entirely new cities to retrofitting initiatives. The two regions of greatest activity were Europe (34) and Asia/Australia (27)").

40 Xuefei Ren, "Green as Urban Spectacle in China" in Federico Caprotti and Li Yu (eds), *Sustainable Cities in Asia* (Routledge 2018) 79.

41 Wu (n 38) 169–171; Drahos (n 17) 165–166.

42 For the government-to-government city project between China and Singapore, see Singapore, Ministry of National Development, Tianjin Eco-City, www.mnd.gov.sg/tianjinecocity/who-we-are, accessed June 12, 2024.

43 Federico Caprotti, *Eco-Cities and the Transition to Low Carbon Economies* (Palgrave Macmillan 2015) 55. See also Federico Caprotti and Ziyue Gong, "Challenging the Eco-City: Residents' Perceptions of Social Sustainability in Tianjin Eco-City, China" in Federico Caprotti and Li Yu (eds), *Sustainable Cities in Asia* (Routledge 2018) 161; Ren (n 40) 80–81.

44 For the literature on China's smart city technologies exports, see, e.g., Matthew S Erie and Thomas Streinz, "The Beijing Effect: China's 'Digital Silk Road' as Transnational Data Governance" (2021) 54(1) NYU J Int'l L and Pol 1, 71; Drahos (n 17) 161–164; Catherine Atha et al, *China's Smart Cities Development* (SOS International LLC 2020) 78, www.uscc.gov/sites/default/files/China_Smart_Cities_Development.pdf, accessed June 12, 2024.

45 See, e.g., Smart and Curran (n 9) 215; Curran and Smart (n 36) 495.

46 Cheng Ting-Fang and Lauly Li, "Huawei Says Smart Business Will Grow Despite US Pressure" (*Nikkei Asia*, October 20, 2020), https://asia.nikkei.com/Editor-s-Picks/Interview/Huawei-says-smart-city-business-will-grow-despite-US-pressure, accessed June 12, 2024.

47 Farah Adilla, "i-City Partners with Huawei to reinvent Next Smart City" (*New Straits Times*, January 20, 2022), www.nst.com.my/business/2022/01/764480/i-city-partners-huawei-reinvent-next-smart-city, accessed June 12, 2024.

Thailand,[48] and Indonesia.[49] Such engagements by China in Asian smart cities are also enhanced by the fact that since 2020 "China has accelerated the international promotion of some of its smart city technologies" and "providing 'anti-epidemic solutions' has become the new selling point for several Chinese tech companies."[50] Indeed, "the COVID-19 pandemic has accelerated the deployment of innovation and technology in urban areas."[51] Although surveillance and monitoring technologies were widely used even before the COVID-19 pandemic, digitalized surveillance technologies for disease tracking and contact tracing are now proliferating.[52]

In addition to China, Singapore has been a pioneer in designing certain types of smart cities, for example, the top-down Smart Nation project. Scholars describe Singapore's initiative as "a state-led initiative orchestrated by civic-minded tech-talent."[53] To be specific, the Singapore government "insources" tech talent instead of outsourcing to private sectors in developing the smart city: "Insourcing involves attracting tech talent to Singapore, instilling technical knowledge and capabilities amongst those responsible for city governance, and thus upgrading the technical competencies of the public sector [of Singapore] more generally."[54] This is a unique state-led approach that avoids outsourcing projects to private firms as "privatization" in smart cities has raised concerns about the increased role of the private sector eroding that of the government, which is viewed as a negative outcome.[55]

Regarding the role of Singapore government, Singapore has another role in the region – leading the smart city movement in ASEAN countries. The next Section III.C turns to this regional aspect of smart cities.

C. *"Technocratic Regionalism": ASEAN and Smart Cities*

In ASEAN countries, "Singapore is highly active in trying to forge a smart cities network and regional platforms."[56] At the 2018 ASEAN Summit, Singapore

48 "Huawei Joins Hands with GLAND to Enable 'Smart City' in Thailand" (*Source: Taiwan External Trade Development Council*, March 3, 2022), www.taiwantrade.com/tradenews/detail.html?newsid=2487840, accessed May 28, 2025.

49 Huawei, "XL Axiata and Huawei Sign MoU on 5G City Joint Innovation" (October 27, 2022), www.huawei.com/en/news/2022/10/5gcity-green5g-ultra-wideband-multi-antenna, accessed June 12, 2024.

50 Alice Ekman and Cristina de Esperanza Picardo, "Towards Urban Decoupling? China's Smart City Ambitions at the time of Covid-19" (2020) EUISS (Brief 10) 1 2, www.iss.europa.eu/sites/default/files/EUISSFiles/Brief%2010%20Smart%20Cities.pdf, accessed June 12, 2024.

51 UN-Habitat (n 20) xxx.

52 Pedro A Villarreal, "International Law and Digital Disease Surveillance in Pandemics: On the Margins of Regulation" (2023) 24(3) German Law Journal 603, 605.

53 Orlando Woods, Tim Bunnell and Lily Kong, "Insourcing the Smart City: Assembling an Ideo-Technical Ecosystem of Talent, Skills, and Civic-Mindedness in Singapore" (2023) 45(5) *Urban Geography* 735, 750.

54 Ibid 736.

55 Voorwinden (n 9).

56 Tai Wei Lim, "Smart Cities in East Asia: ASEAN-China Cooperation in the BRI and Its Digital Nexus" in Yang Yue and Li Fujian (eds), *The Belt and Road Initiative: ASEAN Countries' Perspectives* (World Scientific 2019) 258.

proposed the "ASEAN Smart Cities Network" (ASCN),[57] and to date, twenty-six pilot cities have been launched.[58]

ASEAN has three objectives for smart city development: competitive economy, sustainable environment, and high quality of life.[59] Under these objectives, six areas are targeted for smart city development: (1) civic and social, (2) health and well-being, (3) safety and security, (4) quality of the environment, (5) built infrastructure, and (6) industry and innovation.[60] These targeted areas resonate with the problem-oriented features of Asian smart cities discussed above.

Singapore's leadership has been described as "technocratic regionalism";[61] that is, "[promoting] a technocratic form of regional integration and consolidation," to develop smart city projects across Southeast Asia.[62] Singapore's ambition has motivated other countries in Asia to pursue smart city initiatives. Japan is one of ASEAN's partners supporting smart city development; other partners include South Korea, China, Australia, the US, and the EU.[63]

Hence, whereas China and Singapore have left their strong presence in inter-Asian smart cities, Japan has emerged as an impactful leader as well. Against this backdrop, Section IV focuses on Japan's engagement in smart city projects in ASEAN. It first looks at the development of Japan's smart city policies and then explores smart city cooperation between Japan and the ASEAN countries.

IV SMART CITY COOPERATION BETWEEN JAPAN AND ASEAN

A. *Development of Smart City Policies in Japan*

The Japanese government has only recently shown a strong interest in smart cities; yet in that short time, Japan has become a major player in the Asian region. However, it has made some efforts in the past. In the context of promoting

57 Singapore's Concept Note on ASEAN Smart Cities Network (March 18, 2018), https://asean.org/wp-content/uploads/2019/02/ASCN-Concept-Note.pdf, accessed June 12, 2024.

58 ASEAN Smart Cities Network, Pilot Cities, https://asean.org/our-communities/asean-smart-cities-network/, accessed June 12, 2024.

59 ASEAN, ASEAN Smart City Framework (July 8, 2018) paras 6–8, https://asean.org/wp-content/uploads/2021/09/ASEAN-Smart-Cities-Framework.pdf, accessed June 12, 2024.

60 Ibid paras 13–18. See also Centre for Liveable Cities, *ASEAN Smart Cities Network* (2018) 11, www.clc.gov.sg/docs/default-source/books/book-asean-smart-cities-network.pdf, accessed June 12, 2024.

61 Lily Kong and Orlando Woods, "Scaling Smartness, (De)Provincialising the City? The ASEAN Smart Cities Network and the Translational Politics of Technocratic Regionalism" (2021) 117 Cities 103326 at 1.

62 Ibid.

63 See ASEAN Smart Cities Network, Monitoring & Evaluation Report 2022, https://asean.org/wp-content/uploads/2022/10/2022-ASCN-ME-Report-Final_21Sep2022-for-public.pdf, accessed June 12, 2024; Masaki Okamoto, "Mushrooming Smart Cities in ASEAN Countries and the Unhealthy Multi-Actor Competition" (*Roles Report*, No. 20, 2022), https://roles.rcast.u-tokyo.ac.jp/uploads/publication/file/42/publication.pdf, accessed June 12, 2024.

renewable energy combined with smart grid technologies, the Ministry of Economy, Trade, and Industry (METI) took the lead (starting before the 2011 earthquake, tsunami, and Fukushima nuclear crisis).[64] Such efforts served as a pathway to the current Japan's smart city national policies, and this section discusses three points that mark the Japanese government's increasingly strong engagement in the promotion of smart city policies.

First, Japan's engagement can be found in the Sixth Science, Technology, and Innovation Basic Plan (hereinafter, the Sixth Basic Plan) adopted by the Cabinet in March 2021[65] and covering the period 2021–2025. The Sixth Basic Plan identifies six policies for transforming society in a sustainable and resilient manner, including the development and proliferation of smart cities.[66] The smart city is framed as an "innovation" and a solution for a sustainable and resilient society. This was the first time in the Science, Technology, and Innovation Basic Plan that smart cities were mentioned – the previous Fifth Basic Plan only mentioned the promotion of a "super smart society."[67] Moreover and important for the study of IAL, the Sixth Basic Plan describes the proliferation of smart cities outside Japan, clearly stating that Japan will disseminate the concept of a smart city and export smart-city-related infrastructure and data management systems, particularly with other Asian countries.[68]

The second engagement of the Japanese government relates to the establishment of the concept of smart cities. In April 2021, the Cabinet released the "Smart City Guidebook,"[69] which explains the need for smart cities and the process of development to support smart city efforts. Notably, the Guidebook specifies "three philosophies" and "five principles" of smart cities.[70] The three philosophies are: (1) resident-centric, (2) based on visions/challenges, and (3) collaboration among sections/cities.[71] The first, "resident-centric" framing, actually aligns with the Western smart

[64] See Masaru Yarime and Martin Karlsson, "Examining the Technological Innovation Systems of Smart Cities: The Case of Japan and Implications for Public Policy and Institutional Design" in Jorge Niosi (ed), *Innovation Systems, Policy and Management* (CUP 2018) 398–399; Thomas Feldhoff, "Low Carbon Communities, Energy Policy and Energy Democracy in Japan" in Federico Caprotti and Li Yu (eds), *Sustainable Cities in Asia* (Routledge 2018) 238–239.

[65] The Cabinet Office, Japan, *The Sixth Science, Technology, and Innovation Basic Plan* [The Sixth Basic Plan] (March 2021), www8.cao.go.jp/cstp/kihonkeikaku/6honbun.pdf (in Japanese), accessed June 12, 2024.

[66] Ibid 38–41.

[67] The Cabinet Office, Japan, *The Fifth Science and Technology Basic Plan* (January 2016) 10, www8.cao.go.jp/cstp/kihonkeikaku/5honbun.pdf (in Japanese), accessed June 12, 2024.

[68] The Sixth Basic Plan (n 65) 41.

[69] The Cabinet Office et al, *The Smart-City Guidebook*, Ver. 1.01 (April 2021), www8.cao.go.jp/cstp/society5_0/smartcity/01_scguide_eng_1.pdf, accessed June 12, 2024.

[70] Ibid 9, 13–14.

[71] Ibid 13.

city debate on a "citizen-centric" or "people-centric" approach. According to the Guidebook, the "resident-centric" concept is aimed at "'[improving] well-being' and [taking] a demand side driven approach, in which residents, i.e. primary users, take initiatives, instead of a supply side driven one, in which governments and private companies take initiatives."[72] The "five principles" identified by the Guidebook are explained below in the context of the third instance of the Japanese government's involvement.

Third, the Japanese government has attempted to link smart city policies with data governance concerns, calling for global attention to smart city initiatives from a "data governance" perspective. Smart cities first became an international topic at the G20 Osaka Summit in 2019. Thereafter, the "G20 Global Smart Cities Alliance" was established with the World Economic Forum.[73] In 2020, the Alliance established five principles for smart cities: (1) equity, inclusivity, and social impact; (2) security and resilience; (3) privacy and transparency; (4) openness and interoperability; and (5) operational and financial sustainability.[74] The Japanese government has transferred and adopted these five smart city principles into the 2021 Smart City Guidebook,[75] which illustrates its attempt to align the national smart city policy with global data governance discussions.

B. *Exporting Smart Solutions to ASEAN*

The Japanese government has provided several routes to support the export of smart city technologies and infrastructure to Asia. Four governmental organizations are involved: the Ministry of Land, Infrastructure, Transport, and Tourism (MLIT), METI,[76] the

[72] Ibid. For a case study of the resident-centric approach in Japan, see Zhijian Wang, "Road to Human-Centric Smart City Governance in Japan: The Case of Fujisawa Sustainable Smart Town" (2024) 15(S6) Global Policy 84.

[73] World Economic Forum, *News Releases: World Economic Forum to Lead G20 Smart Cities Alliance on Technology Governance* (June 27, 2019), www.weforum.org/press/2019/06/world-economic-forum-to-lead-g20-smart-cities-alliance-on-technology-governance, accessed June 12, 2024.

[74] The Centre for the Fourth Industrial Revolution Japan, "Making Rules with World Cities: Smart City Policy Roadmap" (February 1, 2021), https://note.com/c4irj/n/nadf562eb2ff4 (in Japanese), accessed June 12, 2024.

[75] *The Smart-City Guidebook* (n 69) 14.

[76] While the METI does not have a particular program to support overseas smart city projects, smart city projects are covered under the program of "Feasibility Study Project for Overseas Deployment of High-Quality Infrastructure." As one example of such a feasibility study under the METI program, Marubeni corporation conducted a "Feasibility Study for the Implementation of Metaverse Service for Overseas Smart City Development" in Ho Chi Minh City, Vietnam. *Marubeni Corporation, News Release* (January 19, 2023), www.marubeni.com/en/news/2023/release/00007.html, accessed June 12, 2024.

Ministry of Environment,[77] and the Japan International Cooperation Agency (JICA).[78] Among these, the most active actors are JICA and MLIT.

JICA is a well-known Japanese institution that offers capacity building and training for foreign local governments via official development assistance (ODA) to support foreign developing countries bilaterally.[79] JICA has been engaged in Asian smart city projects for several years,[80] including famous cases in Bangkok and Jakarta. Additionally, JICA assists small cities such as Siem Reap in Cambodia. Siem Reap has an iconic temple, Angkor Wat, that has been identified as a world heritage site, and tourism has been growing as its main industry.[81] The city needed infrastructure and utilities to cope with an increasing number of tourists from abroad and handle rapid urbanization; therefore, the city sought smart solutions.[82]

As in the Siem Reap case, JICA's smart city assistance is not only about providing technology. The city needed smart city policies, institutions, human workforce, and skills. Thus, JICA focused on the "establishment and human resource development of smart city promotion organization" and the "establishment of institutional framework ... for smart city" by dispatching Japanese experts to foreign local governments.[83]

MLIT is a central actor in the Japanese government that has actively engaged with ASEAN, particularly, the ASCN.[84] Since 2019, MLIT has hosted the annual ASEAN–Japan Smart Cities Network High-Level Meeting. The first meeting was held in Yokohama, Japan, and according to the summary of meeting, the "Japan Association for Smart Cities in ASEAN (JASCA) was established as a framework to facilitate cooperation between ASEAN and Japan, and is composed of potential

77 While the Ministry of Environment's "City-to-City Collaboration for Zero-Carbon Society" program (since 2013) is not directly related to smart cities, the smart city development projects comprise a major part of the program. See, e.g., the Ministry of Environment, *City-to-City Collaboration for Zero-Carbon Society 2020*, www.env.go.jp/earth/coop/lowcarbon-asia/english/project/data/jcm_pamphlet_C2C_2020_EN.pdf, accessed June 12, 2024.

78 For the JICA's smart city cooperation with Asia, see JICA Magazine, Smart Cities for A Brighter Future, No. 2 (October 2021), https://jicamagazine.jica.go.jp/en/cms/wp-content/uploads/2021/08/2110en.pdf, accessed June 12, 2024.

79 JICA, "What We Do" "Types of Assistance," www.jica.go.jp/english/activities/, accessed June 12, 2024.

80 See Marco Zappa, "Smart Energy for the World: The Rise of Technonationalist Discourse in Japan in the Late 2000s" (2020) 51(1–2) IQAS 193.

81 See Ministry of Foreign Affairs, Singapore (2018) *ASEAN Smart Cities Network* 50 ("Siem Reap is looking at a Smart Tourist Management System to assist in handling the increasing number of tourists who visit the city and affect local residents' amenity."), www.clc.gov.sg/docs/default-source/books/book-asean-smart-cities-network.pdf, accessed June 12, 2024.

82 For the JICA's smart city cooperation with Siem Reap, www.jica.go.jp/Resource/project/cambodia/036/outline/index.html (in Japanese), accessed June 12, 2024.

83 JICA, *Smart City Approach: Towards Sustainable Urban Management*, www.jica.go.jp/activities/issues/urban/ku57pq00001gfbsv-att/smartcity_01_en.pdf, accessed June 12, 2024.

84 See (n 57).

Japanese partners, both public and private, from various fields."[85] More specifically, JASCA's web page explains its role that "[JASCA] will proactively and continuously disseminate information on the technologies and experiences that promote Japan's smart cities in ASEAN."[86]

At the second high-level meeting held in December 2020, the MLIT proposed "Smart City Supported by Japan–ASEAN Mutual Partnership" (Smart JAMP), which is an overseas smart city assistance program.[87] Smart JAMP consists of four measures: (1) assisting new project formations, (2) offering financial support, (3) strengthening the relationship between ASEAN members and Japanese firms, and (4) sharing information.[88] Among these, MLIT particularly supports the first measure, engaging with ASEAN countries and cities to form new smart city projects. When MLIT requested proposals from ASEAN countries and cities, thirty-two proposals were raised and nineteen were adopted.[89]

Further, MLIT suggested ASEAN develop the "ASEAN Smart City Planning Guidebook," which was released in March 2022 and aims "to provide practical insights including frameworks and examples, to support stakeholders involved in smart city development in ASEAN."[90] This Guidebook is actually based on Japan's national "2021 Smart City Guidebook" (as explained above).

V DISCUSSION – HOW TO SHAPE THE CONCEPT OF SMART CITIES IN ASIA

Japan's intention seems to be to diffuse smart city ideas and norms into ASEAN. As seen above, MLIT has been supporting project developments in ASEAN; at the same time, it suggested creating the "ASEAN Smart City Planning Guidebook," which was a "transplant" of Japan's Guidebook version. As noted, Japan's Guidebook includes "three philosophies" (including the resident-centric view) and "five principles" (including data governance guidelines) for smart cities.

How has ASEAN responded? It has officially stated that the ASEAN Smart City Planning Guidebook is "[p]repared by [the] Ministry of Land, Infrastructure, Transport and Tourism (MLIT) in Japan [i]n Consultation with the ASEAN

85 MLIT, Summary Record of ASEAN-Japan Smart Cities Network High-Level Meeting, para 6, www.mlit.go.jp/report/press/content/001313066.pdf, accessed June 12, 2024.

86 JASCA, www.jasca2021.jp/, accessed June 12, 2024.

87 JASCA, Smart JAMP, www.jasca2021.jp/cooperative/#smartjamp, accessed June 12, 2024.

88 JASCA, Smart JAMP in detail, www.jasca2021.jp/pdf/SmartJAMP_en.pdf, accessed June 12, 2024.

89 MLIT, The Adopted Smart JAMP Proposals, www.mlit.go.jp/kokusai/content/001408266.pdf (in Japanese), accessed June 12, 2024.

90 ASEAN Smart Cities Network, *ASEAN Smart City Planning Guidebook* (March 2022) 5, https://asean.org/wp-content/uploads/2022/06/ASEAN_SmartCityPlanningGuidebook_en_WEBSITE.pdf, accessed June 12, 2024. See also JASCA, *ASEAN Smart City Planning Guidebook* (March 2022), www.jasca2021.jp/cooperative/, accessed June 12, 2024.

Smart Cities Network (ASCN) and the ASEAN Secretariat."[91] Hence, it appears that ASEAN has accepted the Japanese guidebook to some degree but nonetheless retains the Japanese origin for the guidebook. In other words, there seems to be some level of caution in ASEAN's approach rather than the wholesale incorporation of the Japanese guidebook into its own normative framework.

While the process is not seamless and there are important nation-of-origin distinctions in branding the regulatory and normative bases for Asian smart cities, the diffusion of smart city ideas and norms may eventually lead to the export of Japanese legal infrastructures, which may provoke regulatory competition in Asia. For Japan's MLIT, there are potential regulatory competitors: South Korea and China.[92]

First, there is South Korea's Ministry of Land, Infrastructure and Transport (MOLIT), which has been hosting the "K-City Network Global Cooperation Program," "a new platform and G2G cooperation program for overseas smart city development and export of K-smart city model."[93] Under this program, twelve smart city projects were adopted in 2020 and eleven in 2021,[94] with nine in ASEAN countries. However, as MOLIT's program also focuses on global projects beyond Asia, the extent to which Japan and South Korea are in regulatory competition to export their own smart city models to ASEAN may be unclear.

China is another possible rival. As noted previously, Chinese big-tech corporations such as Huawei have been engaging in Asian smart city projects. Chinese companies' technologies and systems can spread through overseas smart city projects along the "Digital Silk Road" under China's "Belt and Road Initiative."[95] Moreover, the Chinese government is engaged in the ASCN. In 2019, China and ASEAN released the "ASEAN–China Leaders' Statement on Smart City Cooperation Initiative."[96]

91 See the title page of ASEAN Smart Cities Network (n 90).

92 Singapore historically actively exported "the Singapore model of urban development." See Orlando Woods and Lily Kong, "Mobile Cities, Modelling Policies: Importing/Exporting the Singapore 'Model' of Development" in John Rennie Short (ed), *A Research Agenda for Cities* (Edward Elgar Publishing 2017) 206–217. However, currently, Singapore is not regarded as a major country exporting smart cities in Asia.

93 MOLIT, "Launching of 'K-City Network Global Cooperation Program'" (February 13, 2020), https://overseas.mofa.go.kr/viewer/skin/doc.html?fn = 20200214053956512.docx&rs = /viewer/result/202304, accessed June 12, 2024.

94 For the 2020 results, MOLIT News (April 20, 2020), www.molit.go.kr/english/USR/BORD0201/m_28286/DTL.jsp?id = eng0301&cate = &mode = view&idx = 2937&key = &search = &search_regdate_s = &search_regdate_e = &order = &desc = asc&srch_prc_stts = &item_num = 0&search_dept_id = &search_dept_nm = &srch_usr_nm = N&srch_usr_titl = N&srch_usr_ctnt = N&srch_mng_nm = N&old_dept_nm = &search_section = &source = &search1 = &lcmspage = 1, accessed June 12, 2024; for the 2021 results, MOLIT News (June 25, 2021), www.molit.go.kr/english/USR/BORD0201/m_28286/DTL.jsp?id = eng0301&cate = &mode = view&idx = 2979, accessed June 12, 2024.

95 See the literature cited (n 44).

96 ASEAN-China Leaders' Statement on Smart City Cooperation Initiative (November 3, 2019), https://asean.org/wp-content/uploads/2019/11/Final-ASEAN-China-Leaders-Statement-on-Smart-City-Cooperation-Initiative-2.pdf, accessed June 12, 2024.

According to the Statement, ASEAN and China agreed to "support private sector collaboration," "encourage the establishment of mutually beneficial city partnerships between ASEAN cities ... and Chinese cities," and "promote ... encouraging exchanges among related government departments, research institutions, enterprises, and other relevant stakeholders to promote the sharing of knowledge, technology and innovative solutions."[97]

Related to the promotion of "sharing of knowledge, technology and innovative solutions" above, one study pointed out that "China is promoting its smart city expertise through a set of training programmes provided to officials and engineers from foreign countries, particularly developing ones."[98] Indeed, the same study argues, "China is not only training foreign officials on the technical dimension of smart cities (infrastructure, maintenance, etc.) but also, increasingly, on how the government can use this expertise for specific social, political or security purposes."[99]

The COVID-19 pandemic increased opportunities for China to export its own smart city model because the pandemic has expanded and added a new function to smart city development: the need for an urgent response to public health emergencies. Smart city technologies can promote "remote work, online or distance learning, digital and contactless payments, telehealth, online shopping and drone or robot delivery" during health emergencies.[100] Moreover, smart technologies for surveillance and monitoring, which can track people's location and movement, have been useful for managing public safety during pandemics. As another study highlighted, "[t]he public sector has regained unexpected power and trust"[101] in using smart surveillance and monitoring technologies during the pandemic, and "[s]mart-city development will be boosted following COVID-19."[102] At this point, China may successfully export its own smart city model, which is useful for responding to public health emergencies and thus has great appeal for other governments.[103]

As noted, China has been extensively engaged in training foreign officials in smart city governance. This differs from what Japan's MLIT and South Korea's MOLIT

97 Ibid paras 4, 6, 8.

98 Ekman and Picardo (n 50) 5.

99 Ibid.

100 UN-Habitat (n 20) xxx. The literature on smart city development during and after the COVID-19 pandemic is vast. See, e.g., Orlando Troisi et al, "Covid-19 Sentiments in Smart Cities: The Role of Technology Anxiety before and during the Pandemic" (2022) 126 Computers in Human Behavior 106986; Daniel G Costa and João Paulo J Peixoto, "COVID-19 Pandemic: A Review of Smart Cities Initiatives to Face New Outbreaks" (2020) 2(2) IET Smart Cities 64; Jung Won Sonn, Myounggu Kang and Yeol Choi, "Smart City Technologies for Pandemic Control without Lockdown" (2020) 24(2) Int J Urban Sci 149.

101 Klaus R Kunzmann, "Smart City after Covid-19: Ten Narratives" (2020) 56(2) disP – The Planning Review 20, 22.

102 Ibid 27.

103 Ekman and Picardo (n 50) 5.

have been doing for smart city cooperation, mainly assisting overseas smart city project formation. As noted, for Japan, capacity building and training for foreign local governments are within the scope of JICA, which uses ODA to support foreign developing countries bilaterally. JICA's engagement with foreign local governments is possible only after JICA receives official requests for support from foreign (local) governments. Generally, just as "traditional donors have diffused principles, political structures, state reform, and economic adjustment programmes to recipient countries via Official Development Aid,"[104] JICA can also attempt to diffuse Japanese urban development models through smart city cooperation. However, JICA's smart city support may be insufficient to compete with the extensive capacity building offered by China.[105]

Simultaneously, the Chinese government's engagement and big-tech company projects will certainly raise security and privacy concerns regarding smart city development. Arranging the regulatory framework for data governance, including security and privacy issues, is a significant challenge, particularly in Asian smart cities.[106] In terms of concerns over privacy, China's approach differs from that of Japan – Japan can differentiate its overseas smart city projects from China's projects in light of privacy and security concerns.

VI CONCLUSION

This chapter has examined Japan's shaping of the ideas and norms of smart cities in Asian countries, particularly in relation to ASEAN in the context of inter-regional competition. Several methods exist for exporting smart solutions by Japanese governmental organizations, including development cooperation, diffusion of ideas, and regulatory competition. While interactions do not yet entail the export and adoptions of specific Japanese legal infrastructures, the MLIT and JICA are attempting to diffuse the norms, ideas, and governance models of smart cities through cooperation with ASEAN. Japan attempts to shape the idea of smart cities as it seeks to strengthen cooperation with ASEAN countries and highlight

[104] Rubens de S Duarte and Carlos R S Milani, "Southern States in International Development Cooperation: From Contestation to Norm Conception," (2021) 14 Chin J Int Politics 506, 508 (citing Carol Lancaster, *Foreign Aid: Diplomacy, Development, Domestic Politics* (University of Chicago Press 2007) 288; Emma Mawdsley, *From Recipients to Donors: Emerging Powers and the Changing Development Landscape* (Zed Books 2012) 270).

[105] I am grateful to Matthew S Erie for the discussion about China's extensive scale of engagement.

[106] See B Courtney Doagoo, "Smart Cities in Asia: An Introductory Note" in Thanh Phan and Daniela Damian (eds), *Smart Cities in Asia: Regulations, Problems, and Development* (Springer 2022) 9. Data governance is an increasingly common concern among smart cities around the world. For a case of Brazil, see Jhessica Reia and Luã Fergus Cruz, "Seeing Through the Smart City Narrative: Data Governance, Power Relations, and Regulatory Challenges in Brazil" in Blayne Haggart et al (eds), *Power and Authority in Internet Governance: Return of the State?* (Routledge 2021) 219.

advantages over rival countries (i.e., China). More precisely, Japan wants to take the lead in exporting the smart city model associated with the "citizen-centric" approach and the importance of privacy and data protection.[107]

What are the consequences of these interactions? It takes time to observe the effects and consequences of any interaction; in the case of smart cities, implementation takes a decade.[108] Each smart city project encompasses various development pathways; there is no smart city in Asia yet that includes a comprehensive smart "system" achieving all three levels (as illustrated in Section II.A).[109] It remains to be seen how the interactions between Japan and ASEAN will lead to the creation of the Asian smart city model. For future research on IAL of smart cities, it is necessary to look at interactions involving other key actors (i.e., Singapore, South Korea, and China)[110] and examine how the dynamism of interactions affects cooperation, diffusion, and competition in shaping the idea of smart cities in Asia.

[107] For the growing focus on citizen participation in Asia, see, e.g., Bipashyee Ghosh et al, "Smart as (Un)democratic? The Making of a Smart City Imaginary in Kolkata, India" (2022) 40(1) Environ Plann C: Politics Space 318–339.

[108] For the difficulties of implementing smart city projects, Kong and Woods (n 61) 5.

[109] This point is recognized not only in the context of Asia; the smart city literature has also noted in other regions that, far from taking a holistic approach, past smart city initiatives tended to choose only one or two sectors. See, e.g., Tooran Alizadeh, "An Investigation of IBM's Smarter Cities Challenge: What Do Participating Cities Want?" (2017) 63 Cities 70–80.

[110] See, e.g., Si-Ying Tan, Araz Taeihagh and Kritika Sha, "How Transboundary Learning Occurs: Case Study of the ASEAN Smart Cities Network (ASCN)" (2021) 13(11) Sustainability 6502.

14

In the Shadow of Sovereignty

Multiple Pathways of Inter-Asian Legal Influence of China on Hong Kong

Jacques deLisle

I INTRODUCTION

Since Hong Kong's reversion to China in 1997, the former British colony's legal order has reflected sharply increased influence from the now-superordinate People's Republic of China (PRC) and has begun to look more like the Mainland's – particularly in aspects of law that are relatively closely related to politics. The impact of the PRC on the law and legal order of China's first Special Administrative Region (SAR) is an extreme example of the effect of one Asian legal system on another – so much so that Hong Kong might not seem to be a very illuminating or interesting case for the study of "Inter-Asian Law (IAL)." In a formal and fundamental sense, PRC legal influence on Hong Kong is intra-jurisdictional. Amid all the controversies concerning Hong Kong's post-reversion legal trajectory, it is undisputed that the Hong Kong SAR (HKSAR) is part of the PRC and thus subject to domestic law-making by China.[1]

Despite these features – and because of them – the Hong Kong example offers insights into the broader phenomenon of inter-Asian legal influence. In practice, one Asian legal system's capacity to influence another is a matter of degree. Full sovereign powers are, perhaps, qualitatively different, but they also arguably lie at one end of a broad spectrum of power and influence. Beijing has employed a wide range of methods to shape Hong Kong's post-reversion legal order – ones that extend well beyond exercises of sovereign lawmaking powers.[2] These channels are in part

[1] See, e.g., Joint Declaration of the Government of the United Kingdom of Great Britain and Northern Ireland and the Government of the People's Republic of China on the Question of Hong Kong, December 19, 1984, Articles 1–2 (statements by governments of the United Kingdom and the PRC that Hong Kong is under Chinese sovereignty, at least as of July 1, 1997); Basic Law of the Hong Kong Special Administrative Region of the People's Republic of China 1990, Article 1 (declaring the HKSAR "an inalienable part" of the PRC).

[2] For studies illustrating some of the range of methods that the PRC has employed to shape political-system-related aspects of law, see, e.g., Michael C Davis, *Making Hong Kong China* (Columbia University Press 2020); Jacques deLisle and Kevin P Lane, "Hong Kong's Endgame

(but only in part) the product of the distinctive arrangements that created the HKSAR – the Sino-British Joint Declaration that set the terms for Hong Kong's reversion, the PRC constitutional provisions that legally underpin the SAR structure, and the Basic Law of the Hong Kong Special Administrative Region that sets forth terms for the interaction and allocation of authority between the SAR and the central government and their legal systems. The People's Republic of China's influence also flows along other, often less formal, pathways linking the two legal systems. The Hong Kong experience thus provides an especially comprehensive taxonomy of – or field guide to – the many modes of inter-Asian legal influence. Indeed, one of the striking features of the Hong Kong case is the extent to which PRC influence has occurred through mechanisms *other than* the clearly dispositive and in-principle available one of formal lawmaking.

Distinctive features of the China–Hong Kong example also spotlight the complexity of, and some of the challenges in assessing, inter-Asian legal influence. As the more detailed discussion later in this chapter indicates, the relationship between PRC *legal influence* and exportation of PRC *legal models or characteristics* is complicated. Many of the most prominent and salient features of China's influence on the HKSAR's laws and legal order are, at least in a general sense, instances of convergence with PRC templates. Legal changes in Hong Kong that the PRC has influenced, or seems relatively likely to have influenced, have been anti-democratic (as measured against a standard of fully contestatory electoral democracy), illiberal (specifically with respect to civil liberties and political rights), focused on maintaining or fostering political and social order and stability, and unfriendly toward liberal rule of law (including aspects of judicial independence), and so on. Such features are nearly paradigmatic of the PRC legal order. Yet, convergences – even when they are products of PRC lawmaking – are rarely simple transplants. Even where attempts at full imposition of a model or its components would seem feasible, influence has often occurred through more nuanced means. Even some instances of PRC lawmaking for Hong Kong specifically undertake *not* to impose Chinese law or export features of the PRC legal system, in keeping with the promise of autonomy for Hong Kong in legal affairs and continuity with Hong Kong's pre-reversion legal order.

The PRC's legal impact on Hong Kong resonates with the broader discourse of legal transplants and exports of legal models that form the backdrop to the current interest in IAL. The recipient legal order in Hong Kong under PRC rule is largely the product of an earlier and long-recognized type of external imposition or mandated legal borrowing – from the West and from a former colonial power that largely created the Hong Kong legal order that became subject to growing influence from the PRC after 1997. Hong Kong's post-reversion experience as a weak party on the receiving end of legal influence from a much more powerful external source thus

and the Rule of Law (I): The Struggle over Institutions and Values in the Transition to Chinese Rule" (1997) 18 U Pa J Int'l L 195.

echoes its colonial past. As has happened with post-reversion PRC influence, United Kingdom (UK) authorities had shaped Hong Kong law partly in ways that did not track the homeland model. Indeed, illiberal and undemocratic elements in SAR-era Hong Kong law resemble, and in some cases originated during, the period of British rule – a phenomenon that complicates assessments of PRC influence on the SAR legal order.

II PRC LAWMAKING FOR HONG KONG

An especially potent mode of PRC legal impact on the HKSAR is the most formal – and the least obviously relevant to comparative IAL. People's Republic of China lawmakers can, and do, make laws that apply in the HKSAR. The Basic Law is the preeminent example. It is authorized by the PRC constitution, which provides, "The State may establish special administrative regions ... [with] the systems ... to be prescribed by laws enacted by the National People's Congress [NPC] in light of specific conditions."[3] The Basic Law is also provided for by the pact between the PRC and the UK concerning Hong Kong's return to Chinese rule. The Joint Declaration states that "a Basic Law" would be adopted by the NPC to embody the commitments about Hong Kong's future governance, including its legal order, set forth in the Joint Declaration (specifically article 3 and Annex I).[4] As the Constitution and the Joint Declaration envisioned, the Basic Law is an enactment of the PRC's national legislative body.

From the perspective of Hong Kong, the Basic Law is an extraordinarily strong form of PRC legal influence. Although sometimes characterized as the SAR's "mini-constitution," it is, for Hong Kong, more entrenched than a constitution. It is not subject to amendment by the people it governs or the SAR government. The power of amendment lies with the central legislative authorities in Beijing, and the NPC Standing Committee (NPC-SC) may invalidate any SAR law that it finds to be not in conformity to the Basic Law.[5]

Yet, the legal arrangements for the HKSAR include ostensibly serious, arguably legally binding, pledges to limit the PRC's impact on law and the legal system in Hong Kong. In the Joint Declaration – which China regards as a treaty or treaty-like international legal instrument – the PRC declares its "basic policies," which would "remain unchanged for 50 years." Those policies include "a high degree of autonomy" for the SAR "except in foreign and defense affairs," vesting "executive, legislating and independent judicial power, including that of final adjudication" in the SAR, governance by SAR inhabitants chosen in part through local elections

3 Constitution of the People's Republic of China 1982, Article 31.

4 Joint Declaration, Article 3 and Annex I.

5 Basic Law, Articles 11, 17, 158. Proposals for amendment may come from the SAR but only the NPC may enact them.

or consultation, and continuity in social, economic, and legal systems, and liberal civil liberties.[6]

The Basic Law, as promised in the Joint Declaration, would implement those commitments, and its text largely does so. It authorizes the specific types – and the "high degree" – of autonomy described in the Joint Declaration. It charges the SAR with safeguarding the "rights and freedoms" of SAR residents and adopts a list of liberal civil and political rights and the rights set forth in the International Covenants on Civil and Political Rights and on Economic, Social, and Cultural Rights. It also mandates that "the laws previously in force" including "the common law" and the "judicial system previously practiced" be "maintained" (with courts directed to "exercise judicial power independently," and with the "power of final adjudication" given to a new Court of Final Appeal (CFA)). It declares that the "socialist system and policies" of the PRC will not apply to the SAR for fifty years, and grants the SAR government legislative, executive, and judicial power (including final adjudication). It provides for an elected legislature and a consultatively chosen Chief Executive, and declares an "ultimate aim" of selection of legislators and the Chief Executive by universal suffrage (in the case of the Chief Executive, from among candidates nominated "in accordance with democratic procedures").[7] The SAR-enabling provision in the PRC Constitution – in a phrase echoed in the Basic Law and other Hong Kong-specific legal documents – arguably imposes another limitation: The SAR's "systems" are to be framed "in light of specific conditions" in the region.[8]

The Basic Law's promise of restraint on the application of PRC law or the intervention by PRC lawmaking in Hong Kong was notable. At the time of reversion, there were reasons to make such a commitment, including the seriousness with which the PRC government – at least initially – took commitments made in the international treaty-like Joint Declaration, the plausible argument that making and honoring such commitments were vital to Hong Kong's continued economic success, the input that Hong Kong representatives had through the Basic Law Drafting Committee, the heightened concern in Hong Kong and abroad about the potential impact of reversion in the aftermath of the Chinese regime's actions against the protests at Tiananmen Square (and elsewhere in China) in June 1989, as well as Beijing's broader assessment of what served its interests in a successful return of Hong Kong to Chinese rule.[9]

[6] Joint Declaration, Article 3.

[7] Basic Law, Articles 2, 3, 8, 12, 16–19, 27–39, 45, 68, 81, 82, 85–87.

[8] PRC Constitution, Article 31; Joint Declaration Annex I s I; see also Decision of the National People's Congress on the Basic Law of the Hong Kong Special Administrative Region of the People's Republic of China, April 4, 1990.

[9] For examples of these views, see Ji Pengfei, "Explanations on 'The Basic Law of the Hong Kong Special Administrative Region of the People's Republic of China (Draft)' and Its Related Documents" (Address to the 7th National People's Congress, 3rd session, March 28, 1990), www.basiclaw.gov.hk/filemanager/content/en/files/basiclawtext/basiclawtext_doc6.pdf,

In principle (under fundamental tenets of PRC law and approaches to international law) and (increasingly in the post-reversion era) in practice, such commitments cannot reliably constrain China's influence on Hong Kong law and the SAR's legal order. In the PRC view, the Joint Declaration – although accepted as having at least treaty-like status – does not include the contract-like quid pro quo that is characteristic of typical bilateral treaties and that, in the UK view, characterizes the Joint Declaration. This position is amply reflected in the text. While the British provision states, "The Government of the United Kingdom declares that it will restore Hong Kong to the [PRC]" as of July 1, 1997, the parallel Chinese article asserts, "The Government of the [PRC] ... has decided to resume the exercise of sovereignty over Hong Kong" on the same date.[10] In official and orthodox Chinese views, the nineteenth-century treaties that purportedly transferred sovereignty over Hong Kong Island and the Kowloon Peninsula and granted a 99-year lease to the New Territories were "unequal treaties" and, therefore, void *ab initio*.[11] There could be no binding commitment by China concerning the future governance of Hong Kong – including its legal order – *in return for* the UK's surrender of sovereignty over two of the three territorial components of Hong Kong. Tellingly, the provision in the Joint Declaration that sketches the arrangement to be fleshed out in the Basic Law states that what follows are "the basic policies of the [PRC] regarding Hong Kong" which will be implemented through NPC legislation.[12] In recent years, Beijing has declared that the Joint Declaration's "mission was completed" at the moment of reversion and that the Joint Declaration "does not have any binding power on how the central government administers Hong Kong" and thus no longer imposes (if it ever did) obligations on the PRC, enforceable at the behest of the UK.[13]

The Basic Law cannot be, as a matter of PRC constitutional theory, more unamendable than other NPC legislation. The Basic Law itself affirms the NPC's broad powers of amendment (although it purports to limit changes to those that do not contravene the PRC's basic policies regarding Hong Kong).[14] More

accessed July 11, 2024; Albert H Y Chen, "The History of the Drafting and Implementation of the Basic Law of the Hong Kong Special Administrative Region" in Ngoc Son Bui, Stuart Hargreaves and Ryan Mitchell (eds), *Routledge Handbook of Constitutional Law in Greater China* (Routledge 2022); Pui-yin Lo, "The Making of the Hong Kong Basic Law" (2003) 1 Asian Comparative Constitutional Law 99.

10 Joint Declaration, Articles 1, 2.

11 See generally Wang Tieya, "International Law in China: Historical and Contemporary Perspectives" (1990) 2 Receuil de Cours 195, 237–262; Dong Wang, "The Discourse of Unequal Treaties in Modern China" (2003) 76 Pac Aff 399.

12 Joint Declaration, Article 3.

13 Xinhuanet, "China Voices Firm Opposition to UK, G7 Statements over Hong Kong" (March 14, 2021), www.news.cn/english/2021-03/14/c_139809006.htm, accessed July 11, 2024; CGTN, "Sino-British Declaration on HK 'No Longer Has Realistic Significance': Chinese FM" (June 30, 2017), https://news.cgtn.com/news/356b7a4d31517a6333566d54/index.html, accessed July 11, 2024.

14 Basic Law, Article 159.

fundamentally, in the PRC's constitutional order, the NPC has full powers to amend legislation, as well as the constitution itself.[15] If a potentially persuasive legal argument could assert that laws passed pursuant to the SAR provision in the constitution are somehow more deeply entrenched than other NPC legislation (and thus less amenable to discretionary amendment by the NPC), there is no mechanism in PRC law, other than the NPC-SC, to address such a constitutional challenge.[16]

The PRC has not used its powers to amend the Basic Law's main text to affect Hong Kong's legal order. But it has engaged in other lawmaking for the SAR, sometimes with major effects. The PRC constitution, unsurprisingly, applies in the SAR, but presumptively with the limitations adopted in the Basic Law, as legislation consistent with the constitution's rules on SARs. The Basic Law and the Joint Declaration place beyond Hong Kong's authority some areas of law, particularly matters of foreign affairs and national defense. Annex III to the Basic Law, along with subsequent decisions by the NPC-SC, have made a dozen national laws in those and related fields applicable in the SAR.[17] Focused on matters such as national symbols, PRC nationality, maritime rights rooted in international law, and foreign sovereign and diplomatic immunity, such laws have not greatly affected Hong Kong's internal legal order.

In a much more transformative move in 2020, the NPC adopted a National Security Law for the Hong Kong SAR (HKNSL), precipitated by the massive protests that erupted in Hong Kong initially in response to a proposed local ordinance that would have permitted extradition of criminal defendants from the SAR to face prosecution in Mainland PRC courts. With the legislation, PRC lawmakers imposed elements of an illiberal, more PRC-like legal order – and in some instances PRC law itself. The most notable features of the law include: broadly and vaguely defined crimes of secession, subversion, terrorist activities, and collusion with "external" actors to endanger national security in Hong Kong; extensive affirmative obligations of the SAR government to address threats to security, including through establishing an SAR Committee for Safeguarding National Security, accountable to the central government, with broad policy-shaping powers, and with a central government-appointed National Security Advisor; authorization of a central government security force in the SAR and directives to create special SAR police and prosecutorial units; special selection procedures for judges who adjudicate national security cases, including mandatory exclusion of those who have made statements or taken actions "in any manner endangering national security"; permission to suspend a wide range of criminal procedure laws that promise due process (including public trial, jury trial, bail, and restrictions on searches, surveillance, and other investigative

15 PRC Constitution, Articles 2, 57–58, 62, 64.

16 Ibid Article 67.

17 See generally Joint Declaration, Article 3(2) and Annex I, s I; Basic Law, Articles 18–19 and Annex III (as amended in 1998 and 2005).

measures); and the creation in Hong Kong of a central government Office for Safeguarding National Security with extensive powers that supplement those of SAR institutions and that include taking over investigation and prosecution of serious national security cases in Hong Kong and doing so under the PRC's Criminal Procedure Law and in PRC-designated courts.[18]

Following several "Decisions" and "Interpretations" of the Basic Law rebuffing calls from Hong Kong for democratic reforms to election rules,[19] the NPC-SC exercised its lawmaking power to address an especially serious version of a recurring challenge: Pro-democracy candidates had won a landslide victory in elections to local district councils in November 2019, amid the ongoing anti-extradition law and pro-democracy protests and anger over the government's repressive response. In the shadow of the then-newly enacted HKNSL, the NPC-SC in March 2021 amended Basic Law Annexes I and II, which set forth the mechanisms for selecting the SAR Chief Executive and members of the Legislative Council. The amendments shrank the share of the legislature chosen by universal suffrage (to twenty out of ninety seats). They also expanded and restructured the Election Committee to secure control by reliably PRC and SAR government-friendly members, and empowered it to select forty of the ninety members of the legislature (alongside its long-standing role of nominating all Chief Executive candidates). The new rules further required that candidates for the legislature, Chief Executive, and the Election Committee be vetted by the HKNSL-created SAR Committee for Safeguarding National Security and the SAR police's new national security unit.[20]

In sum, when the PRC has influenced Hong Kong law, it has sometimes done so by making PRC law that applies in the SAR. While such moves, tautologically, make SAR law converge with PRC law, the pattern has been more complex in terms of substantive content. In a few relatively narrow contexts, originally PRC-applicable law has been extended to reach the SAR. Broadly, PRC lawmaking for the SAR (including the Basic Law) also has promised – at times, and increasingly hollowly – to forego mandating convergence with PRC law or transformative changes to Hong Kong's inherited legal order. To a large and growing extent, however, Beijing's

[18] Law of the People's Republic of China on Safeguarding National Security in the Hong Kong Special Administrative Region 2020. For critiques of the law, see, e.g., Johannes M M Chan, "National Security Law 2020 in Hong Kong – One Year On" (2022) Academia Sinica Law Journal 39; Surabhi Chopra and Eva Pils, "The Hong Kong National Security Law and the Struggle over Rule of Law and Democracy in Hong Kong" (2022) 50 FL Rev 292; Donald Clarke, "Hong Kong's National Security Law: An Assessment" (China Leadership Monitor Quick Take, July 13, 2020), www.prcleader.org/post/hong-kong-s-national-security-law-an-assessment, accessed July 11, 2024.

[19] These are addressed in the "PRC Interpretations of PRC Law for Hong Kong" section of this chapter.

[20] National People's Congress Standing Committee, Amendment to Annex I, Method for the Selection of the Chief Executive of the Hong Kong Special Administrative Region, Amendment to Annex II, Method for the Formation of the Legislative Council of the Hong Kong Special Administrative Region and Its Voting Procedures, March 30, 2021.

lawmaking has effected changes in the SAR to check democratization and (in Beijing's view) threats to order and security. These measures have altered Hong Kong's law and legal order in ways that make it more closely resemble the Mainland's. Such formal lawmaking is not the only means that China has had available and employed.

III PRC INTERPRETATIONS OF PRC LAW FOR HONG KONG

The NPC-SC has issued five formal "Interpretations" of the Basic Law[21] and one of the HKNSL – exercising powers that Hong Kong-applicable, PRC-made law explicitly grants to the NPC-SC – and several "Decisions" – sometimes explicitly pursuant to the NPC-SC's general powers under the PRC constitution to interpret PRC laws (a category that includes the Basic Law and the HKNSL).[22] These NPC-SC actions are framed as interpretations of law already applicable in – and, thus, binding on – Hong Kong. Formally, they are not PRC-generated changes in Hong Kong Law, in that they purport merely to ascertain and explicate the meaning of the PRC-created Basic Law (or HKNSL). In practice, they have profoundly affected the legal order in Hong Kong, most often in the form of pushing back against calls for, or moves toward, liberal democracy or, in one instance, robust judicial powers. Although not requiring imitation or replication of PRC models, these NPC-SC moves blocked divergence of Hong Kong's legal order from the PRC's in key areas of law.

In 1996, the Preparatory Committee for the HKSAR, exercising powers conferred by the NPC,[23] authorized creation of a Provisional Legislative Council for the soon-to-be-established SAR, thereby derailing the so-called "through train" arrangement by which the final colonial-era Legislative Council would have become the first Legislative Council of the SAR.[24] This move by the PRC-created body gave the

[21] Two of the Interpretations have marginal or highly indirect implications for the issues considered in this chapter and therefore are not discussed: One determined that the replacement for a resigned Chief Executive would only serve out his predecessor's initial term, rather than hold office for a full term; and another addressed the law governing foreign sovereign immunity and related acts of state, which the Basic Law had declared to be beyond the scope of Hong Kong's autonomy.

[22] See Basic Law, Article 58; PRC Constitution, Articles 58, 67(4).

[23] See Decision of the National People's Congress on the Method for the Formation of the First Government and the First Legislative Council of the Hong Kong Special Administrative Region April 4, 1990 (directing the creation of a Preparatory Committee of Mainland and Hong Kong members, responsible for implementing processes for selecting the first Chief Executive, and providing that the first post-reversion Legislative Council would consist of members of the last Legislative Council of the pre-reversion era provided that its selection was consistent with the Basic Law and the present Decision, and that members uphold the Basic Law and pledge allegiance to the SAR and are otherwise qualified to hold legislative office under the Basic Law – upon confirmation by the Preparatory Committee).

[24] See Legislative Council of the Hong Kong Special Administrative Region of the People's Republic of China, The Establishment of the Provisional Legislative Council, www.legco.gov.hk/yr97-98/english/est/estab.htm.

power to select the legislature to the same 400-member Selection Committee that would choose the first SAR Chief Executive. The decision effectively overturned democratizing electoral changes introduced by Hong Kong's last colonial governor, partly on the basis that the reforms violated the Basic Law (or, at least, the PRC's interpretation of it).[25] Those reforms – a last gasp of UK influence on Hong Kong law – had greatly expanded the electorate for the one-half of the legislature's seats that were to be chosen by "functional constituencies," transforming what had been envisioned as a quasi-corporatist arrangement representing sectoral economic interests and economic elites into one in which most employed Hong Kongers would have one vote in a geographic constituency and a second vote in a functional constituency related to their jobs.

In 2004, the NPC-SC's second formal Interpretation of the Basic Law and an NPC-SC Decision issued three weeks later combined to reject proposals from Hong Kong to allow universal suffrage elections for the Chief Executive in 2007 and all seats in the Legislative Council in 2008. The NPC-SC actions affirmed that measures to amend the rules for selecting the SAR's Chief Executive and legislators had to comply with the cumbersome procedures set forth in two Annexes to the Basic Law – on the surface, a rather anodyne point about process, but one that underscored the formidable barriers to democratic changes to electoral laws. More substantively, the NPC-SC Interpretation and Decision determined that there would be no changes to the rules in the near term. The NPC-SC cast the result in part as an interpretation of the principles embodied in the text of the Basic Law (including the Annexes) that changes to election rules would occur only when there is a "need" to change those rules "in light of the actual situation" in Hong Kong and consistent with "gradual and orderly progress" toward the "ultimate aims of universal suffrage."[26]

[25] See, e.g., State Council Information Office of the People's Republic of China, Hong Kong Democratic Progress under the Framework of One Country, Two Systems s II. December 4, 2021, http://english.scio.gov.cn/node_8027477.html, accessed July 11, 2024. This official PRC source – like many others – declared that the electoral reforms violated the "principle of alignment with the Basic Law" as well as the Joint Declaration and the agreements and understandings reached between the PRC and the UK. See also Albert H Y Chen, "The Provisional Legislative Council of the SAR" (1997) 27 HKLJ 1.

[26] Decision of the Standing Committee of the National People's Congress on Issues Relating to the Methods for Selecting the Chief Executive of the Hong Kong Special Administrative Region in the Year 2007 and for Forming the Legislative Council of the Hong Kong Special Administrative Region in the Year 2008, April 26, 2004; Interpretation by the Standing Committee of the National People's Congress of Article 7 of Annex I and Article 3 of Annex II to the Basic Law of the Hong Kong Special Administrative Region of the People's Republic of China, April 6, 2004. The quoted language is primarily from the Decision. Consistent, and largely similar, language is in the Interpretation. The language concerning "in light of the actual situation" and "the principle of gradual and orderly progress" and the "ultimate aim" of "universal suffrage" is in Basic Law, Article 45 (concerning the Chief Executive) and Article 68 (concerning the Legislative Council).

In 2007, the NPC-SC reprised this pattern. It issued a Decision that rejected a new set of Hong Kong proposals for universal suffrage elections of the Chief Executive and the Legislative Council, reaffirmed the need to comply with the existing rules for achieving amendments to election rules, and echoed the 2004 Decision's discouraging tone by stating that changes would be considered "at an appropriate time."[27] In 2014, the NPC-SC determined that the SAR government had submitted a report on electoral reform proposals that met the procedural requirement of the Basic Law Annexes, and it authorized the election of the Chief Executive by universal suffrage in 2017. But the NPC-SC Decision pointedly noted that the position of the Chief Executive in the Basic Law framework meant that any occupant of that office must "love the country" and "love Hong Kong," limited the number of candidates (to two or three), and set a high threshold for nomination (by at least half of the members of a nominating body similar to the Election Committee that had selected the prior Chief Executive). Those requirements meant, of course, a less-than-democratic process that would yield a winner acceptable to Beijing. The Decision also rejected proposals to more thoroughly democratize the process for electing the legislature, keeping the rules for the 2016 election in place for the subsequent round.[28] The 2014 Decision elicited a strong response in Hong Kong, spawning the pro-democracy protests of Occupy Central and the Umbrella Movement.

In 2016, the NPC-SC issued its fourth Interpretation of the Basic Law, again with the effect of making Hong Kong law less democratic. Candidates from the pan-democratic camp who had prevailed in contests for directly elected seats in the 2016 Legislative Council departed from the prescribed text of the oath required by the Basic Law and administered upon taking office. To convey pro-democracy and pro-Hong Kong positions and to signal negative views of the PRC, they supplemented or altered the text. Responding to a request from the SAR government, the NPC-SC interpreted the Basic Law's requirement that officeholders "in accordance with law, swear to uphold the Basic Law ... and swear allegiance to" the SAR and the PRC. The Interpretation decreed that this provision meant that one who "takes the oath in a manner which is not sincere or solemn" or "intentionally reads out words which do not accord with the wording ... prescribed by law" is "disqualified" from assuming the office and has no opportunity to lift the disqualification by

[27] Decision of the Standing Committee of the National People's Congress on Issues Relating to the Methods for Selecting the Chief Executive of the Hong Kong Special Administrative Region and for Forming the Legislative Council of the Hong Kong Special Administrative Region in the Year 2012 and on Issues Relating to Universal Suffrage, December 29, 2007.

[28] Decision of the Standing Committee of the National People's Congress on Issues Relating to the Selection of the Chief Executive of the Hong Kong Special Administrative Region by Universal Suffrage and on the Method of Forming the Legislative Council of the Hong Kong Special Administrative Region in the Year 2016, August 31, 2014.

retaking the oath properly.[29] On the basis of the Interpretation, six democratically elected members were barred from the legislature.

In 1999, the first NPC-SC interpretation of the Basic Law affected – albeit somewhat obliquely and indirectly – another element of Hong Kong's legal order and a different point of contrast with the PRC's legal order: a robust common-law-style notion of constitutional judicial review. The SAR CFA had exercised its powers of judicial review under the Basic Law to strike down SAR ordinances that required persons of Chinese nationality born outside Hong Kong to Hong Kong permanent resident parents to apply for approval from PRC government authorities to enter Hong Kong (as the Basic Law required for people form non-Hong Kong parts of China). The CFA found that the requirement (although consistent with one relevant Basic Law provision) violated a provision of the Basic Law that accords such persons a "right of abode" in Hong Kong because they are "permanent residents" of Hong Kong.[30]

The CFA went beyond overturning the SAR ordinances and – in a move that echoed or exceeded the US Supreme Court's assertion of powers of judicial review in *Marbury v. Madison* – asserted that it had the authority, and duty, to review (and declare invalid) legislative acts by the NPC or NPC-SC for inconsistency with the Basic Law. The NPC-SC Interpretation rejected the CFA's decision on the merits, interpreting the Basic Law as imposing the requirements that were reflected in the local ordinances.[31] Earlier, sharp condemnation of the CFA ruling by PRC legal scholars (understood to represent the central government's views) and an application from the SAR government to the CFA to "clarify" its decision in the case had elicited a statement from the CFA accepting that the NPC-SC had the authority to issue an Interpretation binding on SAR courts and that the CFA "accepts that it cannot question" the NPC's and NPC-SC's "authority . . . to do any act which is in accordance with" the Basic Law.[32]

Much more recently, the NPC-SC issued an Interpretation of the Hong Kong National Security Law that set forth limits to the right to counsel for defendants

[29] Interpretation by the Standing Committee of the National People's Congress of Article 104 of the Basic Law of the Hong Kong Special Administrative Region of the People's Republic of China, 7 November 2016. The SAR government then took local legal action to implement the disqualification. See "Hong Kong Government Disqualifies Four Legislative Council Members" (*Congressional Research Service*, November 16, 2020), https://crsreports.congress.gov/product/pdf/IN/IN11533/2, accessed July 11, 2024.

[30] Basic Law, Article 24; *Ng Ka Ling v. Director of Immigration* [1999] 1 HKLRD 315.

[31] Interpretation by the Standing Committee of the National People's Congress of Articles 22(4) and 24(2)(3) of the Basic Law of the Hong Kong Special Administrative Region of the People's Republic of China, June 26, 1999.

[32] *Ng Ka Ling v. Director of Immigration (II)* [1999] 1 HKLRD 577, 578. See generally Po-Jen Yap, "10 Years of the Basic Law: The Rise, Retreat and Resurgence of Judicial Power in Hong Kong" (2007) 36 CLWR 166, 166–175; Johannes Chan, "Judicial Independence: Controversies on the Constitutional Jurisdiction of the Court of Final Appeal of the Hong Kong Special Administrative Region" (1999) 33 Int'l Law 1015.

charged under the law.[33] Facing charges of colluding with foreign actors to endanger national security, media mogul and pro-democracy activist Jimmy Lai sought representation by an eminent British barrister who was not admitted to practice law in Hong Kong. After SAR courts permitted the lawyer's participation, the SAR government sought, with the approval of the PRC State Council, the NPC-SC Interpretation. The Interpretation decreed that, in the absence of a certificate from the Chief Executive permitting representation, the SAR Committee for Safeguarding National Security (which was created by the HKNSL and accountable to Beijing) had judicially unreviewable authority to determine whether a case involves national security or evidence that implicates state secrets and, where the Committee so determines, to deny overseas lawyers permission to serve as defense counsel because such representation endangers national security.

Through the NPC-SC's Interpretations and Decisions, China has, thus, greatly affected Hong Kong law and the SAR's legal order. It has done so most notably on issues related to democracy and judicial review. By framing its decisions as interpretations of existing law, Beijing has exercised influence without formally creating "new" law for Hong Kong.

Notwithstanding its authority to determine Hong Kong law (whether by enacting or interpreting PRC law for the SAR), China often exerts influence through means that do not depend on exercises of the national government's sovereign power. Even in politically sensitive areas where Beijing has relatively clear goals and where incentives to use methods under PRC authorities' direct control would seem to be strong, the modes of influence are often less formal and determinative.

IV HONG KONG LAWMAKING

Many of the changes in Hong Kong law that have made the SAR's legal order more closely resemble the PRC's are acts of SAR local lawmaking under PRC influence. Such influence has run a gamut from legal mandates, to diffuse and not-fully transparent PRC pressure and preferences – some embraced by local actors. Many examples of local legal change proposed or adopted in post-reversion Hong Kong have contributed to the SAR's move away from liberal democratic or liberal rule of law models and toward a more PRC-style legal regime. A few of the most important and high-profile instances suggest the broader pattern and illustrate the range of forms of influence.

Article 23 of the Basic Law obliges the SAR to "enact laws on its own to prohibit any act of treason, secession, sedition, or subversion against the Central People's Government" and to prohibit theft of state secrets and various forms of foreign influence in SAR politics. China thus imposed a legal obligation on the SAR to

[33] The HKNSL, in Article 65, gives the NPC-SC authority to interpret that law in terms similar to the Basic Law's conferral of authority on the NPC-SC to interpret the Basic Law.

enact local laws, although without specific content or by a particular date. Shortly after being reappointed to a second term, the first SAR Chief Executive Tung Chee-hwa proposed the National Security (Legislative Provisions) Bill 2003 (popularly known as "article 23 legislation"), perhaps reflecting mounting pressure from Beijing[34] or perhaps as an act of preemptive compliance – that is, doing what presumably would please the government in Beijing, to which he was legally accountable and whose support was necessary for his appointment and reappointment. The bill would have amended several Hong Kong criminal and public order ordinances and, as critics charged, gone beyond what article 23 appeared to require in terms of restricting civil and political liberties (including punishment possibly for speech, extraterritorial reach, erosions of criminal procedure protections, and bans on PRC-banned organizations). The bill triggered a furious backlash from pro-democracy Hong Kong political leaders, much of the bar, and the Hong Kong public – more than 500,000 of whom took to the streets in protest of the bill (among other issues) – and foreign governments. The SAR government withdrew the bill, and the controversy played a major role (along with flawed handling of the SARS outbreak) in Tung's resignation in 2005.

In March 2024, in the aftermath of the passage of the HKNSL, the SAR adopted the article 23-implementing Safeguarding National Security Ordinance (Instrument A305). Pressure and influence from Beijing were clear, although the SAR government played a self-proclaimed proactive role as well. SAR Chief Executive Carrie Lam had publicly committed and then reaffirmed a commitment to introduce article 23-implementing legislation in the aftermath of the 2019 protests in Hong Kong (denounced by both SAR and PRC officials for endangering national security), the subsequent PRC enactment of the HKNSL, and the democrats' victories in the local elections (which would later prompt the anti-democratic revisions to laws governing elections to the SAR legislature).[35] More pointedly and specifically, an NPC Decision in 2020 that called for enacting the HKNSL also directed the

[34] For an account of the 2003 bill and controversy, see Carole J Petersen, "Hong Kong's Spring of Discontent: The Rise and Fall of the National Security Bill in 2003" in Fu Hualing, Carole J Petersen and Simon N M Young (eds), *National Security and Fundamental Freedoms: Hong Kong's Article 23 Under Scrutiny* (HKU 2005). For assessments that see the bill as a reflection of PRC pressure or influence, see Wong Yiu-chung, "'Super-Paradox' or 'Leninist Integration': The Politics of Legislating Article 23 of Hong Kong's Basic Law" (2006) 30(2) Asian Perspectives 65; Harvey Stockwin, "Article 23 Stimulates Hong Kong's People Power" (2003) 3(14) Jamestown Foundation China Brief, https://jamestown.org/program/article-23-stimulates-hong-kongs-people-power/, accessed July 11, 2024.

[35] Chun Han Wong, "China's Xi Jinping Voices Support for Hong Kong Leader's Handling of Protests" (*Wall Street Journal*, December 16, 2019); Christian Shepherd, Siddarth Shrikanth and Nicolle Liu, "Beijing Cranks up Level of Condemnation of Hong Kong Protests" (*Financial Times*, July 29, 2019); "CE's Speech in Delivering 'The Chief Executive's 2021 Policy Address' to LegCo (1)" (October 6, 2021), www.info.gov.hk/gia/general/202110/06/P2021100600177.htm, accessed July 11, 2024 (pledge of "taking forward proactively the enactment of local legislation to implement Article 23 of the Basic Law in Hong Kong").

HKSAR to fulfill its "constitutional responsibilities" and "complete the national security legislation" promptly.[36] The SAR legislation cited Basic Law article 23, the 2020 NPC Decision, the HKNSL, and the NPC-SC Interpretation of the HKNSL as imperatives requiring the legislation. The Ordinance's fast-tracked passage, with unanimous support from a legislature devoid of pro-democracy representatives (thanks to earlier PRC-mandated changes in election laws) under the administration of Lam's successor John Lee, had been urged by and drew public praise from PRC authorities.[37]

Much of the content of the 190-article Ordinance echoed, with substantial added detail and with specific amendments to many longstanding Hong Kong ordinances, the HKNSL. Critics in Hong Kong and abroad pointed to features that were consonant with the HKNSL and PRC law (as well as the failed 2003 bill) and arguably went beyond the HKNSL. Concerns included: broad or vague definitions of the crimes of treason, insurrection (and incitement thereto), espionage and improper acquisition, possession or disclosure of state secrets, national-security-endangering sabotage, and external interference that endangers national security; possible criminalization of speech, including political advocacy, disclosure of seemingly unthreatening information to foreigners, and incitement to "disaffection" with the central or local state; broad government powers to ban organizations; authority of the Chief Executive to add, without advance legislative consent, to the list of national security crimes; potential punishments, including for nonviolent offenses, that are much harsher than under inherited colonial laws and that resemble PRC law; expanded investigative powers, free from the ordinarily applicable constraints of Hong Kong law; permissible denial of access to counsel; and extraterritorial reach.[38]

36 Decision of the National People's Congress on Establishing and Improving the Legal System and Enforcement Mechanisms for the Hong Kong Special Administrative Region to Safeguard National Security, May 29, 2020.

37 Address by CE to LegCo on Passage of Safeguarding National Security Bill, Government of the Hong Kong Special Administrative Region Press Releases (March 19, 2024), www.info.gov.hk/gia/general/202403/19/P2024031900717.htm, accessed July 11, 2024; Lily Kuo, "Hong Kong Fast-Tracks Law That Once Drew Protests, Cementing Beijing's Hold" (*Washington Post*, March 20, 2024); Xi Tianqi and Atlas Shao, "Ding Calls to Speed Up Article 23 Legislation" (*China Daily (Hong Kong)*, March 6, 2024), www.chinadailyhk.com/hk/article/379850, accessed July 11, 2024; Xinhua, "Completion of Article 23 Legislation Brings Brighter Future" (March 20, 2024), https://english.news.cn/20240321/7e2585869 90c44cab9790dee4a5f98d8/c.html, accessed July 11, 2024.

38 Tiffany May and David Pierson, "Hong Kong Adopts Sweeping Security Laws, Bowing to Beijing" (*New York Times*, March 19, 2024); Amnesty International, "What Is Hong Kong' Article 23 Law? 10 Things You Need to Know" (March 22, 2024), www.amnesty.org/en/latest/news/2024/03/what-is-hong-kongs-article-23-law-10-things-you-need-to-know/, accessed July 11, 2024; Eric Y H Lai, "Implications of Article 23 Legislation on the Future of Hong Kong" (2024) 24 Jamestown Foundation China Brief, https://jamestown.org/program/implications-of-article-23-legislation-on-the-future-of-hong-kong/, accessed July 11, 2024; Congressional Research Service, "Hong Kong Adopts New National Security Ordinance: Article 23" (April 1, 2024).

The saga of Hong Kong's article 23 legislation illustrates some of the complexities of inter-Asian legal influence. In terms of process, as the foregoing sketch suggests, there are mandates from the central government (which are absent in true inter-jurisdictional cases of legal influence), but the contours of the mandates are uncertain and appear to have been imprecise. Binding directives coexisted with more diffuse forms of political pressure and influence from Beijing and possibly acts of political ambition and favor-currying by local officials – traits that are likely to be found in examples of IAL more typical than the PRC–Hong Kong case. A definitive assessment of the relative importance of the various types of influence is elusive, and the effects may, of course, be synergistic. In terms of substance, the preexisting, largely colonial-era, laws in Hong Kong on matters akin to those addressed in the article 23-implementing legislation and the HKNSL were far from paragons of liberal legality. Indeed, as the section of this chapter on "Influencing the Legal Order (Beyond Laws)" addresses, they have proven capacious enough to be a formidable tool, alongside the post-reversion laws, for prosecuting and stifling the regime's critics, pro-democracy advocates and protesters, and other targets.

The PRC's impact on SAR-enacted local election law has been simpler and more straightforward. When central PRC authorities have approved or required changes in election law in Hong Kong, the SAR has enacted conforming changes. This pattern was most dramatic in 2020–2021 when extensive amendments (in 475 articles) were made to the Legislative Council Ordinance to implement the detailed changes mandated by the NPC-SC's amendments to Basic Law Annexes I and II. The heavily PRC-shaped rules resulted in the disqualification of pro-democracy candidates and a sweeping win for government-supporting candidates in the 2021 elections, which had been postponed, with Beijing's support and quite possibly at its behest, from their scheduled 2020 date. The stated reason was the COVID-19 pandemic but, critics plausibly charged, the goal was to effectuate the election system changes required by the NPC-SC and achieve the electoral outcome sought by Beijing and the SAR government. The SAR review process banned a dozen pro-democracy candidates from the ballot, and the elections produced the legislature that voted unanimously for the 2024 national security ordinance.[39] (In an earlier, broadly similar move, the SAR government implemented the NPC-SC Interpretation concerning legislative oath-taking by taking local legal measures to disqualify four elected legislators.)

[39] Improving Electoral System (Consolidated Amendments) Ordinance 2021; Fernando Cheung, "Why Did Hong Kong Delay Its Election – By a Year?" (*New York Times*, August 20, 2020); Suzanne Pepper, "Covid or Covert? How Beijing Concocted an Election Delay to Reshape Hong Kong's Legislature" (*Hong Kong Free Press*, January 2, 2021), https://hongkongfp.com/2021/01/02/covid-or-covert-how-beijing-concocted-an-election-delay-to-reshape-hong-kongs-legislature/, accessed July 11, 2024; Tony Cheung, Natalie Wong and Kimmy Chung, "Hong Kong Asks China's Top Legislative Body to Resolve Legal Problems with Postponing Elections" (*South China Morning Post*, July 31, 2020); Yanni Chow and Jessie Pang, "Hong Kong Blocks 12 Democrats from Election as China Security Shadow Looms" (*Reuters*, July 30, 2020).

A more complicated case of possible PRC influence on Hong Kong law involves another failed attempt at SAR legislation that was part of the backstory to the national security and election law changes of the early 2020s. The protests in 2019 that evolved into broad pro-democracy and anti-SAR-government movement began in reaction to a proposed amendment to Hong Kong's extradition ordinance backed by Chief Executive Carrie Lam.[40] The existing law concerning extradition specifically excluded extradition to the Mainland. The amendment – proposed in reaction to a case in which a Hong Kong resident had fled back to the SAR from Taiwan and could not be extradited because the two jurisdictions had no extradition agreement – would have given the Chief Executive power, subject to judicial review, to grant extradition requests from any jurisdiction, including the PRC. The bill was withdrawn in the face of sharp criticism and the large-scale protests.

The extent to which the PRC was pushing for such a change to Hong Kong law is contested. Chinese authorities had been frustrated with difficulties in getting hold of persons in Hong Kong accused of violating PRC criminal laws (and were generally believed to have resorted to kidnapping in at least one high-profile case) and publicly supported the legislation after it was proposed.[41] In language notably echoed by Beijing, Lam characterized the proposed amendment as a move to "plug a loophole" in Hong Kong law – a statement that suggested that the existing ordinance's explicit targeting of the PRC was in her view problematic.[42] In terms of substance, the proposed amendment would not have made Hong Kong law more like PRC law: PRC law does not adopt expansive extradition provisions and prohibits extradition of PRC nationals.[43] For opponents of the proposed legislation, the principal problem of PRC legal influence lay not in the prospect that PRC or PRC-like law would enter Hong Kong law but, rather, in the threat that people in

[40] Jacques deLisle, "Hong Kong's Summer of Discontent: Another Battle in the Long War over Autonomy, Democracy, and the Rule of Law" (2019) 63 Orbis 473; T Y Wang, "Hong Kong and the 2019 Anti-Extradition Bill Movement" (2023) 58 J Asian Afr Stud 3; Hiu-fung Chung, "Changing Repertoires of Contention in Hong Kong: A Case Study on the Anti-Extradition Bill Movement" (2020) China Perspectives 57.

[41] See David Lague, James Pomfret and Greg Torode, "How Murder, Kidnappings and Miscalculation Set off Hong Kong's Revolt" (*Reuters*, December 20, 2019), www.reuters.com/investigates/special-report/hongkong-protests-extradition-narrative/, accessed July 11, 2024; Christy Leung, "Extradition Bill Not Made to Measure for Mainland China and Won't Be Abandoned, Hong Kong leader Carrie Lam Says" (*South China Morning Post*, April 1, 2019); Barbara Demick, "Why Did China Kidnap Its Provocateurs" (*New Yorker*, February 16, 2016), www.newyorker.com/news/news-desk/why-did-china-kidnap-its-provocateurs, accessed July 11, 2024.

[42] Transcript of Remarks by CE at Media Session before ExCo Meeting, Government of the Hong Kong Special Administrative Region Press Releases (April 16, 2019), www.info.gov.hk/gia/general/201904/16/P2019041600517.htm, accessed July 11, 2024; Xinhuanet, "Liaison Office of China's Central Government in Hong Kong Voices Support for Hong Kong's Decision to Suspend Fugitive Law Amendments" (June 15, 2019), www.xinhuanet.com/english/2019-06/15/c_138146134.htm, accessed July 11, 2024.

[43] See Extradition Law of the People's Republic of China 2000, Article 8(1).

Hong Kong would become subject to Mainland criminal legal process and prosecution in PRC courts and under PRC laws that did not apply in the SAR.[44]

The People's Republic of China's influence through formally autonomous SAR acts of compliance with PRC directives or preferences – and possible limits to such influence – may also characterize another high-profile legal development in early post-reversion Hong Kong. To be sure, the NPC-SC's Interpretation of the right of abode-related provisions in the Basic Law effectively quashed prospects that the CFA could arrogate to itself *Marbury* or *Marbury*-plus powers of constitutional review and led to the CFA explicitly recognizing the limits to its powers articulated by the Interpretation. But the CFA's statement of compliance was arguably hedged, stating that the Court "accepts that it cannot question" the NPC's and NPC-SC's authority "to do any act *which is in accordance with*" the Basic Law.[45]

V INFLUENCING THE LEGAL ORDER (BEYOND LAWS)

The People's Republic of China's influence on Hong Kong's legal order extends beyond effects on formal lawmaking. A legal order is, of course, much more than the laws themselves. In the SAR, much of the change that has brought convergence with Mainland legal norms and practices has occurred in these other dimensions.

In Hong Kong's executive-led government, the Chief Executive and the Chief Executive's subordinates wield a large share of local power over law and the legal order. The evolving law for selecting Chief Executives has consistently assured that the top office's occupant would be acceptable to Beijing and, in turn, so would the SAR government's stance on legal matters important to Beijing. The shift to universal suffrage for the Chief Executive has not changed that pattern, given the role of the Election Committee in vetting candidates. Some of the Interpretations of the Basic Law discussed earlier in this chapter were sought by the Chief Executive-headed SAR government. The Chief Executive's alignment with Beijing and practices that diverge from liberal rule-of-law norms have been especially pronounced during the tenure of John Lee, who was the SAR Secretary of Security during the crackdown on the 2019–2020 protests and who, as Chief Executive, has presided over the implementation of the HKNSL and the enactment and implementation of related local legislation.[46] Particularly after the 2014 Umbrella

[44] See, e.g., Cora Chan, "Demise of 'One Country, Two Systems'? Reflections on the Hong Kong Rendition Saga" (2019) 49 HKLJ 447; Wang (n 40); Mercy A Kuo, "Hong Kong Extradition Law: The Fallout" (*Diplomat*, June 25, 2019), https://thediplomat.com/2019/06/hong-kong-extradition-law-the-fallout/, accessed July 11, 2024.

[45] *Ng Ka Ling (II)* (n 32) 578 (emphasis added). On this point, see Yap (n 32) 173–174.

[46] See, e.g., Chen Qingqing and Bai Yunyi, "With Highest Level of Support, John Lee Set to Open New Chapter for Hong Kong" (*Global Times*, May 8, 2022), www.globaltimes.cn/page/202205/1265081.shtml, accessed July 11, 2024; Xinhua, "Xi Hears Report from Chief Executives of HK, Macao SARs" (*China Daily (Hong Kong)*, December 18, 2023), www.chinadailyhk.com/hk/article/367288, accessed July 11, 2024. On the pattern of prosecutions and convictions

Movement and the 2019 anti-extradition law protest, the SAR administration undertook large-scale prosecution of movement leaders and protesters for crimes ranging from public order offenses to subversion. For national security cases, such exercises of SAR police and prosecutorial authority occur with additional authority and greater insulation from legal restraints and judicial review – partly thanks to HKNSL-created rules and institutions.

The repeatedly revised rules for the Legislative Council – the SAR's relatively weak legislature – have contributed to a similar trajectory for another principal law-related organ of SAR governance. Election rules, including the large number of seats from functional constituencies and multi-member districts, always limited the share of seats occupied by pan-democratic camp representatives and, thus, legislative opposition to measures that diverged from liberal and democratic norms and converged with the preferences and, to some extent, paradigms of the PRC. Nonetheless, throughout much of the SAR's early history, opposition and the prospect of defeat in the Legislative Council checked illiberal or authoritarian-leaning government initiatives, with the 2003 article 23 legislation being a prominent example. Particularly after the changes that followed the NPC Interpretation disqualifying critical pro-democracy and pro-autonomy elected legislators and the sweeping reforms in 2020 to the election rules – including a nomination process to screen out insufficiently "loyal" candidates – the Legislative Council has been more reliably compliant with the agenda of the Beijing-backed Chief Executive, including passing the article 23-implementing legislation in 2024.

Some of the most striking changes have been in the courts. The CFA is permitted by law to have up to thirty non-permanent judges, including from other common law jurisdictions (in addition to six permanent judges drawn from Hong Kong). The purpose of this arrangement was to assure continuity with Hong Kong's prior legal order and to provide visible reassurance of continuity and autonomy. But the number of foreign non-permanent judges has dwindled to a half-dozen, falling sharply in recent years, including six resignations since 2020. The departures have been interpreted as responses to deterioration of the rule of law and liberal legality in the SAR. In some cases, the exiting jurists tied their decisions explicitly to such concerns (principally to the impact of the HKNSL). Under the regime created pursuant to the HKNSL, foreign judges are not permitted on panels hearing national security cases. Participation by foreign non-permanent judges and citation to foreign – principally common law – precedent has declined steeply in Hong Kong court decisions in recent years, possibly showing the weakening influence of such judges and sources of law.[47]

after the Umbrella and Anti-Extradition Law movements, see the discussion later in this section.

47 See Stuart Hargreaves, "Canaries or Colonials? The Reduced Prominent of the 'Overseas Judges' on Hong Kong's Court of Final Appeal" (2021) 16 ASJCL 187; Nuno Garoupa and

Careful scholarly analyses of SAR court – and especially CFA – decisions have discerned significant shifts in judicial practices. These trends include greater deference to SAR political branches' (as well as the PRC's) actions and choices, approval of reductions in criminal procedure and due process protections, other departures from prior liberal rule of law norms, and broad acquiescence in the erosion of liberal individual rights and Hong Kong's autonomy.[48]

The courts have reliably convicted and upheld convictions for hundreds of defendants involved in political protests, pro-democracy movements, and other political activities for violating inherited colonial and new SAR-era laws prohibiting disruption of public order, subversion and sedition, and new national security crimes (including subversion) introduced from 2020 onward. Major rounds targeted leaders and participants in the Umbrella Movement and the anti-extradition law protests. Shortly after the HKNSL came into force, forty-seven prominent defendants were charged with conspiracy to commit subversion (in violation of the HKNSL) for their roles in planning an informal "democratic primary" that sought to identify pro-democracy candidates for the 2020 elections that were postponed and later held under revised, undemocratic rules. The forty-five who pled guilty or were

Weijia Rao, "Foreign Judges and Foreign Case Citations: A Study of the Hong Kong Court of Final Appeal" (2025) J. L. & Courts 1–26. The meaning of declining citation rates is uncertain. It could reflect innocuous developments such as the post-1997 accumulation of local precedent that is consistent with the jurisprudence of previously more cited foreign cases. Or it could reflect a genuine change in the trajectory of Hong Kong law. As noted in the "Conclusions" section of this chapter, the declining role for foreign judges and law surely suggests a declining emphasis on signaling connection to international liberal-legal norms or continuity with the pre-reversion Hong Kong judicial order.

48 See, e.g., Johannes Chan, "Taking Rights Seriously – The Judiciary at a Challenging Time" (2022) 52 HKLJ 937; Cora Chan, "Rights, Proportionality and Deference: A Study of Post-Handover Judgments in Hong Kong" (2018) 48 HKLJ 51 (finding that SAR courts have become more deferential to PRC and SAR government views in politically sensitive rights cases); Yap (n 32) (arguing that the CFA has "adopted a pragmatic view" toward its role, deferring to the central government on issues that implicate PRC laws or NPC-SC decisions and deferring to the SAR legislative and executive branches on issues involving "law and order" in Hong Kong); Johannes Chan, "Judicial Response to the National Security Law: HKSAR v. Lai Chee Ying" (2021) 51 HKLJ 1 (arguing that the CFA was unduly deferential in accepting that the HKNSL displaced common law presumption in favor of bail in the case of pro-democracy media tycoon Jimmy Lai); Johannes Chan, "A Storm of Unprecedented Ferocity: The Shrinking Space of the Right to Political Participation, Peaceful Demonstration, and Judicial Independence in Hong Kong" (2018) 16 ICON 373 (addressing challenges, following the NPC-SC's Interpretation conceding oath-taking, faced by the CFA in protecting liberal common law values within a "shrinking public space" and "amidst a rising and powerful authoritarian regime" in the PRC); Waikeung Tam, "Judicial Responses to Politically Sensitive Cases in an Authoritarian System" (2024) 138 China Perspectives 57 (finding that, in politically sensitive cases, SAR courts defer to the government, dismiss cases on procedural grounds, and delay effects of judgments unfavorable to the government); but see Albert H Y Chen, "Constitutional Adjudication in Post-1997 Hong Kong" (2006) 15 Pac Rim L & Pol'y J 627 (offering a "positive assessment" of SAR courts' handling of cases, including rights-related cases, in the context of Hong Kong's constitutional relationship with the PRC and the differences between the Hong Kong and PRC legal systems and traditions).

convicted included student leaders, a law professor associated with democratic reform efforts, former members of the Legislative Council and other high-profile pro-democracy politicians, and independent media figures.[49]

Such convictions and the resulting removal from active roles in Hong Kong law and politics, along with the broader changes in Hong Kong's legal order, have led to the chilling, silencing, or departure from Hong Kong of pro-democracy politicians, activists, and liberal and rights-oriented lawyers, and shrinking space for independent media and critical civil society. Those developments, in turn, have weakened forces outside the legal system (narrowly defined) – the larger law-related ecosystem – that might resist trends that have been transforming Hong Kong's legal order.

These patterns in legal and law-related institutions' staffing and functioning reflect China's direct and indirect influence (alongside other, more local factors) on the SAR legal order's movement away from Hong Kong's inherited legal order and the once-promised democratic trajectory in the laws governing its political order – and thus movement toward, at least in a general sense, closer resemblance to the PRC.

VI CONCLUSION: SCOPE, VARIETY, AND COMPLEXITY OF INFLUENCE

Although this chapter covers a large swath of Hong Kong's post-reversion legal trajectory, its scope is in some ways narrow. The foregoing discussion focuses on areas of public law (particularly those most closely adjacent to politics) and formal state institutions (legislative, executive, and judicial) and the laws affecting their composition and powers. If we were to widen the aperture to take in developments in, say, commercial law, or the law- and legal order-shaping activities of non-state actors, or legal changes in areas where Beijing appears to have a less fully developed

[49] See Bill Chappell, "Hong Kong Court Convicts 9 'Umbrella Movement' Organizers of Nuisance Charges" (NPR, April 9, 2019), www.npr.org/2019/04/09/711350340/hong-kong-court-convicts-9-umbrella-movement-organizers-of-nuisance-charges, accessed July 11, 2024; "Hong Kong: Drop Case against 'Umbrella 9'" (*Human Rights Watch*, November 14, 2018), www.hrw.org/news/2018/11/14/hong-kong-drop-case-against-umbrella-9, accessed July 11, 2024; Jun Chan, Eric Yan-ho Lai and Thomas E Kellogg, "The Hong Kong 2019 Protest Movement: A Data Analysis of Arrests and Prosecutions" (Center for Asian Law, Georgetown Law, October 2023), www.law.georgetown.edu/law-asia/wp-content/uploads/sites/31/2023/10/GCAL-HK-2019-ARREST-DATA-REPORT-FINAL-OCT-2023.pdf, accessed July 11, 2024; Tiffany May, "Hong Kong Convicts Democracy Activists in Largest National Security Trial" (*New York Times*, May 29, 2024); Tiffany May, "Hong Kong Editors Convicted of Sedition in Blow to Press Freedom" (*New York Times*, August 28, 2024); K. K. Rebecca Lai, David Pierson and Tiffany May, "How 45 Pro-Democracy Leaders Were Sentenced in Hong Kong's Largest National Security Case" *New York Times*, November 19, 2024. See also Pui-yin Lo, "Reactivated and Re-Energised: The Sedition Offences in 'New Era' Hong Kong" (2022) 52 HKLJ 913; Chan (n 18); Sonny Lo, "Hong Kong in 2020: National Security Law and Truncated Autonomy" (2021) 61 Asian Survey 34.

and urgent agenda, some of the less formal and direct modes of influence that emerge in the foregoing account might well appear more prominent and pervasive. At the same time, the indications of such phenomena even in the areas of law considered in this chapter – where they are less likely to be present – may provide especially strong confirmation of their existence, though not their full scope. At a broader and deeper level, much the same is true of the PRC–Hong Kong experience, viewed in the comparative context of more typical cases of inter-Asian legal influence, where the robust formal and practical power that the PRC wields over the SAR is not present.

First, the PRC–Hong Kong case indicates that the mechanisms of trans-jurisdictional legal influence in Asia are sometimes oblique and opaque, mediated through the recipient jurisdiction's institutions and legal-political actors and reflecting contextual factors. Border-crossing legal influence thus often looks more neo-colonial than colonial, even where one party (Beijing) has plenary sovereign authority to pursue full-blown lawmaking or issue binding government mandates to the other (Hong Kong) and even in areas of law where the stronger party's imperative or temptation to exercise such power seems especially strong. Although this pattern surely reflects the central PRC authorities' calculations of costs and benefits and possible resistance, it also resonates with a broader feature of China's growing legal impact abroad: the relatively low salience of the type of "legal model-exporting" agenda that characterized much of the US- and Western-led drives to promote legal reform abroad during the postwar and post–Cold War eras.[50]

Second, the Hong Kong experience illustrates the complicated relationship between exporting models and influencing legal orders, as well as the difficulty of discerning causation. Even where Beijing could have required Hong Kong to adopt PRC models, and even when PRC institutions made or mandated law for Hong Kong, the result generally was not a simple "transplant" of PRC paradigms. Substantive characterizations are difficult and contestable: As Hong Kong has moved away from aspects of the laws and legal order inherited from colonial times and abandoned progress toward the legal elements of a democratic political order that were imagined in the arrangements for reversion (and nudged forward in the late days of British rule), such divergence might not necessarily or incontestably be characterized as convergence with PRC models. In terms of process, the pathway for Hong Kong's law and legal order toward achieving Beijing's ends of maintaining

[50] See, e.g., Matthew S Erie, "Chinese Law and Development" (2021) 62 Harv Int'l L J 51; Jacques deLisle, "Law and the China Development Model" in S Philip Hus, Yu-Shan Wu and Suisheng Zhao (eds), *In Search of China's Development Model* (Routledge 2011); Jacques deLisle, "The Chinese Model of Law, China's Agenda in International Law, and Implications for Democracy in Asia and Beyond" in Gilbert Rozman (ed), *Democratization, National Identity and Foreign Policy in Asia* (Routledge 2021). On the US and Western approach in an earlier period, see Jacques deLisle, "Lex Americana?: United States Legal Assistance, American Legal Models, and Legal Change in the Post-Communist World and Beyond" (1999) 20 U Pa J Int'l L 179.

social order and stability, illiberal and undemocratic governance, and so on often (although far from always) entailed distinctively Hong Kong (or at least not closely PRC-imitating) lawmaking and law-shaping. The adoption of illiberal or undemocratic legal rules and mechanisms in the SAR includes instances where it is, at best, difficult to untangle the relative importance of demands from Beijing, the more diffuse shadow of Beijing's preferences, and the agendas of local officials and interest groups. In some cases, tools of illiberal, undemocratic, or repressive law were in the toolkit inherited from colonial times and could be used with little adaptation, albeit by different rulers.

Finally, the Hong Kong example spotlights the phenomenon of competition for influence in a world of plural sources of trans-jurisdictional legal influence, with China as a rising influencer. To be sure, the SAR is an extreme case – and arguably the canary in the coal mine – of PRC influence on legal orders beyond the Chinese Mainland. Still, the progression across the SAR's history is broadly instructive. While China's formal authority to shape Hong Kong law has been extremely broad and deep since 1997, Beijing's apparent exertion of influence and practical impact have increased in scope and scale. And PRC/SAR concern with meeting Western or other foreign metrics for the character and quality of the influenced legal order has waned.[51] Therein lie possible lessons that warrant attention from analysts of IAL in an era of China's proclaimed pursuit of "foreign rule of law" [*shewai fazhi*][52] and US–China competition across many fields, including law and transnational legal influence.

[51] Examples discussed in this chapter include the increasingly frequent resort to highly public means and authoritarian content in PRC lawmaking and law-interpreting for Hong Kong, the downplaying of the treaty-like Joint Declaration concerning the SAR's legal order through at least 2047, and the equanimity or indifference with which PRC and SAR authorities have faced the criticism of national security legislation and the departure of foreign judges.

[52] Matthew S Erie, "Foreign Policy Implications for China's Foreign-Related 'Rule of Law'" (2023) 67 Orbis 565; Jacques deLisle, "Xi Jinping's Impact on China's Legal Development: Domestic and International" (*Asan Forum*, October 15, 2015), https://theasanforum.org/xi-jinpings-impact-on-chinas-legal-development-domestic-and-international/, accessed July 11, 2024.

A Beginning

Matthew S. Erie and Ching-Fu Lin

I THE LAW OF THE HORSE

Judge Frank Easterbrook once argued that rather than establish narrowly defined areas of legal research, scholars should stick to the study of general rules, which can be applied to any number of subject areas. The specific target in Judge Easterbrook's crosshairs was cyberlaw, which was ascendant in the 1990s. His argument, and the metaphor within, is worth quoting at length:

> Lots of cases deal with sales of horses; others deal with people kicked by horses; still more deal with the licensing and racing of horses, or with the care veterinarians give to horses, or with prizes at horse shows. Any effort to collect these strands into a course on "The Law of the Horse" is doomed to be shallow and to miss unifying principles. Teaching 100 percent of the cases on people kicked by horses will not convey the law of torts very well. Far better for most students – better, even, for those who plan to go into the horse trade – to take courses in property, torts, commercial transactions, and the like, adding to the diet of horse cases a smattering of transactions in cucumbers, cats, coal, and cribs. Only by putting the law of the horse in the context of broader rules about commercial endeavors could one really understand the law about horses.[1]

Lawrence Lessig responded to Judge Easterbrook's denunciation of cyberlaw as a specialized field of study. Lessig did not defend "the law of the horse," but rather argued that the study of the intersection of law and cyberspace could teach us something that we otherwise would not learn.[2] That something, for Lessig, was that the "architecture" or soft and hardware of cyberspace could itself have regulatory

[1] Frank H Easterbrook, "Cyberspace and the Law of the Horse" (1996) 207 U Chi Legal F 207, 207–208.

[2] Lawrence Lessig, "The Law of the Horse: What Cyberspace Might Teach" (1999) 113 Harv L Rev 501, 502.

effects on behavior, functionally equivalent to law.[3] Lessig elaborated his assertion in his book *Code and Other Laws of Cyberspace* (1999), which opened up whole new fields of scholarship on cyberlaw, the internet, and other digital domains. Lessig showed that the study of cyberlaw was itself generative of new rules of general application. In retrospect, Lessig's argument in "the law of the horse" debate carried the day.

Inter-Asian Law (IAL) may also be dismissed as another "law of the horse."[4] Critics may deem it to be geographically circumscribed and parochial, an exercise in extracting more general legal phenomena and shoehorning them into a regional setting or, worse yet, a dressing up of long-standing relationships in post-colonial language. Seen in such a light, Judge Easterbrook's opprobrium would seem to return; IAL may be "doomed to be shallow and to miss unifying principles." In short, "there is no 'there there'."

Contrary to the above view, we believe IAL is just starting. To be clear, there are important antecedents, for example, the spread of Confucian ideas about ethics, morality, and law from China to Korea as early as the third century CE and several centuries later in Japan. Legal scholars have suggested that these rich historical layers of repeated borrowing and cross-borrowing are productive of "Confucian constitutionalism" in East Asian states.[5] For sure, religio-philosophical traditions that were formative of premodern IAL warrant more scholarly attention.[6] For purposes of this volume, our focus is on the contemporary context for IAL, expounding the idea that whereas IAL is, in many instances, embryonic, it nonetheless is beginning to affect domestic and transnational legal orders. While nascent, IAL will likely only grow in the future. Current trends for global trade and investment devalue globalization and prioritize regionalization or supply chain realignment. These shifting geo-economic conditions, including those found in the Asian region, are poised to foment more IAL. Consequently, IAL provides a lens into what the future may be, extending beyond Asia.

The payoff, then, in studying IAL is to understand the emergence of intra-regional law, including sub-national, national, and transnational levels, outside Euro-America, which potentially has dynamism precisely because the locus of the law is

3 Ibid 507–509.

4 The authors thank Deepa Das Acevedo for this productive provocation.

5 See, e.g., Jiang Qing, *A Confucian Constitutional Order* (Daniel A Bell and Ruiping Fan (eds), Edmund Ryden (tr), Princeton University Press 2012); Sungmoon Kim, *Confucian Constitutionalism: Dignity, Rights, and Democracy* (OUP 2023); Tom Ginsburg, "Confucian Constitutionalism? The Emergence of Constitutional Review in Korea and Taiwan" (2002) 27(4) L & Soc Inquiry 763.

6 For some recent studies, see, e.g., Cuilan Liu, *Buddhism in Court: Religion, Law, and Jurisdiction in China* (OUP 2024) (discussing how an Indian Buddhist campaign for clerical privileges was taken up by Chinese Buddhists); Tom Ginsburg and Benjamin Schonthal (eds), *Buddhism and Comparative Constitutional Law* (CUP 2022) (examining the "Buddhist-constitutional complex" beginning in precolonial times to the present across Asia).

non-Western. More specifically, there are two broad takeaways. First, whereas IAL is not fully divorced from Anglo-American and European civil law and in some instances is derivative from Western law, it features its own normative origins, dynamics, processes, trajectories, and effects. These are worthy of study unto themselves as, to some extent, they fulfill post-colonial historian Dipesh Chakrabarty's charge to "provincialize Europe."[7] Second, IAL may serve as a springboard for a comparative study of intra-regional law. By this, we mean not only IAL, but also inter-Latinx law, inter-African law, and inter-European law, among other post-global futures.[8] In the remainder of this chapter, we first summarize and synthesize the findings of the volume pursuant to the analytical framework proposed in the Introduction: The Emergence of Inter-Asian Law. Next, we expand beyond the findings to suggest the broader significance of IAL and provide an outline for an agenda for future research. Lastly, we propose an agenda for comparative and international study in a period of heightened regionalization.

II ANALYTICAL FINDINGS

IAL shows emerging interactions between and among Asian jurisdictions that are generative of legal, policy, and regulatory innovation. These include both substantive and procedural law. Substantive law reveals a wide range of legal domains, from religious freedom and abortion to corporate law and alternative dispute resolution (ADR) to cybersecurity and artificial intelligence (AI) regulation. Procedural law includes lay assessors as adjunct adjudicators and treaty formation through consensus formation. In each of these examples, law from Asian jurisdictions serves as a normative resource, and it is this law that is subsequently incorporated into the domestic legal framework of the recipient or host state. Yet, in most cases, with possible exceptions like the Association of Southeast Asian Nations (ASEAN) multilateralism, IAL does not lead to a homogenous body of law. Even in extreme cases of export from a hegemon to a weaker jurisdiction, the latter adapts law according to its own institutional framework and policy needs. While the development of a distinct body of law is not an impossibility, for the near term, contextualization, localization, and differentiation will likely characterize the growth and spread of IAL.

Returning to the analytical framework set out in the Introduction to this volume, the chapters provide empirical, doctrinal, and theoretical insights into IAL's origins, mechanisms, and end results. *One*, the focus on types and methods of interaction helps explain how IAL operates, and the contributions offer instructive examples

7 For Charkrabarty, the challenge is to wrest modernity from the grip of the Enlightenment; his approach was to explore political modernity via the Indian peasant. See Dipesh Chakrabarty, *Provincializing Europe: Postcolonial Thought and Historical Difference* (Princeton University Press 2000) 10.

8 See infra text accompanying notes 25–33.

and analyses. The first is various forms of collaboration, cooperation, or joint/collective efforts. These include, pre-eminently, bilateral relationships of, variously, borrowing, appropriating, diffusing, or transplanting law from one jurisdiction to another. Examples include Vietnam's borrowing of ADR models from Singapore (Naiki) and Cambodia, Uzbekistan, and Vietnam's use of Chinese law, including cyber/data as well as constitutional provisions (Erie). Another type of collaboration is various instances of exchange of best practices and regulatory learning (Hans, Lin). A third type is cross-referencing of cases, laws, or soft law (Yew, Das Acevedo, Naiki). A fourth type is multilateralism, which may be more formal as in the case of the Regional Comprehensive Economic Partnership (RCEP) (Hsieh) and Digital Economy Partnership Agreement (DEPA) (Lin) or informal as in the example of the Belt and Road Initiative (Erie).

In addition to the collaborative approach, IAL, specifically, within East Asia, is infused with rivalries. Consequently, there is also a competitive alternative to cooperation. Examples include Singaporean, Chinese, and Japanese actors vying for supremacy in their smart city projects in emerging economies in Southeast and South Asia (Naiki) and, likewise, Chinese, Japanese, Korean, and Taiwanese contesting for optimal regulatory approach to global technology supply chains (Lin). Collaboration and competition are not mutually exclusive; many inter-Asian relationships exhibit both at the same time for different types of legal questions.

Both the collaborative and competitive approaches highlight (in)compatibility between legal systems and reveal two sub-regional clusters. The first cluster is the East Asian civil law systems. China, Japan, Taiwan, and Korea show some readiness to borrow from each other, although historic frictions that survive to this day can shape outcomes. Parallels in constitutional jurisprudence and democratic process in Taiwan and Korea allowed for policy learning during the COVID-19 pandemic crisis (Chang and Lee). Japan and China, in particular, have sometimes emerged as norm exporters. Singapore is a slight outlier in its being a common law system and yet one that has, to some extent, bridged the common law–civil law divide by influencing legal development in such civil law jurisdictions as Vietnam (Linh) and ASEAN states, which are predominantly but not exclusively civil law systems (Naiki). The second cluster is South Asian common law systems. Here, India is the leading exporting state and has influenced development among its neighbors (Tew, Das Acevedo). In the South Asian cluster, we see post-colonial inheritance fostering compatibility between legal systems and creating the conditions for IAL interactions.

Collaboration and competition are not the only types of interaction; contributors also employed IAL interactions in surprising and novel ways that defy such descriptions. For instance, Goto and Puchniak used IAL as a lens for understanding differentiation in corporate law localizations. Pillai employs "IAL as method,"[9]

[9] cf Yoshimi Takeuchi, "Asia as Method" in Richard F Calichman (ed), *What Is Modernity? Writings of Takeuchi Yoshimi* (Columbia University Press 2005) 149–166.

generating hypotheticals that highlight IAL as an imaginative domain that may include such inversions as Nepal operating as normative inspiration for India.

Two, the analytical framework suggests that IAL evolves through different types of actors and intermediaries that facilitate the movement of law within inter-Asia, linking interactions to outcomes. These exist at the sub-national or firm level, for example, company towns (Nguyen) or arbitration centers (Linh). States and their constitutive parts including judiciaries, naturally, comprise a consistent unit for IAL exchanges (Goto and Puchniak, Tew, Das Acevedo, Lin). Transnational networks comprise another type of actor as seen in the examples of networks of officials between home and host states (Erie) or religious networks (Putri and Taylor). Multilateral treaty bodies, whether RCEP (Hsieh), the Singapore Convention (Linh), or DEPA (Lin) may also serve as platforms. Lastly, civil society may also form transnational links, sharing normative resources (Chang and Lee). The density of these overlapping actors and intermediaries comprises one of the defining elements of inter-Asia.

Three, IAL leads to diverse effects, consequences, and even conflicts. First, in the wake of the US–China trade war, deglobalization, and the sidelining of the World Trade Organization, other multilateral, mega-preferential, and plurilateral agreements have taken root, and many of these are in Asia. These include the Comprehensive and Progressive Agreement for Trans-Pacific Partnership, RCEP, and the Asia-Pacific Trade Agreement. Pursuant to anti-globalization, which is causing a downsizing in international law globally, from "mini-deals"[10] to "micro international law,"[11] inter-Asia is becoming the site for a recalibrated and chastened yet nevertheless vibrant international trade and investment law,[12] which in turn fosters new forms and vectors of IAL.

Beneath this layer of international economic law, the coupling of "regional international law"[13] with the resilience of Asian economies[14] means that global supply chains, which are already rooted across inter-Asia, will most likely continue to deepen and expand despite the global headwinds and geopolitically driven realignment. As Mae Nguyen shows in her chapter, inter-Asian company towns that support such supply chains have become centers for multi-layered contracting,

[10] Kathleen Claussen, "Trade's Mini-Deals" (2022) 62 Va J Int'l L 315.

[11] Katrin Kuhlmann, "Micro International Law" 61 Stanford J Int'l L (2025).

[12] See, e.g., Pasha Hsieh, "New Investment Rulemaking in Asia: Between Regionalism and Domestication" (2023) 22 World Trade Rev 173; Soonjun Cho and Jürgen Kurtz, *Investing the ASEAN Way: Theories and Practices of Economic Integration in Southeast Asia* (CUP 2022).

[13] Artur Simonyan, "Regional International Law Revisited: Eurasian International Law" (2023) 31 Mi St Int'l L Rev 283.

[14] World Bank Group, "East Asia and Pacific: Resilient Growth in Turbulent Times" (October 7, 2024), www.worldbank.org/en/news/press-release/2024/10/07/east-asia-and-pacific-resilient-growth-in-turbulent-times, accessed May 23, 2025 (quoting Manuela V. Ferro, Vice-President of the World Bank for East Asia and the Pacific, "Countries in the East Asia and the Pacific Region continue to be an engine of growth for the world economy.")

including contracts that use the local host state law as governing law.[15] Following global trends, these supply chains may be shifting, but they are doing so within the region (e.g., from China to Vietnam). That said, regionalization or decentering might not come easily, as institutional inertia and path dependency persist.

As a result of the commercial activity within the region, as Linh demonstrates in her chapter, the regional centers for dispute resolution, namely, Hong Kong and Singapore, have attained not only regional pre-eminence but also international renown. Second-tier cities, including Seoul, Shenzhen, Tokyo, Dubai, Kuala Lumpur, and Shanghai, are gaining ground, followed by third-tier cities like Jakarta, Ho Chih Minh City, Bangkok, Nur-Sultan, and others. The inter-Asian dispute resolution ecosystem is extraordinarily active, if not over-crowded. These centers are engaging through soft law, cross-training, and institutional and regional promotion. While many of these centers will fail, others will continue to thrive and ascend the international rankings.[16]

In addition to intra-regional lawmaking and dispute resolution, there are two other observations from the studies. First, and somewhat surprisingly, many of the IAL interactions have not resulted in convergence or harmonization. In fact, interactions have, in several instances, caused increased differentiation as local host states incorporated normative resources within their existing legal, political, and economic frameworks. Chapters by Das Acevedo, Tew, and Goto and Puchniak most clearly exemplify what the latter term "strategies for adaptation and localization." In a similar vein, in her chapter, Naiki shows that whereas ASEAN states were open to Japanese guidelines as a template for their own smart city guidelines, they also explicitly labeled them as Japanese, which Naiki interprets as an intentional act of distancing. In short, IAL interactions do not lead to legal sameness; country-of-origin matters, including for transplanted norms.

Second, and perhaps less surprisingly, regional heavyweights like China cause legal and regulatory spillovers in neighboring jurisdictions. DeLisle creates a taxonomy of these influences in the example of the People's Republic of China (PRC) and the Hong Kong Special Administrative Region (SAR). These influences are not reducible to transplants and represent a spectrum from formal impositions of PRC law to PRC pressure on Hong Kong lawmakers to adopt measures within the SAR framework in light of PRC interests. The PRC–Hong Kong story is a strong case for IAL, even if the political relationship between the two polities (i.e., the SAR is technically part of the PRC) makes the relationship unique.

Despite that uniqueness, some of the informal nature of PRC–Hong Kong IAL is replicated in China's relationships with sovereign states in Central Asia and

[15] Henry Gao and Gregory Shaffer, "The Role of Law in Chinese Value Chains" (2021) 19 J Ch Econ & Bus Studies 197.

[16] Matthew S Erie, "The New Legal Hubs: The Emergent Landscape of International Commercial Dispute Resolution" (2020) 60 Va J Int'l L 225, 243, 251, 297.

Southeast Asia, as Erie shows in his chapter. The transnational networks that Erie's study points to are also consequences of China's economic and political clout in those countries. Yet, contrary to the Hong Kong example, countries like Vietnam have a much higher degree of sovereignty than the SAR. Their incorporation of Chinese-inspired legal, regulatory, and institutional innovations may not necessarily benefit the PRC; rather, they may use them to bolster their own sovereignty and even contest Chinese encroachments through, for example, their own version of data localization.

In summary, just as IAL movements may lead to greater localization rather than convergence across borders, so too may borrowing from regional powers augment differentiation instead of simply feeding neo-imperial projects although greater legal interactions can also create the conditions for economic interdependence.

III BROADER SIGNIFICANCE

The wider value of IAL is to suggest not the narrative of the "decline of the West and the rise of the rest" popularized by certain Asian autocrats; instead, Asian jurisdictions – collectively and in competition with one another – are building local, regional, and transnational law to address issues of practical and theoretical importance. These include greater commercial ties, corporate governance, multilateralism, resolution of conflicts, infrastructure development, public order pertaining to religious freedom, women's rights, and constitutionalism, authoritarian creep, digital economy, and advanced technologies like AI and those in smart cities. In creating law to address such concerns, Asian jurisdictions are not exclusive. IAL is not monopolistic; rather, it integrates Western and global law influences, as seen in such examples as AI governance (Lin) and court reforms (Hans). Asian law is thus one referent among many in an increasingly complexified sourcing of law globally.

IAL shows that legal origins are becoming more diversified. Moving away from the conventional typology of common law originating from England and civil law from France, Germany, and Switzerland, IAL demonstrates the growing importance of China (Erie, Lin, DeLisle, Naiki), India (Yew, Das Acevedo, Pillai), Japan (Hans, Naiki), Singapore (Linh, Naiki, Goto and Puchniak), and Saudi Arabia (Putri and Taylor). Further, IAL shows greater and intensified hybridization and pluralization of legal origins, including not only common law and civil law but also religious law and digital law. Law travels horizontally (Erie, Putri and Taylor) and vertically (Hsieh, Lin).[17]

[17] For examples of the less familiar vertical movement of laws, see Jacques deLisle, "Lex Americana? United States Legal Assistance, American Legal Models, and Legal Change in the Post-Communist World and Beyond" (1999) 20 U Pa J Int'l Econ L 179, 292; Kim Lane Scheppele, "The International Standardization of National Security Law" (2010) 4 J Nat'l Sec L & Pol'y 437, 440–441; Ngoc Son Bui, "Vertical Law and Development" (2021) 54 Cornell

Diversification of sourcing law may shape legal flows and outcomes, including the trajectories of legal development in host states. Authoritarian forms of law, for instance, may gain popularity alongside liberal law. Globally, democratic and liberal systems are undergoing backsliding in confronting populist pressures;[18] in concert, authoritarian legal systems may possibly gain appeal among low-income states featuring non-liberal or weak democracies. While it is not easy to infer causal relationships between stagnant or retrograde democracies and surgent authoritarians, it is clear that established democratic states face new competition in the form of authoritarian versions of legal development overseas.[19] China is the most prominent actor in this new competition, but there are others including Singapore. India, the other major Asian power, and the would-be largest democracy in the world, has undergone its own slow slide into illiberal politics.[20] While de-democratization appears to be a global trend, the stakes are particularly high in Asia given its combination of major economies, demographic size, and fragile political systems. Deepening authoritarianism in China and illiberalism in India darken the prospects for IAL as a form of autochthonous democratic law.

IV AGENDA FOR FUTURE RESEARCH

IAL is in no way limited to the thematic areas covered in this present volume. For instance, one area of law that requires further study is the role of religio-philosophical traditions, whether Confucianism, Buddhism, or other traditions, in promoting IAL.[21] Given the centrality of the family to private law in Asia, family law also warrants elaboration.[22] Of equal relevance are culture, gender, community, village/folk/customary law, and social movements across Asian jurisdictions, intra-

Int'l L J 1, 5–7. See also, Mark Tushnet and Bojan Bugaric, *Power to the People: Constitutionalism in the Age of Populism* (OUP 2022).

18 Laurent Pech and Kim Lane Scheppele, "Illiberalism Within: Rule of Law Backsliding in the EU" (2017) 19 Cambridge YB Euro LS 3; Tom Ginsburg, "Democratic Backsliding and the Rule of Law" (2018) 44 Ohio NU L Rev 351.

19 Matthew S Erie, "Chinese Law and Development" (2021) 62 Harv Int'l L J 51.

20 Priya Chacko, "The Right Turn in India: Authoritarianism, Populism, and Neoliberalism" (2018) 48 J Contemp Asia 451; Maya Tudor, "Why India's Democracy is Dying" (2023) 34 J Democracy 121.

21 See (n 5–6). See also Weng Li, "Philosophical Influences on Contemporary Chinese Law" (1996) 6 Ind Int'l & Comp L Rev 327; Iza R Hussin, *The Politics of Islamic Law: Local Elites, Colonial Authority, and the Making of the Muslim State* (Chicago University Press 2016); Michael Gilsenan, "Topics and Queries for a History of Arab Families and Inheritance in Southeast Asia: Some Preliminary Thoughts" in Eric Tagliacozzo (ed), *Southeast Asia and the Middle East: Islam, Movement, and the Long Durée* (National University of Singapore 2009) 199–234.

22 See, e.g., Rama Hyeweon Kim, "Historicizing Same-Sex Marriage Debate in the Legal Periphery: Savigny, Nakagawa, and the Korean Marriage" (2024) 33 Minn J Int'l L 155.

regional environmentalism and climate change innovations, as well as the structure and power in financial regulation, transfer of control, and cross-border consumer protection. All such fields have their historical roots, and because of this, the legal histories of IAL are also ripe for scholarly exploration.[23]

Further, this volume's thematic organization into the four sections – commercial law, constitutional law, law's movements, and emerging problems – is by no means static. It is meant only to provide an entry into the areas of IAL. Each thematic section deserves further and sustained attention, not to mention the overlap or intersection between these thematic discourses. To take one example, given the primacy of business and commercial law in the region, more work needs to be done on consumer law, competition law, corporate law, and insolvency law. Finance law, too, is a sprawling field in Asia, ranging from informal markets to shadow banking to venture capital and alternative development finance, each of which has cross-border elements.[24] Each of these invites both multi-scalar and multi-disciplinary approaches.

Beyond substantive (or procedural) areas of law specific to IAL, the concept on which IAL is based – intra-regional legal interactions – invites a broader comparative intra-regional approach. How this volume unpacks and contextualizes IAL's unique characteristics and diverse origins and patterns of influence that shape its contours may also serve as a methodological lens for or at least shed light on other emerging regional developments. One could think of, for example, "Inter-European law," "Inter-African law," and "Inter-Latinx law." Each one shows both internal interaction within the respective region and broader effects internationally.

To provide a thumbnail sketch of each, Inter-European law is not reducible to EU law, the paragon of regional law and which has had spillover effects more globally.[25] Inter-European law is the interaction of European state legal systems, an interaction with a long history.[26] More in line with IAL, other post-colonial regions may demonstrate even more interactions and international influence. Inter-African law includes both regional law and influences on international law. For the former, an example is the possibility for African Union Law to

[23] For recent studies, see Kalyani Ramnath, "Intertwined Itineraries: Debt, Decolonization, and International Law in Post-World War II South Asia" (2020) 38 L & Hist Rev 1; Rohit De, "The Jurisprudence of Decolonization: The Postcolonial Career of D N Pritt and the Practice of Rebellious Lawyering" (2023) 14(1) Humanity 121.

[24] Nafay Choudhury, "Transacting on Trust: The Regulation of Trade Credit by Afghanistan's Money Exchangers" (2022) 32 Transnat'l L & Contemp Problems 341; Shen Wei, *Shadow Banking in China: Risk, Regulation and Policy* (Elgar 2016); Lin Lin, *Venture Capital in China* (CUP 2021); Ming Wan, "Japan and the Asian Development Bank" (1995) 68(4) Pacific Affairs 509.

[25] See Anu Bradford, *The Brussels Effect: How the European Union Rules the World* (OUP 2020).

[26] See, e.g., Tamar Herzog, A *Short History of European Law: The Last Two and Half Millenia* (Harvard University Press 2018) 212.

produce a continent-wide legal system.[27] For the latter, at the international level, African scholars have examined the extent to which the "Africanization" of inter-African investment agreements offers a viable alternative to conventional international investment law.[28]

Inter-Latinx law is an active field of legal engagement, cross-fertilization, and regional law. There are numerous instances of a country within the region serving as a model for legal reform in neighboring countries. Examples include the invocation of an "unconstitutional state of affairs" first used by Colombian courts and subsequently borrowed by Brazilian counterparts[29] and Mexico's constitutional provision on prioritizing workers' claims vis-à-vis secured creditors, which has influenced the constitutions of other Latin American states.[30] In the Caribbean, states have followed one another in modifying transplanted UK legislation in the field of family law. Examples there include de facto relationships, constructive trusts, and the statue of children.[31] Tracy Robinson has written, "The new states looked at their neighbours and built ideas of Caribbean legal kinship as much as they turned to common law countries in the Global North as a traditional and practical resource."[32] Still, inter-Latinx law, like IAL, may demonstrate continued inheritance from and incomplete decentering of established models. For instance, in the digital trade space, Latin American countries have had difficulty moving away from the approach introduced by the United States.[33]

[27] See, e.g., Olufemi Amao, Michèle Olivier and Konstantinos D Magliveras (eds), *The Emergent African Union Law: Conceptualization, Delimitation, and Application* (Oxford University Press 2022).

[28] See, e.g., Olabisi D Akinkugbe, "Africanization and the Reform of International Investment Law" (2021) 53 Case W Res J Int'l L 7.

[29] For example, see Carlos Bernal-Pulido, "The Constitutional Protection of Economic and Social Rights in Latin America" in Rosalind Dixon and Tom Ginsburg (eds), *Comparative Constitutional Law in Latin America* (Edward Elgar 2017) 325–342. At the international level, Latin American countries have sought to integrate greater protection of traditional cultures in the intellectual property provisions of their trade agreements. These efforts have led to new treaties including the Treaty on Intellectual Property, Genetic Resources and Associated Traditional Knowledge. See, e.g., World Intellectual Property Organization, "WIPO Member States Adopt Historic New Treaty on Intellectual Property, Genetic Resources and Associated Traditional Knowledge" (May 24, 2024), www.wipo.int/pressroom/en/articles/2024/article_0007.html, accessed May 23, 2025.

[30] Kevin E Davis, Mariana Pargendler and Maria Eduarada Lessa, "Legal Heterodoxy in the Global South: Priority of Workers versus Secured Creditors in Insolvency" in Kevin E Davis and Mariana Pargendler (eds), *Legal Heterodoxy in the Global South: Adapting Private Law to Local Contexts* (Cambridge University Press 2025).

[31] See Tracy Robinson, "Remaking Family Property Law in the Anglo Caribbean" in Margaret Briggs and Andy Hayward (eds), *Research Handbook on Family Property and the Law* (Edward Elgar 2024) 463, 466, 473, 476.

[32] Ibid 479.

[33] Fábio Morosini, Lucas Tasquetto and Marília Maciel, "Navigating the Digital Divide: Challenges and Strategies for Latin American Countries in E-Commerce and Data Governance Regulation" (*LAPEG Paper*. No. 1, November 2024).

Each one of these prospective fields could reveal the historical and contemporary aspects of interactions to challenge long-standing conventions in the study of comparative and international law. Going forward, IAL and its parallels may offer pathways to reconsider and reconfigure comparative and international law from the perspective of former peripheries, which may now be emerging as new centers in times of deglobalization and regional realignment.

Index

For EU product safety concerns, contact us at Calle de José Abascal, 56–1°, 28003 Madrid, Spain or eugpsr@cambridge.org.

www.ingramcontent.com/pod-product-compliance
Ingram Content Group UK Ltd.
Pitfield, Milton Keynes, MK11 3LW, UK
UKHW021928120426
469821UK00020B/467

* 9 7 8 1 0 0 9 5 8 0 6 0 1 *